Presented To   Aug 2012
   Williston City Library
by the
   Williston Rotary club
      in honor of:
BILL MOYERS JOURNAL

Doug Taylor
Oscar Halvorson

ALSO BY BILL MOYERS

BILL MOYERS JOURNAL

The Conversation Continues

Bill Moyers

Edited with
Michael Winship

Photographs by
Robin Holland

THE NEW PRESS

NEW YORK
LONDON

Requests for permission to reproduce selections from this book should be mailed to: Permissions Department, The New Press, 38 Greene Street, New York, NY 10013.

Published in the United States by The New Press, New York, 2011
Distributed by Perseus Distribution

LIBRARY OF CONGRESS CATALOGING-IN-PUBLICATION DATA

Moyers, Bill D.
    Bill Moyers journal : the conversation continues / Bill Moyers ; edited by Michael Winship ; photographs by Robin Holland.
        p. cm.
    Includes bibliographical references and index.
    ISBN 978-1-59558-624-7 (hc. : alk. paper) 1. United States--Civilization--1970- 2. United States--Politics and government--1989- 3. United States--Politics and government--1945-1989. 4. National characteristics, American. 5. Democracy--United States. 6. United States--Social conditions--1980- 7. Civilization, Modern--1950- 8. Interviews--United States. I. Winship, Michael. II. Title.
    E169.12.M68 2011
    973.92--dc22
                            2011007597

The New Press was established in 1990 as a not-for-profit alternative to the large, commercial publishing houses currently dominating the book publishing industry. The New Press operates in the public interest rather than for private gain, and is committed to publishing, in innovative ways, works of educational, cultural, and community value that are often deemed insufficiently profitable.

www.thenewpress.com

Book design and by composition by the Influx House
This book was set in Garamond

Printed in the United States of America

10 9 8 7 6 5 4 3 2

CONTENTS

INTRODUCTION

As the French aristocrat Alexis de Tocqueville came off the boat in New York in 1831 to begin his famous tour of the fledgling America, he was greeted with tumult. Had there been a tourist bureau at the dock, the banner of greeting might have read: "Welcome to democracy! Protect your own sanity. Bring earplugs."

Even now, all these years later, that tumult—the cacophony of a fractious, insatiable, and rambunctious people—is no less bewildering. Our national dissonance continues to play havoc with journalists trying to make sense of it. When we returned to PBS with *Bill Moyers Journal* in the spring of 2007, we knew that, as always, we were in for a romp, arduous yet invigorating. Our time on the air coincided with momentous events: the final years of the Bush White House, the turbulent 2008 election campaign that culminated in the election of America's first African American president, the first fifteen months of the Obama administration (including fierce national debates over health care, financial reform, and the escalation of the war in Afghanistan), and the worst global economic meltdown since the Great Depression.

We covered all of these as journalists, not oracles. But events that seemed singular, even isolated, turned out to be part of a procession with consequences not immediately discernible. It is now evident that the independent-minded thinkers we kept talking to foresaw much of what the country is experiencing today. Simon Johnson and James K. Galbraith told us that in the aftershocks of the financial earthquake those responsible for it would continue to prosper, resisting new regulations and picking profit from the

ruins of the lives they had helped shatter. Wendell Potter, the health insurance executive turned health care reformer, prepared us for the glass-
half-empty compromise that would follow. The physician-turned-activist
Margaret Flowers, while heartening in her willingness to organize and
advocate, anticipated the futility of fighting, much less hoping, for public
health insurance that would make Medicare available to all.

The Washington Post's Robert Kaiser described how the power of money
and lobbyists, given their greed and political clout, would undoubtedly
frustrate true reform. The historian Andrew Bacevich, West Point graduate
and Vietnam veteran, warned that the excesses of empire and hubris were
reaching a point of no return. Sam Tanenhaus, Victor Gold, Ross Douthat,
and Mickey Edwards spoke about the death of traditional conservatism but
saw in its throes the rage that emerged in Tea Party candidacies and the resurgence of the right in the 2010 midterm elections.

This is a book of ideas and—we hope—stimulating conversation, one
you can dip into at will. It exists because the issues and ideas we discussed
remain pertinent in the here and now; their significance did not end when
the closing credits rolled. We still must struggle with the deep and systemic
corruption of power and money and the vast chasm of inequality between
rich and poor that is the consequence of that corruption. As James K.
Galbraith said recently, our democracy increasingly is one ruled by an "extremely small number of the extremely fortunate, which is not a democracy
at all."

These stories and conflicts do not die. The health care reform story is far
from over, as the Republican leadership and the Chamber of Commerce
vow to have it changed or completely repealed—read "destroyed." And we
continue to look away as American soldiers die in Afghanistan; we worry
about poverty, hunger, and the quality of the food we eat; the degeneration
of our cities and the education system; race politics and injustice; human
rights and torture during an age of terrorism; the war between Palestinians
and Israelis; aging in America; capital punishment and a blighted penal system; the conflict over gay marriage; and the politicization of our courts. All
of these matters are reflected in these pages.

We also know that too much tumult is hard on the nerves. And while the
political upheavals and economic woes were foremost on just about everyone's mind, we at the *Journal* took regular breaks to protect our—and our
viewers'—sanity. Indeed, our first guest was Jon Stewart, whose wit is a con-

tagious conveyor of wisdom; our last was the writer Barry Lopez, who never mentioned politics but left us thinking about how to endure the bleakness it sometimes visits upon us and how to seek the justice that truly should be its end. In between these two, Robert Bly, Nikki Giovanni, W.S. Merwin, Martín Espada, and John Lithgow read poetry and opened breathing room amidst the clamor and dissonance around us; Jane Goodall brought a smile to the heart as she talked about what chimpanzees teach us about coping with the tumult; Maxine Hong Kingston quickened our longing for books of peace; and E.O. Wilson reminded us, amidst all the clashing of political egos and gnashing of pundit teeth, that it's "the little things that run the world." When we did return to politics, as duty so often required, there were harbingers of hope—from the historians Howard Zinn and Nell Painter to the populist Jim Hightower, who spoke of Americans in our past who did not give up when democracy was on the ropes. Their fighting spirit might once again turn the past to prologue.

These are a few of the conversations awaiting you within these pages; in some cases small changes have been made for accuracy and clarity. There were many other interviews—especially those focused so exclusively on the week's events—that we could not include, but each of them is available for viewing: Just go to our website at pbs.org/moyers. All were of value and we are thankful for each one.

This book, like the *Journal* itself, is the love's labor of many. Neither would have happened except for the leadership of our executive editor, Judith Davidson Moyers, and our executive producers, Judy Doctoroff O'Neill and Sally Roy. They fielded a remarkably talented team of so many standouts that we can't mention them all, but we are especially indebted to Rebecca Wharton and Ana Cohen Bickford for their ability to recognize and recruit some of the best thinkers in the country to appear on the broadcast. Helen Silfven and Ismael Gonzalez worked for months to help bring this book to fruition. Robin Holland took the wonderful portraits that graced the broadcasts, our website, and now these pages.

There wouldn't have been a *Journal* in the first place except for the individuals and organizations that provided the funding and asked nothing in return but the best journalism we could offer. They include John and Polly Guth and The Partridge Foundation; the Park Foundation; the Marisla Foundation; the John D. and Catherine T. MacArthur Foundation; the Fetzer Institute; the Herb Alpert Foundation; Marilyn and Bob Clements and The Clements Foundation; The Kohlberg Foundation; Bernard and Audre Rapoport and the Bernard and Audre Rapoport Foundation; Barbara Fleischman; Lillian and Jon Lovelace; the Orfalea Family Foundation; the Public Welfare Foundation; The Cornelia and Michael Bessie Foundation; and our sole corporate sponsor for twenty years, Mutual of America Life Insurance Company.

The John D. and Catherine T. MacArthur Foundation, the Public Welfare Foundation, the Herb Alpert Foundation, and the Marisla Foundation provided special funding for the creation and publication of this book. We are especially grateful to Marc Favreau and the team at The New Press for wanting to continue the conversation.

—Bill Moyers and Michael Winship

BILL MOYERS JOURNAL

JON STEWART

Someone asked why I invited Jon Stewart to be the first guest on the Journal's premiere in 2007. "Because Mark Twain isn't available," I answered. I was serious. Like Twain, Stewart has proven that truth is more digestible when it's marinated in humor.

He and his writers craft political commentary the way Stradivarius made violins. Exquisitely. Just watch The Daily Show. Or, on a dark and stormy night, when the news from Washington has your stomach churning and your nerves jangling, dip into their book, America (The Book): A Citizen's Guide to Democracy Inaction. You will instantly feel better. My favorite entry is their "inspirational" story of how the media "transformed itself from a mere public necessity into an entertaining profit center for ever-expanding corporate empires." Unfortunately, this account will make you weep as much as laugh. Stewart regularly reminds us how the press botches the world, often deliberately. Witness his spot-on put-downs of Fox News, CNBC's coverage of the global financial crisis, and the vapid bombast of CNN's late and unlamented Crossfire, which came to an end soon after Stewart appeared on it and said, in effect, "Shame on you!"

The Daily Show's humor would be funny enough even if it weren't true, but truth is satire's spermatozoon, and where it lands it leaves us not only laughing but thinking. Jon Stewart says he is just a comic, but I don't think so. Look at his appeal to people who are alienated from American electoral politics. The

"Rally to Restore Sanity and/or Fear" that he and Stephen Colbert threw in Washington the Saturday before Election Day 2010 drew a quarter of a million people to the National Mall. His on-air support—and scathing attacks on opponents—of the health care legislation for 9/11 responders were considered critical to its passage by Congress. An appearance on The Daily Show *has become a campaign stop for any national candidate willing to face Stewart's barbed but respectful—and always well-informed— questioning.*

Three days before Stewart appeared on the premiere of the Journal, *he interviewed Senator John McCain on* The Daily Show. *McCain, in fact, had been his most frequent political guest, but this was surely one appearance he would like to take back. The senator had just returned from a visit to Iraq and he began the conversation with a "one of the boys" joke about planting an IED— the insurgents' weapon of choice against American soldiers—under Stewart's desk. There were groans from the audience. Stewart then went to work on him with the skeptic's scalpel, and McCain, seemingly baffled by the facts of the war so readily brandished by Stewart, withered before our eyes. When the interview ended, one could imagine the inept candidate for president that McCain would turn out to be. It took Stewart to reveal what over the years the Sunday talk shows had helped McCain to conceal—that he was just another flesh-and-blood politician, skilled at manipulating the press to serve his own ambition, and not the anticipated messiah.*

A few years ago, Leslie Moonves, the president of CBS, said he could foresee a time when Stewart would replace Katie Couric as anchor of CBS Evening News. *In fact, when Americans were asked to name the journalist they most admired, Stewart was right up there—tied in the rankings with Brian Williams, Tom Brokaw, Dan Rather, and Anderson Cooper.*

No kidding.

—Bill Moyers

———✦———

You've said many times, "I don't want to be a journalist, I'm not a journalist."

And we're not.

But you're acting like one. You've assumed that role. The young people who work with me now think they get better journalism from you than they do from the Sunday morning talk shows.

I can assure them they're not getting any journalism from us. If anything, when they watch our program we're a prism into people's own ideologies. This is just our take.

But it isn't just you. Sometimes you'll start a riff, you'll start down the path of a joke, and it's about Bush or about Cheney, and your live audience will get it, they'll start applauding even before they know the punch line. And I'm thinking, "Okay, they get it. That's half the country." What about the other half of the country—are they paying attention? If they are, do they get it?

We have very interesting reactions to our show. People are constantly saying, "Your show is so funny, until you made a joke about global warming, which is a serious issue, and I can't believe you did that. And I am never watching your show again." You know, people don't understand that we're not warriors for their cause. We're a group of people who write jokes about the absurdity that we see in government and the world and all that, and that's it.

We watched the McCain interview you did. Something was going on in that interview that I have not seen in any other interview you've done with a political figure. You kept after him. What was going on in your head?

In my head?

Yes.

"Are his arms long enough to connect with me if he comes across the table?" I don't particularly enjoy those types of interviews, because I have a great respect for Senator McCain, and I hate the idea that our conversation became just two people sort of talking over each other, at one point. But I also, in my head, thought I would love to do an interview where the talking points of Iraq are sort of deconstructed—sort of the idea of, "Is this really the conversation we're having about this war, that if we don't defeat al-Qaeda in Iraq, they'll follow us home? That to support the troops means not to question that the surge could work? That what we're really seeing in Iraq is not a terrible war, but in fact just the media's portrayal of it?"

I saw McCain shrivel.

Eight minutes on *The Daily Show*.

But something happened. You saw it happen to him. What you saw was evasive action.

He stopped connecting and just looked at my chest and decided, "I'm just going to continue to talk about honor and duty and the families should be proud," all the things that are cudgels emotionally to keep us from the conversation, but things that weren't relevant to what we were talking about.

So many people seem to want just what you did, somebody to cut through the talking points and get our politicians to talk candidly and frankly.

Not that many people. You've seen our ratings. Some people want it. A couple of people download it from iTunes. The conversation that the Senate and the House are having with the president is very similar to the conversation that McCain and I were having, which was two people talking over each other and nobody really addressing the underlying issues of what kind of country do we want to be, moving forward in this? And it's not about being a pacifist or suggesting that you can never have a military solution to things. It's just that it appears that this is not the smart way to fight this threat.

Your persistence and his inability to answer without the talking points did get to the truth—that there's a contradiction to what's going on in that war that they can't talk about.

That's right. There is an enormous contradiction, and it is readily apparent if you just walk through a simple sort of logic and simple rational points. But the thing that they don't realize is that everyone wants them to come from beyond that contradiction so that we can all fix it. Nobody is saying, "We don't have a problem." Nobody is saying that "9/11 didn't happen." What they're saying is, "We're not a fragile country. Trust us to have this conversation, so that we can do this in the right way, in a more effective way."

Why is the country not having this conversation, the kind of conversation that requires the politicians who are responsible for the war to be specific to the concerns of the American people?

Because I don't think politics is any longer about a conversation with the country. It's about figuring out how to get to do what you want. The best way to sell the product that you want to put out there. It's sort of like dishwashing soap, you know, they want to make a big splash, so they decide to have more lemon, as though people are going to be like, "That has been the problem with my dishes! Not enough lemon scent!"

There seems a detachment emotionally and politically in this country from what is happening.

It's very hard to feel the difficulties that the military goes through. It's very hard to feel the difficulties of military families, unless you're in that environment. And sometimes you have to force yourself to try and put yourself in other people's shoes and environment to get the sense of that. One of the things that I think government counts on is that people are busy. And it's very difficult to mobilize a busy and relatively affluent country, unless it's over really crucial—you know, foundational issues, that come, sort of, as a tipping point.

"War? What war?"

War hasn't affected us here in the way that you would imagine a five-year war would affect a country. Here's the disconnect: that the president says that we are in the fight for a way of life. This is the greatest battle of our generation, and of the generations to come. Iraq has to be won, or our way of life ends, and our children and our children's children all suffer. So what I'm going to do is send ten thousand more troops to Baghdad.

So there's a disconnect there. You're telling me this is the fight of our generation, and you're going to increase troops by 10 percent. And that's going to do it? I'm sure what he would like to do is send four hundred thousand more troops there, but he can't, because he doesn't have them. And the way to get that would be to institute a draft. And the minute you do that, suddenly the country's not so damn busy anymore. And then they really fight back, then the whole thing falls apart. So they have a really delicate balance to walk between keeping us relatively fearful, but not so fearful that we stop what we're doing and really examine how it is that they've been waging this.

But you were thinking this before you got McCain.

Sure, yes, this happened with McCain because he was unfortunate enough to walk into the studio. The frustration of our show is that we're very much outside any parameters of the media or the government. We don't have access to these people. We don't go to dinners. We don't have cocktail parties. You've seen what happens when one of us ends up at the White House

Correspondents' Dinner; it doesn't end well. So he was the unlucky recipient of pent-up frustration.

You know, the media's been playing this big. CNN, USA Today...

Well, they've got twenty-four hours to fill. You know, how many times can Anna Nicole Smith's baby get a new father?

But what does it say about the press that the interview you did became news? And, in a way, reflected on the failure of the "professional" journalists to ask those kinds of questions?

I don't know if it really reflects on the failure of them to ask. I think, first of all, for some reason, everything that we do or Stephen does—Stephen Colbert—is also then turned into news. The machine is about reporting the news, and then reporting the news about the news, and then having those moments where they sit around and go, "Are we reporting the news correctly? I think we are." And then they go, and the cycle just sort of continues. I don't know that there was anything particularly astonishing about the conversation, in that regard.

Have you lost your innocence?

What? Well, it was in 1981, it was at a frat party... oh, I'm sorry... You know, I think this is gonna sound incredibly pat, but I think you lose your innocence when you have kids, because the world suddenly becomes a much more dangerous place. There are two things that happen. You recognize how fragile individuals are, and you recognize the strength of the general overall group, but you don't care anymore. You're just fighting for the one thing. And then you also recognize that everybody is also somebody's child. It's tumultuous.

Your children are how old?

Two and a half and fourteen months.

So, has it been within that period of time that you made this transformation from the stand-up comic to a serious social and political critic?

I don't consider myself a serious and social political critic.

But I do. And I'm your audience.

I guess I don't spend any time thinking about what I am, or about what we do means. I spend my time doing it. I focus on the task and try and do it as best we can. And we're constantly evolving it, because it's my way of trying to make sense of all these ambivalent feelings I have.

I watched the interview you did with the former Iraqi official, Ali Allawi. And I was struck that you were doing this soon after the massacre at Virginia Tech. It wasn't your usual Daily Show *banter. I said, "Something's going on with Stewart there." What was it?*

Well, first of all, you know the process by which we put the show together is always going to be affected by the climate that we live in. And there was a pall cast over the country. But also you're fighting your own sadness during the day. We feel no obligation to follow the news cycle. In other words, I felt no obligation to cover this story in any way, because we're not, like I said, we're not journalists. And at that point, there's nothing sort of funny or absurd to say about it. But there is a sadness that you can't escape, just within yourself. And I'm also interviewing a guy who's just written a book about his experience living in Iraq, faced with the type of violence that we're talking about on an unimaginable scale. And I think that the combination of that is very hard to shake.

And I know that my job is to shake it, and to perform. It wouldn't be a very interesting show if I just came out one day and said, "I'm going to sit here in a ball and rock back and forth. And won't you join me for a half hour of sadness?"

But that wasn't performance when you were wrestling with the sadness you were feeling with him.

Well, I thought it was relevant to the conversation. I was obviously following the Internet headlines all day. And there was this enormous amount of space and coverage given to Virginia Tech, as there should have been. And I happened to catch sort of a headline lower down, which was "Two Hundred People Killed in Four Bomb Attacks in Iraq." And I think my focus was on what was happening here versus sort of this peripheral vision thing that caught my eye. I felt guilty.

Guilty?

For not having the empathy for their suffering on a daily basis that I feel sometimes that I should.

Do you ever think that perhaps what I do in reporting documentaries about reality and what you do in poking some fun and putting some humor around the horrors of the world feed into the sense of helplessness of people?

No. I mean, again, I don't know, because I don't know how people feel. And you know, the beauty of TV is, they can see us, but we can't see them. I think that if we do anything in a positive sense for the world, it's to provide one little bit of context that's very specifically focused, and hopefully people can add it to their entire puzzle to give them a larger picture of what it is that they see. But I don't think it's a feeling of hopelessness that people feel. If they're feeling what we're feeling, it's that this is how we fight back. And I feel like the only thing that I can do, and I've been fired from enough jobs that I'm pretty confident in saying this, the only thing that I can do, even a little bit better than most people, is create that sort of context with humor. And that's my way of not being helpless and not being hopeless.

Is Washington a better source for jokes now that the Democrats are in the majority?

It's more fun for us, because we're tired of the same deconstructed game.

Yeah, I saw that piece you did on the Democrats debating how to lose the war.

Right, exactly. This has been six years, you know; we're worn down. And I look forward to a new game to play, something new. I mean, the only joy I've had in that time is having Stephen's show come on the air and sort of give us a different perspective. And, you know, because it's made of the same kind of genetic material as our show. It feels like it's also freshened up our perspective and kind of completed our thought.

You could take me on as a correspondent.

We would love to take you on as a correspondent. You know, the pay is pretty bad.

Yeah, well, this is PBS. What would my assignment be? Would you want me to be your senior elderly correspondent?

I would like you to just sit in my office, and when I walk in, just lower your head and go, "That was ugly." ∿

MICHAEL POLLAN

For a brief moment, reformers thought Barack Obama might include America's corrupted food chain in the "agenda for change" that he would take to Washington as president. Time magazine had published a scathing indictment of our agricultural system as "a welfare program for the megafarms that use the most fuel, water and pesticides; emit the most greenhouse gases; grow the most fattening crops; hire the most illegals; and depopulate rural America." Asked for his position, Obama told Time that the way we produce our food is "partly . . . contributing to type 2 diabetes, stroke and heart disease, obesity, all the things that are driving our huge explosion in health care costs." The farm lobby roared in protest. Obama buckled and took it back, saying he was "simply paraphrasing" an article he read.

And what an article! A bombshell landing right in the middle of the presidential campaign less than a month before the election, in the form of a nine-page open letter in The New York Times Magazine from journalist and omnivore Michael Pollan. He warned Obama and Republican candidate John McCain that significant progress on health care, energy independence, and climate change depends on something they "barely mentioned during the campaign: food." The article triggered such a response that an online movement sprang up calling on President-elect Obama to name Michael Pollan secretary of agriculture.

A pity it didn't happen. Pollan would have brought to Washington the activist zeal of Upton Sinclair and the same canny zest for making food both tasty and appealing that Julia Child brought to her kitchen. National magazines had tabbed him among the one hundred most influential people in the world, as well as one of the seven top thought leaders. He has written four bestselling books on food, including, most recently Food Rules: An Eater's Manual. *I wanted to know where he would have started if Obama had yielded to Pollan's legions of admirers and made him secretary of agriculture.*

—Bill Moyers

How about that: Secretary Pollan?

I would be so bad at that job.

Why?

I have an understanding of my strengths and limitations. You have to understand that the Department of Agriculture, this $100-billion-a-year behemoth, is a captive of agribusiness. They're in the room making policy there. When you have a food safety recall over meat, sitting there with the secretary of agriculture and his chief of staff is the head of the National Cattlemen's Beef Association.

It's all worked out together. The department is part of the problem. They're also very dependent on the legislation that the House and Senate Agricultural Committees cobble together. So I think you'd get swallowed up there very easily. If Obama wants to make change in this area, we'll need a food policy czar in the White House, because the challenge is not just what we do with agriculture, it's connecting the dots between agriculture and public health, between agriculture and energy and climate change, agriculture and education.

You need someone who can take a global view of the problem and realize that it's an interdisciplinary problem. And if you hope to make progress in all these other areas, you have to make sure that if the surgeon general is going on about the epidemic of type 2 diabetes, you don't want to be signing farm bills that subsidize high-fructose corn syrup at the same time.

Because?

High-fructose corn syrup contributes mightily, as do all sugars, to type 2 diabetes. And we are subsidizing cheap sweeteners by subsidizing corn. You have a war going on between the public health goals of the government and the agricultural policies. Only someone in the White House can force the realignment of those goals. For a start, what we're after is looking at these commodity programs. Essentially the five crops we subsidize are corn, wheat, soy, rice, and cotton. We'll leave cotton out because we don't eat too much of it, although we do eat some cottonseed oil. Our farm policy for many years has been to increase production of those crops and keep the prices low.

And we have cheaper prices and plenty of food today.

You can walk into a fast-food outlet and get a bacon double cheeseburger, french fries, and soda for less than what you would get paid for an hour of work at the minimum wage. In the long sweep of human history, that's an amazing achievement. But we've learned that overabundant, too-cheap food can be as much a problem as too little food.

Look at the health care crisis. We're all eating 300 more calories a day than we were twenty-five years ago. We've gone from 2,000 or 2,300 to 2,600, something like that. We all weigh on average ten pounds more. And lo and behold, we have a serious epidemic of obesity, type 2 diabetes, heart disease, diet-related cancers. All these chronic diseases that kill us pretty reliably in America are adding more than $250 billion a year to health care costs. They are the reason that the generation being born now is expected to have a shorter life span than their parents, that one in three Americans born in the year 2000, according to the Centers for Disease Control, will have type 2 diabetes. That is a serious sentence. It takes several years off your life. It means an 80 percent chance of heart disease. It means you are going to be spending $14,000 a year in added health costs. So this is all about how we're eating.

And you're saying this is primarily the result of what we eat?

Yes. There are other factors, obviously. A sedentary lifestyle. Cane workers in Cuba can eat 6,000 calories of sugarcane a day, yet they don't get diabetes because they burn it off. We don't burn it off. So exercise is an issue, although exercise hasn't changed dramatically in this same period that our public health has declined so much. When you have monocultures of corn and soy in the fields, which is what we have because of our farm policy, you end up with a fast-food diet, because those crops are the building blocks of fast food. We turn the corn into high-fructose corn syrup to sweeten the sodas. We also turn the corn into cheap feedlot meat. The soy we also turn into cheap feedlot meat and hydrogenated soy oil, which is what our fast food is fried in. It has trans fats, known to be lethal. We are basically subsidizing fast food.

I laughed when I read in your New York Times Magazine *article, "When we eat from the industrial food system, we are eating oil and spewing greenhouse gases." Now, Michael, I don't ever remember sitting down to a meal of yummy petroleum.*

Well, we are eating oil and we obviously don't see it.

How so?

How do you grow those giant monocultures of corn and soy? As soon as you plant a monoculture, which basically is lots of the same thing year after year, you risk depleting the fertility of the soil. How do you replenish the fertility? Fertilizer. How do you make fertilizer? It's made with natural gas, diesel oil. So we actually have to spread huge quantities of oil or fossil fuels on our fields to keep the food coming.

When you grow a monoculture, you also get lots of pests. They love monocultures. You build up the population of the pests by giving them a vast buffet of exactly what they've evolved to eat. So how do you get rid of them? You use pesticides made from fossil fuels. When you grow corn and soy, you then have to process it. And so it takes ten calories of fossil fuel energy to produce one calorie of food—to make a Twinkie or something like that. It's a very fuel-intensive process.

Look, nobody wants to see food prices go up. Nobody wants to see oil prices go up. But we understand that we are not going to change our energy economy unless we start paying a higher price for oil. We are not going to improve our health around food unless we pay the real cost of food.

Cheap food is actually incredibly expensive. Farm subsidies—that's $25 billion a year spent to make food cheap. You look at the pollution effects—nitrates in the water, moms who can't use tap water because their kids get blue baby syndrome from nitrogen in the water. You look at the public health costs. You look at the cost to the atmosphere—the food system is the single biggest contributor to greenhouse gases.

You claim that we use more fossil fuel in producing food than we do in any other activity, including driving to work.

It's more than personal transportation, absolutely. And you know, we don't see that when we look at our food system.

You told us that food connects not only to health care but also to energy independence, to climate change, to national security—how do all the dots connect?

Well, when you have a big globalized food system based on a very small number of crops, first, you're moving food everywhere. I mean, the supply chains of food are just absurd. We're catching so-called sustainable salmon in Alaska. We ship it to China to get filleted and then we bring it back here. That's how cheap Chinese labor is. We're not going to be able to do that much longer. We're selling sugar cookies to the country of Denmark, and we're buying sugar cookies from the country of Denmark. And Herman Daly, the economist, said, "Wouldn't it be more efficient to swap recipes?" I mean, these absurdities can't continue. So energy is deeply implicated in the system. Any system that uses a lot of energy is going to produce a lot of greenhouse gas. Plus livestock also produce huge amounts of greenhouse gas.

National security? Well, there's a tremendous danger when you centralize your food supply. Having a highly centralized food system such as we have, where one hamburger plant might be grinding forty or fifty million burgers in a week, where one pre-bagged salad plant is washing twenty-six million servings of salad in a week, that's very efficient, but it's also very precarious, because if a microbe is introduced into that one plant, by a terrorist or by accidental contamination, millions of people will get sick. You don't want to put all your eggs in one basket when it comes to your food safety. You want to decentralize. Tommy Thompson, when he was departing as secretary of health and human services, said one of the big surprises of his time in Washington was that no terrorist had attacked the food supply because, and this is a quote, "it would be so easy to do."

The politicians might say, "Look what's happening on Wall Street, look what's happening to people's 401(k)s. Look what's happening to people's security—

their real physical security is in great jeopardy. This is what they're scared about. And you're asking me to talk about food."

If you really care about dealing with climate change; if you really care about dealing with the health care crisis, which is going to mean getting health care costs down; if you really care about feeding the rest of the world, because our agricultural policies are taking food out of the mouths of people in Africa and throughout Asia, our ethanol policies in particular—you can't escape the question of food.

Food is the shadow issue over all those other issues. You're only going to get so far with health care costs unless you look at the diet. Let's look at the school lunch program. This is where we're feeding a big part of our population. We are essentially feeding them fast food and teaching them how to eat it quickly. We could spend a dollar or more per day per child and work on the nutritional quality of that food. And let's require that a certain percentage of the school lunch spending in every school district has to be spent within a hundred miles to revive local agriculture, to create more jobs on farms.

You will have a healthier population of kids who will perform better in the afternoon after that lunch. You will have the shot in the arm to local economies by helping local agriculture. And you will teach this generation habits about eating that will last a lifetime.

Right now the school lunch program is a disposal scheme for surplus agricultural commodities. When they have too much meat, when they have too much cheese, they send it to the schools, and they dispose of it through our kids' digestive systems. Let's look at it in a different way. This should be about improving the health of our children, so maybe the program belongs in Health and Human Services, maybe it belongs in Education. Get the Department of Agriculture's hands off it.

As with so much in politics, the initial conditions or rules determine the outcome. If you fill your Agriculture Committee with representatives of commodity farmers and you don't have urbanites, you don't represent eaters, okay? If you don't have people from New York City on these committees, you are going to end up with the kind of farm bills we have, a piece of special-interest legislation. It shouldn't even be called the Farm Bill. It should be called the Food Bill. It's about us. It's not just about them.

It sounds so reasonable, but once again politics and human nature intervene. What are the political obstacles to making that happen?

Well, the commodity groups are one of the most well-organized lobbies on the Hill. And the Farm Bureau, which purports to represent farmers, actually represents agribusiness. So I'm not saying it's going to be easy. But I also feel that there is a political movement rising. It's a very young movement. (If anyone's talking about me for agriculture secretary, that's a measure of how young it is! But it's rising.) There are millions of mothers concerned about food, about the school lunch program, about what's on sale in the supermarket. There's enormous concern about food safety. There is the security issue. There are many facets to this movement. It's still inchoate, and politicians have not recognized the power that is there for the seizing.

I will make a confession. I like to take my grandkids to McDonald's occasionally, okay? Given the human nature at play here, how do you convince us that we're contributing to climate change, we're contributing to a precarious national security, we're contributing to bad health? What would you say to move us to change?

Well, the first thing I would say is, I'm not a Puritan about food. I'm not a zealot about it. There is something called special-occasion food that we have in our house, and it's kind of understood that sometimes you enjoy your fast food. You have your Twinkie. People have done this for thousands of years. There's nothing wrong with doing it. Our problem is we've made special-occasion food everyday food and that one in three American children is at a fast-food outlet every single day. And that's where you get into trouble.

How did you get from the writer's attic at Harper's *magazine to a man with dirt between your toes?*

My path was through the garden. I loved gardening from a very young age, and liked growing food for myself. From there it was kind of an easy step to an epiphany on a feedlot and on a potato field when I was doing a piece of journalism. I was driving down Route 5 in California, which links San Francisco to L.A. And it was a beautiful golden fall day. Suddenly this stench came up. I couldn't believe the smell. I didn't know what it was because everything around me looked exactly the same. And I drove a little longer. The landscape, which had been gold, turned black. And it was a feedlot that's right on the highway, on both sides of the highway.

Suddenly I was in this nightmare landscape where there were mountains of manure the size of pyramids, and mountains of corn the size of pyramids, and black cows as far as you could see. I was like, "Wow, this is where my meat comes from?" I had no idea. And that was when I decided I owe it to myself, I owe it to my readers, and my family, to figure out where my food comes from.

You said in your letter to the president-elect that the first family should "eat locally." What did that mean?

Well, look, the president's bully pulpit is a very important thing. And, you know, I think the first family could set an example by whom they appoint White House chef. Is it someone who's really associated with this local food movement who would not only cook wonderful, healthy food for them, but who, at state dinners, would kind of shine a light on some of the best farmers in this country and elevate the prestige of farming? I also think that we need, in addition to a White House chef, a White House farmer.

Are you suggesting that the president should rip up the South Lawn?

Not all of it. They've got seventeen acres to play with. I don't know exactly how much, but I'm saying five acres. Put in a garden, an organic garden. Hire a good farmer to grow food there. I think that would send a powerful message. This has happened before. Eleanor Roosevelt put a victory garden at the White House in 1942, over the objections of the Department of Agriculture, who thought it was going to hurt the food industry if people started growing food at home. You know, God forbid.

Some things never change.

Yes, I know. But she persisted, and she said, "This is really important for the war effort. I want to encourage people to grow food." She put in this garden, and by the end of the war, there were twenty million victory gardens in America. People were ripping up their lawns, planting vegetables, raising chickens, and by the end of the war, 40 percent of the fresh produce in America was being produced in home gardens. So it's not trivial, it could make a tremendous contribution, especially in hard times.

We have some people right here in urban New York who are growing gardens.

You know, a lot of people talk about the elitism of the food movement, and they think about Whole Foods and people shopping at upscale farmers' markets. But there is another face to this food movement. There is a real crisis in the inner city over access to fresh produce. And we know that the distance from a source of fresh produce is a predictor of health.

Example: West Oakland, California, is an area that has about twenty-six convenience stores, liquor stores that sell processed food, and not a single supermarket. No source of fresh produce. You might get some onions and potatoes in that convenience store, but that is it. Yet it's full of fast-food outlets. So in effect you have a fresh-food desert. And that is one of the reasons that people in the inner city have such higher rates of diabetes. There is a demand for fresh and healthier food that's not being served.

Oddly enough, government policy helped get the fast-food outlets into the city—via well-intentioned Small Business Administration loans to encourage minority business ownership. The easiest business to get into is opening a fast-food franchise in the inner city; our government helped that happen. Again, for good reasons. We need similar programs to encourage the supermarkets to come in, so there is a source of fresh produce. Or draw in the farmers' markets. Why not offer every food stamp recipient a voucher redeemable at a farmers' market for fresh, wholesome food? At a stroke, that would draw farmers' markets into the inner city and improve the diet. Not just the number of calories people are getting, but the quality of those calories.

But with urban sprawl, with so many acres of farmland being turned over to development, most of us live a long way from a farmers' market.

I agree that, since the '50s, a lot of the local farms have been paved over with houses. We need to protect the land that remains because, when the oil runs out, we're going to need to be able to feed ourselves from within one hundred, two hundred, three hundred miles. One of the more significant things that happened when we had this oil price spike last summer is the price of moving a box of broccoli from the Salinas Valley in California, where most of it is grown, to the Hunts Point Market here in New York went from $3 to $10.

When that happened, two or three of the big growers in California started buying farmland in New England. See, they get that, in the future, we're going to need to grow food closer to where people live. And broccoli grows really well anywhere in this country. So we need to look at high-quality farmland close to cities like New York and realize that it's as precious as, say, a wetland, which we wouldn't let you develop unless you could really prove the need to develop a wetland. We need to protect farmland, and we're going to need different solutions in different parts of the country.

We need to recognize that what people in Iowa are really growing there is cattle feed. It looks like corn and beans, but 40 to 50 percent of that grain is going to feed cattle and hogs. So what if we cut out all the transportation, the middleman, and actually put animals back on those farms? Let them grow really high-quality, grass-fed beef. You know, that is some of the best agricultural land in the world, and so we grow meat, back on the land, sustainably. It's not all or nothing. We need to let a thousand flowers bloom. We need to try many things in many places to figure out what works.

Okay, give me a list of what we can do to make a difference.

If you've got space, plant a garden, and if you don't, look into a community garden where you might rent a little bit of space. Cook. Simply by starting to cook again, you declare your independence from the culture of fast food. As soon as you cook, you start thinking about ingredients, you start thinking about plants and animals, and not the microwave, and you will find that your diet, just by that one simple act, is greatly improved. You will find that you are supporting local agriculture, because you'll care about the quality of ingredients. And whether you're cooking or not is one of the best predictors for a healthy diet. People with more money generally have healthier diets, but affluent people who don't cook are not as healthy in their eating as poor people who still cook. Very, very important. If you don't have pots and pans, get them.

People say they don't have time, and that's an issue. I am saying that we do need to invest more time in food. Food is just too important to relegate to these ten-minute corners of our lives. You know, we watch cooking shows like crazy on television. We've turned cooking into a spectator sport. If you would merely invest the time you spend watching cooking shows in actually cooking, you would find you've got plenty of time to put a meal on the table.

Are you suggesting that we're going to have to learn to slaughter our own pigs? I don't have a fridge large enough for a whole hog.

I actually think buying a freezer, Bill, is a really good investment, because that's how you can take advantage when there are deals at the farmers' market. I actually think hunting is a very sustainable form of meat production in a lot of places, where we have way too many whitetail deer. I know that this will offend some people. But by hunting and growing some of your own food, you make yourself a real producer. It sounds kind of sweet and old-lady-like, but gardens are very powerful things.

My garden now is only ten feet by twenty feet, but it produces so much produce I need to give much of it away. I have to spend time figuring out how to get rid of it. By gardening, you will obtain some of the healthiest, freshest food you can possibly get. It is the shortest food chain of all. And it teaches certain habits of mind that I think are really, really important. You know, the philosopher Wendell Berry had a phrase. He said, you know, we're afflicted by this "cheap-energy mind," because cheap energy has allowed us to outsource so much in our lives. We do our job, and for everything else, we have a specialist who provides it. They entertain us, they feed us, they clothe us. We don't do anything for ourselves anymore. It's one of the reasons that when we look at climate change, we feel so helpless, because we can't imagine doing any more for ourselves.

Well, as soon as you start gardening, you've found a cure for the cheap-energy mind. You're suddenly realizing, "Hey, I can use my body in support of my body. I have other skills. I can feed myself if I needed to." And that is a preparation, I think, for the world we may find ourselves in. But it's very empowering to realize that you're not at the mercy of the supermarket.

We have 6.7 billion people on this earth, needing to be fed. If we put into effect what you're talking about, do you think that we have a system that will produce enough food?

As long as the sun still shines, there is the energy to produce food. When people ask, "Can we feed the world sustainably?" the thing we need to remember is that about 40 percent of all the grain we're growing in the world, which is most of what we grow, we are feeding to animals. So there's an awful lot of slack there. There is plenty of food, if we organize our agriculture in a proper way.

The "Can we feed the world?" argument has been used for fifty years to drive the industrialization of agriculture. It is agribusiness propaganda by people who are not particularly interested in feeding the world. They're interested in driving up productivity on American farms. Yes, some want to export food. ADM and Cargill want to ship it out to other places, but basically, they want their raw materials as cheap as possible, and you need overproduction to achieve that. If you're producing that McDonald's hamburger or Coca-Cola, you're dependent on corn and soy, and the cheaper they are, the more profit you're going to make.

I'm sorry that I can't persuade you or convince you to take the job. You would be a provocative secretary of agriculture.

Well, that's probably a good word for it. ∽

LOUISE ERDRICH

Every once in a while, a book so possesses me that I happily give up a couple of consecutive nights of sleep—as well as the evening news broadcasts and late-night talk shows—to finish it.

That's what happened when I opened the novel Shadow Tag *by Louise Erdrich. She might have been writing about any of us, trying to negotiate our complex familial and sexual longings, but Gil and Irene, the troubled and fiercely passionate couple whose story is the heart of* Shadow Tag, *also contain traces of the DNA of the Native American clans we met in Erdrich's first novel,* Love Medicine.

This is Erdrich's secret—she makes their story our story, although they may have descended from Ojibwe chieftains and we from Scottish clansmen. Erdrich grew up Catholic on the endless plains of the Dakotas, the daughter of a French Ojibwe mother and a German American father. To this day she will willingly show you the old confessional stall that she keeps in her nifty bookstore—Birchbark Books—in Minneapolis. But she will just as quickly introduce you to some of the phrases she recently learned in classes that she is taking to help preserve the Ojibwe language. Such surprises make this "emissary of the between-world" the quintessential American.

—Bill Moyers

When I opened Shadow Tag *and read the first page, it was like stepping onto a high-speed train that didn't stop until it reached its destination. And even then I didn't want the trip to be over. It's a masterpiece of suspense and character. Where did the idea come from?*

I wanted to write a suspense novel. I like that kind of narrative. And I wanted to do exactly what you picked out about it. I wanted to have a reader start it and keep reading it and want to know what happens in the end.

Where did the title come from?

Did you play shadow tag when you were a child?

Yes, that's where you try to step on the shadow of the other—

The other person's shadow.

Yes.

If you grow up in a place where you can play outdoors, under a street lamp, you can play late into the night. And that's what I did. I had that title in mind for many, many, many years until it occurred to me that if the shadow selves in a relationship were to interact somehow, they would be playing shadow tag. I don't mean only the darker sides of people, but I also mean the dream sides, the subterranean sides that we don't know. We don't always know what our actions are going to be in respect to another person, and somehow, in this setting, in the book, the shadow selves of the family begin to interact.

There is a moment with the husband and wife—Gil and Irene—when we sense the layer of deception that is at the heart of their marriage. We realize she both hates him and she loves him.

They're very intertwined. Gil is a painter. And Irene is often his subject. He's an artist . . .

And most of his paintings are of her, at different stages and in different poses. You're revealing the story of a stolen identity—how a man steals his wife's image and power.

And it's also a book about diaries and about doubles. I love the German word *doppelgänger*, by the way. That image kept coming back to me and then into this book.

Irene is keeping two diaries.

She realizes that he is secretly reading her diary, so she begins to write a second diary, one that's false.

She's writing lies deliberately for him to read.

She's manipulating him.

Manipulating him. Which leads me to ask how much of marriage involves holding back a part of ourselves?

About half.

The shadow half?

No, I think the shadow half is very important to show in a marriage. This doesn't happen often. We wait and hold back that half until we're absolutely secure with each other. You can't completely immerse yourself in another human being.

You're also writing about love, survival, and memory. Those themes that the reader understands come from your American Indian past. Memory is very important to the survival of Native Americans.

Memory is all. Memory is where the language resided, because it was an oral language. The stories were not written down. I have to say that as you said that, the image of my father came into my mind. I thought about the letters he's written me. He's written me hundreds, maybe thousands of letters over my lifetime. And his letters are really the treasures of my life. They take in whole pieces of memory, and they're his gift to me. He described everything that was happening around him.

You keep returning to this Native American imagery in your past.

That is one of the reasons Native American people puzzle other people. Why is that so strong with them? Why don't they just become like the rest of us? What is it that's so important in their culture that they cling to it so? I think this has to do with the belongingness and the sense of peace that I feel among other Native people, this sense of community, where I'm in the comfort of a very funny, grounded people who are related to everything that's around them. And that's why being Ojibwe or Anishinabe is so important to me. I'm very proud, very comfortable with it.

You heard Ojibwe spoken when you were growing up.

Oh, yes, my grandfather spoke Ojibwe. He had his medicine bundle as he prayed, and he would walk in back of the house and stand in the woods before he went a little way into them. I would stand behind him and listen to him praying. And as I grew up, I thought that Ojibwe was like Latin, a ceremonial language. And it wasn't until I was in my teens that I walked into a situation where people in a store were all speaking Ojibwe. They were laughing and having a good time, and I wanted to know what the jokes were. I wanted to get the jokes. And one day I said to myself: "I have to know this language." When I moved to Minnesota, I found there was a thriving, determined movement, a grassroots movement, to revitalize the Ojibwe language. Now, I've never come to be a competent speaker, I have to say that right now. But even learning the amount of Ojibwe that one can at my age is a life-altering experience.

How so?

You see the world in a different way. You're working in a language in which there is a spirit behind it. I think it has to do with Ojibwe being one of the indigenous languages of this continent. You see the forms of things that were named long, long ago. And you see the forms of things that have been named relatively recently.

Give me an example of what you're talking about.

Okay, I'll read from this book. It's for the Ojibwe immersion schools, a vocabulary project.

> Mii sa go da-gaagiigidowaad, da-anama'ewaad, da-ozhibii'igewaad endaso bebezhig debendaagozid.

Now, that's a translation by Rose Tainter of the First Amendment to the U.S. Constitution. You know, Native Americans put their deepest trust in the United States government. And they teach their children about their relationship to that government.

After all their bad experiences with a government constantly going back on its word, breaking its promises?

After all those bad experiences, yes. Native Americans first fought in World War I before they had citizenship. The American flag comes out first at every powwow. There's a heart-to-heart feeling about the government that we are nation-to-nation with you. It's a sense of equality, that you will recognize us, that we did not vanish as you thought. We survived. We exist. We have our language. We have your words in our language. We have your constitution in our language.

And your children are learning Ojibwe?

Yes. For that sense of community, peace, comfort, and because this speaks to our background. I'd love to meet my ancestors. I'd love to be able to speak to them. There's a teaching that after you die you're going to be asked what your name is in Ojibwe. You will have to give your name. And you will speak to the spirit if you want to go to that place of your ancestors. Otherwise, you will go to the Christian heaven, which doesn't seem like much fun.

And the difference?

You can do all sorts of things in your Ojibwe heaven that you can't do in the Christian heaven. You can gamble. You can make love. You can eat. It's a world where there are no sad consequences to any pleasurable thing you do, a world like this one, but without the pain.

When you reach the other side and you're asked your name in Ojibwe, what are you going to say?

I have two Ojibwe names. The first is my grandfather's name for me. The second name, Kinewgonebiik, means "the feather of the golden eagle." But I don't know that I'm going to reach the other side, Bill. I keep shifting my spiritual beliefs about an afterlife.

Well, you may have to invoke your Catholic past, right? Your German side of the family.

That's the beauty of being a mixed person. Assuming there's a German afterlife, I'll just have to think fast.

You have that capacity. Your cultures keep competing within your imagination, don't they?

They do. They do.

And the ideas in this book—they come from this constant interplay between these many cultures?

I live on the margin of just about everything, Bill. I'm a marginal person, and I think that is where I've become comfortable. I'm marginally there in my Native life, and marginally German. I'm always a mother. That's my first identity, but I'm always a writer, too. I have to write. I have a very fractured inner life.

Your first nonfiction was about your pregnancy and your child's birth, the first year of that child's life, The Blue Jay's Dance. *What was the metaphor there?*

It was a blue jay's dance of courage in front of a hawk. I saw it from the window as I was nursing my baby. I kept feeders, and all sorts of birds came down. I saw a blue jay. And then a hawk swooped down on it. The blue jay knew it was doomed, but it started to dance at the hawk. And the hawk was startled. The blue jay was confusing it. This dance of an inferior bird against a superior raptor finally so mortified the hawk that it flew away.

This is the mother's role, the blue jay's dance to keep the aggressive threats at a distance, right?

I never really thought of it exactly that way. Yes, it's the advantage so many of us have, in a small way. It's the advantage of behaving in a surprisingly courageous fashion when the odds are completely against you.

Which is what mothers do.

I've seen it—many do.

And it comes through in Shadow Tag, *with Irene.*

Yes.

There's this prescient kid in the family named Stoney.

Yes.

And he comes to a profound truth in this one short passage. Will you read it for us?

> Irene bent over and held her son. With her arms locked, she backed up to the living room couch and toppled them both onto the pillows. Stoney tightened his arms around Irene, still sobbing so harshly that he couldn't form words. There was nothing to do but stroke his sun-shot hair. Soon Irene could feel the hot tears soak through her shirt.
>
> What is it? What is it?
>
> The crying began all over again with the same miserable force. Then Stoney quit.
>
> I don't want to be a human, he said. His voice was passionate. I want to be a snake. I want to be a rat or spider or wolf. Maybe a cheetah.
>
> Why, what's wrong?
>
> It's too hard to be a human. I wish I was born a crow, a raccoon, or I could be a horse. I don't want to be human anymore.

"It's too hard to be human." This is a six-year-old speaking. Unpack that. What are you saying through him?

That we rationalize ourselves out of shame. We can rationalize anything away as we get older and older, but a child hasn't that capacity yet. And when the shame hits, he's knocked over. The truth of shame can do that. And it's what comes back to us. This is what happens to everybody. There's going to be a time, no matter who we are, that we participate in the very oldest of human sorrows. We are at one with other people in our loss, in our shame, and we come to the very limit of who we are as people. We face that part of ourselves that we never wanted to look at. And then we experience shame the way a child experiences it. It's one of those moments that link us with other human beings. At least I think so.

There's something else that comes up here, too, which is that no matter how much a parent loves a child, you can't protect the child from the cruelty of the world.

No. Well, a mother is a frayed net, you know. We stretch ourselves over everything we can, but there are holes all over the place where things get through. And we do everything, fathers and mothers. We try so hard. But we can't do it all. We can't completely protect our children, obviously. I do want things to be ordinary for my children. Routine can be a good thing. I want things to be simple, so they can cope. But that's not what the world is like, and that's not even what they want. They want to grow in every way that they possibly can, and that's going to involve pain.

That conflict—the reality in your stories—reminds me that a well-known reviewer said that with each successive novel Louise Erdrich is writing, she's writing more like Ernest Hemingway, William Faulkner, Albert Camus. That's a heavy burden.

If I thought that way, I wouldn't be able to do a thing.

No, but some reviewers do. And they expect your next novel to be Hemingway, Camus, Faulkner.

Just got to be Erdrich. I can't do anything else. Let me read you something else. There are many writers who are more deserving of that sort of praise, but I don't think many of them have as many children, or as messy a house, as I do. I wrote a poem and called it "Advice to Myself":

ADVICE TO MYSELF

Leave the dishes.
Let the celery rot in the bottom drawer of the refrigerator
and an earthen scum harden on the kitchen floor.
Leave the black crumbs in the bottom of the toaster.
Throw the cracked bowl out and don't patch the cup.
Don't patch anything. Don't mend. Buy safety pins.
Don't even sew on a button.
Let the wind have its way, then the earth
that invades as dust and then the dead
foaming up in gray rolls under the couch.
Talk to them. Tell them they are welcome.
Don't keep all the pieces of the puzzles
or the doll's tiny shoes in pairs, don't worry
who uses whose toothbrush or if anything

matches, at all.
Except one word to another. Or a thought.
Pursue the authentic—decide first what is authentic,
then go after it with all your heart.
Your heart, that place
you don't even think of cleaning out.
That closet stuffed with savage mementoes.
Don't sort the paperclips from screws from saved baby
   teeth
or worry if we're all eating cereal for dinner
again. Don't answer the telephone, ever,
or weep over anything that breaks.
Pink molds will grow within those sealed cartons
in the refrigerator. Accept new forms of life
and talk to the dead
who drift in through the screened windows, who collect
patiently on the tops of food jars and books.
Recycle the mail, don't read it, don't read anything
except what destroys
the insulation between yourself and your experience
or what pulls down or what strikes at or what shatters
this ruse you call necessity.

Now I know how it is you're so prolific. That's real discipline!

In my case, I suspect it has to do with a small, incremental, persistent, insect-like devotion to putting one word next to the next word. It's a very dogged process. I make myself go upstairs, where I write, whenever I can. And I never have writer's block. If I went up there and had writer's block, I think I'd lose my mind. I have to get up to my papers and my books and my notebooks—I am always jotting things down, by the way. And I just keep going.

You've come such a long way from those days when you were a waitress, a signal woman at a construction site. You kept getting a lot of rejection slips when you first started writing. When you got rejection after rejection, why did you keep writing? And what do you say to young writers about keeping it up despite a slap in the face?

I kept writing because I grew up as a Catholic. The one place we were allowed to be emotional and to really talk about ourselves was in the confessional. You're safe there, in the darkness. And you begin to think, "Well, I have a sacred part of me—like the priest, who is supposed to be a conduit to God—that can also receive these unknowable emotions." Eventually I began to write about what was innermost. Sometimes I was astonished at what I read that I had written down, because I didn't mean to have written some of those things. I'm from a small town, as you know, and sometimes mothers come up to me in my daughters' grade schools, they look at me, and they say, "It must be unique, living in your head. How could you write that?" I don't know why the filter is not there, but I have to be as truthful as I can. I have to get as close to the bare truth as I can.

The truth of what?

Experience. When I talked about the insulation between yourself and your experience—back to what we were saying about a child—you don't develop this insulating skin until you begin to be hurt, over and over, until you begin to rationalize, over and over. But when you can go back to it as an adult in writing, you get inside that skin and just hang on for dear life. I loved writing because of that. I'm able to live in a world where I can be expressive and I can be truthful about emotion and about human nature.

Did you want to be a priest when you were growing up?

I wanted the power of the priest. The priest had a great deal of power. A lot of the women who taught me were Franciscan sisters. They could have been happier as priests. Their power was thwarted.

The theme to many of your stories.

Thwarted female power. Yes.

And identities, often stolen by the men in their lives.

Often.

That helps me understand the story in The Last Report on the Miracles at Little No Horse.

About Father Damien, yes.

Father Damien was secretly a woman.

Yes, having worn the habit of a sister, a nun, and knowing that she's called to be a priest—well, she is a very good priest. She wore her disguise well. The best priest I ever wrote about.

She sacrificed her female identity.

Yes, she did. But she lived as the priest. She was able to do that.

Do you have an assured faith now?

I go through a continual questioning. And I think that is my assurance—if I were to let go of my doubt, I believe that I would somehow have surrendered my faith. My job is to address the mystery. My job is to doubt. My job is to keep searching, keep looking. We don't understand works of art when we see them. We see the greatest works of art through a glass darkly. They're very difficult for us to understand. So with this great work of art in which we're all participating—this life—the Great Artist has made beauty and terror and death and cruelty and humor and mystery part of who we are. As well as commerce and politics and all the rest. Everything is part of this mystery.

So who is God in Ojibwe?

Gichi-Mandidoo or Gizhe Manidoo. The great kind spirit, the spirit that looks after all of the good in the world but also looks after all that is painful in the world. The Creator.

So God is life.

"Endless forms most beautiful." ∾

NIKKI GIOVANNI

When she heard about the shootings, Nikki Giovanni had a flash: could the killer be that odd young man who had once sat in her class? She was off campus that spring day in 2007 when Seung-Hui Cho, an English major at Virginia Tech, suddenly turned violent, murdering thirty-two people and wounding twenty-five before killing himself. Heading back to the stricken community, Giovanni heard his name and knew it was so: he had attended her poetry class. The next day she was asked to speak at a memorial service for the victims. Her words brought thousands to their feet in a tearful standing ovation—a moment, someone said, "of profound healing." Here are some excerpts:

Nikki Giovanni reading from:

WE ARE VIRGINIA TECH
(16 APRIL 2007)

We know we did nothing to deserve it

But neither does the child in Africa
Dying of AIDS

Neither do the Invisible Children
Walking the night away

To avoid being kidnapped by a rogue army

Neither does the baby elephant watching his community
Be devastated for ivory
Neither does the Mexican child looking for fresh water. . . .

We are Virginia Tech. . .

We will continue
To invent the future
Through our blood and tears
Through all this sadness . . .

We will prevail.

Watching on C-SPAN, I wondered how many others remembered, as I could, the younger Nikki Giovanni, bursting on the scene in the incendiary '60s, a time of bitter divides and wounds that would not heal. A student activist at Fisk University in Nashville, a soul mate of Angela Davis and James Baldwin, a founding member of the Black Arts Movement, the "Princess of Black Poetry."

POEM FOR FLORA

and she would learn . . .

how god was neither north
nor south east or west
with no color but all
she remembered was that
Sheba was Black and comely

and she would think

i want to be
like that

All these years later, the "Princess" has ripened into a strong, handsome woman of hard-won, sturdy experience, the University Distinguished Professor of English at the school that now turned to her, desperately in need of solace and courage. And she did not let them down. The words she gave them that *day are now the closing pages in a collection of her poems that she calls, simply,* Bicycles.

—*Bill Moyers*

—◦◦◦—

You came through with the right words in that memorial service for the victims at Virginia Tech. Your words truly met the moment. How do you explain to yourself the power of words at such a time?

They let us know we're not alone. I think what words do is acknowledge that we're human and we hurt. So you don't have to pretend you're not hurting. You can admit you have a hole in your heart. Go back to 9/11. People were posting poems all over the Internet, because they were trying to find a way to connect, to say, "This hurts, but we're not alone. Someone else is sharing this pain." And this thing that happened at Virginia Tech, it was an incredibly sad time for us. The only thing I could do to make sense out of it was to connect these dots. And the only thing to connect the dots was love. Because no matter what else is wrong with you, good wine and good sex will make you feel better. I don't know if I'm allowed to say that on this show.

You are granted permission.

Well, good, because, you know, sixty-five-year-old women are not finished.

I hope not. Why did you turn to the metaphor of bicycles? What do they have to do with tragedy, drama, loss, death?

Well, tragedy and trauma are wheels. And they're always with us, aren't they? They're always spinning around, on the perimeters of life, like tragedies. They just spin around and spin around. And so what you're trying to do is bring them together. And when you bring them together you've got the bar, right? So you have a vehicle. Now, when I grew up, you learned to ride a bicycle by getting on a bicycle. Which means you're going to fall off. And love and life and bicycles are about trust and balance. It's about riding it and believing that this thing that doesn't make sense for you to be on, can move. And we see it here. This is such a great city—I love Manhattan. And I miss it in my dreams sometimes. But when we see the messengers on their bikes, in a frenzy of traffic, that's just trust and balance. It's beautiful watching them on their bicycles. But that's what we do in our relationships. It's the same bike. Our relationships need trust and balance.

So have you learned to ride a bicycle?

I did. An emotional bicycle. I saw the spinning wheels because I was spinning. I was being hurt by things that had nothing to do with me. I was being hurt because my sister had a lung tumor that had metastasized. And I will go to my grave believing my mother died because she didn't want to bury my sister, because there was nothing wrong with my mother until it was evident that my sister was not going to make it. And I say it all the time: the only reason I want to go to heaven is to tell those two women, "You did it to me again." Because they were always leaving me, Bill. I was a baby. Remember Robert Louis Stevenson:

> BED IN SUMMER
>
> In winter I get up at night
> And dress by yellow candlelight.
> In summer, quite the other way,
> I have to go to bed by day.
>
> I have to go to bed and see
> The birds still hopping on the tree . . .

And I had to go to bed at nine o'clock. Mommy would bathe us at seven. And then we'd sing or tell stories. Then she would come and get my sister, about nine-thirty, and I would hear her: "Is she asleep?" And my sister would say, "I think so." And then they would sneak out. So when they up and died, I said, "They did it again. They left me again." I had to write my way out of it.

Let's hear "Bicycles."

> BICYCLES
>
> Midnight poems are bicycles
> Taking us on safer journeys
> Than jets
> Quicker journeys

Than walking
But never as beautiful
A journey
As my back
Touching you under the quilt

Midnight poems
Sing a sweet song
Saying everything
Is all right
Everything
Is
Here for us
I reach out
To catch the laughter

The dog thinks
I need a kiss

Bicycles move
With the flow
Of the earth

Like a cloud
So quiet
In the October sky
Like licking ice cream
From a cone
Like knowing you
Will always
Be there

All day long I wait
For the sunset

The first star
The moon rise

I move
To a midnight

Poem
Called
You
Propping
Against
The dangers

I love that one.

My favorite of your poems is "Choices." Would you read it?

Oh, certainly.

CHOICES

if i can't do
what i want to do
then my job is to not
do what i don't want
to do

it's not the same thing
but it's the best i can
do

if i can't have
what i want then
my job is to want
what i've got
and be satisfied
that at least there
is something more
to want

since i can't go
where i need
to go then i must go
where the signs point
though always understanding
parallel movement
isn't lateral

when i can't express
what i really feel
i practice feeling
what i can express
and none of it is equal
i know
but that's why mankind
alone among the mammals
learns to cry

Where did that one come from?

From the book I wrote while my father was dying, *Cotton Candy On a Rainy Day*. Burying my dad was a sad affair because I wasn't that close to him. But my mother liked him, and I liked my mother. So I figure, maybe she knows something I don't know. But when I buried Mommy, I knew that I was going into a place where there was no one that I could talk to. When your mommy's gone, there's no one who's going to enter that boat that you row by yourself back to that place where your deepest fears reside.

There are many somber books born of grief. Here's one of love born of grief. Yours is a book of love poems.

Well, what else is going to make you smile at a time like that? The writing of it makes me smile. What else will get you through? And you start to dress better, start to take care of yourself again. Now, let me digress to say I'm a freak for how food looks. I will not eat ugly food. I'm an American and will not starve to death, so I do not have to eat ugly food. I refuse to do drive-through. I am not a grazer, I am not a cow. You eat. You sit down. You put a napkin there. And it has to have the colors. If you're having a steak, then you'll want a few little carrots because they are yellow and look good. And maybe a little broccoli. When my uncle died, my aunt Ag was very sad. And I called her and said, "Ag, what'd you have for dinner?" She said, "Oh, I just had a bowl of cereal." I said, "You can't do that. You have to plate your food." So in bad times I want good-looking food. Have massages. It feels great, somebody rubbing oil in your back. Bill, you have to do things to re-mind yourself that it's a really good idea to be alive.

Okay, I hear you. But do you think a lot about death? The campus where you teach was stalked by death. You lost your mother and your sister in the same approximate time. You've lost a lung, right?

Yes. Yes.

To cancer?

I was glad to give that up. It was a bad lung. Nasty. Mean lung. It was my left lung. I didn't need it. I have another one.

Does all of this cause you at sixty-five to think about death?

No, Bill, I think I fell in love.

You fell in love?

Oh, yeah. Absolutely. It is wonderful. And when you're in love you just keep thinking of things that are wonderful to do. Life is a good idea.

All right. So tell me what it takes to write a love poem.

A generous spirit and a willingness to make a fool of yourself.

It takes those to love, too.

That's love.

You've written that love is about you and not the beloved. And you said that's very important to remember as you're writing a poem. Why?

Because it's your trip. I've always been amazed that you can break up with somebody, and that somebody will say to you, "If you leave me, I'm going to kill you." Now, logic says, if I'm dead, you still didn't get me. Right? See what I'm saying? I learned a long time ago, because I just fell madly in love, and I don't mind saying this, his wife knows it, with Billy Dee Williams. Billy is so good-looking. If I was forty years younger I'd be in love with Barack Obama. But I realized that it had nothing to do with Billy Dee. Being in love has nothing to do with how the person feels about you. It has to do with how you feel about yourself.

Okay, but loving someone who doesn't love you can be a source of pain.

No, that's just because you're expecting something that you can't have. That kind of love is crazy. And it's going to go away. It's like a cold. So the important thing to ask yourself is not what can that person do for me, but what can I do? I've got the light, what do I do with it?

I must say, some of your poems reek with desire.

Oh, desire is there. You fall in love, there's always desire. But, also, there's a lot of longing. And I realize that a lot of this book still has a lot to do with my mother. I miss the safety. And I think one is never so unsafe as when one's mother is not there to put her arms around you. Your mom just makes you safe, you know? Your mother just says, "It's going to be all right." No matter what it is, you say, "Yeah." So I really had to stop myself, on April 16, from picking up the phone because after that tragedy on the campus, I wanted to hear my mother's voice. But I stopped. She wasn't there.

When the killings occurred you wanted to talk to your mom?

Yeah. I did. Because I knew she'd make sense out of it for me.

How about reading "Everything Good Is Simple"?

EVERYTHING GOOD IS SIMPLE

Everything good is simple: a soft boiled egg . . . toast fresh from the oven with a pat of butter swimming in the center . . . steam off a cup of black coffee . . . John Coltrane bringing me "Violets for My Furs"

Most simple things are good: Lines on a yellow legal pad . . . dimples defining a smile . . . a square of gray cashmere that can be a scarf . . . Miles Davis *Kind of Blue*

Some things clear are complicated: believing in a religion . . . trying to be a good person . . . getting rid of folk who depress you . . . Horace Silver *Blowing the Blues Away*

Complicated things can be clear: Dvořák's *New World* Symphony . . . Alvin Ailey's *Revelations* . . . Mae Jemison's ride in space . . . Mingus *Live at Carnegie Hall*

All things good are good: poetry . . . patience . . . a ripe tomato on the vine . . . a bat in flight . . . the new moon . . . me in your arms . . . things like that

I like that.

It's a nice poem.

And then there's "Give It a Go?"

"Give It a Go?" is just an old lusty poem. I love it.

GIVE IT A GO

I like to polish
Silver
Rub the paste in
Let it set
Then shine shine shine

Even as a little girl
I loved to wash
Grandmother's crystal
Watch the light bounce
Off of the edges
Of the glasses

We were taught
Never to use clear
Fingernail polish
But trim our nails
To a respectable length
And buff them
With lamb's wool

I wipe my bathroom
Mirror after each shower
And always shine my faucet

In order to properly care for things
They must be loved
And touched

Want to give it
A go?

I'm game.

That's a shout-out to Prince Charles and Camilla.

Oh?

Yes. Because there's a story that Camilla said to Charles: "You know, my grandmother was the mistress of your grandfather. Want to give it a go?" So I did this poem as a shout-out to Charles. I'm a big fan of Charles. I think he's a great kid. And had a lot on him to be, what, is he fifty-five years old? To spend your life waiting for your mother to die so that you can do what you were born to do. That's a burden. So I did a shout-out to Charles.

I like the whimsy. But I have to say, these poems are a long way from your days as a young revolutionary.

Indeed.

Did you know love then? Or was it the love of the cause? The passion of the commitment?

Young people do things differently. And I did what I thought I should do. I'm proud of what I did then. But look at what the hip-hop generation has done—elected a president. Barack Obama's president of the United States. This is something that we would only dream of. One of the poems here in *Bicycles* is a poem I did for Huey Newton, who was a wonderful young man. Here's Huey registering voters, sponsoring school programs. Huey was about the politics. Martin Luther King Jr. was about justice for the world. Martin would be happy, I'm sure, that the United States has elected this fine young man. But he would still weep for the children dying of malaria and hunger around the world. He wanted a just earth. And his job went beyond the bus boycott. His job was to change the earth. He's way bigger. He's way bigger.

What do you think about all the talk that Obama's election means we've moved into a postracial world?

Well, I think as much as people don't like it, yes.

Is that feasible—desirable—that we don't think of race anymore?

Oh no, no, we think of race. But we now don't think that race means an automatic exclusion, as it once did. There's going to be lots of racist things that are going to happen. I mean, we've already seen a young man get shot in the back in Oakland, California. The young baseball player gets shot in his own driveway. We still have a way to go before this is really a postracial time. We'll always see race. When we look at a Barack Obama, we are looking at a man of color. If we just go back even ten years, when we looked at Tiger Woods, maybe fifteen years ago, I remember Tiger saying, "I'm not really black." Well, it was fine with me, because if you don't want to be black, you don't have to be. But it made me want to call up and say, "Tiger, baby, have you looked in the mirror lately?"

So it's not that we don't see race but that race is now an enhancement. Right now somebody is saying, "My daughter can be president of the United States." Maybe the first Chinese American president of the United States will be a woman. We've opened up the world.

What opened up your world?

Largely my grandmother. She was a great old girl. I adored her. When Grandmother walked, I'd be right behind her. If she stopped, I would bump into her. I wrote the poem "Knoxville, Tennessee" for Grandmother—it's a love poem, too. I never feel safe, Bill. I'm always looking for safe places. And I always felt safe with Grandmother. Also, she wanted to change the world. She wasn't ambitious for money and stuff. But she wanted to make an impact. And she fought very hard in Knoxville, Tennessee, to make changes for black folks. Her drive made me want to make a difference.

Where did your adoration of words come from?

Oh, probably Grandpapa. He was a Latin teacher. He graduated from Fisk University and taught at Austin High School. Grandpapa was twenty years older than Grandmother when they met—talk about a crazy love. He fell in love with her. Unfortunately, he was married, and Grandmother wouldn't have any truck with him. She wouldn't let him make love to her because— well, I used to hear them talk, later, when I lived with them, and she told him, "John Brown Watson, if I had let you kiss me"—that was the metaphor for making love, but it meant something more, you know—"you would never have married me." And Grandmother was right. So he divorced his wife and married her. But he's twenty years older, and by the time we came along, Grandpapa was an old man and not one to suffer fools gladly. I never knew why Grandpapa spent time with me. But he would say, "Nikki, let's go look at the stars." We'd go out and he would say, "That's Orion's Belt. That's the Big Dipper." And then he would explain the heavens. He read all of the myths to me.

He saw something.

Yes. I mean, I don't know. But that's where I got whatever I got. My father's a big talker, so if you put together my grandfather's intellectual interests with my father's bullshitting, I think you end up with a Nikki.

You wrote a poem once to specifically empower girls.

Because girls are always sitting around listening to stupid things that boys say. And half the games girls play: "Little Sally Walker, what is she doing? She's rising to the east, looking for the one she loves the best. What's her name? Snow White. And she's going to go to sleep until 'one day my prince will come.'" You get sick of that. You get a girl who can spin flax into gold, and her father then takes her up to the prince to say, "You should marry my daughter. She can spin flax into gold." Now I ask you, Bill, what does she need with him? If she can spin flax into gold, she didn't need the prince. So I wrote "ego-tripping" as a shout-out to how wonderful it is to be a girl, to be complete within yourself.

Let's hear it.

EGO-TRIPPING (THERE MAY BE A REASON WHY)

I was born in the congo
I walked to the fertile crescent and built
  the sphinx
I designed a pyramid so tough that a star
  that only glows every one hundred years falls
  into the center giving divine perfect light
I am bad

I sat on the throne
  drinking nectar with allah
I got hot and sent an ice age to europe
  to cool my thirst

My oldest daughter is nefertiti
  the tears from my birth pains
  created the nile
I am a beautiful woman

I gazed on the forest and burned
  out the sahara desert
  with a packet of goat's meat
  and a change of clothes
I crossed it in two hours
I am a gazelle so swift
  so swift you can't catch me

  For a birthday present when he was three
I gave my son hannibal an elephant
  He gave me rome for mother's day
My strength flows ever on

My son noah built new/ark and
I stood proudly at the helm
  as we sailed on a soft summer day

I turned myself into myself and was
  jesus
  men intone my loving name

  All praises All praises
I am the one who would save

I sowed diamonds in my back yard
My bowels deliver uranium
  the filings from my fingernails are
  semi-precious jewels
  On a trip north
I caught a cold and blew
My nose giving oil to the arab world
I am so hip even my errors are correct
I sailed west to reach east and had to round off
  the earth as I went
  The hair from my head thinned and gold was

    laid across three continents

    I am so perfect so divine so ethereal so surreal
    I cannot be comprehended
      except by my permission

    I mean . . . I . . . can fly
      like a bird in the sky . . .

I wrote this for little girls, Bill, but the joy of my life was watching a couple of little kindergarten boys recite it for me once. I realized it was a good poem because the boys didn't feel excluded from it. When you can do something like that and little boys say, "I was born in the congo"—whoa, wait a minute, we might have something here.

What was the turning point in your life? What was the hinge?

I think maybe it's still ten years down the pike. I haven't hinged yet. I haven't thought about it like that.

No, but you start out as this passionate, incendiary, controversial activist. "The Princess of Black Poetry," it was said.

Yeah. That was nice. I'm still passionate. I just don't try to censor myself as I go through things. I was never an ideologue.

What were you?

I was just a woman looking at the world, trying to find a way to be happy and to be safe and to make a contribution. And in order to do that, a lot of bush had to be cut down. I don't think I cut down any trees. I'm a big fan of trees. But there were a lot of weeds out there. And racism, poverty, just basic prejudice against women. Prejudice against any number of things. And so you go through one field after another, and you say to yourself: "I have got to knock some of these weeds down." That's all I was trying to do. I was just trying to be me. ❧

ANDREW BACEVICH

Our finest warriors are often our most reluctant warmongers. They have seen firsthand the toll war exacts. They know better than anyone that force can be like a lobster trap that closes with each stage of descent, making escape impossible. So it was when the liberal consensus lured America into Vietnam during the '60s, and again after 9/11, when neoconservatives clamored for the invasion of Iraq. With the notorious ferocity of the noncombatant, the neocons banged their tin drums and brayed for blood, as long as it was not their own that would be spilled.

One old warrior looked on sadly, his understanding of combat's reality tempered by twenty-three years in uniform, including service in Vietnam. A graduate of West Point, Andrew Bacevich retired from the military to become a professor of history and international relations at Boston University, a public thinker who has been able to find an audience across the political spectrum, from The Nation *to* The American Conservative *magazines. In several acclaimed books, including* The New American Militarism: How Americans Are Seduced by War, Washington Rules: America's Path to Permanent War, *and his bestselling* The Limits of Power: The End of American Exceptionalism, *Bacevich speaks truth to power, no matter who's in power, which may be why he reaches both the left and the right.*

We spoke in the middle of the 2008 presidential campaign, just as The

Limits of Power *was published. Bacevich supported Barack Obama's candidacy but believes that Obama's commitment of more troops to Afghanistan was a deadly mistake.*

—*Bill Moyers*

⸎

You began The Limits of Power *with a quote from the Bible, the book of Second Kings, chapter 20, verse 1: "Set thine house in order." Why that admonition?*

I've been troubled by the course of U.S. foreign policy for a long, long time. I wrote the book in order to sort out my own thinking about where our basic problems lay. And I reached the conclusion that our biggest problems are within.

I think there's a tendency on the part of policy makers and probably a tendency on the part of many Americans to think that the problems we face are problems that are out there somewhere, beyond our borders. And that if we can fix those problems, then we'll be able to continue the American way of life as it has long existed. I think that's fundamentally wrong. Our major problems are at home. You begin healing yourself by looking at yourself in the mirror and seeing yourself as you really are.

You write: "The pursuit of freedom, as defined in an age of consumerism, has induced a condition of dependence—on imported goods, on imported oil, and on credit. The chief desire of the American people," you write, "is that nothing should disrupt their access to these goods, that oil, and that credit. The chief aim of the U.S. government is to satisfy that desire, which it does in part through the distribution of largesse here at home (with Congress taking a leading role) and in part through the pursuit of imperial ambitions abroad."

In other words, you're saying that our foreign policy is the result of a dependence on consumer goods and credit.

Our foreign policy is not something simply concocted by people in Washington, D.C., and then imposed on us. Our foreign policy may be concocted in Washington, D.C., but it reflects the perceptions of our political elite about what we the people want. And what we want, by and large, is to sustain the flow of very cheap consumer goods. We want to be able to pump gas into our cars regardless of how big they happen to be, in order to be able to drive wherever we want to be able to drive. And we want to be able to do these things without having to think about whether or not the books balance at the end of the month or the end of the fiscal year. And therefore, we want an unending line of credit.

You write that what will not go away is "a yawning disparity between what Americans expect and what they are willing or able to pay."

One of the ways we avoid confronting our refusal to balance the books is to rely increasingly on the projection of American military power around the world to maintain this dysfunctional system, or set of arrangements, that have evolved over the last thirty or forty years.

But it's not the American people who are deploying around the world. It is a very specific subset of our people, this professional army. We like to call it an all-volunteer force, but the truth is, it's a professional army, and when we think about the tasks we assign that army, it's really an imperial army. We need to step back a little bit and ask ourselves, how did it come to be that places like Iraq and Afghanistan should have come to seem critical to the well-being of the United States of America?

There was a time, seventy, eighty, a hundred years ago, when we Americans sat here in the Western Hemisphere and puzzled over why British imperialists sent their troops to places like Iraq and Afghanistan. We viewed that sort of adventurism with disdain. Today this has become part of what we do.

How is Iraq a clear manifestation, as you say, of this "yawning disparity between what Americans expect and what they are willing or able to pay"?

Let's think about World War II, a war that President Roosevelt told us was essential to U.S. national security, and was. President Roosevelt said, because this is an important enterprise, the American people would be called upon to make sacrifices. And indeed, the people of the United States went off to fight that war in large numbers. On the home front, people learned to get by with less. It was a national effort.

None of that's been true with regard to Iraq. I mean, one of the most striking things about the way the Bush administration has managed the global war on terror, which President Bush has compared to World War II, is that there was no effort made to mobilize the country, there was actually no effort even made to expand the size of the armed forces. Just two weeks or so after 9/11 the president said, "Go to Disney World. Go shopping." There's something out of whack here. The global war on terror, and Iraq as a subset of the global war on terror, is said to be critically important, on the one hand. Yet on the other hand, the country basically goes about its business, as if, really, there were no war on terror, and no war in Iraq ongoing at all.

So it is, you write, "seven years into its confrontation with radical Islam, the United States finds itself with too much war for too few warriors—and with no prospect of producing the additional soldiers needed to close the gap."

We're having a very difficult time managing two wars that, in a twentieth-century context, are actually relatively small.

You also say: "U.S. troops in battle dress and body armor, whom Americans profess to admire and support, pay the price for the nation's collective refusal to confront our domestic dysfunction." What are we not confronting?

The most obvious, blindingly obvious, question is energy. It's oil. I think historians a hundred years from now will puzzle over how it could be that the United States of America, the most powerful nation in the world, as far back as the early 1970s, came to recognize that dependence on foreign oil was a problem, posed a threat, compromised our freedom of action, and then did next to nothing about it. Every president from Richard Nixon down to the present has declared, "We're going to fix this problem." And none of them did. The reason we are in Iraq today is because the Persian Gulf is at the center of the world's oil reserves. I don't mean that we invaded Iraq on behalf of big oil, but the Persian Gulf region would have zero strategic significance were it not for the fact that that's where the oil is.

Back in 1980, President Carter promulgated the Carter Doctrine. He said the Persian Gulf had enormous strategic significance to the United States. We were not going to permit any other country to control that region of the world. That set in motion a set of actions that militarized U.S. policy and led to ever deeper U.S. military involvement in the region. The result has been to postpone the day of reckoning. Americans are dodging the imperative of having a serious energy policy.

And this is connected to what you call "the crisis of profligacy."

Well, we don't live within our means. The individual savings rate in this country is below zero. As a nation, we assume the availability of an endless line of credit. But as individuals, the line of credit is not endless; that's one of the reasons why we're having this current problem with the housing crisis, and so on. And my view would be that the nation's assumption that its line of credit is endless is also going to be shown to be false. And when that day occurs it's going to be a black day indeed.

You call us an empire of consumption.

I didn't create that phrase. It's a phrase drawn from a book by a wonderful historian at Harvard University, Charles Maier. The point he makes in his very important book is that when American power was at its apex after World War II, through the Eisenhower years, into the Kennedy years, we made what the world wanted. They wanted our cars. We exported our television sets, our refrigerators—we were the world's manufacturing base. He called it an "empire of production."

Sometime around the 1960s there was a tipping point when the "empire of production" began to become the "empire of consumption." When the cars started to be produced elsewhere, and the television sets, and the socks, and everything else. And what we ended up with was the American people functioning primarily as consumers rather than producers.

And you say this has produced a condition of profound dependency, to the extent that, and I'm quoting you, "Americans are no longer masters of their own fate."

Well, they're not. I mean, the current debt to the Chinese government grows day by day. Why? Because of the negative trade balance. Our negative trade balance with the world is something on the order of $800 billion per year. That's $800 billion of stuff that we buy, so that we can consume, that is $800 billion more than the stuff that we sell to them. That's a big number, even relative to the size of our economy.

You use a metaphor that is intriguing. American policy makers "have been engaged in a de facto Ponzi scheme intended to extend indefinitely the American line of credit." What's going on that resembles a Ponzi scheme?

This continuing tendency to borrow and to assume that the bills are never going to come due. I testified before a House committee on the future of U.S. grand strategy. I was struck by the questions coming from members that showed an awareness, a sensitivity, and a deep concern about some of the issues that I tried to raise in the book.

How are we going to pay the bills? How are we going to pay for the entitlements that are going to increase year by year for the next couple of decades, especially as baby boomers retire? Nobody has answers to those questions. So I was pleased that these members of Congress understood the problem. I was absolutely taken aback when they said, "Professor, what can we do about this?" I took this as a candid admission that they didn't have any answers, that they were perplexed, that this problem of learning to live within our means seemed to have no politically plausible solution.

You say that the tipping point between wanting more than we were willing to pay for began in the Johnson administration. "We can fix the tipping point with precision," you write. "It occurred between 1965, when President Lyndon Baines Johnson ordered U.S. combat troops to South Vietnam, and 1973, when President Richard M. Nixon finally ended direct U.S. involvement in that war." Why do you see that period as so crucial?

When President Johnson became president, our trade balance was in the black. By the time we get to the Nixon era, it's in the red. And it stays in the red down to the present. As a matter of fact, the trade imbalance essentially becomes larger year by year.

So I think that it is the '60s generally—the Vietnam period—that was the moment when we began to lose control of our economic fate. And most disturbingly, we're still really in denial.

You describe another fateful period between July 1979 and March 1983. You describe it, in fact, as a pivot of contemporary American history. That includes Jimmy Carter and Ronald Reagan, right?

Well, I would be one of the first to confess that I think that we have misunderstood and underestimated President Carter. He was the one president of our time who recognized, I think, the challenges awaiting us if we refused to get our house in order.

Talk about his speech on July 15, 1979. Why does that speech resonate so strongly?

This is the so-called Malaise Speech, even though he never used the word *malaise* in the text. It's a very powerful speech, because President Carter acknowledges that our dependence on oil poses a looming threat to the country. If we act now, he says, we may be able to fix this problem. If we don't act now, we're headed down a path along which not only will we become increasingly dependent upon foreign oil, but we will have opted for a false model of freedom. A freedom of materialism, a freedom of self-indulgence, a freedom of collective recklessness. The president was urging us to think about what we mean by freedom. We need to choose a definition of freedom that is anchored in truth, he argued, and the way to manifest that choice was by addressing our energy problem. Carter had a profound understanding of the dilemma facing the country in the post-Vietnam period. And, of course, he was completely derided and disregarded.

And he lost the election.

Exactly.

This speech killed any chance he had of winning reelection. Why? Because the American people didn't want to settle for less?

They absolutely did not. And indeed, the election of 1980 was the great expression of that, because in 1980, we have a candidate, perhaps the most skillful politician of our time, Ronald Reagan, who says, "Doomsayers, gloomsayers, don't listen to them. The country's best days are ahead of us."

"Morning in America."

It's "Morning in America." You don't have to sacrifice; you can have more of everything. All we need to do is get government out of the way and drill more holes for oil. The president led us to believe the supply of oil right here in North America was infinite.

You describe Ronald Reagan as the "modern prophet of profligacy, the politician who gave moral sanction to the empire of consumption."

To understand the truth about President Reagan is to appreciate the extent to which our politics are misleading and false. Remember, he was the guy who came in and said we need to shrink the size of government. But government didn't shrink during the Reagan era, it grew. He came in and he said we need to reduce the level of federal spending. He didn't reduce it. It went through the roof. The budget deficits for his time were the greatest we'd experienced since World War II.

And wasn't it his successor, his vice president, the first President Bush, who said in 1992 that the American way of life is not negotiable?

This is not a Republican thing, or a Democratic thing. All presidents, all administrations are committed to that proposition. Now, I would say that probably 90 percent of the American people today likewise concur. They insist that the American way of life should not be not up for negotiation.

What I would invite them to consider is this: if you want to preserve the American way of life, then you need to ask yourself, what exactly is it you value most? I believe that if we want to preserve that which we value most in the American way of life, then we will need to change the American way of life. We need to modify or discard things that are peripheral in order to preserve those things that possess real importance.

What do you value most?

I say we should look to the Preamble to the Constitution. There is nothing in the Preamble to the Constitution that defines the purpose of the United States of America as remaking the world in our image, which I view as a fool's errand. There is nothing in the Preamble to the Constitution that provides a basis for embarking upon an effort, as President Bush has defined it, to transform the greater Middle East, a region of the world that incorporates something on the order of a billion people.

I believe that the framers of the Constitution were primarily concerned with the way we live here, the way we order our affairs. They wanted Americans as individuals to have an opportunity to pursue freedom, however defined. They wanted Americans collectively to create a national community so that we could live together in some kind of harmony. And they wanted future generations to be able to share in those same opportunities.

The big problem, it seems to me, with the current crisis in American foreign policy is that unless we change our ways, the likelihood that our children and our grandchildren are going to enjoy the opportunities that we've had is very slight. Why? Because we're squandering our power. We are squandering our wealth. To the extent that we persist in our imperial delusions, we're also going to squander freedom itself, because imperial policies end up enhancing the authority of the imperial president, thereby providing imperial presidents with an opportunity to compromise freedom even here at home. We've seen that since 9/11.

The disturbing thing that you say again and again is that every president since Reagan has relied on military power to conceal or manage these problems that stem from the nation's habits of profligacy, right?

That's exactly right. And again, this is another issue where one needs to be unsparing in fixing responsibility as much on liberal Democratic presidents as conservative Republican ones. I think that the Bush administration's response to 9/11 in constructing this paradigm of a global war on terror, in promulgating the so-called Bush Doctrine of preventive war, in plunging into Iraq—an utterly unnecessary war—will go down in our history as a record of recklessness unmatched by any other administration.

But that doesn't really mean that Bill Clinton before him, or George Herbert Walker Bush before him, or Ronald Reagan before him were all that much better. They all have seen military power as our strong suit. They all have assumed that by projecting power, by threatening to employ power, we can fix the world. Fix the world in order to sustain this dysfunctional way of life that we cling to at home.

This brings us to what you call the political crisis of America, and you say, "The actual system of governance conceived by the framers . . . no longer pertains."

I am expressing in the book what many of us sense, even if few of us are ready to confront the implications. Congress, especially with regard to matters related to national security policy, has thrust power and authority to the executive branch. We have created an imperial presidency. Congress no longer is able to articulate a vision of what is the common good. Congress exists primarily to ensure the reelection of its members.

Supporting the imperial presidency are the various institutions that comprise the national security state. I refer here to the CIA, the Joint Chiefs of Staff, the Office of the Secretary of Defense, the other intelligence agencies. These have grown since the end of World War II into a mammoth enterprise. But the national security state doesn't work. Despite all the money it spends and the people it employs, the national security state was not able to identify the 9/11 conspiracy. It was not able to deflect the attackers on 9/11. The national security state was not able to plan intelligently for the Iraq War.

The national security state has not been able to effectively prosecute this so-called global war on terror. So as the Congress has moved to the margins, as the president has moved to the center of our politics, the presidency itself has come to be, I think, less effective. The system is broken.

You write that no one in Washington knows what they're doing, including the president.

What I mean specifically is this: The end of the Cold War coincided almost precisely with the first Persian Gulf War. Americans saw Operation Desert Storm as a great, historic, never-before-seen victory. It really wasn't.

Politically and strategically, the outcome of that war was far more ambiguous than people appreciated at the time. Nonetheless, the war itself was advertised as this great success, demonstrating that the Pentagon had developed a dazzling new American way of war. This new American way of war ostensibly promised to enable the United States to exercise military dominion on a global basis in ways that the world had never seen.

The people in the Pentagon developed a phrase to describe this. They called it "full-spectrum dominance," meaning that the United States was going to demonstrate outright supremacy, not just capability, across the full spectrum of warfare. This became the center of the way that the military advertised its capabilities in the 1990s.

The whole thing was fraudulent. To claim that the United States military could enjoy such dominance flew in the face of all of history. Yet in many respects, this sort of thinking set us up for how the Bush administration was going to respond to 9/11. If you believe that the United States military is utterly unstoppable, then a global war to transform the greater Middle East might seem plausible. Had the generals been more cognizant of the history of war, and of the nature of war, then they might have been in a better position to argue to Mr. Rumsfeld, then the secretary of defense, or to the president himself, "Be wary. Don't plunge in too deeply." Recognize that force has utility, but that utility is actually quite limited. Recognize that when we go to war, almost inevitably unanticipated consequences will follow, and they're not going to be happy ones.

Above all, recognize that when you go to war, it's unlikely there will be a neat, tidy solution. It's far more likely that the bill that the nation is going to pay in lives and in dollars is going to be a monumental one. My problem with the generals is that, with certain exceptions—one could name General Shinseki . . .

Who said we are going to need more than half a million men if we go into Iraq. He was shown the door for telling the truth.

By and large, the generals did not speak truth to power.

One of the things that comes through in your book is that great truths are contained in small absurdities. And you use the lowly IED, the improvised explosive device, or roadside bomb, that's taken such a toll on American forces in Iraq, to get at a very powerful truth.

Wars are competitions. Your enemy develops capabilities. And you try to develop your own capabilities to check him and gain an advantage. One of the striking things about the Iraq War, in which we had been fighting against a relatively backward or primitive adversary, is that the insurgents have innovated far more adeptly and quickly than we have.

The IED provides an example. It began as a very low-tech kind of primitive mine, and over time became ever more sophisticated, ever more lethal, ever more difficult to detect. Those enhancements in insurgent IED capability continually kept ahead of our ability to adapt and catch up.

And I think you say in your book that it costs the price of a pizza to make a roadside bomb. This is what our men and women are up against in Afghanistan.

The point is that war is always a heck of a lot more complicated than you might imagine the day before the war begins. And rather than imagining that technology will define the future of warfare, we really ought to look at military history.

And what do we learn when we look to the past?

Preventive war doesn't work. The Iraq War didn't work. Therefore, we should abandon the Bush Doctrine of preventive war. We should return to the just-war tradition, which permits force only as a last resort, which sees war as something that is justifiable only when waged in self-defense.

How, then, do we fight what you acknowledge to be the real threat posed by violent Islamic extremism?

I think we need to see the threat for what it is. Sure, the threat is real. But it's not an existential threat. The nineteen hijackers that killed three thousand Americans on 9/11 didn't succeed because they had fancy weapons, because they were particularly smart, or because they were ten feet tall. They succeeded because we let our guard down.

We need to recognize that the threat posed by violent Islamic radicalism, by terrorist organizations like al-Qaeda, really is akin to a criminal conspiracy. It's violent and dangerous, but it's a criminal enterprise. Rooting out and destroying the conspiracy is primarily the responsibility of organizations like the FBI, and of our intelligence community, backed up at times by Special Operations Forces. That doesn't require invading and occupying countries. One of the big mistakes the Bush administration made, and it's a mistake we're still paying for, is that the president persuaded us that the best way to prevent another 9/11 is to embark upon a global war. Wrong. The best way to prevent another 9/11 is to organize an intensive international effort to dismantle that criminal conspiracy.

In fact, you say that instead of a bigger army we need a smaller, more modest foreign policy, one that assigns soldiers missions that are consistent with their capability. "Modesty"—I'm quoting you—"implies giving up on the illusions of grandeur to which the end of the Cold War and then 9/11 gave rise. It also means reining in the imperial presidents who expect the army to make good on those illusions."

People run for the presidency in order to become imperial presidents. The people who are advising these candidates, those who aspire to be the next national security advisor, the next secretary of defense, yearn to share in exercising this great authority. They're not running to see if they can make the Pentagon smaller.

I was in the White House back in the early '60s, and I've been a White House watcher ever since. I have never come across a more distilled essence of the evolution of the presidency than in just one paragraph in your book.

You write, "Beginning with the election of John F. Kennedy in 1960, the occupant of the White House has become a combination of demigod, father figure, and, inevitably, the betrayer of inflated hopes. Pope, pop star, scold, scapegoat, crisis manager, commander in chief, agenda setter, moral philosopher, interpreter of the nation's charisma, object of veneration, and the butt of jokes . . . all these rolled into one." I would say you nailed the modern presidency.

I think the troubling part is that the president has become what we have instead of genuine politics, instead of genuine democracy. The cult of the presidency has hollowed out our politics and, in many respects, has made our democracy a false one. We're going through the motions of a democratic political system, but the fabric of democracy really has worn very thin.

Would the imperial presidency exist were it not for the Congress?

No, because the Congress, since World War II, has thrust power and authority onto the presidency.

Here is what I take to be the core of your analysis of our political crisis. You write, "The United States has become a de facto one-party state, with the legislative branch permanently controlled by an Incumbents' Party." And you write that every president "has exploited his role as commander in chief to expand on the imperial prerogatives of his office."

One of the great lies about American politics is that Democrats genuinely subscribe to a set of core convictions that make Democrats different from Republicans. And the same thing, of course, applies to the other party. It's not true.

I happen to define myself as a conservative. But when you look back over the past thirty or so years, said to have been a conservative era in American politics, did we get small government? Do we get balanced budgets? Do we give serious, as opposed to simply rhetorical, attention to traditional social values? The answer's no. The truth is that conservative principles have been eyewash, part of a package of tactics that Republicans employ to get elected and to then stay in office.

And yet you say that the prime example of political dysfunction today is the Democratic Party in relation to Iraq.

Well, I may be a conservative, but I can assure you that in November of 2006 I voted for every Democrat I could find on the ballot. And I did so because the Democratic Party, speaking with one voice at that time, said, "Elect us. Give us power in the Congress, and we will end the Iraq War."

The American people, at that point adamantly tired of this war, did empower the Democrats. And Democrats absolutely, totally, completely failed to follow through on their promise.

You argue that the promises of Harry Reid and Nancy Pelosi proved to be empty. Reid and Pelosi's commitment to forcing a change in policy took a back-seat to their concern to protect the Democratic majority.

Could anybody disagree with that?

This is another one of my highlighted sentences: "To anyone with a conscience, sending soldiers back to Iraq or Afghanistan for multiple combat tours while the rest of the country chills out can hardly seem an acceptable arrangement. It is unfair, unjust, and morally corrosive." And yet that's what we're doing.

Absolutely. And I think—I don't want to talk about my son here.

You dedicate the book to your son.

My son was killed in Iraq. That's a personal matter. But it has long stuck in my craw, this posturing of supporting the troops. There are many people who say they support the troops, and they really mean it. But what exactly does it mean to support the troops? It ought to mean more than putting a bumper sticker on the back of your car. I don't think we actually do support the troops. What we the people do is we contract out the business of national security to approximately 0.5 percent of the population, about a million and a half people who are on active duty. And then we really turn away. We don't want to look when our soldiers go back for two or three or four or five combat tours. That's not supporting the troops. That's an abdication of civic responsibility. And I do think there's something fundamentally immoral about that.

Again, I think the global war on terror, as a framework of thinking about policy, is deeply defective. But if the global war on terror is a national priority, then why isn't the country actually supporting it in a meaningful, substantive sense?

Are you calling for a reinstatement of the draft?

I'm not, because I understand that, politically, the draft is an impossibility. And to tell you the truth, we don't need to have an army of six or eight or ten million people. What we need is to have the country engaged in what its soldiers are doing. That simply doesn't exist today.

Despite your and your wife's loss, you say in this powerful book what to me is a paradox. You say that "ironically Iraq may yet prove to be the source of our salvation." Help me to understand that.

We Americans are going to have a long argument about the Iraq War, not unlike the way we had a very long argument about the Vietnam War. And that argument is going to cause us, I hope, to ask serious questions about where this war came from and what it has meant. How did we come to be a nation that fancied our army capable of transforming the greater Middle East?

What have been the costs that have been imposed on this country? Hundreds of billions of dollars. Some project $2 to $3 trillion. Where is that money coming from? How else could it have been spent? For what? Who bears the burden? Who died? Who suffered loss? Who's in hospitals? Who's suffering from PTSD? And was it worth it? There will be plenty of people who are going to say, "Absolutely, it was worth it. We overthrew a dictator." But I hope and pray that there will be many others who will make the argument that it wasn't worth it.

My hope is that Americans will come to see the Iraq War as a fundamental mistake. That it never should have been undertaken. And that we're never going to do this kind of thing again. That might be the moment when we will look at ourselves in the mirror. And we will see what we have become. And perhaps undertake an effort to make those changes that will enable us to preserve for future generations that which we value most about the American way of life. ∽

Robert Wright

When hysteria broke out over the building of an Islamic cultural center near the site of the 9/11 attacks in New York, right-wing Christians and Jews—and the politicians who kowtow to them—sounded as if they were holding all Muslims collectively guilty of terrorism. We were once again reminded why trying to understand religious experience is crucial to navigating the treacherous waters of the twenty-first century.

I thought back to my conversation a year earlier with Robert Wright, who had just published his book The Evolution of God. *He told me, "Religion will be the medium by which people express their values for a long time to come, so it's important to understand what brings out the best and worst in it."*

Wright, the founder of Bloggingheads.tv, is known as a journalist of big ideas. In The Moral Animal, *published in 1994, he argued that the biological process of natural selection that determines the fate of a species can create a more ethical human society. Six years later, in* Nonzero, *he used game theory to speculate that modern society doesn't have to be a win-lose proposition.*

For The Evolution of God *he spent almost a decade charting the history of belief, from the Stone Age to the present, examining how societies mingled and interacted over the centuries. Call it a religious version of globalization: the gods that have been the most successful—that have attracted the most believers around the world—are those, according to Wright, that can shed their early vengeful incarnations and adapt into a more universal, more benevolent form. This was good news for a change, holding out the possibility that despite the competition between monotheistic fundamentalists, we may be able to evolve beyond the religious wars. His book arrived swiftly on the bestseller list despite a paucity of advance publicity—a tribute to the following that Wright has gained through his fearless search for the moral underpinnings of society. Of course, the evolution of God is no purely abstract exercise for him. As a kid in Texas he was buckled to the Bible Belt—"born again," as the saying goes. It was the first step of his own journey into the understanding of religious experience, one that has kept on evolving ever since.*

—Bill Moyers

So here's the journalistic lede I would use if I were reviewing your book: Robert Wright has made a convincing case that as circumstances change, God has changed, because the story of God is intrinsic to the human story. But what Wright has not done is to make a convincing case that God exists.

I would say it's hard for anyone to make a convincing case that God exists in the sense of pointing to evidence. And I don't really try to do that. I mean, I do argue that there is evidence of some sort of larger purpose unfolding through the workings of nature. But that doesn't tell you much about what might have infused the purpose.

As I read your book, I kept thinking that for a long time now, human beings have been yielding great power over their lives to a supreme being whose existence they can't prove. What is there in human nature that does that?

I don't think there's a kind of God gene, or that religion was designed in by natural selection because it helps us survive and reproduce. Back at the beginning of religion, the main purpose seems to have been to explain to people why good things happen and why bad things happen and how you increase the number of good things.

It doesn't initially serve a moral purpose, in our sense of the term. So it's not about discouraging theft or discouraging lying or anything. It's about people trying to figure out why disease afflicts them sometimes. Why they lose wars sometimes and win them. They come up with theories that involve gods. And then they try to manipulate the gods in ways that will make things better.

So did God begin as a figment of the human imagination?

I would say so. Now, I don't think that precludes the possibility that as ideas about God have evolved, people have moved closer to something that may be the truth about ultimate purpose and ultimate meaning.

In my earlier writings about evolutionary psychology, one thing that became clear to me is that the human mind is not designed to perceive ultimate truth or even truth in a very broad sense. I mean, the human mind was designed by natural selection to get genes into the next generation, to do some things that help you do that, like eat and reproduce. The human mind is not designed to perceive truth that goes beyond this narrow part of the material world.

But there was something in even the primeval brain that was able to conceive of the supernatural, something beyond the perceived workings of nature.

Yes. Very early on, apparently, people started imagining sources of causality, things out there making things happen. And early on there were shamans who had mystical experiences that even today a Buddhist monk would say were valid forms of apprehension of the divine or something. But by and large I think people were making up stories that would help them control the world.

I chuckled when you compared the shamans of early times—the first religious experts, we might say—to stockbrokers today. Each claiming to have special insights into a great and mysterious force that shapes the fortunes of millions of people.

Right. Some serious economists have argued that you're better off throwing darts at a list of stocks on the wall than listening to any broker in particular. And yet we continue to pay them tremendous credence.

I think what that shows is that whenever you don't understand what it is that's influencing very momentous events, you will pay attention to anyone who credibly says they have the answer. And I think that's in the beginning of shamanism. That's what's going on. People say, "I understand the will of all these gods."

What does that say about human nature that we will turn to an intermediary?

I guess it says that we get a little desperate when we're faced with actual ignorance, and mistakes matter. But it's certainly true that this just pervades society, not only in the religious realm but in financial markets, and things like that.

The gods of the market have failed, of course, again. We're living through that period right now, when there is no God on Wall Street anymore. But the God of Abraham thrives. What does it say about us that this ancient religion still has a vitality and a vibrancy?

I think it's a tribute to the evolutionary power of cultural change. And it shows us how God has adapted to varying cultural circumstances, because the God that is believed in now, first of all, assumes many different forms, even among believers.

I mean, the difference between the God I was brought up with in the Southern Baptist church and the way God would be conceived by an Anglican priest are very different. And similarly, there's been change over time. The fact that God can adapt accounts for His longevity. And at crucial points during that evolution, He acquired features that have proved very attractive.

The Christian doctrine of individual salvation, of an eternal afterlife, if you qualify, certainly helped the church flourish. It was picked up by Islam, by Muhammad, who was in touch with these doctrines, and has proved very popular. Look at the number of Christians and Muslims around today. So the very appealing parts of God endure, and I think the adaptation accounts for some of the real moral growth.

So if we are propelled along by natural selection, is it okay to say that God is a product of natural selection?

The God that I show evolving is undergoing a process very analogous to natural selection. New traits arise, and if they succeed in enhancing the power of God by, for example, attracting new believers, then they remain. And if they don't work for one reason or another, they fall by the wayside. So God has evolved very much the way the human organism evolved through natural selection, yes.

But you go to considerable lengths in here to make sure that we remember gods are products of cultural evolution, not biological evolution.

Cultural evolution is a much messier process than biological evolution. You and I can point to the source of our genes very easily: our parents and then their parents and so on. It's very easy to see the channels of influence. I'm not going to transmit any genes to you in the course of this conversation. It doesn't work like that.

But with cultural evolution, either of us could actually influence the ideas in our heads through conversation. Let's go back to the Roman Empire, when the Christian God is kind of in flux and is taking shape. It's not just a question of who, so to speak, his ancestor was. His ancestor was the God of the Israelites.

We know that. But meanwhile he can be picking up traits from all kinds of gods in the environment. And in fact, one thing I argue is that maybe the idea of individual salvation and being rewarded with a blissful afterlife if you live your life here right, may have come from one of the Egyptian cults that was competing with Christianity in the Roman Empire.

That's why it's hard to disentangle who's influencing whom. I mean, you can go back there and read the texts written by adherents of the so-called mystery religions, the Greco-Roman mystery religions. They describe a born-again experience that sounds very much like one a Christian might describe today. And it's really not clear who was copying whom back then.

Your own perception of God has evolved. As a child, God was real to you, right?

Very much.

Nine years old and you had a born-again experience of your own?

I went to the front of the church. I had been under the influence of a visiting evangelist at a Baptist church in El Paso, Texas, whose name was Homer Martinez. He was good. And I'll tell you how he made his reputation: by getting people like me to go up to the front of the church.

Walk the aisle, as we said.

It was a spontaneous thing. My parents weren't there. I went up to the front of the church and accepted Jesus and was baptized some weeks later. Then

I encountered the theory of evolution, and I had come from a creationist environment, so that was a kind of irreconcilable threat to my faith. The theory of natural selection seemed very compelling to me. And my parents even brought a Southern Baptist minister over to the house at one point when I was in high school to try to convince me that evolution had not happened. It didn't work.

But I'll tell you one thing I have not lost is that I've never lost the sense that I'm being judged by a being. If you're brought up believing that a god is watching you, it's a powerfully ingrained thing. And I think just in a vague kind of way I still feel that.

But does one need the God experience to have that?

I know plenty of conscientious people who don't believe in God. On the other hand, it seems to me not necessarily bad for the conscience to assume belief in a personal God. I mean, if you believe that there is a moral axis to the universe, okay. If you believe in moral truth—

And do you?

Yes, I do. I believe that there's a purpose unfolding that has a moral directionality. I have barely the vaguest notion of what might be behind that and whether it could be anything like a personal God or an intelligent being or not. That's another question. I don't know. But I will say, whatever is behind it, if something is, it's probably something that's beyond human conception.

One thing quantum physics has told us is A, that the way we're thinking about electrons is wrong. And B, the human mind is probably not capable of thinking about them really accurately. Okay? And yet thinking about them in this crude way and drawing little things that you say are electrons, given the constraints on the mind, it's all we can do, and it's useful.

Well, you might say that in the moral realm, given the constraints on human cognition, believing in a personal God is a pretty defensible way to go about orienting yourself to the moral axis of the universe, which wouldn't mean that a personal God exists.

An imagined personal God is accountable for our conscience, then?

I think, roughly speaking, evolutionary psychologists know how the conscience actually evolved. In other words, we can explain it plausibly in terms of natural selection. It gets back to these mutually beneficial relationships. Natural selection seems to have equipped us to enter into friendships. And part of that equipment seems to be because friendships are mutually beneficial. They're good. I mean, friendless people don't do well in society.

And one of the tools it seems to have given us is that we feel guilty if we neglect a friend or betray a friend. So these feelings of guilt and these feelings that there is some kind of moral truth out there that sometimes we fall short of are explicable in terms of natural selection. I don't think you need a god to explain that.

On the other hand, if you separately conclude that there is such a thing as moral truth and you want to try to use your conscience, which certainly is imperfect as natural selection shaped it, it's not by itself a reliable guide to moral conduct. And so if you want to shape the conscience in a way that makes it a better guide to moral truths, religious belief is certainly defensible and may be a valid way to do that.

But you're not saying that one has to be religious to be moral?

Absolutely not. One of my own closer contacts with, I would say, a form of consciousness that's closer to the truth than everyday consciousness came at a Buddhist meditation center. These were essentially secular Buddhists, and that was the context of the experience.

Through the meditative practice performed intensively for a week—no contact with the outside world, no speaking, five and a half hours of sitting meditation a day, five and a half hours of walking meditation a day—I reached a state of consciousness that I think is closer to the truth about things than the form of consciousness that is natural for human beings.

Was it a consciousness with an ethical and moral issue in it or was it a state of being? Of simple acceptance?

It absolutely had ethical implications because it involved much broader acceptance of other beings and it involved being less judgmental of other beings. I mean, it reached almost ridiculous extremes, looking down at weeds and thinking, "I can't believe I've been killing those things. They're actually as pretty as the grass. Prettier." But in the realm of humanity, by the end I was being very much less judgmental about people I would see on the street.

And my focus moved away from myself. I think that is movement toward the truth. The basic illusion natural selection builds into all of us is that we are special. If you were natural selection, that's obviously something you'd want to build into animals, right? Because that's how you get them to take care of their own and get their genes into the next generation. But it really is an illusion, and it's more fraught with ethical implications than we realize. It just suddenly blinds us to the truth about people, I think.

I do find more people like you who are seeking a spiritual practice without a governing deity presiding over it.

Yeah, it seems to work. These people, though—even these secular Buddhists, I would say—they do believe in a transcendent source of meaning. They believe that there's something out there that is the moral truth, and they are aligning themselves with it.

I know that we can't be precise, but in the larger sense was there a moment when God became a capital G?

There is this very curious word in the Bible, in the Hebrew version of the Bible, or what Christians would call the Old Testament: *Elohim*. It literally is the plural of the generic noun for "gods." Elohim is at this point becoming a proper noun, and so I would say it's not only God with a capital *G*, if this theory is right, but there's also a notion called the Godhead. It comes out of Hinduism, among other places, where the idea is that all the gods are manifestations of a single, underlying divine unity. And it may be that that notion of the Godhead is being hinted at in this particular language of God, this particular language for talking about God that's emphasized after the exile.

How do you relate that to the fact that, as you say again and again in here and as all of us know, the three great faiths all embraced the slaughter of infidels?

Right. They do. In the Koran, on one page Muhammad, or God speaking through Muhammad, is advising Muslims to greet unbelievers by saying, "You've got your religion, we've got ours." On another page it says, "Kill the infidels wherever you find them." Similarly, in the Bible, at one moment, God is advising the Israelites to completely wipe out nearby peoples who worship a foreign god. On another page, you've got the Israelites not only suggesting peaceful coexistence to a people who worship a foreign god but invoking that god to validate the relationships. So they say, "Your god gave you your land, our God gave us our land, can't we get along?"

The question is, why does God seem to be in these different moods? Why the mood fluctuations? I think the answer is actually good news, that when people feel that they can gain through peaceful collaboration or coexistence with another people, by and large they will find tolerance in their doctrines. Whereas when they feel threatened by a people in material terms, or there's a threat to their values, they're going to be more likely to find belligerence in their scriptures. And I think that's what was going on in ancient times, when God seemed to be changing moods.

Although all of that is in the pasts of these religions and surfaces periodically even today, the good news is that when people find themselves in a kind of interdependent relationship, when they see that they can gain through collaboration or that they don't need to be threatened, then doctrines of tolerance tend to emerge.

Are you suggesting that the character of God is ultimately defined by the conduct and interpretation of God's followers?

That is what God is, a construct. He consists of the traits that are attributed to Him at any given time by people. Now, that doesn't mean that theology can't get us closer to the truth about something that may deserve the term *divinity*. But yes, I think in the first instance, God is an illusion, and I'm tracing the evolution of an illusion.

Where do you come out in the old conflict among those who say that religion is good for people and those who say religion serves power? You know, Marx's argument that religion is a tool of social control.

I think religion is like other belief systems in that people will try to use it to their advantage. That's human nature. We all try to game the system. And if there are huge discrepancies in power, the powerful will try to use religion to their advantage. I don't think it has to be that way, and I think that often religion comes in a benign and good form. I think there's a kind of danger in being too cynical about religion. I think there's a danger in thinking that the so-called religious conflicts are fundamentally about religion and that without religion they wouldn't be here. For example, Richard Dawkins has said if it weren't for religion, there would be no Israel-Palestine conflict.

I think, A, that's not true. That conflict started as an essentially secular struggle over land. And B, it leads us to throw up our hands and say, "Well, what can you do? As long as people are religious, there's no point in addressing any grievances or rearranging the facts on the ground to try to make things better." I think there's been a dangerous overemphasis on the negative effects of religious belief in the modern world, although it has many negative effects.

I don't find any traces of cynicism in your book. In fact, I want to ask you about something you say toward the end: "Human beings are organic machines that are built by natural selection to deal with other organic machines. They can visualize other organic beings, understand other organic beings, and bestow love and gratitude on other organic beings. Understanding the divine, visualizing the divine, loving the divine—that would be a tall order for a mere human being." But we've not given up trying, have we?

No. And I think, you know, in a way we shouldn't. I mean I think if there is something out there called moral truth, we should continue to try to relate to it in a way that brings us closer to it.

Out there?

Did I say that?

Yeah, you've said it several times.

I should be careful. *Transcendent* is a very tricky word. And I get into trouble with hard-core materialists by using it because people think, "Oh, you mean spooky, mystical, ethereal stuff." I don't know exactly what I mean by *transcendent*. I may mean "beyond our comprehension." I may mean "prior to the creation of the universe" or something. I don't know. But I do think that the system on earth is such that humanity is repeatedly given the choice of either progressing morally in the sense of accepting more people into the moral circle or paying the price of social chaos.

We are approaching a global level of social organization, and if people do not get better at acknowledging the humanity of people around the world in very different circumstances, and even putting themselves in the shoes of those other people, then we may pay the price of social chaos.

After exploring thousands of years of how belligerent the great faiths can be, I expected to find you shrouded in pessimism. But at the end, you seem to put

a light in the window. And a glow comes from it of some hope that these re-
ligions, these great faiths, can overcome millennia of belligerence and accom-
modate one another.

Well, they have shown the ability to do that. I think one of the more encouraging facts about the history of Judaism, Christianity, and Islam is that
if you ask, "When were they at their best? When did doctrines of tolerance
emerge?" I answer that they were best in periods that were in some ways
analogous to a modern globalized environment.

In the ancient world the closest analogue to the modern globalized world
is an empire, a multinational platform. And I think all three religions have
shown their ability to adapt constructively to that kind of environment.
That doesn't mean they'll do it now. The moral progress that is needed is
not assured. But all three of them have this adaptive capacity that's been
proven.

You say it's going to take an extraordinary amount of smart thinking to deal
with this world that's on the verge of chaos. A world—and a chaos—to which
the great faiths have contributed.

In a certain sense the prophets of all three Abrahamic faiths got one thing
right that is applicable to this situation in the modern world. What all of
them were saying was that salvation is possible so long as you align yourself
with the moral axis of the universe.

Now, they meant different things by salvation. In the Hebrew Bible, they
often meant social salvation. In Christianity and Islam they might be more
inclined to mean individual salvation. And of course they didn't say the
moral axis of the universe. They said God. But to them God *was* the moral
axis of the universe.

But I think when you put it abstractly like that, it applies to the modern world. In other words, if we want to secure the salvation of the global
social system of the planet, if we want salvation in the Hebrew Bible sense
of the term, we do have to move ourselves closer to what I would call the
moral axis of the universe, which means drawing more of humanity into
our frame of reference. Getting better at putting ourselves in their shoes.
Expanding the realm of tolerance. And it has to happen symmetrically. It's
not enough for just the Muslim world or just the West to do it. But I do
think it has to happen.

You make me think that perhaps, in your head, God is the reasoning principle through time.

Interestingly, there is this idea of the *logos*.

"In the beginning was the Word," is how the New Testament, the book of John, translates it.

Yes, "the Word" in that passage is the translation of the Greek term *logos*. And in a way, the term reappears in the Koran when Muhammad says Jesus is the Word of God. But it also has an important place in Jewish thought. In fact, one of the thinkers I fastened onto in the book is an ancient thinker who I think is a pretty good candidate for modern theology. Philo of Alexandria was a Jew who lived around the time of Jesus except in a much more urban environment. And he had access to Greek philosophy. He had this idea that God is the *logos*, that this kind of logic is the animating spirit through history. And from a modern point of view, he said some things that look remarkable.

He said history was moving toward this world of tremendous interdependence and that part of God's plan was to make it so that individual peoples and even individual species would need one another, would be dependent on one another. And that as history wore on, that would become truer and truer. As a result, the world would move toward this kind of unity.

I think, in terms of logic animating history, that's a reasonably modern way to think of the divine. If you want to construct a theology that I would say can be rendered in a way that is compatible with modern science, I think Philo of Alexandria is a good place to start.

I keep coming back, though, to what you instructed us in this book when you talk about how everything we do and our response to it are affected by a brain which has not been prepared by natural evolution for the complexity of the social order today. And you say, "The way the human mind is built, antipathy can impede comprehension. Hating protesters, flag burners, and even terrorists makes it harder to understand them well enough to keep others from joining their ranks."

It's a tricky balance to strike because on the one hand, understanding terrorists and how they became terrorists, which is in our interests if we want to discourage the creation of more terrorists, tends to involve a kind of sympathy that in turn can lead you to say they are not to blame for what they did.

You don't want to say that because, as a practical matter, you have to punish people when they do bad things. So you don't want to let go of the idea of moral culpability, but you do need to put yourself in their heads. And that is really a great challenge in the modern world.

Are human beings likely to grow out of their need for God?

I think it's going to be a long time before a whole lot of them do, if they do. Religion will be the medium by which people express their values for a long time to come, so it's important to understand what brings out the best and the worst in it. And I think the answer to that question depends partly on how abstractly you define religion. You know, there is this William James quote that religion is the idea that there is an unseen order and our supreme interests lie in harmoniously adjusting ourselves to that order. It's a good definition because it encompasses the great variety of things we've called religion, and not many definitions do. If you define religion that way, I think it'll probably be with us forever. Because if you define religion that way, I'm religious, and if I qualify, that's defining it pretty broadly. ∾

DAVID SIMON

Watching movie and television versions of Charles Dickens's novels, I often have imagined him back from the beyond, only this time living in America, putting his remarkable powers of observation to the dramatization of life in our inner cities. Then one day, while screening some episodes of HBO's The Wire, *it hit me: Dickens is back and his pseudonym is David Simon.*

What Charles Dickens learned walking the streets and alleys of Victorian London, Simon saw and heard over twelve years as a crime reporter for The Baltimore Sun. *He turned his experiences first into a book and the NBC television series* Homicide, *then the HBO series* The Corner. *Next, with Ed Burns, a real-life cop turned teacher, he created* The Wire. *Their meticulous and brutally honest storytelling made Baltimore a metaphor for America's urban tragedy. During its five seasons,* The Wire *held up a mirror to an America many of us never see, where drugs, mayhem, and corruption routinely betray the promise of "life, liberty, and the pursuit of happiness" that is so ingrained in our political DNA.*

For The Wire *and his other work, David Simon recently received a MacArthur Fellowship, the half-million-dollar, no-strings-attached grant that honors singular creativity and innovation. In the last few years, Simon also has produced* Generation Kill, *a brutal and realistic depiction of combat in Iraq, and* Treme, *a series that dissects post-Katrina New Orleans much as*

The Wire *did Baltimore. Yet "when television history is written," one critic wrote, "little else will rival* The Wire." *Nor, when historians come to tell the story of America in our time, will they be able to ignore this Dickensian portrayal of America's expendable lives.*

—Bill Moyers

———

There is a fellow in city government here in New York who's a policy wonk and a die-hard Wire *fan. He was hoping I would ask you the one question on his mind: "David Simon has painted the most vivid and compelling portrait of the modern American city. Has he walked away from that story? And if he has, will he come back to it?"*

I've walked away from the *Wire* universe. It's had its five years. Stories have a beginning, middle, and end. If you keep stuff open-ended and you keep trying to stretch character and plot, they eventually break or bend.

What is it about the crime scene that gives you a keyhole, the best keyhole perhaps, into how American society really works?

You see the equivocations. You see the stuff that doesn't make it into the civics books, and you also see how interconnected things are. How connected the performance of the school system is to the culture of a street corner. Or where parenting comes in. The decline of industry suddenly interacts with the paucity and sort of fraud of public education in the inner city. Because *The Wire* was not a story about America, it's about the America that got left behind.

I was struck by something that you said. You were wrestling with this one big existential question. You talked about drug addicts who would come out of detox and then try to steel-jaw themselves through their neighborhood. And then they'd come face-to-face with the question—which is . . . ?

"What am I doing here?" You know, a guy coming out of addiction at thirty, thirty-five, because it often takes to that age, he often got into addiction with a string of problems, some of which were interpersonal and personal, and some of which were systemic. These really are the excess people in America. Our economy doesn't need them—we don't need 10 or 15 percent of our population. And certainly the ones who are undereducated, who have been ill-served by the inner-city school system, who have been unprepared for the technocracy of the modern economy, we pretend to need them. We pretend to educate the kids. We pretend that we're actually including them in the American ideal, but we're not. And they're not foolish. They get it. They understand that the only viable economic base in their neighborhoods is this multibillion-dollar drug trade.

I did a documentary about the South Bronx called The Fire Next Door *and what I learned very early is that the drug trade is an inverted form of capitalism.*

Absolutely. In some ways it's the most destructive form of welfare that we've established, the illegal drug trade in these neighborhoods. It's basically like opening up a Bethlehem Steel in the middle of the South Bronx or in West Baltimore and saying, "You guys are all steelworkers." Just say no? That's our answer to that? And by the way, if it was chewing up white folk, it wouldn't have gone on for as long as it did.

Can fiction tell us something about inequality that journalism can't?

I've wondered about that, because I did a lot of journalism that I thought was pretty good. As a reporter, I was trying to explain how the drug war doesn't work, and I would write these very careful and very well-researched pieces, and they would go into the ether and be gone. Whatever editorial writer was coming behind me would then write, "Let's get tough on drugs," as if I hadn't said anything. Even my own newspaper. And I would think, "Man, it's just such an uphill struggle to do this with facts." When you tell a story with characters, people jump out of their seats, and part of that's the delivery system of television.

Is it because we are tethered to the facts, we can't go where the imagination can take us?

One of the themes of *The Wire* really was that statistics will always lie. Statistics can be made to say anything. You show me anything that depicts institutional progress in America: school test scores, crime stats, arrest reports, anything that a politician can run on, anything that somebody can get a promotion on, and as soon as you invent that statistical category, fifty people in that institution will be at work trying to figure out a way to make it look as if progress is actually occurring when actually no progress is. I mean, our entire economic structure fell behind the idea that these mortgage-backed securities were actually valuable, and they had absolutely no value. They were toxic. And yet they were being traded and being hurled about, because somebody could make some short-term profit. In the same way that a police commissioner or a deputy commissioner can get promoted, and a major can become a colonel, and an assistant school superintendent can become a school superintendent, if they make it look like the kids are learning and that they're solving crime. That was a front-row seat for me as a reporter, getting to figure out how once they got done with them the crime stats actually didn't represent anything.

And you say statistics are driving the war on drugs, though.

Stats, you know, dope on the table. "We've made so many arrests." I mean, under one administration they used to ride around Baltimore and say, "If we can make fifty-four arrests a day, we'll have an all-time record for drug arrests." Some of the arrests, it was people sitting on their stoops and, you know, loitering in a drug-free zone, meaning you were sitting on your own steps on a summer day. Anything that is a stat can be cheated, right down to journalism. And I was sort of party to that.

So I would be watching what the police department was doing, what the school system was doing, you know, looking outward. But if you looked inward you'd see that the same game is played everywhere, that nobody's actually in the business of doing what the institution's supposed to do.

Many people could see what you saw simply if we opened our eyes. And yet the drug war keeps getting crazier and crazier, from selling guns to Mexico's drug cartel to cramming more people into prison even though they haven't committed violent crimes. Why don't the policies change?

Because there's no political capital in it. There really isn't. The fear of being called soft on crime, soft on drugs. The paranoia that's been induced. Listen, if you could be draconian and reduce drug use by locking people up, you might have an argument. But we are the jailing-est country on the planet right now. Two million people in prison. We're locking up less-violent people. More of them. The drugs are purer. They haven't closed down a single drug corner that I know of in Baltimore for any length of time. It's not working. And by the way, this is not a Republican-Democrat thing, because a lot of the most draconian stuff came out of the Clinton administration, this guy trying to maneuver to the center in order not to be perceived as leftist by a Republican Congress.

Mandatory sentences, three strikes—

Loss of parole. And again, not merely for violent offenders, because again, the rate of violent offenders is going down. Federal prisons are full of people who got caught muling drugs and got tarred with the whole amount of the drugs. It's not what you were involved in or what you profited from. It's what they can tar you with. You know, a federal prosecutor, basically, when he decides what to charge you with and how much, he's basically the sentencing judge at that point. And that's, of course, corrupting. Again, it's a stat.

It's also clear from your work that you think the drug war has destroyed the police.

That's the saddest thing in a way, again, because the stats mean nothing. Because a drug arrest in Baltimore means nothing. Real police work isn't being done. In my city, the arrest rates for all major felonies have declined, precipitously, over the last twenty years. From murder to rape to robbery to assault.

Because to solve those crimes requires retroactive investigation. They have to be able to do a lot of things, in terms of gathering evidence, that are substantive and meaningful police work. All you have to do to make a drug arrest is go in a guy's pocket. You don't even need probable cause anymore in Baltimore. The guy who solves a rape or a robbery or a murder, he has one arrest stat. He's going to court one day. The guy who has forty, fifty, sixty drug arrests, even though they're meaningless arrests, even though there's no place to put them in the Maryland prison system, he's going to go to court forty, fifty, sixty times. Ultimately, when it comes time to promote somebody, they look at the police computer. They'll look and they'll say, "This guy made forty arrests last month. You only made one. He's the sergeant" or "That's the lieutenant." The guys who basically play the stat game, they get promoted.

In the third season of The Wire, *police major Bunny Colvin tells some people in the hood that he wishes he could tell them the fight against drugs will get better, but if he did, it would be a lie. Is it futile?*

Again, we have to ask ourselves a lot of hard questions. The people most affected by this are black and brown and poor. It's the abandoned inner cores of our urban areas. As we said before, economically, we don't need those people; the American economy doesn't need them. So as long as they stay in their ghettos and they only kill each other, we're willing to pay for a police presence to keep them out of our America. And to let them fight over scraps, which is what the drug war, effectively, is. Since we basically have become a market-based culture, that's what we know, and it's what's led us to this sad dénouement. I think we're going to follow market-based logic right to the bitter end.

Which says?

If you don't need 'em, why extend yourself? Why seriously assess what you're doing to your poorest and most vulnerable citizens? There's no profit to be had in doing anything other than marginalizing them and discarding them.

But here's the problem for journalism. When we write about inequality, we use numbers that are profound but numbing. Here's something I just read: over the past twenty years, the elite 1 percent of Americans saw their share of the nation's income double, from 11.3 percent to 22.1 percent, but their tax burden shrank by about one-third. Now, those facts tell us something very important: that the rich got richer as their tax rates shrank. But it doesn't seem to start people's blood rushing.

You start talking about a social compact between the people at the bottom of the pyramid and the people at the top, and people look at you and say, "Are you talking about sharing wealth?" Listen, capitalism is the only engine credible enough to generate mass wealth. I think it's imperfect, but we're stuck with it. And thank God we have that in the toolbox. But if you don't manage it in some way that incorporates all of society, if everybody's not benefiting on some level and you don't have a sense of shared purpose, national purpose, then it's just a pyramid scheme. Who's standing on top of whose throat?

Why do you think, David, that we tolerate such gaps between rich and poor?

You know, I'm fascinated by it. Because a lot of the people who end up voting for that kind of laissez-faire market policy are people who get creamed by it. And I think it's almost like a casino. You're looking at the guy winning, you're looking at the guy who pulled the lever and all the bells go off, all the coins are coming out of a one-armed bandit. You're thinking, "That could be me. I'll play by those rules." But actually, those are house rules. And most of you are going to lose.

After all these years do you have the answer?

Oh, I would decriminalize drugs in a heartbeat. I would put all the interdiction money, all the incarceration money, all the enforcement money, all of the pretrial, all the prep, all of that cash, I would hurl it as fast as I could into drug treatment and job training and jobs programs. I would rather turn these neighborhoods inward with jobs programs. Even if it was the urban equivalent of FDR's CCC—the Civilian Conservation Corps—if it was New Deal–type logic, it would be doing less damage than creating a war syndrome. The drug war is war on the underclass now. That's all it is. It has no other meaning.

There's very little the police can do.

You talk honestly with some of the veteran and smarter detectives in Baltimore, the guys who have given their career to the drug war, including, for example, Ed Burns, who was a drug warrior for twenty years, and they'll tell you, this war's lost. This is all over but the shouting and the tragedy and the waste. And yet there isn't a political leader with the stomach to really assess it for what it is.

So whose lives are less and less necessary in America today?

Certainly the underclass. There's a reason they are the underclass. We're in an era when you don't need as much mass labor; we are not a manufacturing base. People who built stuff, their lives had some meaning and value because the factories were open. You don't need them anymore. Unions and working people are completely abandoned by this economic culture, and, you know, that's heartbreaking to me. I've been a union member my whole life and I guess I belong to a little gilded union now. A gilded guild.

The Writers Guild.

The Writers Guild, yes, but I was a member of the Newspaper Guild before that, and I thank them for letting me earn an honest living. Without them, God knows what we would have been paid in Baltimore. But I look at what's happened with unions. Ed Burns says all the time that he wants to do a piece on the Haymarket.

The Haymarket bombing in Chicago, in 1886.

Yes. The bombing, that critical moment when American labor was pushed so much to the starving point that they were willing to fight. And I actually think that's the only time when change is possible, when people are actually threatened to the core, and enough people are threatened to the core that they just won't take it anymore. Those are the pivotal moments in American history, I think, when something actually does happen.

In Haymarket, they were fighting for the eight-hour workday. It sounded radical at the time, but it's basically a dignity-of-life issue. You look at things like that, you look at the anti–Vietnam War effort in this country. You had to threaten middle-class kids with a draft and with military service in an unpopular war for people to rise up and demand an end to that unpopular war. I mean, it didn't happen without that. So on some level, as long as they placate enough people, as long as they throw enough scraps from the table that enough people get a little bit to eat, I just don't see a change coming.

Did this great collapse we have experienced confirm the reporting you had done about what happens when an economic system creates two separate realities?

I couldn't have conceived of something as grandiose as the mortgage bubble, when you finally look at what caused that, and the sheer greed and the stupidity of that pyramid scheme. We didn't know it was as corrosive as it was. We didn't know it was rotted out that much. But we knew there was something rotten in the core. And we knew it from what we were looking at, in terms of Baltimore, and how Baltimore addressed its problems.

Politics is supposed to be about solving the situations you describe. But it's constantly creating its own reality, right?

It's about money and it's about advancement. As a reporter, I got to see some politics. I wasn't a political reporter per se, but I got to see enough of city politics to absorb it. And Ed Burns taught in the Baltimore city school system and pulled all that through the keyhole for season four of *The Wire*. I got to see the war on drugs. I got to see policing as a concept. And I got to see journalism.

And when it came to explaining complicated and sophisticated systems and trying to say, "This is what's going on and if we change this or do that, or if we actually implement this policy, we can, you know . . ." The hard work of looking at it systemically, there was no incentive to do it, and nobody did it, and that's as true in Baltimore today as when I started as a reporter, and I think it's true in America.

I remain indebted to those reporters who go where I can't go, who talk to people I can't reach, and come back with news I need to know. And as you say, you were spit out by the forces at work in the journalistic world. And now journalism is spitting out reporters like teeth.

Left and right. You know, listen, I was not the last. That's true. And it's heartbreaking. And I say this with no schadenfreude just because I got a TV gig. It's heartbreaking what's happening, and I feel that the republic is actually in danger.

There is no guard now assessing anything qualitatively, no pulling back the veil behind what an official will tell you is progress, or is valid, or is legitimate as policy. Absent that, no good can come from anything. Because there is an absolute disincentive to tell the truth.

You recently told The Guardian in London: "Oh, to be a state or local official in America"—without newspapers—"it's got to be one of the great dreams in the history of American corruption."

Well, I was being a little hyperbolic.

But it's happening.

Yes. It absolutely is. To find out what's going on in my own city I often find myself at a bar somewhere, writing stuff down on a cocktail napkin that a police lieutenant or some schoolteacher tells me, because these institutions are no longer being covered by beat reporters who are looking for the systemic. It doesn't exist anymore.

"We were doing our job, making the world safe for democracy. And all of a sudden, terra firma shifted, new technology. Who knew that the Internet was going to overwhelm us?" I would buy that if I wasn't in journalism for the years that immediately preceded the Internet. I took the third buyout from *The Baltimore Sun*. I was about reporter number eighty or ninety who left, in 1995, long before the Internet had had its impact. I left at a time when *The Baltimore Sun* was earning 37 percent profits.

We now know this because it's in bankruptcy and the books are open. All that R&D money that was supposed to go into making newspapers more essential, more viable, more able to explain the complexities of the world went to shareholders in the Tribune Company. Or the L.A. Times Mirror Company before that. And ultimately, when the Internet did hit, they had an inferior product that was not essential enough that they could charge online for it.

I mean, the guys who are running newspapers over the last twenty or thirty years have to be singular in the manner in which they destroyed their own industry. It's even more profound than Detroit in 1973 making Chevy Vegas and Pacers and Gremlins and believing that no self-respecting American would buy a Japanese car. Except it's not analogous, in that a Nissan is a pretty good car, and a Toyota is a pretty good car. The Internet, while it's great for commentary and froth, doesn't do very much first-generation reporting at all. The economic model can't sustain that kind of reporting. They had contempt for their own product, these people.

The publishers. The owners.

You know, for twenty years, they looked upon the copy as being the stuff that went around the ads. The ads were God. And then all of a sudden the ads were not there, and the copy, they had had contempt for. They had actually marginalized themselves. I was being a little flippant with *The Guardian*, but what I was saying was, you know, until they figure out the new model, there's going to be a wave of corruption.

Are you cynical?

I am very cynical about institutions and their willingness to address themselves to reform. I am not cynical when it comes to individuals and people. And I think the reason *The Wire* is watchable, even tolerable, to viewers is that it has great affection for individuals. It's not misanthropic in any way. It has great affection for those people, particularly when they stand up on their hind legs and say, "I will not lie anymore. I am actually going to fight for what I perceive to be some shard of truth."

You know, over time, people are going to look at *The Wire* and think, "This was not quite as cynical as we thought it was. This was actually a little bit more journalistic than that. They were being blunt. But it was less mean than we thought it was." I think, in Baltimore, the initial response to seeing some of this on the air was, "These guys are not fair and they're mean. And they're just out to savage us." But it was a love letter to Baltimore.

You said to the students at Loyola College in Baltimore some years ago, "I want you to go and look up the word oligarchy." *Well, I did just that. I took your advice. I looked it up.*

Uh-oh.

It means "government by the few." Or "a government in which a small group exercises control for corrupt and selfish purposes." Is that what you saw in Baltimore?

I was speaking nationally, but yes. We are a country of democratic ideas and impulses, but it is strained through some very oligarchical structures. One of which could be, for example, the United States Senate. Or I look at the Electoral College as being decidedly undemocratic. I don't buy into the notion that "one man, one vote" is not the most fundamental way of doing business. And, ultimately, when I look at the drug war—listen, the only reason that alcohol and cigarettes, which do far more damage than heroin and cocaine, are legal is that white people, and affluent white people at that, make money off that stuff. Philip Morris, if those guys had black and brown skin and were in the Mexican state of Chihuahua, they'd be hunted. Or maybe not anymore; maybe they'd be in control of the Mexican state of Chihuahua. That's another story. . . .

I look at that, and I say, "Yes, money talks." The idea that what the most people want is best for the most people, the utilitarian sense of democracy still applying in American life—I just don't see a lot of evidence for that.

So is this what you mean when you say The Wire *is dissent?*

Yes. It is dissent. It is saying, "We no longer buy these false ideologies. And the false motifs you have of American life." I look at this and I think to myself, if only you stand up and say, "I'm not going to be lied to anymore," that's a victory on some level, that's a beginning of a dynamic. Can change happen? Yes. But things have to get a lot worse.

If I could put a lede on the body of your work—your journalism, your articles, your essays, your speeches, your books, your television series—it would be this: David Simon says America's not working for everyday people who have no power. And that's the way the people with power have designed it to work.

Right. I mean, it would be one thing with an oligarchy if they were doing a better job of it. I would be okay with that.

Making the trains run on time.

Right, but everything from Iraq to Wall Street to urban policy to the drug war, I look at it all and I say, "You know, these guys really couldn't do much worse." New Orleans was such a beautiful metaphor for the hollowness at the core of American will, you know? To have seen the president of the United States take the plane down and look out his window and say, "Oh my God, it must be twice as bad on the ground." Twice as bad? Really? It's failure of will and imagination and I see it across the board, and I just think, in a way, *The Wire* is an editorial. It's an angry op-ed, as if Frank Rich was given, you know, twelve hours of airtime to rant.

Are you, as someone said, "the angriest man in television"?

I saw that. It doesn't really mean much. The second-angriest guy is, you know, by a kidney-shaped pool in L.A. screaming into his cell phone because his DVD points aren't enough. But I don't mind being called that. I just don't think it means anything. How can you have lived through the last ten years in American culture and not be? How can you not look at what happened on Wall Street, at this gamesmanship that was the mortgage bubble, that was just selling crap and calling it gold? Or watch a city school system suffer for twenty, twenty-five years? Isn't anger the appropriate response? What is the appropriate response? Ennui? Alienation? Buying into the great-man theory of history—that if we only elect the right guy? This stuff is systemic. This is how an empire is eaten from within.

But I don't think these good individuals you talk about—the individual who stands up and says, "I'm not going to lie anymore"—I don't think individuals

*know how to crack that system, how to change that system. Because the system
is self-perpetuating.*

And beautifully moneyed. I don't think we can. And so I don't think it's going to get better. Listen, I don't like talking this way. I would be happy to find
out that *The Wire* was hyperbolic and ridiculous, and that the "American
Century" is still to come. I don't believe it, but I'd love to believe it, because
I live in Baltimore, and I'm an American. I want to sit in my house and see
the game on Saturday along with everybody else. But I just don't see a lot of
evidence of it.

*Do you really believe, as you said to those students at Loyola, that we're not
going to make it?*

We're not going to make it as a first-rate empire. And I'm not sure that that's
a bad thing in the end. Empires end, and that doesn't mean cultures end
completely, and it doesn't even mean that for nation-states. If you looked
at Britain in 1952 and what was being presided over by Anthony Eden and
those guys, you'd have said, "Man, what's going to be left?" But Britain's still
there, and they've come to terms with what they can and can't do.

   Americans are still sort of in an age of delusion, I think. A lot of our foreign policy represents that. And this notion that the markets were always
going to go up, and that once we had invested stocks to death, we could create some new equity out of nothing.

*You are a reporter, not a prophet, but who do you think is going to tell us now
what the facts are that we can agree on? Is it going to be television? Is it going
to be fiction? Is it going to be journalism?*

I don't know. I mean, I think ultimately a little of it's going to come from
everywhere. You know, there have been novels that I read that I thought
were genuine truth-telling. And there have been journalistic endeavors that
have really come close to being brilliant and blunt and honest, in a variety
of formats. And there has been some film and some television. But it's not
like everybody's rushing to make *The Wire*. I've pretty much demonstrated
how not to make a hit show, you know? I make a show that gets me on Bill
Moyers.

   There are about 749 different shows, dramas and comedies, on television right now, and 748 of them are about the America that I inhabit, that

you inhabit, that most of the viewing public, I guess, inhabits. There was only one about the other America. And it was arguing, passionately, about a place where, let's face it, the economic rules don't apply in the same way. Half of the adult black males in my city are unemployed. That's not an economic model that actually works. ∾

VICTOR GOLD

Fifty years ago, Vic Gold and I were both young idealists who voted for John F. Kennedy for president. Except for our awe of the Alabama football legend "Bear" Bryant, that's probably the last time we ever agreed on anything until now. I went on to serve in the Kennedy administration and then in the White House with President Lyndon Johnson. Vic Gold became a speechwriter and advisor to Senator Barry Goldwater. We were pitted against each other in 1964 when Goldwater challenged Johnson for the presidency and lost. Vic has never forgiven me for the television ads we ran against his candidate, even though I left the White House three years later to atone for my sins and have been a journalist ever since (a bigger sin, perhaps, in Vic's eyes).

He went into public relations and to soldier on in other Republican campaigns, including working with Richard Nixon's vice president, Spiro Agnew, in 1970, when Agnew went after journalists. He called us "nattering nabobs of negativism." Along the way, Vic became a confidant of the first George Bush, helping on his campaigns and in the writing of the soon-to-be president's autobiography, Looking Forward. He also wrote a political satire with his old friend Lynne Cheney, the former vice president's wife, called The Body Politic.

In 2007, this longtime Republican insider wrote a book with a title that almost all of us who started in politics, no matter our affiliation, wish we had *claimed first. Because sooner or later—and this is what Vic Gold and I have in common today—most of us think the party of our youth has fallen into the wrong hands—his, into the hands of ideologues; mine, into the hands of its bankrollers. The title is* Invasion of the Party Snatchers, *but in Vic's case, the subtitle says it all:* How the Holy-Rollers and the Neo-Cons Destroyed the GOP.

Believe it or not, after all these years, when Vic Gold came to the studio, we were meeting for the first time.

—Bill Moyers

———— ❦ ————

Do you remember what the great liberal journalist Pete Hamill said about Barry Goldwater?

This is the first time I've said this publicly, but Pete Hamill inspired my book.

Well, here's exactly what you quote Pete Hamill: "No democracy can survive if it is wormy with lies and evasions. That is why we must cherish those people who have the guts to speak the truth: mavericks, whistle-blowers, disturbers of the public peace. And it's why, in spite of my own continuing (though chastened) liberal faith, I miss Barry Goldwater."

I have never met Pete Hamill. But when I read in the *L.A. Times* that Pete Hamill had said that he wished we had a Barry Goldwater around now, I said to myself, "He's right." And I worked for Goldwater! So I'm going to write something about why we have abandoned the principles he represented.

I never met Barry Goldwater. Back in 1964 he was the guy on the other side to beat. He did shoot from the hip, and was mobilizing the fringe, including the old Confederacy, on the wrong side of the civil rights movement. But in later years I came to admire his candor. Who's speaking like Barry Goldwater today?

I don't know if a Barry Goldwater could exist in today's political world because of the sound bite mentality, the appealing to the base, which you find in both parties. If you look at the candidates today—what I call the Stepford candidates on both sides in these debates—the only two who are speaking clearly are the ones people think of as the kooks. On the Democratic side they ask Mike Gravel, "Do you think English should be the official language?" He says, "Yes." The others say, "No, not the official language, the national language." And I say: "What the devil is the national language? Why don't they just say no?" And on the Republican side you have Ron Paul, who was the only candidate who is antiwar and pro–civil liberties, and he really opposes what the Bush administration is doing to civil liberties—and they call him a kook. If Senator Goldwater were around, he'd probably throw up his hands at the whole process and not run.

Why do you think candidates can't speak their mind today?

It's the system. Look, if you have to win Iowa, you have to come out for ethanol. And if you don't, that finishes you. You're compromised right there. Then you've got to go over to New Hampshire and you've got to sign a pledge: no taxes. If you don't say "no taxes," you're going to lose New Hampshire. You get killed there. And then you will not make the cover of *Time* and *Newsweek*, and that'll be your ruin. So that's what does it.

You said you wrote this book because you were angry. Why were you angry?

Goldwater did seem to be a clarion voice, a clear voice. What did Goldwater and the conservative movement at that time stand for? They stood for limited government. Now, when I say "limited government," I mean limited power of government. What Arthur Schlesinger ultimately described as the imperial presidency under Nixon. Of course, Nixon picked up where John Kennedy and Lyndon Johnson left off, and he expanded the imperial powers of the presidency and the imperialization of the country, and now you've got the neocons and the religious right claiming we should be policemen for the world.

Do you feel threatened by the holy rollers—as you call them—and the neocons?

I am a nonconformist. I have always been a nonconformist. When I was with Goldwater, I was a nonconformist. We thought the conformists were on the other side. The fact is that what the religious right demands is conformity. Purely and simply, they would like to establish a theocracy. And the paradox is that the neocons are not religious. But they have a mission. They think we have a moral mission in the world. The United States is the leading nation in the world, it's the superpower in the world, our mission is to democratize the world. Benevolent hegemony is what they want. Some of them are theocons, by the way.

Well, the neocons and the religious right have used each other.

They've used each other, but they take the same position, benevolent hegemony: "We're going to teach people all over the world the way it should be."

Barry Goldwater wrote back in 1994: "The conservative movement is founded on the simple tenet that people have the right to live life as they please, as long as they don't hurt anyone else in the process." And he went on to declare that "the radical right has nearly ruined our party." What's your take on that?

The interesting thing is if you go back to the Goldwater campaign and read his speeches, the word *spiritual*—the spiritual side of mankind—is very much in every speech. He accused President Johnson and the Johnson administration of being materialistic. Goldwater spoke of the whole man, so he used the word *spiritual* and he used the word *God*.

Now, Republican conservatives understand what it means to keep government out of the boardroom, but what they don't seem to understand is keeping government out of the bedroom, out of our private lives. Goldwater understood that. If you had told me and if you had told Barry Goldwater that we would one day have an office in the White House called the Office of Faith-Based Initiatives—what kind of Orwellian language is that? Faith-based initiatives? That's the Office of Religion. The Office of Religious Outreach. How do you put that in the White House?

The Terri Schiavo case seems to have been a turning point in all of this. The moment people like you really began to be aroused was when the religious right took that case to the White House.

Well, think of what it was aside from the emotional side. Think of what it meant constitutionally and in terms of conservative principles. The hypocrisy of the Tom DeLays and people like him who had always been against activist judges. "We don't want these activist judges interfering"—right? Here, state courts had decided this thing. And Republicans in Congress pass a law which takes it out of state jurisdiction and turns it over to the federal court. And President Bush—who waited four days before he visited

New Orleans after Katrina—interrupts his vacation in Crawford, Texas, to immediately fly back to sign this bill. A bill that takes the case out of state hands and puts it in federal hands. The pitiful thing was they take this personal family tragedy and elevate it to a national case.

Goldwater over the years openly supported the rights of gay men and women. He voted consistently to protect a woman's choice concerning abortion. He championed the separation of church and state, and he was as concerned about the religious right as liberals. I began to ask, "Who's the conservative here and who's the liberal?" Did the Goldwater Republicans then desert him? Did they leave him? Is that what happened?

No, they didn't leave him. They now feel we can't win an election unless we have the theoconservatives, the religious right, with us. These are our ground troops. These are our storm—but when you take them in, it changes the character of the party. You win, but do you win on the principles that you once stood for?

Well, they won twice, 2000 and 2004.

They won. You said, "They won." That's what I think a lot of conservatives like me have discovered. I voted for George Bush in the year 2000, but there were a lot of defections in 2006. There were a lot of conservative Republicans like me who wanted to lose in 2006 and then come back to the kind of reform we believe in.

Back in 2001, you wrote the profile of the new vice president, Dick Cheney, for the official inauguration program. You called him "a man of gravitas with a quick and easy wit; a conservative who will see a road less traveled; a political realist who sees his country and the world around him not in terms of leaden problems but golden opportunities."

That's the person I knew. I mean, I wasn't writing bull.

So what happened to him?

That is one of the great mysteries. I quote Madame de Staël: "Men do not change, they unmask themselves." As you know, power can change people. When I was in the army I remember that when I got my sergeant stripes they told me, "Now we're going to find out what kind of person you are." So Cheney becomes vice president of the United States. Maybe all this has been a very good masquerade he's been putting on, because this is not the Dick Cheney any of us knew. If you recall, when George W. Bush was elected, everybody said, "Well, George may be inexperienced, but we have a good stable person in Dick Cheney." And now—he's bombs away. Intransigent on everything.

You're very angry in the book about the war.

Yes.

Why?

Because I feel for those kids—and they are kids—over there. They are getting killed every day, and their lives are being wasted. Politicians say, "Oh, no, they're heroes." But their lives are being wasted. And while they're getting killed, we have white-tie dinners at the White House. The president says this is total war. Where is the sacrifice? I know what a total war is like. You know what a total war is like. I feel for the families of the kids who are over there and the people who are getting killed in a war. Every day that passes, every day that passes there are more of them going to be killed to no end.

Well, back in the Johnson years, the war in Vietnam, especially 1965 when we escalated the war so dramatically, there were white-tie dinners, dances at the Smithsonian. There was a disconnect then. You wrote a piece once about how presidents get isolated. You said they have to burst the bubble of celebrity and sycophancy.

Oh, yes.

George W. Bush has disappeared into the presidency, hasn't he?

He's acting a role. But, you know, have their feet touched the ground? This is the thing that I wonder—is this a real-life thing to them? This happened to Clinton. It becomes a celebrity thing to them. And they get carried away by it.

You're also angry in the book about Attorney General Alberto Gonzales and the Justice Department.

I think it's a corrupted Justice Department. When I say "corrupted," I don't mean dollars and cents. I mean corrupted in terms of our constitutional values. You've heard some of the prosecuting attorneys who were fired now speaking out about exactly what's going on up there. When you corrupt the justice system—the Justice Department is the most important department of government in terms of protecting our constitutional values—well, there need to be investigations. And I knew there wouldn't be with the Republicans controlling Congress. I say let these investigations happen.

Did I just hear you say you want the Democrats to win in November 2008?

I'd say open up the book. Open up the book. I wasn't the only one. Listen, if these same people had won in 2006 following the 2004 mandate, with the war and everything that was going on in the Bush White House—if they win again, my God, we'll be at war with Iran in two weeks.

But both of us agree that the parties are now captives of big wealthy interests, don't we?

You're talking about the people who put up the money for their campaigns? Absolutely. They're captive because their only interest is "How do we get reelected?" And after they get reelected, well, they want to make money. You don't make money inside Congress anymore. There's K Street.

They become lobbyists.

For the first time in my lifetime we have an attorney general—John Ashcroft—who leaves office and establishes his own lobbying firm.

Do you sometimes feel like a dinosaur standing in a lake that's drying up around your ankles?

Well, I'll put it to you this way. I am reading more and more histories of the 1940s and '50s and listening to Frank Sinatra music and Bobby Darin.

Are we winding up here at the end as old curmudgeons?

I don't want to be an old curmudgeon. You remember the old play *Waiting for Lefty*? Well, I'm waiting for Righty. And for a rebirth of Goldwater. I don't see him around. ❧

NELL PAINTER

During a decisive period in the 2008 campaign for the Democratic presidential nomination, Hillary Clinton stopped off at a chain restaurant in Ohio and posed with waitresses in a gesture of working-class solidarity. Barack Obama showed up at a titanium factory, meeting with workers in hard hats as the cameras rolled. Each knew the margin of victory could come from working people who had once been solidly Democratic but now felt abandoned by a party that has become as enthralled as Republicans with hedge fund managers, investment bankers, and corporate lobbyists.

As these photo ops played out on the evening news and across the Internet, eyes must have widened in moneyed suites where a blue-collar job is valued only if it's being shipped overseas. Were Clinton and Obama, whose campaign coffers overflowed like Christmas stockings with Wall Street cash, turning against their benefactors? Or were they just feigning a little populism for the sake of the bleachers?

The mainstream media figured that must be it—a temporary deviation from the corporatism that Democrats practice in a Washington far removed from roadside diners and factory floors. "Before Votes, Democrats Deliver Populist Appeals," read a headline in The New York Times, as if it were but a realistic nod to the vulgar concerns of everyday people trying to make a living. The Columbia Journalism Review politely weighed in: "Before this gets out of *hand, big media needs to stop using the word 'populist' to describe Democrats' economic programs and their appeals to voters. . . . Reporters and headline writers don't need to be historians-on-deadline to know that the word 'populist' has no widely agreed-upon definition, but plenty of negative associations." Meanwhile, the quintessential Beltway oracle David Broder was actually praising Sarah Palin for "her pitch-perfect populism." One could hardly fail to note a double standard at work here: populism on the right, good; populism on the left, dangerous.*

So exactly what is populism, anyway? Merriam-Webster's defines a populist as "a member of a political party claiming to represent the common people." Defined that way, no wonder both Democrats and Republicans are eager to grab the mantle and rub a little dirt on their freshly acquired denim jeans and work shirts. But there actually was a populist political party, known as the People's Party, in the late nineteenth century. Until it was finally squashed, these populists challenged the power of monopolistic corporations, big trusts, the railroads, and banks. Many of the party's goals—a graduated income tax, election of senators by direct vote, civil service reform, the eight-hour workday, pensions—eventually won public approval, culminating in the Progressive era that followed in the early years of the twentieth century.

The historian Nell Irvin Painter tells this vital story in her book Standing at Armageddon: A Grassroots History of the Progressive Era. *Until her recent retirement Painter was one of the most popular teachers at Princeton University. She also is a past president of the Organization of American Historians, the largest professional society dedicated to the teaching and study of American history.*

—*Bill Moyers*

———

It seems that everybody's throwing around the word populism.

And it sounds as if they're throwing it around as a dirty word. If it is a dirty word, they don't know what they're talking about.

Why do they think it's a dirty word?

I think they think it's a dirty word because in their understanding of it, populism pits Americans against each other, as if we would all be one happy family, hand in hand, if it weren't for populist agitators. You know, every time politicians start talking about what's needed for working people or, heaven forbid, poor people, and how their interests are different from people who have a lot of money, critics accuse them of "populism." But if you go back to the late nineteenth century, when rich people decided what to do and expected workers and others to go along with it, a lot of ordinary people weren't having it. They stood up and declared that their interests were not the same as the plutocracy—the people with all the money.

In the new edition of your book you quote the populist orator and presidential candidate William Jennings Bryan on how America can be a democracy—

Or an empire.

But not both.

Well, he was right. And we've become an empire. That happened in the twentieth century with one war after another. Running an empire doesn't square with what regular people have to face every day—health care, making a living. Especially ever since the Cold War we have become what my colleague Lizabeth Cohen calls "a consumers' republic." The populists, on the other hand, talked about a producers' republic. And our interest as consumers and our interest as citizens may be different. As citizens, we need to pay for bridges, roads, education, colleges. But these are not the kind of things Americans are going to buy as consumers. Yet we need them as citizens. There's a difference.

What's still relevant about that early populism?

We need to remember that the ideas put forward by the populists in the late nineteenth century were considered harebrained. Crank ideas. But by the early twentieth century, those ideas, many of them, had been realized. The income tax, the direct election of senators, the whole regulatory state of the twentienth century had their roots in that early populism.

Populists feared monopolies and wanted to control their power, wanted to check the big industrial giants, the money trusts.

That's right. Remember that what we call laissez-faire capitalism didn't look kindly on government interference. The populists, however, said that government should serve the people, not just the corporations and the very wealthy.

What does it say to you that income inequality, which was a big issue in the Populist Era, grew significantly in the last year for which we had data, 2005? The top 1 percent of people received the largest share of national income since 1928, the year before the big crash.

Yes. It's frightening, isn't it?

And what does that say to you?

It says, "Oh! We're going to have another damn depression." That's what it says to me. And then I remember that we have a lot of safeguards in place that were not in place in 1929 and are in place now because of the disaster of the Great Depression. But then again, many of those safeguards have been weakened, particularly over the last quarter century or so. I think that's what we see in the credit crunch. It started with subprime mortgages but spread throughout the whole financial sector because of the lack of regulation.

There's a story this week that says the vast majority of African American and Latino families who have entered the middle class are either borderline or at high risk of falling out of the middle class altogether. This report, published by Brandeis University, says about 95 percent of African American and 87 percent percent of Latino middle-class families don't have enough net assets to meet their essential living expenses for even three months if their source of income disappears.

Yes. Yes. We're not just seeing income disparities. We're seeing huge wealth disparities. Wealth is family assets. Your house. Your car. Your savings. Your retirement. Your life insurance. Your cash. It's that very money that you can use in unusual times, whether a breadwinner loses a job, whether somebody falls ill, whether a child has to go to college or graduate school. To have the wealth to be able to get by month by month, that's crucial to stay in the middle class or to move up. So many families are short of wealth. Some time ago I was asked by some Democratic senators what can be done about the situation of struggling black families. And I said, "People need jobs. People need jobs." If I were running the world, I would call back Franklin Roosevelt, and people would have jobs.

What might the populists of old be saying to us about all this?

"Who does the government serve? Who should it serve?" Bill, I believe government can work for people. That's at the heart of election reform, public financing of elections. Do we let the free market run amok as if it were good for all of us? No, it's not necessarily good for all of us. Because we get tainted food, dangerous toys, diseased cattle processed into hamburger. We need to call up some of those questions that the populists were asking a hundred years ago—and some of the answers, too.

What about the title of your book, Standing at Armageddon? *Why did you choose that?*

Because so many people in the late nineteenth and early twentieth century actually felt that their world was collapsing around them. The end of their world was at hand. *Standing at Armageddon* actually comes from Teddy Roosevelt. When he was running as the Progressive Party candidate for president in 1912, he rallied his delegates by saying: "We stand at Armageddon, and we battle for the Lord."

Interesting, isn't it, that Teddy Roosevelt and his cousin Franklin Roosevelt, both men of means, championed the cause of people against the big corporations?

Because they realized that not standing up to gross economic power risked ruining this country, risked incredible disorder, risked asking for Armageddon. Theodore Roosevelt came to say that he couldn't just let the bankers and the railroads call the tune. They would run the country into the ground. Franklin Roosevelt in the Great Depression, with the strikes and marches, realized once again that government would have to step in on the side of ordinary people.

Are we standing at Armageddon today?

In the sense of a revolution? No. We're too big for that. One of our safeguards is our huge size. Everything takes a lot of time. So in that sense, we're not standing at Armageddon. However, we certainly are standing at a critical moment when we decide whether or not to continue, in William Jennings Bryan's terms, as an "empire," or whether we want to return to our roots as a democracy. A very critical moment. ∾

JIM HIGHTOWER

Nell Painter looks at populism as an historian; Jim Hightower writes about it as a journalist and lives it as an activist—or, by his own definition, "a populist agitator." On his home page he modestly refers to himself as "America's #1 Populist." He's earned the title over a prolific lifetime of battling Big Money, including two terms as Texas agriculture commissioner, a job he took to heart by standing up for small farmers and consumers. He was then overwhelmed by the deep pockets of a vindictive agribusiness, in a campaign orchestrated by Karl Rove for the current Texas governor Rick Perry.

Undaunted and unbowed, Hightower has kept on battling the principalities and powers of corporate America as the publisher of The Hightower Lowdown, *a newsletter as well researched and highly readable as the work of the early muckrakers. The* Lowdown *has won both the Alternative Press Award and the Independent Press Association Award for best national newsletter.*

Hightower also broadcasts daily commentaries on radio, writes a newspaper column, makes scores of speeches every year, and turns out bestselling books with eye-catching titles: Thieves in High Places: They've Stolen Our Country and It's Time to Take It Back; If the Gods Had Meant Us to Vote They Would Have Given Us Candidates; There's Nothing in the Middle of the Road But Yellow Stripes and Dead Armadillos; *and* Swim Against the Current: Even a Dead Fish Can Go with the Flow.

He grew up where populism once flourished, in northeast Texas, in a family of small-business owners, tenant farmers, and, in his parlance, "just plain folks."

—Bill Moyers

———— ∿ ————

Populism began in Texas, right?

It did. In 1877, out near Lampasas, in central Texas. Farmers sitting around a table much like this. Getting run over by the banks and by the railroad monopolies, not unlike what's happening today. People were being knocked down by corporate power. And that power was initially the banks that gouged them. Usurious rates of lending. Farmers live on credit, you know; they were getting stuck with 20 percent, 25–30 percent, and they were going to go broke. And they said, "We've got to do something." That issue has come up so much throughout history. We've got to do something. And people figure it out. This became the most extensive and successful mass grassroots movement ever in this country around economic issues. It didn't begin as a political movement. They found ways to get credit, establish their own credit system, bypassing the banks. They created their own supply system—seed, fertilizer, and that sort of thing—and then their own marketing system. They also began to build a cultural movement around it. They educated people. They had a speakers' bureau. And it was an intellectual movement. It was an education movement, cultural movement, economic movement. Then it became political. They elected candidates across the country, New York to California.

Yes, the movement spread from Texas to Kansas and—

Up to the plains states. And over into the upper Midwest. And then east and then west and then down through the South. So it was everywhere. A very powerful movement.

They were the first to call for the direct election of senators, to oppose all subsidies to corporations. They called for pensions for veterans. They wanted to corral the power of lobbyists and end all subsidies to corporations. What do we owe them?

We owe them imitation. We owe them the continuation of the spirit that saw we do not have to just accept what is handed to us. We can battle back against the powers. But it's not just going to a rally and shouting. It's organizing and thinking and reaching out to others, and building a real people's movement.

How does the Tea Party differ from the people you're talking about?

Here's what populism is not. It is not just an incoherent outburst of anger. And certainly it is not anger that is funded and organized by corporate front groups, as the initial Tea Party effort was, and as most of it is still today, though there is legitimate anger within it, in terms of the people who are there. But what populism is at its essence is a determined focus on helping people be able to get out of the iron grip of the corporate power that is overwhelming our economy, our environment, energy, the media, government. That's one big difference between real populism and what the Tea Party is. Real populists understand that government has become a subsidiary of corporations. So you can't say, "Let's get rid of government." You need to be saying, "Let's take over government."

You're often described as a progressive. Why don't you call yourself a liberal?

The difference between a liberal and a progressive is the liberals want to assuage the problems that we have because of corporate power. Populists want to get rid of corporate power. An example is what's happening, right now, with the Wall Street "reform" that's in Washington.

I heard quotation marks around that word reform.

Here come the Democrats again, just weaker than Canadian hot sauce, you know? Offering a little reform. I saw one of the senators, a Democrat, saying, we're going to have a robust disclosure program. Oh, good. They're going to tell us the banks are stealing from us. So liberals want to—

To regulate the banks.

Yes, yes. Rather than bring them down to size. When you're too big to fail, you're too big, period. And now they've become not only too big to fail, but too big to care.

So when you identify yourself as a populist, what are you saying?

I'm saying that the central issue in politics is the rise of corporate power. Overwhelming, overweening corporate power that is running roughshod over the workaday people of the country. They think they're the top dogs and we're a bunch of fire hydrants, you know? And they can do what they want to us. What's been missing is, what can we do about it? It's about the long haul. The target is not government; it's those who are pulling the strings of government, those corporate lobbyists and the money that the corporate executives and now corporations directly can put into our campaigns.

Because of the recent Supreme Court decision, Citizens United?

Yes. *Citizens United,* which is really a black-robed coup by five men on the Supreme Court. And Bill, there's another fraud. These people on the Supreme Court call themselves conservatives and the media goes along with it. There's nothing conservative at all about that decision to allow corporations to be "people" and to contribute all the money that they want out of their corporate treasuries into our campaigns. That is a usurpation of democratic power.

You wouldn't call them conservative, what would you call them?

I would call them traitors to the democratic ideal of the self-government of people.

In your books and speeches you describe a political landscape that has been radically altered.

And both political parties have been a part of this. But the altering has been done by the corporate interests. They have changed the way our economy works. They beat up on labor unions. So now they can fire at will. They can offshore. They can downsize. They can do what they want with the workers.

You quote a Wall Street honcho who says, "American business is about maximizing shareholder value. . . . You basically don't want workers."

Exactly. And that's what's happening. They've changed the whole dynamic of power in our economy. It is now concentrated in these corporate suites. They have the lobbying power. They make financial contributions to Congress. Enormous power. Already corporations have amassed almost half a billion dollars for the 2010 elections.

And that doesn't count what's going to come with the Supreme Court decision allowing all that money from the corporate treasuries to be unleashed on candidates. Already the U.S. Chamber of Commerce is spending more money than both the Democratic national party and the Republican national party combined.

So let's pass an amendment that says, "No, a corporation cannot contribute its money to politics." In fact, originally most of the state charters in the country prohibited any corporate involvement in politics whatsoever. The founders, Jefferson and Madison, feared corporate power, because they knew it could amass unlimited amounts of money and overwhelm the government. They advocated strict standards for performance, because a corporation is a selfish entity that has no public responsibility. It was a dangerous threat, and it has to be not only strictly regulated but also structured in such a way that serves us rather than vice versa.

So many people in high places fear populism. They see it—

Of course.

—as a menace to their position. Take a look at these comments from several politicians.

> *SENATOR JUDD GREGG: Well, the problem we have is that there's populist fervor, sort of this Huey Long attitude out there that says that all banks are bad and that the financial system is evil and that as a result we must do things which will basically end up reducing our competitiveness as a nation. . . .*

> *MAYOR MIKE BLOOMBERG: And the real danger here is that we write a bill based on populist reaction: "I'm going to get those SOBs," because of a financial crisis, which, incidentally, they may or—they had something to do with but were not the only ones responsible for.*

> *SENATOR BOB CORKER: Look, we—this is important stuff. This isn't about populist ideas, and this isn't about a political issue. We're going to have to live with this. It's going to affect our competitiveness around the world in big ways.*

They're afraid of you.

Absolutely. If ignorance is bliss, these people must be ecstatic, because they don't have a clue about what's going on in the countryside. It is not just populist anger. It's information. It's education. People are informed. They know what's going on. And despite Senator Gregg's comments there, people do not hate all banks. They know the difference between Goldman Sachs and the local community bank. They know the difference between JPMorgan Chase and their credit union. They know who's serving the community and who is not. And who's offering financial products that actually serve our society and those that are just gimmicks to further enrich the rich.

You were very influenced in your own populist beliefs by your father. What was it he said?

Everybody does better when everybody does better.

Which means?

That means that instead of tinkle-down economics that we've been trying for the last thirty years in this country—"Let's just help the rich and then the rest of us will enjoy a seven-course dinner, which turns out to be a possum and a six-pack"—let's spread the prosperity around.

He was a small-business owner. He had the Main Street newsstand in Denison, Texas, a wholesale magazine business. He and my mother ran it, giving us a middle-class possibility. But he never thought that he did that by himself, you know? He knew there was something called the New Deal that was on his side. He was always having to battle the banks, and then ultimately battle Walmart and the chain stores. He knew about the power of the oil lobby down in Austin and the legislature. Now, he thought he was a conservative. But when you talk to him about these issues, he sounded like a William Jennings Bryan radical. He wanted to go get them. And that's the kind of politics the Democratic Party has to have. Because that's why the Democratic Party exists. Not to be friends of the corporate interests. Not to represent Goldman Sachs. But to challenge those corporate interests on behalf of everybody else.

I heard someone say this morning that the Republicans work for Wall Street and the Democrats are afraid to work against them.

Isn't that strange? It's odd to me that we've got a president who ran from the outside and won and now is trying to govern from the inside. You can't do progressive government from the inside. You have to rally those outsiders and make them a force to come inside.

I grew up in Denison, Texas. A small town. I was a small guy. So I learned early on, you should never hit a man with glasses. You should use something much heavier. And our heavy weight is the people themselves. The other side has the fat cats, but we've got the alley cats. And we need to organize them and bring them inside. But I'll tell you right now, the Democrats don't really organize the grassroots. They'll say, "Well, write your congressman or send an email or make a call."

Send $5 on the Internet.

Yeah, exactly. But people are our strength. And we have to organize that strength in strategic ways and in tactical ways. Jesse Jackson said something strong. He said, we might not all have come over on the same boat, but we're in the same boat now. That's a powerful political reality. When people grasp that, they can see the possibility of getting together and doing something.

Corporations are here to stay. They do employ millions of people. And many of them do good things in the country, like Mutual of America, which supports this broadcast.

Well, let's support those that support good things. But let's also do something else. And that is devise alternatives. There's a huge cooperative movement in America that you almost never hear about. There are co-ops running some 72,000 businesses today. Most of them are consumer co-ops. There are insurance co-ops. There are health care co-ops. There are food co-ops, of course. There are banking co-ops. There are all kinds of cooperatives out across the country. And those entities have hundreds of millions of people participating in them. Members.

You never hear about this movement. I've worked with a number of them. There's a great one in Madison, Wisconsin. The Union Cab Cooperative. A bunch of cabbies going broke back in the '70s. Getting treated like Kleenex by the manager. And so they formed a union. The owner said, "Well, to hell with that. I'm not dealing with any union. I'll just sell the thing." But the workers said, "Okay, we do the work here. We do the dispatching and the driving and mechanical work. We could run it." They created a co-op. They had a lot of ups and downs. But over the next thirty years, they were able to make it. And it's the most successful cab company in all of Wisconsin. They get the highest consumer approval rating. I learned about this because I rode a cab to the airport in Madison once. And the guy turned around—full body, by the way—to look at me in the back. And he said, "You know you're in a union cab?" And I said, "No, I didn't." And then he told me the story. He said he was one of the original founders. That he had been able to put his two kids through college driving a cab because the owners were the workers themselves, and doing a great service to the public.

It's been interesting to watch you over these thirty years. You've suffered defeat. You were beaten in your last race by the man who's now been governor of Texas longer than anyone in history, whose campaign manager was—

Karl Rove.

A lot of what you want for America hasn't happened. Yet you haven't given up.

Well, it could be stupidity. But I'm a lucky duck. I travel a whole lot. I give a lot of speeches. And that takes me all across the country on a regular basis. I've been just about everyplace that's got a zip code, I think. And what I find in every one of those places is someone or some group of someones who is in rebellion. Not just ranting but actually organizing others and taking on some aspect of this corporate power. And winning. I see victories just about every week across the country in my travels. You can go anywhere and you see victories. Some of them political, but most of them in terms of civic action. People engaged in and making a difference in their communities. You want to see the populist movement where it actually is today, it's in the communities.

And they keep you going?

Yes, exactly. I go all the way back to Thomas Paine, of course. That was kind of the ultimate rebellion. The media tool was a pamphlet or a broadside. The great men wrote the Bill of Rights and the Constitution and the Declaration of Independence. But they didn't create democracy. Their work made democracy possible, but what created democracy was Thomas Paine and Shays' Rebellion, the suffragists and the abolitionists and on down through the populists, the labor movement, including the Wobblies. Tough, in-their-face people. Mother Jones, Woody Guthrie, the cultural aspect of it as well. Martin Luther King and Cesar Chavez.

They were agitators. They extended democracy decade after decade. Now it's down to us. You know, sometimes we get in the midst of these fights. We think we're making no progress. But you look back, we've made a lot of progress. And you've seen it. And I have. That agitator, after all, is the center post in the washing machine that gets the dirt out. We need a lot more agitation. That's the only thing that succeeds from a progressive side in changing politics in America.

What do you mean when you say the water won't clear up until we get the hogs out of the creek?

That's it. That's right. They are in the creek. And they're fouling our environmental, political, and economic waters. And you don't get a hog out of the creek, Bill, by saying, "Here, hog, here, hog." You got to put your shoulder to it and shove it out of the creek. ∼

RICHARD GOLDSTONE

There's a scene I remember from Harper Lee's novel To Kill a Mockingbird. *A neighbor is talking to the children of Atticus Finch, the attorney in a sleepy southern town who has just bravely but unsuccessfully defended an African American man against a false charge of rape. "I simply want to tell you that there are some men in this world who were born to do our unpleasant jobs for us," she says. "Your father's one of them."*

To fight for justice when your voice seems alone against prevailing opinion, to stand up and speak truth when others cower—these are the "unpleasant jobs," tasks of conscience, from which Judge Richard Goldstone has never shirked. Born and raised in South Africa, he rose to senior positions in the judiciary and wrote laws that helped to undermine apartheid, heading a commission to investigate the vicious behavior of white security forces. The United Nations named him to lead its investigation of war crimes in the former Yugoslavia, where ethnic cleansing had produced the deadliest violence in Europe since World War II. Then came the prosecution of genocide after the slaughter of almost a million people in Rwanda, followed by the independent inquiry he led into war crimes in Kosovo.

In 2009, he took on the greatest challenge of his legal career. For years, Hamas militants had fired rockets into southern Israel from Gaza, those 139 square miles separating Israel and Egypt that are recognized as Palestinian *territory. Israel retaliated in December 2008 with the aptly named Operation Cast Lead: twenty-two days of fierce military action targeting Gaza. More than twelve hundred Palestinians died. Three Israeli civilians and ten soldiers were killed. When the Israeli military withdrew, Gaza was left devastated and reeling from the loss of life and the destruction of homes, hospitals, schools, and mosques. The United Nations Human Rights Council called for an investigation, which Goldstone agreed to lead only after demanding that the mission's mandate be expanded to include charges against Hamas as well as Israel. The Israeli government nonetheless refused to cooperate, arguing that the mission was biased from the beginning.**

Over the next several months Goldstone and his team threaded their way through a minefield of accusation and denial. The resulting 575-page report, scorching in detail, accused both the Israel Defense Forces and Hamas of war crimes and possibly crimes against humanity. While condemning Palestinian rocket attacks, the report reserved its harshest language for Israel's treatment of civilians in Gaza. Goldstone said, "These attacks amounted to reprisals and collective punishment and constitute war crimes. The government of Israel has a duty to protect its citizens. That in no way justifies a policy of collective punishment of a people under effective occupation."

Goldstone came under strident criticism. He was accused of running a "kangaroo court," of denying Israel's right to defend itself, and of misusing "the language of human rights and international law . . . to isolate and demonize Israel." Outwardly he seemed unfazed by the firestorm. A week after the UN's Human Rights Council officially endorsed his findings, we had this conversation.

—Bill Moyers

—◦◦◦—

Let me put down a few basics first. Do you personally have any doubt about Israel's right to self-defense?

---

*As of publication, the Office of the Israel Defense Forces' Military Advocate General has launched forty-eight criminal investigations alleging abusive behavior by IDF troops, resulting in the convictions of two soldiers for using a Palestinian child as a human shield—they received three-month suspended sentences—and another for stealing a credit card from a Gaza resident and withdrawing money from his account.

Absolutely not. In our approach to our mission and in our report, the right of Israel to defend its citizens is taken as a given.

The report in no way challenges Israel's right to self-defense.

Not at all. What we look at is how that right was used. We don't question the right.

Do you consider Hamas an enemy of Israel?

Anybody who's firing many thousands of rockets and mortars into a country is, I think, in anybody's book, an enemy.

Were those rocket attacks on Israel a threat to the civilians of Israel, to the population of Israel?

Absolutely. The people within the range of those rockets and mortars in southern Israel and Sderot and Ashkelon have been living under circumstances of tremendous terror. Schoolchildren in particular, women and men, have less than forty-five seconds to seek shelter when the Israelis know that rockets are coming. The fact that the death toll in southern Israel wasn't higher is really happenstance. It's remarkable that none of those rockets caused a great deal more death and injury than they did.

And Israel, in your judgment, was justified in trying to put an end to those rocket attacks.

Absolutely. No country can be expected to accept that with equanimity.

You're Jewish, and a Zionist. In your case, when you say, "I'm a Zionist," what does that mean?

It means that I fully support Israel's right to exist. And that the Jewish people should have their own national homeland, in Israel.

Why, then, as a Jew and a Zionist, concerned for Israel's survival, did you agree to stand in judgment on Israel's action in Gaza?

It was a question of conscience, really. I've been involved in investigating very serious violations in my own country, South Africa, and I was castigated by many in the white community for doing so. I investigated serious war crimes in the Balkans, and the Serbs hated me for that. I was under serious death threats, both in South Africa and in respect to the Balkans. Then

I went on to Rwanda, and many people hated me for doing that. I've been a co-chair of the International Bar Association's Human Rights Institute, and for the last five years I've been sending letters of protest weekly to governments in China, Syria, Bangladesh, Sri Lanka—you name it—complaining about violations of human rights. So I've been involved in this work for the last fifteen years or so, and it seemed to me that being Jewish was no reason to treat Israel exceptionally, to say that because I'm Jewish, it's all right for me to investigate everybody else but Israel.

You have so many ties to Israel. You were on the board of Hebrew University.

I still am. That's correct.

So you had to know you were going to antagonize a lot of your friends.

That's correct, but I also have the support of many of my friends. It's something that goes both ways, but antagonizing friends was inevitable—in respect to this investigation and previous investigations.

Your report basically accuses Israel of waging war on the entire population of Gaza.

That's correct.

There are allegations in here—some very tough allegations—of Israeli soldiers shooting unarmed civilians who posed no threat; of shooting people whose hands were shackled behind them; of shooting two teenagers who had been ordered off a tractor that they were driving, apparently carrying wounded civilians to a hospital; of hundreds, maybe thousands of homes destroyed, left in rubble; of hospitals bombed. It's a damning indictment of Israel's conduct in Gaza.

Well, that conduct was outrageous, and there should have been outrage. The response to this report, by the way, has not been to deal with the substance of those allegations. I've really seen or read no detailed response in respect of the actual incidents on which we report.

Why is that?

I don't know. I suppose people hate being attacked. There's a knee-jerk reaction to attack the messenger rather than deal with the message. And I think this is typical of that response. I certainly don't claim infallibility. But I would like to see a response to the substance of the report, particularly the attack on the infrastructure of Gaza, which seems to me to be absolutely unjustifiable.

What did you see with your own eyes when you went there?

I saw the destruction of the only flour-producing factory in Gaza. I saw fields plowed up by Israeli tank bulldozers. I saw chicken farms for egg production completely destroyed. I met with families who lost their loved ones in homes in which they were seeking shelter from the Israeli ground forces. I had to conduct very emotional and difficult interviews with fathers whose little daughters were killed, whose families were killed. It was a very difficult investigation, and will give me nightmares for the rest of my life.

What makes these particular acts war crimes?

With humanitarian law, it's fundamentally what's known as the "principle of distinction." It requires all people involved—commanders, troops, all people involved in making war—to distinguish between civilians and combatants. And then there's a question of proportionality. One can, in war, target a military target. And there can be what's euphemistically referred to as "collateral damage," but the "collateral damage" must be proportionate to the military aim. If you can take out a munitions factory in an urban area with a loss of one hundred lives, or you can use a bomb twice as large and take out the same factory and kill two thousand people, the latter would be a war crime, the former would not.

Who is to say so? Who is to make that distinction?

That distinction must be made after the event. I think the military must be given a fairly wide margin of appreciation, in the sense of room for mistakes, and ultimately it's a question of looking at the intent, at any question of negligence on the part of the people who make the decision.

You wrote, "The military operation [in Gaza] was a result of disrespect for the fundamental principle of 'distinction' in international humanitarian law." So in layman's language, the distinction is between—

Between combatants and innocent civilians.

And you're saying Israel did not make that distinction in many of these incidents.

That's correct.

Did you find evidence that it was deliberate on their part?

We did. We found evidence in statements made by present and former political and military leaders who said, quite openly, that there's going to be a disproportionate attack. They said that if rockets are going to continue, we're going to hit back disproportionately. We're going to punish you for doing it. And that's not countenanced by the law of war.

So they were doing, on the ground, what they had announced earlier that they intended to do.

Well, certainly. One thing one can't say about the Israel Defense Forces is that they make too many mistakes. They're a very sophisticated army. And if they attack a mosque or attack a factory, and over two hundred factories were bombed, there's just no basis to ascribe that to error. That must be intentional.

The Israelis admit that they bombed some of what you call civilian targets in your report, but they argue that because Hamas is the elected leadership in Gaza, some of those facilities are, in fact, part and parcel of the Hamas infrastructure.

Right. Well, there's certainly room for difference of opinion in respect to some of them. We had a look, for example, at the legislative assembly in Gaza. Now, the legislative assembly consists of members of Hamas in the majority, but also opposition parties. And certainly, as we understand international humanitarian law, to bomb the legislative assembly is unlawful. It's not a military target, it's a civilian target. Let's take an example closer to home. If the United States is at war it would be legitimate to bomb the Pentagon; I would suggest it would be illegitimate to bomb the Congress.

We did bomb the Bundestag in Germany, during World War II. The Allies—

I think the standards of World War II are a little outdated. Since then we've had the 1949 Geneva Conventions and the 1977 additional optional protocols to the Geneva Conventions. The law has moved considerably. I don't believe one can judge a war in 2008 and 2009 by the standards of the 1940s.

But what about Hiroshima and Nagasaki? The United States deliberately incinerated two cities with atomic bombs, knowing that tens of thousands of civilians, including women and children, would perish.

Times have changed, the law has changed. And I have little doubt that if a similar situation arose today, it's highly unlikely that there would be the use of nuclear power in respect to cities, or the civilian toll that we saw in Hiroshima and Nagasaki.

What's the heart of the Geneva Conventions and those protocols?

Again, it's to give heightened protection to civilians, not only in international armed conflict, but also in non-international armed conflict. So the whole topic has expanded considerably, under the guidance and the guardianship of the International Committee of the Red Cross. It's important to bear in mind that the 1949 Geneva Conventions is the first international instrument that's been ratified by every single member of the United Nations, so that's the law. It's not only treaty law, but it's become customary international law.

And it applies to a situation like Gaza?

Absolutely. And it applies, as we held in our report, clearly to Israel as a state party to the Geneva Conventions, and it applies also to Hamas as a non-state party, under customary international law.

During your investigation, did you find war crimes by Hamas?

Oh, indeed. We found the firing of many thousands of rockets and mortars at a civilian population to constitute a very serious war crime. Possibly, we said, crimes against humanity.

But Hamas is not a party to the Geneva Conventions, right?

Well, it can't be, because it's not a state party. But Hamas is bound by customary international law and by international human rights law, and that makes it equally a war crime to do what it's been doing.

Some critics say that by focusing more on the actions of the Israelis than on those of the Palestinians, you are in essence making it clear who you think is the more responsible party here.

I suppose that's fair comment, Bill. I think it's difficult to deal equally with a state party, with a sophisticated army like Israel's, with an air force and a navy, and the most sophisticated weapons that are not only in the arsenal of Israel, but manufactured and exported by Israel, on the one hand, and, on the other, with Hamas using improvised, imprecise armaments. It's difficult to equate their power. But that having been said, one has to look at the actions of each and judge the criminality, or the alleged criminality, of each. That's the reason our main recommendation is to urge both sides to look at themselves, to conduct their own internal investigations—criminal investigations—and to prosecute and punish the people responsible.

Was it possible to distinguish between militants and civilians among the casualties in Gaza?

I can't believe that the Israeli intelligence doesn't enable them to do so, certainly to a higher degree. I'm not suggesting that there can be any infallibility. But I'll give you an example. We spoke to the owner of a home in Gaza City. He said he looked out of his window and saw some militants, whether Hamas or other Palestinian groups, setting up their mortar launchers in his yard. He ran out and said, "Get out of here. I don't want you doing this here. You're going to endanger my family, because [the Israelis] are going to bomb. Get out." And in fact, they left. Whether that was typical or atypical, I don't know. But assuming the militant had disobeyed him, assuming they had launched the rockets over the objections of the household owner and his family, and disappeared, it would be a war crime, as I understand it, for Israel to have bombed the home of that innocent household that did not want this to happen.

The Israelis would maintain that many of those militants in Gaza were embedded in homes, hospitals, schools, and the like.

Well, we couldn't cover the field. There were really hundreds of incidents. We chose thirty-six. And it could have been thirty-six hundred.

Why those thirty-six?

Because they seemed to represent the most serious—the highest death toll and the highest injury toll. And they appear to represent situations where there was little or no military justification for what happened. We didn't want to investigate situations where we would be called upon to second-guess decisions made by Israel Defense Force leaders or soldiers in what's called the "fog of battle." It's really unfair to do that, especially without hearing the other side. So we tried to concentrate on issues that seem to be less likely to be justifiable by applying those standards.

Did you find evidence that Israel tried to avoid targeting civilians?

In some cases, yes. We gave Israel full credit for some of the leaflets that were dropped in Rafah which were specific. They announced, "During such-and-such a period, we're going to be bombing between X street and Y street, and A street and B street. Get out for your own safety." And that saved a lot of innocent lives.

But many hundreds of thousands of other leaflets were really unhelpful. They were dropped in many parts of Gaza warning, "We are going to be bombing. Get out of your homes." Didn't say when. Didn't say where. And also didn't say where people should go. It's such an overcrowded civilian area—one and a half million people, in a tiny area, with closed borders. There was little action families could take to react to that sort of warning.

I didn't know until I read your report that the Israelis had actually made a hundred thousand calls to telephones in Gaza and said, in effect, "Get out." They were giving the occupants a chance to move.

Well, first, move to where? And second, in consequence of the overwhelming majority of those warnings, there was no attack. So they were causing confusion and terror rather than saving lives.

But confusion and terror are part of war, right?

No, there shouldn't be confusion and terror applied to a civilian population. If you're going to give warnings, they should be specific.

But when the terrorists, the militants, whatever one wants to call them, are known to be embedded in those tight, concentrated areas, what's the other army to do?

It's to launch commando actions to get at the militants and not the innocent civilians. And there's an element of punishment here: if one looks at the attacks on the infrastructure, on the food infrastructure, one sees a pattern of attacking all of the people of Gaza, not simply the militants.

Why did they bomb the infrastructure so thoroughly?

We've found that the only logical reason is collective punishment against the people of Gaza for voting into power Hamas, and a form of reprisal for the rocket attacks and mortar attacks on southern Israel.

If they were interested only in stopping the rockets, did they have to destroy the land?

No, this was a political decision, I think, and not a military one. I think they were telling the people of Gaza that if you support Hamas, this is what we're going to do to you.

Give me some more examples of what you see as a pattern in the destruction of the infrastructure.

I'd start with the bulldozing of agricultural fields, apparently pretty randomly. It wasn't as though these farms were owned by Hamas militants. I haven't seen that allegation made. Then there's the bombing of some two hundred industrial factories—the only flour-producing factory, the water supply facilities of Gaza, the sanitation facilities, which caused an overflow of filth and muck into neighboring farmland.

Do you know if these were targeted, or were they the consequence of spontaneous actions aimed at militants?

Clearly, there can be no question of militants running two hundred factories. We know from our investigation that the owner of the flour factory, in fact, had one of the rare documents issued by Israelis allowing the owner to go into Israel and deal with Israeli counterparts. He received a warning to evacuate, he evacuated his staff, nothing happened. They went back. He then made inquiries through a friend in Israel, who contacted the Israel Defense Forces, and was told, "Don't worry. They're not going to bomb your factory." They went back. A few days later, he gets another telephone call through the switchboard—not to him directly: "Evacuate." He again makes inquiries. "Don't worry. We're not going to bomb." So they go back. Nothing happens. Then there's a third warning to evacuate. They evacuate—and this time the Israelis bomb the factory. Now, the Israelis know who they're deal-ing with; they'd given him that document allowing him to go into Israel. This is the sort of conduct that indicates to us an intent to punish civilians in Gaza for what their leaders were complicit in doing.

It's difficult for us in the United States to understand this intimacy of self-destruction: a Gaza factory owner calls a friend in Israel, who calls the mili-tary, and then he calls back to the factory.

It's the sort of evidence that has some credibility to it. It's not the sort of evidence that this man is going to concoct.

As you conducted your investigation, what were your standards of evidence?

We spoke to well over a hundred witnesses. We obviously didn't take at face value everything we were told.

One criticism of your effort is that those witnesses were supplied by Hamas militants.

That's not correct. We made our own inquiries and we decided who we would see. We weren't given a list by Hamas or anybody else. We chose incidents—thirty-six out of hundreds. We chose the people we wanted to see, and there was no Hamas presence anywhere we talked to these people. There were malicious statements to the effect that militants were around, but I can give you every assurance that it didn't happen. And I can assure you that if it did happen, I wouldn't have been prepared to continue to op-erate under those situations. I would have insisted that they leave. And if I couldn't achieve that, I would have abandoned the investigation.

Was there a moment when you thought, "Why am I doing this?"

Oh, there've been frequent moments. I was, quite frankly, nervous going into Gaza. I had nightmares about being kidnapped. It was very difficult, es-pecially for a Jew, to go into an area controlled by Hamas. So I went in with a certain amount of fear and trepidation. But I was struck by the warmth of the people we met and dealt with in Gaza. My fears were put aside.

Why do you do these things?

Well, I think one accepts these duties and obligations, not knowing where they're going to lead. And then one has to do one's duty.

Yes, but why do you have to do your duty?

I think it's one's experience. I got involved in the antiapartheid movement in South Africa because of my anger and frustration at the unfairness of racial oppression. I was privileged to be able to get involved and make a difference. And then, solely because of pressure from Nelson Mandela, I found myself getting involved in the war crimes tribunal in the former Yugoslavia. I didn't want to do it. But he twisted my arm—he's a very good arm-twister—and I found myself in Bosnia. Then the UN Security Council asked me to do Rwanda. The Swedish prime minister asked me to do Kosovo. Kofi Annan asked me to do the oil-for-food investigations at the UN. These were all difficult, difficult inquiries. I must confess that I got a tremendous amount of satisfaction from doing work that put me into a position of working with absolutely outstanding people. Really, one thing leads to the other.

But on this most recent occasion you have been accused by some right-wing Jews in Israel of betraying your people. This is different, isn't it?

It's different, but it's symptomatic of the same disease, which is a form of racism. Why should my being Jewish stop me from investigating Israel? I just don't see it. I think a friend should be open to criticism from friends. I think it's more important. I think true friends criticize their friends when they do wrong things.

Israelis claim that if you hold them to the standard that you have just de-scribed, any democracy that's fighting terrorism is likely to find itself dragged into an international court of justice. Do you consider that a valid concern?

No. Absolutely not. Take the United States fighting wars in Kosovo and Iraq and Afghanistan. They have certainly at a high level gone to extremes to protect innocent civilians. Where they've made mistakes, and mistakes have been made—in Kosovo, in Iraq, in Afghanistan—apologies have followed. The United States, in general, has accepted and tried its best, with the assistance of military lawyers, to avoid violating international humanitarian law. So it seems to me this is a smokescreen. I've no doubt that the laws of war are sufficient to cover the situation of fighting what is now termed "asymmetric war." It's not easy; I concede that. But there's a line over which you just don't transgress without clearly violating the law.

Israelis point out they live in a sea of animosity and, if they took your findings to heart, they would not be able to root out the terrorists that surround them.

I just don't accept that, Bill. I don't accept that the destruction of the food infrastructure is necessary to fight terrorism from Gaza.

Here's what Israeli prime minister Benjamin Netanyahu said at the United Nations: "A democracy legitimately defending itself against terror is morally hanged, drawn and quartered, and given an unfair trial to boot. By these twisted standards, the UN Human Rights Council would have dragged Roosevelt and Churchill to the dock as war criminals. What a perversion of truth. What a perversion of justice. . . . The same UN that cheered Israel as we left Gaza, the same UN that promised to back our right of self-defense now accuses us, my people, my country, of being war criminals. And for what? For acting responsibly in self-defense? For acting in a way that any country would act with a restraint unmatched by many. What a travesty. Ladies and gentle-men, Israel justly defended itself against terror. This biased and unjust report provides a clear-cut test for all governments. Will you stand with Israel? Or will you stand with the terrorists?" What were you thinking as you just lis-tened to that?

I was thinking that it's a complete misunderstanding, and a lack of ap-preciation of what humanitarian law is all about. Again, it's no answer to say that there's a right of self-defense. As I said to you, I accept the right of Israel, absolutely, to defend itself. But let me give you an exam-ple. Assuming the United States, in fighting the Taliban, started bombing the whole food infrastructure of the people in the area where the Taliban thrives—plowing up fields, bombing food factories, and so on. I don't be-lieve that this would be accepted as legitimate by the people of the United States.

Do we need to change the rules of war in fighting terrorism?

Not at all, and you know, it struck me when I heard Prime Minister Netanyahu suggest that the law of war needs to be changed—it seemed to me to contain an implicit acceptance that they broke the law as it now is, and that's why it needs to be changed.

From the outset, Israel refused to cooperate with you. Israel would not even let you in the country to conduct investigations. How could you expect to do a good job with only one side of the story?

Naively, I must confess, I believed Israel would cooperate. I thought that I had obtained an even-handed mandate, really for the first time, from the Human Rights Council. I really expected the Israeli government to seize this opportunity of using an even-handed mission to its advantage. And I pleaded with the Israeli government—in one letter directly to Prime Minister Netanyahu, I said, "Please meet with me. Tell me how you want us to implement the mandate. Give us advice as to how we should go about it." I assumed they'd do that.

Did you hear from him?

The final refusal came some two and a half months later, after we were busy, involved, committed. It seemed to me too late to withdraw at that stage.

Your report recommends that both Israel and Hamas conduct their own investigations, and that if there are war crimes alleged and proven, that those perpetrators—Israelis or Hamas—be taken to the International Criminal Court.

No. They should be punished in their own countries. Only if there are no investigations should the International Criminal Court become the court of last resort. If nations investigate their own war crimes in good faith, then the International Court has no jurisdiction. If Israel and Hamas conduct good-faith investigations, that's the end of criminal investigations at the international level.

So what is Israel afraid of?

Well, I can only assume they're afraid of an even-handed, good-faith investigation proving that serious war crimes were committed. That, they don't want.

Do you think Hamas will likely do an investigation itself?

There would be tremendous pressure on them to do that, if Israel did.

You said recently that to understand international justice, you have to understand the politics of international justice. What do you mean?

Well, without the political will we wouldn't have had an international war crimes tribunal for the former Yugoslavia. That was a huge departure. If you think about what's happened between 1993 and 2009, there's been a rapid development of this idea. Nobody anticipated a permanent International Criminal Court now with more than a hundred nations actively involved, including every member of the European Union. Japan. One wouldn't have expected that.

But none of that would have happened without political will, and particularly the political will of the United States. It was the Clinton administration, and particularly Secretary of State Madeleine Albright, who drove that whole policy. Without Madeleine Albright there wouldn't have been a Yugoslavia tribunal, there wouldn't have been a Rwanda tribunal, and Kofi Annan wouldn't have been encouraged to call a diplomatic conference to set up an International Criminal Court. Without political will on the part of the United States, these things wouldn't have happened.

Why does the world need an International Criminal Court?

It really is a question of principle. Until 1993, war criminals literally had impunity. They didn't have to fear justice at home, because at home they were usually war heroes and not war criminals. And there wasn't a single international court with jurisdiction over them. There were no individual nations that were prepared to use universal jurisdiction against war criminals. That's changed. War criminals have trouble traveling around many countries of the world. One of the things worrying the Israeli government is that if they don't have their own investigation, they're going to face investigations in some of the European countries and some of the African countries, including my own country, South Africa. So there are a lot of political reasons to indicate that it's in their interest to conduct their own domestic investigation.

Not everyone has been critical of your report. The Financial Times—*a very respected British-based newspaper—ran an editorial saying that "Goldstone's Gaza report is balanced. Israel is not alone in the dock; it simply looms larger." It's hard to understand why Israel is so vociferously opposed to what you call a necessary act of justice.*

The only reason they've given has come from Defense Minister Ehud Barak, who says that an independent investigation would somehow downgrade the military's own investigation of itself. Well, that would be a good thing. One thing that disturbs me about the internal military investigation is that seven months after the end of the war, there's been only one successful prosecution against a soldier.* He stole a credit card—and this has become fodder for cartoonists, considering the plethora of alleged war crimes. What also concerns me is that in only one case, as far as I've read, has the military even approached the victims in Gaza. Obviously, to have a full investigation, one needs to hear both sides.

The Israelis say that they hold their military accountable and that there's no government better at investigating the actions of its own military.

In secrecy? I like to quote the late Supreme Court Justice Brandeis, who said the best disinfectant is sunlight. Israel's investigations happen in the dark. And even with the best good faith in the world on the part of the military investigators, the victims are not going to accept decisions that are taken in the dark.

But aren't Israelis fearful of a United Nations that historically has been biased against the country?

Yes, but I would go out of my way to meet that head-on, and not to simply put one's head in the sand and say, "Well, the United Nations is biased; I'm going to ignore it." That's not the way one succeeds in the modern world.

The Financial Times *says it is your reputation and your methods that the Israeli government fears.*

The only thing they can be afraid of is the truth. And I think this is why they're attacking the messenger and not the message.

Why do you think a report like this is essential to the peace process in the Middle East?

It's been my experience that in the aftermath of serious human rights violations, you cannot get enduring peace if you leave rancor among the victims.

---

*See footnote on p. 111.

What victims need is acknowledgment. They need official acknowledgment that they have been wronged. Whether that's done by Truth and Reconciliation Commissions, as we did in South Africa, or through domestic prosecutions or international prosecutions, official truth-telling is an essential building brick to lasting peace. ∽

ROBERT BLY

I can't imagine the world without Robert Bly, and fortunately, because of his long and prolific life, I don't have to. Like the iconoclast H.L. Mencken, who went on working "for the same reason that a hen goes on laying eggs," Robert Bly never ceases to think, write, and engage. Thankfully, we will always have his amazing legacy of work to nourish us. In fact, the University of Minnesota had to create special quarters to contain his eighty thousand pages of hand-written notes, journals spanning fifty years, audio and television programs—including several he and I have done together—and all the awards and other memorabilia accumulated over his long and creative life.

Bly's international bestseller Iron Man, his interpretation of the fairy tales of the Brothers Grimm, inspired men the world over to use those and other primal stories to probe deep and complex issues of gender. And apart from his own books, poems, and essays, there are the literary magazines he founded that introduced us to giants of poetry hardly known in America: Chile's Pablo Neruda; the Spaniard Antonio Machado; Kabir, the weaver-poet of India; and of course the great Islamic mystic Rumi.

Behind the gruff exterior of a Norwegian woodsman, Bly is a sweetie; I can never forget the night he strummed his dulcimer and sang for our children at the dinner table, or the troubadour songs he performed at my wife Judith's sixty-fifth birthday, a celebration shared with another kindred soul, the noted

Rumi interpreter Coleman Barks. Above all, he is a man of courage and conviction. During the '60s, Bly organized writers to oppose the Vietnam War, and when he won the National Book Award for The Light Around the Body, *he donated the money to the resistance. "It's quite appropriate to write poems against war," he told me, "and it's proper not to be disappointed if nothing happens." Soon after his eightieth birthday he brought some of his recent poems to our studio.*

—Bill Moyers

—⁓—

When we first met, you were barely fifty. Let me ask you to read some stanzas you read then.

> I have wandered in a face, for hours,
> Passing through dark fires . . .
>
> . . . and I am drawn
> To the desert, to the parched places, to the landscape of
>   zeros . . .
>
> I can't tell if this joy
> is from the body, or the soul, or a third place!

It's good you remember that. Instead of talking about "the divine," it's much simpler to say, "There is the body, then there's the soul, and then there's a third place."

Have you figured out what that third place is? Thirty years have passed since you spoke those lines.

It's where all of the geniuses—all the lovely people and the brilliant women—go. And they watch over us a little bit. Once in a while, they'll say, "Drop that line. It's no good." Sometimes when you do poetry, especially if you translate people like Hafez and Rumi, you go almost immediately to this third place. But we don't go there very often.

Why?

I suppose it's because we think too much about our own houses and our own places. Maybe I should read a Kabir poem here.

Kabir?

The poet from India. Fifteenth century. Here's what he wrote:

> Friend, hope for the Guest while you are alive.
> Jump into experience while you are alive!
> Think ... and think ... while you are alive.
> What you call "salvation" belongs to the time before death.
>
> If you don't break your ropes while you're alive,
> do you think
> ghosts will do it after?
>
> The idea that the soul will join with the ecstatic
> just because the body is rotten—
> that is all fantasy.
> What is found now is found then.
> If you find nothing now,
> you will simply end up with an apartment in the City
>   of Death.

I was going through Chicago one time with a young poet, and we were re-writing this. His translation was: "If you find nothing now, you will simply end up with a suite in the Ramada Inn of death." How about that?

> If you make love with the divine now, in the next life
> you will have the face of satisfied desire.
>
> So plunge into the truth, find out who the Teacher is,
> believe in the Great Sound!
>
> Kabir says this: When the Guest is being searched for,
>   it is the intensity of the longing for the Guest that
>   does all the work.
> Look at me, and you will see a slave of that intensity.

See, they don't use the word *God*. It's capital-G *Guest*. He's one of the true religious ones, Bill. One of the deep ones.

You've been working a lot lately in the poems of Islam.

Yes. Muslims have a great literature and fantastic poets. Rumi and Hafez, of course, have been the guiding lights—Rumi especially—of much of American poetry for some years now. It seems to me we should be able to give thanks for the genius that is there, despite what's happened in recent years. Take this fourteenth-century Persian poem:

THE WORLD IS NOT ALL THAT GREAT

The stuff produced in the factories of space and time
Is not all that great. Bring some wine, because
The sweet things of this world are not all that great . . .

The true kingdom comes to you without any breaking
Of bones. If that weren't so, achieving the Garden
Through your own labors wouldn't be all that great.

In the five days remaining to you in this rest stop
Before you to go to the grave, take it easy, give
Yourself time, because time is not all that great . . .

You Puritans on the cold stone floor, you are not safe
From the tricks of God's zeal: the distance between the
   cloister
And the Zoroastrian tavern is not, after all, that great.

And the last stanza is:

The name of Hafez has been well inscribed in the books,
But in our clan of disreputables, the difference
Between profit and loss is not all that great.

You see how he is withdrawing all our obsessions? "I've got to get this done. I don't have much time left." He's a tremendous spiritual poet. And as I say, I like geniuses.

Rumi was a genius.

Yes, he was. I'll give you one I translated.

THE EDGE OF THE ROOF

I don't like it here, I want to go back.
According to the old Knowers
if you're absent from the one you love

even for one second that ruins the whole thing!

> There must be someone . . . just to find
> one *sign* of the other world in this town
> would be enough.

I feel that in Minneapolis. "Just to find one *sign* of the other world in this town would be enough."

> You know the great Chinese Simurgh bird
> got caught in this net . . .
> And what can I do? I'm only a wren.

> My desire-body, don't come
> strolling over this way.
> Sit where you are, that's a good place.

> When you want dessert, you choose something rich.
> In wine, you look for what is clear and firm.
> What is the rest? . . .

The rest is television.

> What is the rest? The rest is mirages,
> and blurry pictures, and milk mixed with water.
> The rest is self-hatred, and mocking other
>   people, and bombing.

> So just be quiet and sit down.
> The reason is—you are drunk,
> and this is the edge of the roof.

It's a good poem, even for the United States right now. Somebody should say to George W. Bush, "This is the edge of the roof. And you're drunk. Just be quiet and sit down."

Your adult life has been bracketed by two long wars: Vietnam and Iraq. You wrote poems against Iraq, and you wrote poems against Vietnam. And both wars went on, despite your poetry. Poetry didn't stop the war.

No, it's never been able to do anything of that sort. It merely speaks to the soul, so the soul can remember. It's quite proper to have poems against the war. And it's proper not to be disappointed if nothing changes. Is it okay if I read what is probably the first poem I wrote against the Iraq War in August of 2002?

This was before the invasion.

Yes.

> CALL AND ANSWER
> AUGUST 2002
>
> Tell me why it is we don't lift our voices these days
> And cry over what is happening. Have you noticed
> The plans are made for Iraq and the ice cap is melting?
>
> I say to myself: "Go on, cry. What's the sense
> Of being an adult and having no voice? Cry out!
> See who will answer! This is *Call and Answer*!"
>
> We will have to call especially loud to reach
> Our angels, who are hard of hearing; they are hiding
> In the jugs of silence filled during our wars.

I was thinking of Grenada. Remember we invaded Grenada? 1983. Why did we do that? Who remembers?

> Have we agreed to so many wars that we can't
> Escape from silence? If we don't lift our voices, we allow
> Others (who are ourselves) to rob the house.
>
> How come we've listened to the great criers—Neruda,
> Akhmatova, Thoreau, Frederick Douglass—and now
> We're silent as sparrows in the little bushes?

It's a very bad pun, but I left it in. "We are silent as sparrows in the little bushes?"

> Some masters say our life only lasts seven days.
> Where are we in the week? Is it Thursday yet?
> Hurry, cry now! Soon Sunday night will come.

And Sunday night came when we bombed Baghdad. "Where are we in the week? Is it Thursday yet? Hurry, cry now! Soon Sunday night will come."

Why isn't there more outcry?

If there were a draft, the outcry would be just as great as it was in the Vietnam War. But Bush decided to use those with the least education in the country to fight the war. Many of the people getting killed are the sons of people in northern Minnesota—places like that—who don't have any access to protest. And it was a disastrous choice.

Back in 1969, when you accepted the National Book Award, you gave your $1,000 prize to the resistance against Vietnam. You said, "As Americans, we have always wanted the life of feeling without the life of suffering. We long for pure life, constant victory. We've always wanted to avoid suffering, and therefore, we are unable to live in the present." Still true?

Yes. Isn't that amazing that it's the people in Washington who make these decisions who aren't suffering at all? The suffering ones are those young men with a poor education and poor opportunities for jobs who needed to escape somehow from the trap of American life, and so they go there and get their legs and arms blown off.

You went to Iran a few months ago.

Yes, we went to the gravesite of Hafez, the great poet. We got up early, and at about eight o'clock in the morning, children started to come. Maybe third-grade children. And they stood around the little tomb and sang a poem by Hafez. Really charming. And then they went away, and now some fifth graders came. And they stood around the tomb and sang a poem of Hafez. And of course, every poem of Hafez is connected with a tune, so you teach the children the tune, and then they have the poem. So I said to myself, "Isn't that unbelievable? And why don't we do that? Why don't we go to the grave of Walt Whitman and have children come there?"

I don't have an answer. Why don't we?

Because we don't love Walt Whitman, or we don't love him in the way that the Iranians love their poets. Wouldn't it be wonderful if children could go to Walt Whitman's grave and recite little poems? You'd bring the poets into the heart, instead of having them in your head in graduate school. And that's what you do with children. You bring children in, and get them associated with the heart when they're very small, and then they can feel it all through their lives.

You told me many years ago that you tried to write a poem every day. Do you still do that?

Yes. It's a joyful thing. Well, I get a few stanzas done every day, anyway.

Here's one I like. Read it, please.

THINGS TO THINK

Think in ways you've never thought before.
If the phone rings, think of it as carrying a message
Larger than anything you've ever heard,
Vaster than a hundred lines of Yeats.

Think that someone may bring a bear to your door,
Maybe wounded or deranged; or think that a moose
Has risen out of the lake, and he is carrying on his antlers
A child of your own whom you've never seen.

When someone knocks on the door, think that he's about
To give you something large: tell you you're forgiven,
Or that it's not necessary to work all the time, or that it's
Been decided that if you lie down no one will die.

And that's for you, too, isn't it? "When someone knocks at the door, think that he's about to give you something large: tell Bill Moyers that you've been forgiven, that it's not necessary for you to work all the time or that it's been decided that if you lie down, then no one will die." Well, that's a beautiful quality, the feeling that it isn't right for you to lie down, Bill, but I'm glad you're still working all the time.

Thank you. But what about this one? You read this one to me many moons ago. I wonder if it still resonates with you.

FOR MY SON NOAH, TEN YEARS OLD

Night and day arrive, and day after day goes by
and what is old remains old, and what is young remains
   young and grows old.

The lumber pile does not grow younger, nor the two-by-
   fours lose their darkness;
but the old tree goes on, the barn stands without help so
   many years;
the advocate of darkness and night is not lost.

The horse steps up, swings on one leg, turns his body;
the chicken flapping claws up onto the roost, its wings
   whelping and walloping,
But what is primitive is not to be shot out into the night
   and the dark,
and slowly the kind man comes closer, loses his rage, sits
   down at table.

That's the second stanza. When I was about thirty-five or forty or so on, and
I had children, I realized that what is primitive in me should not be shot
out all the time into the dark. "Slowly the kind man comes closer, loses his
rage." Some of it. "Sits down at table."

So I am proud only of those days that pass in undivided
   tenderness,
when you sit drawing, or making books, stapled, with messages to the world,
or coloring a man with fire coming out of his hair.

This is for my son, Noah.

Or we sit at a table, with small tea carefully poured.
So we pass our time together, calm and delighted.

*I remember the first time I came to see you, back in the late '70s. You were liv-
ing in Moose Lake, Minnesota.*

Yes. I still live there. Same cabin. We have a house in Minneapolis, but I
sometimes go back up to Moose Lake when I want to be by myself.

What's your favorite poem from up there?

From the North?

How about "After Drinking All Night with a Friend"?

Oh, that's good. I like that one, too. I wrote it in the early 1960s. A friend—
Bill Duffy—and I went up to a lake.

AFTER DRINKING ALL NIGHT WITH A FRIEND, WE GO OUT IN THE BOAT AT DAWN TO SEE WHO CAN WRITE THE BEST POEM

These pines, these fall oaks, these rocks,
This water dark and touched by wind—
I am like you, you dark boat,
Drifting over water fed by cool springs.

Beneath the waters, since I was a boy,
I have dreamt of strange and dark treasures,
Not of gold, or strange stones, but the true
Gift, beneath the pale lakes of Minnesota.

This morning also, drifting in the dawn wind,
I sense my hands, and my shoes, and this ink-—
Drifting, as all of the body drifts,
Above the clouds of the flesh and the stone.

A few friendships, a few dawns, a few glimpses of grass,
A few oars weathered by the snow and the heat,
So we drift toward shore, over cold waters,
No longer caring if we drift or go straight.

You make me think of those lines from a poem in your book My Sentence Was a Thousand Years of Joy. *You write:*

Robert, those high spirits don't prove you are
A close friend of truth; but you have learned to drive
Your buggy over the prairies of human sorrow.

Oh, thanks for bringing that one back. I like it, too. Now I have to read it for you before we quit. "Stealing Sugar from the Castle"—this has the word *joy*.

STEALING SUGAR FROM THE CASTLE

We are poor students who stay after school to study joy.
We are like those birds in the India mountains.

I am a widow whose child is her only joy.

The only thing I hold in my ant-like head
Is the builder's plan of the castle of sugar.
Just to steal one grain of sugar is a joy!

Translating great poetry, you know, is a way of stealing sugar.

The only thing I hold in my ant-like head
Is the builder's plan of the castle of sugar.
Just to steal one grain of sugar is a joy!

This is from *Beowulf.*

Like a bird, we fly out of darkness into the hall,
Which is lit with singing, then fly out again.
Being shut out of the warm hall is also a joy.

I am a laggard, a loafer, and an idiot.

One of my boys said to me, "Dad, you're not a loafer."

I am a laggard, a loafer, and an idiot. But I love
To read about those who caught one glimpse
Of the face, and died twenty years later in joy.

I don't mind you saying I will die soon.
Even in the sound of the word soon, I hear
The word you which begins every sentence of joy.

"You're a thief!" the judge said. "Let's see
Your hands!" I showed my callused hands in court.
My sentence was a thousand years of joy.

Are you happy at eighty?

I'm happy at eighty. But I can't stand as much happiness as I used to.

That's because you're Lutheran.

Maybe one day out of the week I'll become depressed—but the rest of the time, especially if I'm writing poetry, I'm never depressed.

What depresses you?

Who knows? Depression comes up from underneath. And it just grabs you. It's an entity on its own. We are built for depression in a way. Because the *nafs* is so strong in us it doesn't want us to be happy and give away things. It wants us to pull back inside and say, "My mother wasn't good enough to me. My father wasn't good enough to me." You know that whole thing.

Who knows when or if we'll see each other again? Let's bring the circle around. Because when I first met you thirty years ago you told me this was a poem that had marked you. Remember it?

Oh, yes.

> I live my life in growing orbits
> which move out over the things of the world.
> Perhaps I can never achieve the last,
> but that will be my attempt.

Well, that's very '60s, isn't it? This is Rainer Maria Rilke, translated from the German.

> I am circling around God . . .

The word made him nervous. So he said,

> . . . around the ancient tower,
> and I have been circling for a thousand years,
> and I still don't know if I am a falcon, or a storm,
> or a great song.

Genius poem, isn't it? Genius.

> I am circling around God, around the ancient tower,
> and I have been circling for a thousand years,

You know, Bill, there's a part of you that has been circling for a thousand years.

And you.

Yeah.

And all of us.

Oh, yes. And that wonderful energy that you can see in a human face even when walking down the street. Something's still there—circling around God, around the ancient tower. "And I have been circling for a thousand years, and I still don't know if I am a falcon"—which means someone who goes in and grabs things and steals them—"or a storm, or a great song."

Oh, yes. ❧

JEREMY SCAHILL

More than 630 companies were hired by the United States to help implement the occupation of Iraq. By 2007, their 180,000 employees outnumbered America's 160,000 troops. Of those men and women for hire, 48,000 worked for private security firms. Their presence, The New York Times *reported*, marked "a critical change in the way America wages war: the early days of the Iraq War, with all its Wild West chaos, ushered in the era of the private contractor, wearing no uniform but fighting and dying in battle, gathering and disseminating intelligence and killing presumed insurgents."

The most publicized of these companies was Blackwater—a name that became so notorious it ultimately was changed by its owners to Xe Services. Very few Americans had even heard of the company until the spring of 2004, when four Blackwater contractors in Fallujah were killed in an ambush, their bodies mutilated, burned, dragged through the streets, then hanged from a bridge. Photographs of the grisly scenes flashed instantly around the world. American military forces quickly launched a bloody house-by-house assault on Fallujah aimed at driving insurgents from the city, and congressional investigators and journalists were soon digging into Blackwater's history and operations.

None was more meticulous than Jeremy Scahill, the independent investigative reporter who has twice received the George Polk Award for journalistic achievements. His book, Blackwater: The Rise of the World's Most Powerful

Mercenary Army, *was published in March 2007, almost three years to the day since the killing of the four contractors.* The New York Times *called it "a crackling exposé."*

News from Iraq further propelled the book up the bestseller list. On September 16, 2007, while escorting a convoy of State Department officials to a military base, Blackwater guards opened fire on Iraqis in Baghdad's Nisour Square, killing seventeen civilians. According to military reports, the shooters used excessive force without provocation, and the FBI concluded that they had violated rules in effect for security contractors.

Iraq revoked Blackwater's authority to operate there, and the company was suddenly an international pariah. Its founder and chief executive officer, Erik Prince, who had rarely been seen in public, went before an ineptly run congressional hearing and tried to portray his company as the latest incarnation in a long and accepted tradition of contract soldiering—mercenaries. Skeptics weren't buying it, and the secretive Prince uncharacteristically agreed to a series of televised interviews. Jeremy Scahill, who had burrowed deep below Blackwater's spin, was fascinated by the Prince media blitz.

—Bill Moyers

—⟳—

You have been watching the interviews of Erik Prince on television. What's the message?

Let's remember, this is a guy who prior to the September 16 shooting in Baghdad had only done one television interview ever. And that one was right after 9/11 on Fox News with Bill O'Reilly. He told O'Reilly that after 9/11, the phone's been ringing off the hook at Blackwater. Other than that, this is a guy who hasn't really appeared in public. So it was unusual to see him appear before the Congress and do this blitzkrieg of interviews. The message was very clear. He was trying to say, we're a patriotic American company, we're Americans protecting Americans. But there is also something that reminded me of Jack Nicholson in *A Few Good Men* where he boasts about eating his cereal meters away from Cubans who want to kill him. When Erik Prince uses terms like "the bad guys" and "our blood runs red, white, and blue," he's saying, look, you don't understand, American people, what we're doing for you. While you're enjoying comfort here in the United States, we're over there protecting our men and women in uniform, our diplomats. I think he wants to increase the mystique about the company and the operations of Blackwater.

Do you think he was motivated, and his PR firm was motivated, in part because he didn't do that well at the recent hearings before Congress into this shooting?

I think that for years Blackwater has made a very serious strategic error in how they've handled their publicity. And now we're seeing the company go on the offensive. I think Erik Prince held his own in front of the Congress. I attribute that largely to the fact that the Democrats didn't really do their homework on him. Here you have the man who owns the company providing the largest private army on the U.S. government payroll in Iraq. A billion dollars in contracts. Twenty-seven of his men are killed in Iraq. We don't know how many people he killed. No private actor in the occupation of Iraq has had more of a devastating impact on events in Iraq than Blackwater. But at the hearings you see Democrats flipping through the pages while Prince was testifying.

If you go to the CBS News website reporting on Lara Logan's interview with him, the headline reads: "Blackwater Chief Welcomes Extra Oversight." Could that have been the message? Look, this was a terrible thing that happened over there. But we really want you—the State Department, the government, the military—to hold us more accountable.

There's a very Orwellian vibe to all of this. Blackwater says they're not a mercenary company. Erik Prince calls that a slanderous term. We're not even in the private military company business, he says. We're in the business of peace because peace matters. In fact, Blackwater recently left the mercenary trade association. They had been a leading member and funder of it. It's called the International Peace Operations Association. And the logo is a cartoon sleeping lion. It's so incredibly Orwellian. They have been pushing this "hold us accountable" line for years because it looks great on paper. There are going to be laws that govern the use of private military companies, but in reality they are totally unenforceable.

Why?

The idea is that U.S. civilian law is going to apply to contractors on the battlefield. Democrats say let's send an FBI field office over to Baghdad to monitor 180,000 contractors. But there are more contractors in Iraq right now than there are U.S. soldiers. The idea is that the FBI will go around Iraq, investigate crimes committed by contractors, interview witnesses, presumably in very dangerous places, and then arrest the individuals in question, bring them back to the United States, and prosecute them in a U.S. civilian court. I mean, I've never heard a more insane plan. So, what that bill will give Erik Prince and other mercenary companies is the opportunity to sit down and say, there are laws that govern us, we're accountable under U.S. law, when they know that it only exists on paper. There will be a few token prosecutions, but it's impossible to monitor the activities of 180,000 personnel.

How did you get interested in this story?

I started going to Iraq in 1998. I went in the weeks leading up to the Clinton administration's attack on Baghdad in December of '98. I had actually spent a fair bit of time in the city of Fallujah. It was a place that I knew well. And, as you know, on March 31, 2004, four Blackwater operatives were ambushed and killed in Fallujah, their bodies dragged through the streets, burned, strung up from a bridge.

The American public recoiled from those images.

Right. Initial reports were that civilian contractors had been killed, that these were water specialists or engineers being dragged through the streets. Then it emerged that in fact they were mercenaries working for a private company called Blackwater USA. We watched as the Bush administration then began to escalate the rhetoric, and it became clear that they were going to lay siege to the city of Fallujah. What happened in the aftermath is well known. The U.S. military was ordered to destroy the city. Hundreds of Iraqi civilians were killed, a number of U.S. troops. I began from a very simple question: How on earth were the lives of four corporate personnel—not U.S. soldiers, not humanitarian workers—used to justify the destruction of an entire Iraqi city? That siege had an incredibly devastating impact on events on the ground in Iraq. It gave rise to the Iraqi resistance. Fueled it. Attacks escalated against U.S. forces.

*How would our diplomats be protected if it weren't for the private security con-
tractors? The army is stretched thin. Isn't there a role for these people?*

The fact is that the U.S. military has not historically done the job that
Blackwater is doing. That was done through diplomatic security. But in
Iraq, you're talking about the occupation of a country. And without these
private sector forces, without companies like Blackwater, Triple Canopy,
and DynCorp, the occupation wouldn't be tenable. The 180,000 contractors operating in Iraq alongside 170,000 U.S. troops represents a doubling
of the occupation force. What this does is it subverts the citizenry of the
United States. You no longer have to have a draft. You don't have to depend
on your own citizens to fight your wars.

*What do these private contractors make compared to American soldiers on the
ground?*

It varies widely depending on the company, depending on their role, depending on their nationality. If you're a former Navy SEAL or a Delta Force
guy working for Blackwater, you can make about $600 a day for your work
in Iraq. We're talking six-figure salaries. Some of these guys working for
private military companies make as much as General Petraeus, if not more.
He makes about $180,000 a year. Average troops on the ground are be-
ing paid $40,000 a year to be in the exact same war zone as the men from
Blackwater. And they're wearing the American flag on their shoulder, not
the Blackwater logo.

*Didn't I read somewhere that one of our generals said we couldn't be in Iraq
without Blackwater and these other companies?*

General Petraeus himself has been guarded by private contractors in Iraq.
What message did it send for the general who's overseeing the surge in Iraq
to be guarded at times not by the U.S. military but by private forces? Erik
Prince likes to describe Blackwater as a sort of Federal Express of the national security apparatus. He says if you want a package to get somewhere,
do you send it through the post office or do you send it through FedEx?
Fact is, in the coalition that's occupying Iraq, the U.S. military is the junior
partner to these private companies. There are over 170 mercenary companies like Blackwater operating in Iraq right now. That's almost as many na-

tions as are registered at the UN. This isn't just about Iraq. It's also about looting the U.S. treasury.

What does it say that these mercenaries, this "peace and stability industry," have become so essential?

I think we're in the midst of the most radical privatization agenda in our nation's history. We see it in schools, in the health care system, in prisons. And now we're seeing it full-blown in the war machine. The very existence of the nation-state is at stake here, because you have companies now that have been funded with billions of dollars in public money using that money to then build up the infrastructure of private armies, some of which could take out a small national military. The old model used to be that if a company wants to go into Nigeria, for instance, and exploit oil, they have to work with the junta's forces to do that. Now you can just bring in your own private military force, which is a publicly traded mercenary outfit. They've been in Colombia for years. The Colombian government receives $630 million a year to fight the so-called war on drugs. Of that $630 million, half of it goes to U.S. war contractors. They've been in the Balkans. They're all over the place. They're in Bolivia, they're in Ecuador. Blackwater recently won a $15 billion contract that it will share with four other companies to fight terrorists with drug ties.

I was struck that no one confronted Prince about the specifics of his private army. How do you explain that?

I'm not sure why they didn't do it. This is a man who is building up nothing short of a parallel national security apparatus. He not only has his Blackwater Security, which is deployed in Iraq, he has a maritime division and an aviation division. He recently started his own privatized intelligence company called Total Intelligence Solutions that's headed by a thirty-year veteran of the CIA, Cofer Black, the man who led the hunt for Osama bin Laden and who oversaw the extraordinary rendition program. This is the man who promised President Bush that he would have his operative in Afghanistan chop off Osama bin Laden's head, place it in a box with dry ice, and then have it hand-delivered to President Bush. He's now the number two man at Blackwater USA. And he's heading up this private intelligence company called Total Intelligence Solutions. Blackwater won a

$92 million contract from the Pentagon to operate flights throughout central Asia. This is a company that is manufacturing surveillance blimps and marketing them to the Department of Homeland Security. They have their own armored vehicle called the Grizzly. Blackwater's going to be around for a very long time.

And yet Prince said they're just a very "robust temp agency." Sort of like Kelly girls.

I really don't know what to say to that. These are the guys who have worked inside of Afghanistan. They've been responsible for so much death and destruction in Iraq. Erik Prince likes to portray Blackwater as this sort of apple-pie, all-American operation. Yet his company has recruited soldiers from all around the world and deployed them in Iraq. Some are Chilean commandos who trained and served under Augusto Pinochet, the dictator of Chile. Blackwater worked with a Chilean recruiter who had been in Pinochet's military, and they hired scores of Chileans, brought them to North Carolina for evaluation, and then sent them over to Iraq. Chile was opposed to the occupation of Iraq. It said, no, we won't join the coalition of the willing. And so Blackwater goes in and hires up soldiers from a country whose home government is opposed to the war, and deploys them in Iraq. Blackwater has hired Colombian soldiers and paid them $34 a day to be in Iraq as well. They've hired Bulgarians, Fijians, Poles.

But he objects to that term, mercenary?

He says it's slanderous.

I was intrigued to learn that the CEO of the public relations agency that is handling Prince—Burson-Marsteller—was also Hillary Clinton's top campaign strategist, Mark Penn.

PR companies are also mercenaries and oftentimes work for the highest bidder.

They're not shooting people, though.

No, no, no. But they're mercenaries in the sense that they'll rent their services out to anyone. And once you're defending Erik Prince, then you become part of his operation. I also think that it was a strategic choice to go with the company with Mark Penn because of his connection with the Democrats and Hillary Clinton. For so many years we had a Republican-dominated Congress. Blackwater was certainly the beneficiary of the Republican monopoly in government. But this system is now bipartisan. When Hillary Clinton's husband was in the White House, he was an aggressive supporter of the privatization of the war machine. Bill Clinton used mercenary forces in the Balkans.

Few journalists seem to want to press Prince deeply on his political connections. What can you tell us about those connections?

There are two things at play here. There's the funding of congressional candidates. Erik Prince has given a quarter of a million dollars to Republican candidates. He also gave money to the Green Party to defeat Democratic candidates in the 2006 election cycle. So he's a pretty committed supporter of the Republican Party. But what I think is more interesting is Erik Prince's connection to the radical religious right. His father built up a very successful manufacturing empire called Prince Manufacturing. The invention that they were best known for is the now ubiquitous lighted sun visor. You pull down the visor in your car and it lights up; you have a bit of Blackwater history riding around in your vehicle. Prince grows up in this household where he watches his father using that business as a cash-generating engine to fuel and fund the rise of the Republican revolution of 1994, and also of several of the core groups that make up the radical religious right. His dad gave the seed money to Gary Bauer to start the Family Research Council. They were very close to James Dobson and his Focus on the Family "prayer warrior" network. Erik Prince was in the first team of interns that Gary Bauer took on in Washington at the Family Research Council, and Erik Prince's sister Betsy married Dick DeVos, heir to the Amway corporate fortune, big supporter of conservative causes and owner of the Orlando Magic basketball team. Together, these two families merged in the kind of marriage that was commonplace in the monarchies of old Europe. And together they formed this formidable behind-the-scenes power player in radical right-wing politics in this country. As a young man Erik Prince interns in George H.W. Bush's White House but complains it's not conservative enough for him. So he backs Pat Buchanan in his insurgency campaign in 1992. These are the people that peppered the landscape of young Erik Prince's life. He also interned for Dana Rohrabacher, a former speechwriter for Ronald Reagan, now a congressman from California. It's interesting that Rohrabacher

issued a defense of Erik Prince after his congressional testimony and said
that Prince is going to go down in history as a hero, just like Oliver North.

*You write, "What is particularly scary about Blackwater's role in a war that
President Bush labeled a 'crusade' is that the company's leading executives are
dedicated to a Christian-supremacist agenda."*

I believe that Erik Prince is an ideological foot soldier. And I do believe that
he's a Christian supremacist. I think it's very easy to explain that. Look, this
is the guy who gave half a million dollars to Chuck Colson, the first person to
go to jail for Watergate, who has now become a very prominent evangelical
figure and an advisor to President Bush. And one of the leading executives
of Blackwater, Joseph Schmitz, is an active member of the Military Order of
Malta, a Christian militia dating back to the Crusades. I believe that these
men do have an agenda that very closely reflects a Crusader mentality.

*You write about the revolving door. Cofer Black, head of counterintelligence
at the CIA, leaves the government, goes to work as the number two man at
Blackwater. Guys leave the Pentagon and go to work for him.*

It's not a revolving door. It's a bridge. They go back and forth. Blackwater
has emerged almost as an armed wing of the administration in Iraq. It
doesn't work for the Pentagon; it works for the State Department. If I were
Ambassador Ryan Crocker, I wouldn't want to come within ten countries
of the Blackwater bodyguards. When your bodyguards become more of a
target than you, maybe it's time to get a different security detail.

And maybe you're one of the families at that Nisour Square shooting where seventeen people were killed and over twenty-five others were
wounded. Blackwater walks around bragging about how they haven't lost a
single principal; all of their "nouns" have been kept alive, as they call it. But
at what price to the U.S. soldiers in Iraq? I've heard from so many soldiers,
veterans, who tell me, "We're in a village somewhere. And things are going
fine with the Iraqis. And we've reached the point where they're not attacking us anymore. And we feel like there's some goodwill that's been generated." This is an exact story that a translator attached to the Special Forces
unit told me in an email recently. "Then the PSD guys, the personal security
detail guys, come whizzing through with their VIP and they shoot up the
town. And the Iraqis in town don't understand that there's a difference between the private forces and the military. And then they conduct revenge

attacks against us." So the misconduct of these forces is having a blowback effect on the active-duty military.

Is it also true that some of our soldiers in Iraq are "going Blackwater"?

That's the slang. Even if you're going to work for Triple Canopy or DynCorp, the slang of the day is "going Blackwater," which means that you're jumping from active-duty military to the private sector. You are going to be in the same war zone, but you're going to make a lot more money. The troops I talked to also say that these guys are sort of the rock stars of the war zone. They've got better equipment than us, they have better body armor. You talk to these kids and some of them say, I was in Ramadi at the worst time in 2004, and I never stepped foot in an armored vehicle. We're bolting steel plates and putting down sandbags on the ground to protect against IEDs. And then the Blackwater guys whiz by with their six-figure salaries and their wraparound sunglasses. The message is, my country is sending me over here for $40,000 a year, my mom's back home trying to raise money to buy me some real body armor, and then I see these guys whiz by with their six-figure salary wearing the corporate logo instead of the American flag? Or the other reaction is, I want to be like that. I don't want to be over here working for the Third Infantry Division. I want to go and work for Blackwater or Triple Canopy.

Is there a domestic threat implicit in this?

Bill, I was in New Orleans in the aftermath of Hurricane Katrina, and I think I saw a real window into the possible future. I was standing on a street corner in the French Quarter on Bourbon Street and I was talking to two New York City police officers who had come down to help. This is just a couple of days after the hurricane hit. And this car speeds up next to us, a compact, no license plates on it. Three massive guys get out of it. They have M4 assault rifles, bulletproof vests, khakis, wraparound sunglasses, baseball caps. And they say to the cops, "Where are the rest of the Blackwater guys?" I didn't even hear the answer. I couldn't believe what I was hearing. They get back in their vehicle and they speed off. I said to this cop, "Blackwater? You mean the guys in Iraq and Afghanistan?" They said, "Oh, yeah. They're all over the place down here." And I said, "I'd like to talk to them. Where are they?" And they said, "You can go either way on the street." So I walked a little bit deeper into the French Quarter. Sure enough, I encountered some

Blackwater guys. And when I talked to them, they said that they were down there to confront criminals and stop looters.

Who called them in?

This is an interesting story. Erik Prince sent them in there with no contract initially. About 180 Blackwater guys were sent to the Gulf. They got there before FEMA, the Federal Emergency Management Agency, before there was any kind of a serious operation in the city at all.

Within a week, Blackwater was given a contract from the Department of Homeland Security's Federal Protective Service to engage in security operations inside of New Orleans. They were pulling in $240,000 a day. Some of these guys had just been in Iraq two weeks earlier guarding the U.S. ambassador. Now they're in New Orleans. They told me they were getting paid $350 a day, plus a per diem.

When I got a copy of Blackwater's contract with the Department of Homeland Security, it turns out that Blackwater billed U.S. taxpayers $950 per man per day in the hurricane zone. Now, the math on this stuff is always complicated, and Erik Prince and his men are very good at drawing up charts and just saying there's this detail and that detail. The Department of Homeland Security then did an internal review and determined that it was the best value to the taxpayer at a time when the poor residents of New Orleans were being chastised for how they used their $2,000 debit cards that often didn't work. But even scarier than seeing the Blackwater operatives on the streets of New Orleans were the two Israeli commandos who had been brought in by a wealthy businessman in New Orleans, and set up an armed checkpoint outside of his gated community. They were from a company called Instinctive Shooting International, ISI. I talked to them. They tapped on their automatic weapons and said, "Over in our country, when the Palestinians see this, they're not so afraid because they're used to it. But you people, you see it, and you're very afraid." They were almost proud of the fact that I was rather in awe seeing Israeli commandos patrolling a U.S. street, operating an armed checkpoint.

Once upon a time, companies and others hired Pinkerton guards. But never on this scale, right?

It was like Baghdad on the Bayou down there in New Orleans. The poor drowned, they were left without food, called looters when they took perishable goods out of a store when they were in dire need. The rich bring in mercenaries to guard their properties or their businesses or their hotel chains. I think it's a window into what happens in a national emergency. In this country, the poor are left to suffer, and the rich bring in their mercenaries.

The Wall Street Journal reports that Erik Prince is laying plans for an expansion that would put his gunmen in hot spots around the world doing far more than guard duty.

They certainly have intimated that they would be willing to go into Darfur, for one. Blackwater executives said, you send us in, and it'll be "Janjaweed-be-gone!" Janjaweed are Islamic forces in the Sudan. They've been pushing this for a while. This is a gateway into a very lucrative feeding trough, known as the peacekeeping budget.

But suppose they could go in there as mercenaries and bring an end to that conflict. Get food in for those refugees in a way that the United States government can't do.

What does that say, though, about the structure of the world? What does it say about nation-states and international institutions? The last thing needed in Darfur is more private guns. Who's to say that's what would happen if Blackwater gets sent into Darfur in the first place? Who's going to be monitoring them and overseeing them?

But Erik Prince has been saying, "We want more accountability. We welcome it."

This is something that I find fascinating. When Blackwater was sued for wrongful death after the four guys were killed in Fallujah in March of '04 and then the Afghanistan plane crash,* the legal argument that Blackwater put forward was an interesting one: "We can't be sued." They said they should enjoy the same immunity from civilian litigation that's enjoyed by the U.S. military.

---

*On November 27, 2004, a small aircraft designated "Blackwater 61" crashed into a mountain in Afghanistan, killing three U.S. Army personnel and the three Blackwater crew members. Investigators cited the cause as pilot error and inexperience. The widows of the military men sued Blackwater for wrongful death and, in 2010, reached an undisclosed, out-of-court settlement.

At the same time, their lobbyists and spokespeople are waxing poetic in the media about how it would be inappropriate to apply the Uniform Code of Military Justice, the court-martial system, to Blackwater because they're civilians. So when it's convenient, we're part of the U.S. total force, part of the war machine, and should be treated like the military. And when it's not convenient, oh, we can't be subjected to military law, because we're actually civilians.

One of the really disturbing stories out of Iraq in the last year involving Blackwater was that last Christmas Eve inside of the heavily fortified Green Zone, a drunken, off-duty Blackwater contractor allegedly shot and killed a bodyguard for the Iraqi vice president, Adel Abdul-Mahdi. This individual was whisked out of Iraq within thirty-six hours. He actually returned to the region working in Kuwait for another contractor with the Pentagon. The killing happened on December 24, 2006. February of 2007, he's back in the Middle East working for another U.S. military contractor. He hasn't been charged with any crime whatsoever. We understand now that the Justice Department is investigating. The Iraqis clearly labeled it a murder, and it created a major rift between Baghdad and Washington. Imagine if an Iraqi bodyguard shot and killed a bodyguard for Dick Cheney and then the Iraqis just whisked him out of the United States. I mean, what would happen? What message does this send?* What does it say that in four years of occupation, involving hundreds of thousands of contractors, not a single one of them has been prosecuted? Either we have tens of thousands of mercenaries in Iraq who are actually Boy Scouts, or something is fundamentally rotten with that system.†

What about these suits that were filed by some of the survivors of the four contractors who were killed in Fallujah?

---

*In October 2010, the Justice Department announced that after a four-year investigation it lacked sufficient evidence to file homicide charges against the Blackwater employee.

† Since our conversation, according to *The New York Times*, October 21, 2010: "Justice officials noted that the government had had a number of successful prosecutions against contractors in Iraq and Afghanistan, including several for sexual assaults and other violent crimes. More than 120 companies have been charged by the Justice Department for contract fraud and related crimes in Iraq, Afghanistan and Kuwait, officials said."

I've gotten to know those four families very well over these years of work-ing on this story. They're military families, very patriotic. Some of them are pretty conservative Republicans. And these men were all veterans of the U.S. military. Scott Helvenston was one of the youngest people ever to complete the Navy BUDS training program, the Basic Underwater Demolition/ SEAL program. He was one of the guys killed there. These guys were killed on March 31, 2004. The families didn't presume any malice on the part of Blackwater; they thought it was a patriotic American company and that their loved ones were continuing their military service through the private sector in Iraq. When they were killed, the families wanted answers as to what happened, and they began calling Blackwater. Some of the families asked to see a copy of the company's investigation of that incident. Donna Zovko, the mother of Jerry Zovko—they're Croatian immigrants—sat down with Blackwater executives at their compound in North Carolina.

When she asked to get that document and look at it, she claims that a Blackwater representative stood up at the table and told her it's a classified document and you'll have to sue us if you want to see it. Donna Zovko starts to become friends with Katy Helvenston, whose son was also killed in Fallujah. The two of them begin comparing notes. And they're scouring media reports. Then they start to look at the photos. And they realize their sons weren't really in armored vehicles there. They start to put together the pieces. And what emerged was a lawsuit.

In January 2005, the families of those four men—Wesley Batalona, Michael Teague, Jerry Zovko, and Scott Helvenston—filed a groundbreak-ing wrongful-death lawsuit against Blackwater, charging that the com-pany had sent those men into what was arguably the most dangerous city in the world at the time in unarmored vehicles, without heavy weaponry, and without the opportunity to do a twenty-four-hour risk assessment, all of which they said were in the contract governing their mission that day. Blackwater fought back ferociously, and the case is caught up in legal limbo right now. But it's being watched very closely by all of the other war compa-nies, because it's like the tobacco litigation of the '90s. If that one domino goes down, it starts a chain reaction.

Doesn't Erik Prince, as a businessman, have to worry about finding new mar-kets? The State Department has said that when his contract outside the Green Zone in Iraq expires next May, Blackwater's not likely to be a contestant for a new contract. There seems to be a tacit understanding between Blackwater and the government that, given the shootings in September and all the controversy, they'd quietly slip away.

You know what, though? In the midst of all of this chaos and crisis of image for Blackwater, the company continues to win very lucrative government contracts. I don't even think the business in Iraq represents the most lucrative aspects of the company's business. It's just the highest-profile. There's an affiliate company called Greystone that has been registered offshore in Barbados. It's being portrayed as sort of a traditional mercenary outfit, and is pushing services to Fortune 500 companies. Look at the guest list for the kickoff ceremony for Greystone: the governments of Croatia and Uzbekistan, the International Monetary Fund, corporations. Government business for Blackwater is tremendously important. They do an enormous volume of business in the training of law enforcement and of the military. They have been involved with training foreign forces as well. Jordanian attack helicopter crews, for example. They've been deployed in Azerbaijan. But the corporate business is going to be a major part of Blackwater's future.

What does this foreshadow for the future?

It's really scary. I see this as a real subversion of democratic processes in this country and a subversion of the sovereignty of nations around the world.

Isn't it also a way to keep protest at home against the war in Iraq and other wars from rising to the level of—

Oh, absolutely. It masks the human toll of the war in terms of American lives. Because the contractor deaths are not counted in the official tolls, nor are their injuries, and it also masks the true extent of the occupation when over half of your occupation force comes from the private sector. President Bush almost never talks about it. He doesn't have to own it in front of the American people. He's having enough trouble owning the 170,000 troops that are over there right now. This is a real revolution in terms of U.S. politics. They're taking billions of dollars in public money, and they're privatizing it.

As you know, the Pentagon can't make campaign contributions. The State Department can't give campaign contributions. Blackwater's executives can give contributions. These companies are taking billions of dollars from the government, and the money is making its way back into the campaign coffers of the very politicians that make the meteoric ascent of these companies possible. This is tearing away at the fabric of American democracy. ∼

Jeremy Scahill returned to the Journal *almost five months after Barack Obama was sworn in as president. Leaks inside Washington suggested the new administration would increase the number of private contractors in both Iraq, where Obama had pledged to draw down combat troops, and Afghanistan, where he intended to escalate the war.*

Either way, mercenaries working for American companies abroad had become essential personnel on two fronts, confirming once again that the only winners in war are the people made rich by it. Xe, the company formerly known as Blackwater, continues. Erik Prince has moved to Abu Dhabi.

—◦◦◦—

Since we last talked there's been a spike in private contractors in both Iraq and Afghanistan.

What we're seeing under President Barack Obama is old wine in a new bottle. He is sending one message to the world, but the reality on the ground, particularly when it comes to private military contractors, is that the Bush policies are still in place. Right now there are 250,000 contractors fighting the wars in Iraq and Afghanistan. That's about 50 percent of the total U.S. fighting force, which is very similar to what it was under Bush. Having said that, when Barack Obama was in the Senate he was one of the only people willing to take up this issue. And he put forward what became the leading legislation on the part of the Democrats to reform the contracting industry. I give him credit for doing that, because he saw this as an important issue before a lot of other political figures did. He spoke up at a time when a lot of people were deafeningly silent on this issue. As president, he has tried to implement greater accountability structures. We now know, in a much clearer way than we did under Bush, how many contractors are on the battlefield. He's attempted to implement some form of rules governing contractors, including greater accountability when they do commit crimes. All of these things are a step in the right direction. But, ultimately, these companies are still carrying out inherently governmental functions, and that includes carrying a weapon on battlefields.

Obama inherited a quagmire from the Bush administration. What's he to do?

There's no question that Obama inherited an absolute mess, but the reality is that he is escalating the war in Afghanistan and maintaining the occupation of Iraq. If Obama was serious about fully ending the occupation of Iraq, he wouldn't allow the United States to build a colonial fortress that they're passing off as an embassy in Baghdad. Bill, this place is the size of eighty football fields. Who do you think will run the security operation for this eighty-football-field-sized embassy? Mercenary contractors.

You're suggesting that we will be leaving a large mercenary force there.

Absolutely. In fact, you're going to have a sizable presence of U.S. forces in the region. We've seen reports from Jim Miklaszewski, NBC News's Pentagon correspondent, quoting military sources saying that they expect to be in Iraq fifteen to twenty years in sizable numbers. Afghanistan is going to become Obama's war. If the United States, as President Obama says, doesn't want a permanent presence in Afghanistan, why allocate a billion dollars to build a fortress-like embassy, similar to the one in Baghdad, in Islamabad, Pakistan, and another complex in Peshawar? Obviously there will be an increase in mercenary forces, expanding the U.S. military presence there.

Walter Pincus, an investigative reporter at The Washington Post *for thirty or more years now, also reports that these contracts indicate how long the United States intends to remain in Afghanistan. He pointed, for example, to a contract given by the Corps of Engineers to a firm in Dubai to expand the U.S. prison at Bagram in Afghanistan.*

Right. Look, even as President Obama regularly says, "We're going to have Guantánamo closed by early next year," we see an expansion at Bagram. They're spending $50 million on it. You have hundreds of people held without charges. You have people being denied access to the Red Cross in violation of international law. And you have an ongoing position by the Obama administration, formed under Bush, that these prisoners don't have the right to habeas corpus. There are very disturbing signals being sent with Afghanistan as a microcosm. Not to mention these regular attacks that we're seeing inside of Pakistan that have killed hundreds of civilians with robotic drones since 2006.

Afghanistan underscores the fact that the military is actually stretched very thin. Do you think the American people have any idea how their tax dollars are being used in Afghanistan?

No. No idea whatsoever. We've spent $190 billion on the war in Afghanistan, and some estimates say that within a few short years, it could end up at half a trillion dollars. I think most Americans are not aware that many of their dollars being spent in Iraq and Afghanistan are going to for-profit corporations there. These are companies that are simultaneously working for profit and for the U.S. government. That is the intricate linking of corporate profits to an escalation of war that President Eisenhower warned against in his farewell address.

The rise of "the military-industrial complex." You wrote that the Defense Department paid the former Halliburton subsidiary KBR more than $80 million in bonuses for contracts to install what proved to be very defective electrical wiring in Iraq. Senator Byron Dorgan called that wiring shoddy and unprofessional. Why did the Pentagon pay for it when it was so inferior?

This is perhaps one of the greatest corporate scandals of the past decade, the fact that Halliburton, which was once headed by former vice president Dick Cheney, was essentially given keys to U.S. foreign policy and allowed to do things that proved dangerous for U.S. troops. This was a politically connected company that won its contracts because of its political connections.

The army hired a master electrician, according to congressional testimony, to review electrical work in Iraq. He told Congress that KBR's work in Iraq was "some of the most hazardous, worst-quality work" he'd ever inspected. And that his own investigation found improper wiring in every building that KBR had wired there.

And we're talking about a huge number of buildings. This should be an utter scandal that should outrage every single person in this country. And yet you find little mention of this in the corporate media.

Do you get discouraged writing about corruption that never gets cured?

I don't believe that it necessarily doesn't get cured. I'm very heartened by the fact that we have a very vibrant new independent media landscape developing right now. I once put in the tagline of an article that I wrote early on in the Obama administration that I pledge to be the same journalist under Barack Obama that I was under President Bush. It's time to take off the Obama T-shirts. This is a man who's now in charge of the most powerful country on earth. The media in this country has an obligation to treat him the way we treated Bush in terms of being critical of him. I feel like many Democrats have had their spines surgically removed these days, as have a lot of journalists. The fact is that when you are killing civilians, even unintentionally with these robotic drones, in what is perceived to be an indiscriminate way, you're going to give rise to more people who want to attack the United States.

The argument is that these drones are enabling the United States military to kill the bad guys without exposing Americans to danger. There's truth in that, right?

These drones sanitize war. It means that we increase the number of people who don't realize war is hell on the ground. And it means that wars are going to be easier in the future because it's not as tough of a sell.

You will find agreement among people who say war is hell, but you'll also find a lot of people in this country, a lot of Democrats and Republicans, who say Jeremy Scahill is wrong. That we need to be doing what we're doing in Afghanistan because if we don't, there'll be another attack like 9/11 on this country.

I think that what we're doing in Afghanistan increases the likelihood that there's going to be another attack, because we're killing innocent civilians regularly. When the United States goes in and bombs Farah Province in Afghanistan and kills civilians, it has a ricochet impact. The relatives of those people are going to say maybe they did trust the United States, maybe they viewed the United States as a beacon of freedom in the world, but you just took that guy's daughter, you just killed that guy's wife. That's one more person who is going to line up and say, "We're going to fight the United States." We are indiscriminately killing civilians, according to the UN Human Rights Council. That should be a collective shame that we feel in this society. ∽

SARA LAWRENCE-LIGHTFOOT

The sociologist and educator Sara Lawrence-Lightfoot has dubbed that quarter century of life between the ages of fifty and seventy-five "the third chapter." There are 76 million Americans in that category, with more arriving all the time: reportedly, another baby boomer turns fifty every 7.6 seconds. For her book The Third Chapter, *Lawrence-Lightfoot traveled the country gathering the stories of men and women who have taken new paths in the penultimate chapter of their lives and discovered that it can be a real page-turner—an exhilarating time of passion, risk, and adventure.*

Her own life has been a continuing course in adult education. I first interviewed her for my series World of Ideas *when she was a young professor at Harvard. During her thirty-nine years on the faculty there she has earned an international reputation as a teacher, researcher, and writer, winning the prestigious MacArthur Fellowship (popularly known as the "MacArthur genius award") and Harvard's George Ledlie Prize for research that makes the "most valuable contribution to science, or . . . the benefit of mankind." Among her several other books are* I've Known Rivers, *which explores creativity and wisdom through the lens of "human archaeology";* The Essential Conversation: What Parents and Teachers Can Learn from Each Other; *and my favorite,* Balm in Gilead, *about her mother, the pioneering child psychiatrist Dr. Margaret Lawrence.*

When Sara Lawrence-Lightfoot retires she will become the first African American woman in Harvard's history to have an endowed professorship named for her.

—*Bill Moyers*

⁓◦⁓

Here you are now, writing about aging. What are you trying to tell us?

Several years ago at almost every cocktail party, dinner party, professional conference, and meeting, someone would lean into me for what I began to call confessional moments. Something they were truly excited about, passionate about—a new adventure for them. Their voice held both extraordinary passion and excitement, but at the same time some reticence. It was as if they weren't sure we should take too seriously what they were talking about. Yet it couldn't be denied—they felt deeply about it. I began to wonder what these moments were about. The closer I listened, the more I realized they were talking about new learning in their lives, new adventures they were taking, new risks. And here's the thing—their commentary about these moments was so much more excited than talking about their work, or even, at that particular moment, talking about their family. I wanted to know the text and the subtext of these confessional moments. I decided to investigate, and I realized they were on a search for meaning, for purposefulness, in the penultimate chapter of their lives. Something resonated with me about this, and I began to research what I call "the third chapter"—the years between fifty and seventy-five.

And what did you find?

That we're ready for something new; that all of us, to some degree, experience burnout. Burnout is not about working too hard, or working too diligently, or being overcommitted. Burnout is about boredom. In some ways it's about moving beyond the boredom to compose, to invent and reinvent the path that we're on.

Yet you say that while they would talk excitedly and with passion about this vision, this confessional moment, there was a note of fear in their voices.

Right. I think two things are happening there. One is that we are still a youth-obsessed culture, and we tend to think we should be in retreat at this stage of life. But these stories that I was hearing were about moving out, taking an adventure, going against the cultural norms embedded in most of our lives. The other thing is that it's hard to leave these roles that have given us status, responsibility, maybe also influence and power. Those roles have become comfortable. To go on this new journey feels terrifying at first.

One of the interesting revelations in your book is your emphasis on how the pendulum has swung back and forth toward aging. There was a time, in the early days, when Americans powdered their wigs in order to look older. Then came a time when aging was considered an incurable disease, to be treated in old folks' homes. But now you describe this growing old—aging—as a time of great excitement and adventure and passion. What's happened to bring about this change in our perception of the elderly?

We're living longer. That's one big piece. The arc of our lives has changed enormously. We're not dying at fifty. We are, if we're lucky, living to eighty, eighty-five, ninety. So this period that I'm talking about, between fifty and seventy-five, is a penultimate period. It offers us the opportunity and the challenge of doing something meaningful. This is perhaps the transformative time of our lives, the most exciting, in terms of new learning. Limitless in its opportunities.

A lot of people don't experience it this way because the cultural shifts and the institutional shifts haven't yet happened to encourage them, meaning that most people really do see this time, as I said earlier, as a time of retrenchment. They don't enjoy the beauty, the wisdom, the experience that come with aging. We continue to look at younger people as those who have the energy and drive and new ideas, right? Now, I must say that Erik Erikson, my favorite developmental psychologist from way back in the early 1950s, talked about the stages of life across time. He talked about this third chapter as the penultimate of eight stages, the next to the last. And he said, even back then, that each one of these stages is characterized by a crisis, a crisis of whether we're going to move forward, progress, or whether we're going to move back, regress. This is always the tension at each of our developmental stages, between progression and regression. And in our third chapter the crisis is between what he calls "generativity" and "stagnation." Sounds very dramatic, right? Generativity has to do with using your energies to serve, teach, mentor, express yourself through art, to innovate, give something to society, and to leave a legacy. Stagnation, on the other hand, means stasis, redundancy, caution. I'm going to stay right here and make my mark in an individual pursuit.

There's something of a cultural and political factor in this. It was in 1935, during Franklin Roosevelt's New Deal, that the Social Security Act was passed, and people were told they have a "right to retire."

And a lot of people have experienced quitting work as a kind of death. But the forty people whose lives I trace in the book did not decide to retire but to go on doing meaningful work, figuring out ways to be productive, creative, innovative, and purposeful.

You acknowledge that these forty people do not represent the majority of people in this country. They're affluent. They have the means to make choices, to go this way and not that way. But there are six, seven, eight million people over fifty-five in this country who are living in poverty. They don't have choices.

Right. Well, we think they don't have choices. I do talk about perceived abundance, how we experience the choices in our lives. A factory worker who's been laid off from his job in Madison, Wisconsin, tells me that he and his wife went to the flea market every single Saturday with their stuff, trying to trade it or sell it, so that they could put food on their table and continue to feed their family. One Saturday, he saw these strange and interesting sculptures and pieces of art made by artists who were bringing their creations to the flea market. And he said, "You know what? I could do that. I'm a welder. I'm good with metal. I can do that." And he went home and began playing around with the metal in his house. It so happens that he has loved dinosaurs ever since he saw *Jurassic Park*. And he begins to create these animals, these sculptures. He takes them back to the flea market. People become interested. He sells them for almost nothing. It catches on. And by the time he's talking to me, he's telling me that he's gotten his first gig with an art gallery. So his innovation, his resourcefulness, and ultimately his pride in his own creativity come through. This is a factory worker.

You say there's a difference between this new learning we have to do when we enter the third chapter and the old, narrow cognitive learning of the classroom. What's the difference?

Almost everyone that I talked to for this book, even if they had been very successful students in school, even if they had very successful careers by traditional standards, talked about the fact that the learning that goes on in the third chapter is often contrary, a contradiction to the ways in which they were taught and excelled in school. School taught us to move quickly with speed, to be singular in our ambitions, to be competitive, not waste time, not show failure or weakness. And in the third chapter, they talk about risk-taking and collaboration as cultural aspects of learning. We need to fail in order to discover the best way that we can learn. As one person said to me, "I've had to unlearn old school habits."

To make a fool out of ourselves, in your words.

Absolutely. To be willing to fail and make a fool out of ourselves, at least in the short run. And, of course, the ingredient that's so important, which is humor, being able to laugh at ourselves. Lighten up. Not worry about our facade and our persona, but really just get into the process.

One of these people tells you that she's learned that patience is a major gift of life. That it's so important to do things slowly. She says she had forgotten this over the course of her life.

That's right. She's a filmmaker. And she talked about the fact that it was always rush, rush, rush. And her parents had insisted on "quickly, quickly, quickly." Always being the best by shooting your hand up first, by making it to the front of the class.

And what she realized in her third chapter was how glorious it was to slow down. How glorious it was to be able to be reflective, to be meditative. My favorite thing about this period is restraint. How wonderful it is—this is my own revelation—how wonderful it is to know when not to talk, when not to move forward. When it's best to listen and sit back. When it's best to just witness and observe. That slowness of pace offers us the opportunity to see things newly, to discover things that we hadn't seen before, to take the small, incremental steps rather than expect the large leaps forward.

You write that you looked into the eyes of these people and saw your own reflec-

tion, with confessional moments of your own. Are you having to unlearn some things that have made you the success you are?

As I say, these boundaries are arbitrary. As a scholar, writer, and researcher, each one of the books I write is really a new quest for me. I'm able to engage in new learning. And that's a huge, huge luxury, to follow your curiosities without many constraints. There are careers that sustain your curiosity throughout. But there are ways in which my approach has shifted within the context of my institution. I can feel it at a faculty meeting.

I used to reject the idea that I needed to mentor other people. It seemed to make me feel old to establish myself as a mentor and guide. Now I embrace this notion. I know it's important that I let myself be a mentor to my younger colleagues, that I work with and support them. That I tell them stories about my own life and my own career. And here's something else I've discovered in terms of restraint—if I'm in a senior faculty meeting now, I speak once. I listen.

How uncharacteristic!

Well, I've learned that timing is important. When I speak is important. But this way of engaging in a conversation means more listening. It also offers some historical perspective, and that's important. I'm likely to say what I think. Really be very honest, very clear. I'm much less cautious. Those two things come together, a kind of courage to speak your mind and speak your heart and to say where your ideas come from, even if they don't come from cognition. And the idea of waiting and choosing your moment.

Is it true that you went canvassing, knocking on doors last fall in the presidential campaign, with a twenty-four-year-old?

Yes. I did. One of the things I talk about in this book is the need to engage in more cross-generational encounters, discourse, conversation, and movements.

But that's so hard to do, because we are separated into our different realities.

I think that's absolutely true. But one example that I found so exciting, of working with young people, and young people working with old people in a common project, was this Obama campaign. In New Hampshire, three or four times, I went with a young kid from Dartmouth with whom I was paired, and I kept on wishing that I was a fly on the wall, or an ethnographer, watching us navigate our relationship and our encounters.

How so?

Because this was a kid who had voluminous knowledge about politics and facts, who was incredibly energetic, who had great ideas. He was completely urgent and impatient and a terrible listener. And also someone who had stereotyped all of New Hampshire. He thought they were backwoods, rural, country people. Republicans. Surely they hadn't thought deeply about these matters! And his job was to feed them the information, right? And not expect them to change. My approach was to begin by listening to them, not assuming that I knew who they were just because I knew where they lived. Not beginning with a stereotype, but expecting that they had the capacity to think deeply as well. And so negotiating our relationship means I had to help him wait. Help him listen. On the other hand, I needed to experience his energy, his drive, and his optimism.

Clearly, he had more energy than you.

He had more energy. But his impatience often depleted his energy. Because he was so impatient to get the message across.

You quote throughout your book the poet Nikki Giovanni. She has a poem in which she says, "There are sounds which shatter the staleness of lives, transporting the shadows into the dreams." Most people I know, young or old, want to shatter the staleness. What have you learned about how to do that?

One of the things I heard in people's stories touched on the dynamic of loss and liberation. Most people had to go back to childhood stories in order to begin to explain the ways in which they were able to move forward into new learning in the third chapter of life. In their early youth they might have felt unsupported, undernourished, maybe even neglected and abused. So they had to return to that place of hurt, to try to understand it. Not to blame anyone but to try to understand it. Whether that's a metaphoric return, or whether that's literally going back to Ohio and walking up the steps of their father's house and knocking on the door and talking to him honestly about what they had experienced as a small child. That actually happened. It's part of moving beyond those early negative experiences, if you had them. At least I experienced it with these forty people as a very common theme. Some of them discovered those early hurts in the process of my interviewing. The story they had told many, many times before, which was the positive, affirmative, optimistic story, had a dark underbelly they had ignored. Discovering that underbelly revealed their reasons for now moving forward.

What do they tell you had enabled them to go forward?

Let me just give you an example. There's a public health doctor, sixty-seven years old, from a middle-class African American family. He's someone who has always worked very, very hard, most of the time in West Africa, to eliminate malaria. He takes his work very seriously, and he has begun to take voice lessons, which he loves. I asked him, "Why voice lessons?" He begins to tell the story of sitting in his mother's arms, at age six, every Sunday, listening to the Metropolitan Opera. And he loves this moment, because he's sitting in his mother's arms, and because there's nothing more glorious or radiant than the resonant voices of these opera singers. And he says to his mother one day, "Mom, that's what I want to be. I want to be an opera singer." She doesn't respond verbally. But what he remembers, in conversation with me, is the sort of dismissive look that she gave him. And he says with tears in his eyes, now talking to me, that she seemed to be telling him opera singers were sissies, right? He retreats immediately. He never raises that again. He goes on to become a wonderful public health doctor, giving to the world. And at age sixty-five, he takes the big leap of faith and begins to take voice lessons, realizing that this is resonant from this early denial. He experiences what he calls "a liberation I've never felt." And the real kicker in this story is that he discovers in conversation with me that this learning to use his diaphragm, learning to make the sound come up through his body channel, not only feels liberating in that sense, but discovering his voice, his new voice, at sixty-seven, has helped him become a better doctor.

And in contrast, there's a woman in your book named Pamela, a psychologist and an activist, who talks very poignantly about wanting, in this stage of her life, to do "the radical thing," to make a difference. And she's disillusioned to find that the solutions seem out of reach. That it's harder for her to rally people to a collective sense of responsibility than she had thought it would be. That neither government nor private institutions are designed to prepare to help her make a difference.

This is someone who is progressive, who's been an activist all of her life. She really sought to make a difference. And what she discovers, at sixty, is that she's worried about death. Many of the people in her family have died early. She sees the finiteness of her life. And she wants to take on something big. She wants government and hospitals and the whole medical and psychological establishment to respond to the veterans coming back from Iraq and Afghanistan. To recognize that they're not crazy, that they've been through a trauma of huge, profound significance. And she can't get this message across. She feels as if the institutions, the government, the hospitals, the medical establishment, are not recognizing their trauma. And she feels enormously frustrated.

Is she going to spend the third chapter sullen and resigned?

No. She's keeping on pushing, but our conversations gave her an opportunity to really weep at the fact that she really is, as she put it, "at my most powerful now. I have the most to give. I'm wiser. My voice is strong. My influence should be great, and I feel it diminished."

You hear a lot when you listen, and your listening empowers the people talking to you. Does it strike you that there are not enough people who listen?

Oh, absolutely. Absolutely. There are two things that came out of this book. One is curiosity. And that's often dampened or muted in school, as I said earlier—you know, when somehow children stop asking the primary questions: "So, where did he go? Then what happened? Why do you feel that way?" The other important thing is listening. The value of young people listening to old people, old people listening to young people, having a real discourse with respect and with empathy.

That twenty-four-year-old in New Hampshire. What does he want to do with his life and what did he learn from you about what he could do?

I hope he learned from me that he will have many chances to remake himself. There will be many chapters and many challenges. I think the other thing that we talked a lot about is the importance of welcoming those moments when we fail as the time to pick ourselves up and move on. Welcome those moments—I hope he learned that from me.

The people in your book don't talk much about death. Why is that? Was that deliberate on your part?

No. it wasn't. I think Pamela is one of the few people in the book who talk about death. The others were too busy living.

But surely they have to think in the back of their mind, they can see the grains of sand going down the hourglass.

There is an expression of such urgency in their work, in their new work, and in their new learning—this notion of limited time is very much in the mix. They experience the paradox of emerging patience during this period of their lives and the sense of time moving on—of urgency.

Are you feeling that sense of urgency? You're only sixty-four. To me, that's just adolescence.

Well, I certainly am feeling the curiosity. I'm feeling the urgency. I'm feeling the patience. I'm feeling the courage to ask questions that may not have been asked before, to say what it is I need to say. It isn't that I think I'm invincible at all, but these qualities, I think, have deepened during this period of my life. They help me move forward in my own third chapter.

People talk openly about their own fears. What are you afraid of, at this stage?

Sometimes I'm afraid of loneliness. Even though I'm surrounded by a glorious family and friends and have lots of love.

So why fear loneliness?

What I experience when I look at people in their fourth chapters is the possibility of isolation. There's the certainty that as you grow older, your friends will disappear, they will die. And I look at my mother, who's ninety-four, who is deeply curious about the world around her. Who's using this stage and chapter of her life to give forward. Her mind is vital and alive. She's a fabulous listener—

Hold it right there a second—what do you mean, she's giving forward?

Giving forward. I talk about it in the book as a way of serving and contributing to society. Giving back seems to be something of an anachronism. It's like looking backwards. This is being in the present and looking toward the future, trying to figure out a way of giving and serving that fits the contemporary cultural context.

But is she lonely?

She's very much in the world and engaged in the world. But in the meantime, at ninety-four, most of her friends have died. And I see that as an inevitable and profound loneliness. And so that's one of the things that I worry about, for all of us.

You finished this manuscript shortly before the great economic collapse.

Yes.

How do you think the new reality would change the answers people gave you? We talked about how they have the means to afford to make this change, make this turn into the third chapter. How do you think the great collapse would change their answers?

Well, I don't know that it would change them very much. All of us, I think, have to innovate when resources are diminished. The capacity to innovate is very much what these people are talking about. Innovation, creativity in a time when we have less. We are forced therefore to do more with less, to figure out ways of combining our resources, of collaborating, of innovating. I remember a time in my life when I was at my lowest, and my mother said, "Sweetheart, out of this suffering will come creativity." And she was right. I don't mean to be idealizing this at all, but I think there are ways—even at a place like Harvard, which has lost 30 percent of its endowment—there are ways in which this reduction in our resources forces us to think more dynamically, more creatively, about how we can shape a new legacy in this time of sacrifice.

You make me think particularly about the baby boomers. Not all the people in your book are boomers, but some are. The baby boomers grew up in a period of prosperity, of relative abundance. They saw themselves as powerful actors who wanted to shape the culture and paradigm of their era. And they brought considerable resources and wealth to the challenge. Now the rug has been pulled out from under them. I wonder how they are reacting to the new reality.

Well, it's true. I think it's part of what we did as baby boomers. In our younger years we were audacious, we were entitled, we felt empowered. We stopped the Vietnam War, right? We felt that we grew the women's movement. We were engaged in civil rights activities. We made a difference. And it seems to me that even with the rug pulled out from under us, we still have this feeling about ourselves. We still believe that we can make a difference. We still believe that we can come up with good ideas that might help solve today's toughest problems. But we are not the owners of this intellectual capital or this cultural capital. And that's why I talk about bringing people together, crossing the generations to solve the country's and the world's problems. ∿

JOHN LITHGOW

One of the memorable scenes in American theater occurs in Arthur Miller's
All My Sons *when Joe Keller's son Chris discovers that the father he adores is
guilty of a dreadful crime that cost the lives of twenty-one young pilots during
World War II. A hardworking manufacturer, family man, and all-around
"nice guy," Joe Keller had shipped defective parts to the military and engaged
in a long cover-up of his malfeasance. He even let his partner take the rap and
go to jail while keeping the crime a secret.*

*In a recent Broadway revival of the drama, as the moment of revelation ar-
rived and the scales fell from the son's eyes, the emotional reckoning exploded
like a volcano, sucking the oxygen out of the theater. The audience visibly
winced; seconds passed before we could breathe again. Mind you, Miller set his
play in 1947, but ever since we invaded Iraq in 2003 we've been reading about
similar profiteering by American contractors—of faulty electrical wiring leading to injury and death, of deficient armor, black markets, and, as ever, cover-
ups. It's as if Miller created Keller to stalk every generation, haunting us with
damnable reminders of human nature, the betrayal of self and others, the loss
of trust, and the fall of honor.*

*In this revival, Keller was memorably played by John Lithgow. Yes, that John
Lithgow: the aging, punch-drunk prizefighter in* Requiem for a Heavyweight;
the French diplomat madly in love with a Chinese opera diva—in reality, a

man—in M. Butterfly; *the football player turned transsexual in* The World According to Garp; *Dr. Emilio Lizardo in the cult classic* Buckaroo Banzai; *the gentle Iowa banker in love with Debra Winger in* Terms of Endearment.

Name your villain, and odds are Lithgow's your man, too. He played psychopaths in Blow Out *and* Cliffhanger *("Kill a few people, they call you a murderer. Kill a million and you're a conqueror") and a brutal, rival serial killer in the Showtime series* Dexter, *for which he received a 2010 Emmy Award. My grandchildren thrilled to hear him as the evil Lord Farquaad in* Shrek. *And millions became fans when he played Dr. Dick Solomon, the lunatic leader of aliens come to study earth, in* 3rd Rock from the Sun *(another performance for which he won the Emmy Award—three times, in fact).*

He's a man of so many parts you can take your pick, but I'll stick with his role as Joe Keller, a performance that I can imagine causing even playwright Arthur Miller to hold his breath. Lithgow, by the way, is quite a writer in his own name, with a love of language that is evident in his bestselling children's books and The Poets' Corner, *a kind of chapbook of his favorite poetry. We live in the same building and encountered each other in the lobby as both of us returned from that evening's performance of* All My Sons. *He is such a good fellow that he naturally said yes when I asked him for this interview.*

—*Bill Moyers*

———∿∿———

There's that scene in All My Sons—*a gut-wrenching revelation—when a son learns the awful truth about his father. The night I was there, the whole audience was stunned. How do you explain that scene to yourself?*

The scene comes probably about ninety minutes into the play, after the first act, and the audience has gotten to know these two men when, to all appearances, their relationship was warm and wonderful; they are shadowboxing and roughhousing. Joe Keller, the father, is one of those neighborhood great guys—you see him playing with one of the kids from next door—and his son adores him. He has an idolatrous relationship with him. Arthur Miller sets that up, and then, when he's thirty-two, the scales fall from the boy's eyes. To see his father's failing hits him like a ton of bricks, and there is this incredible emotional rupture.

The audience gasps and winces. At a moment like that, when you're onstage holding an audience like that, are you smiling to yourself and saying, "I got 'em again"?

Yes, I am. That's my guilty secret. It's a great pleasure to torture an audience like that.

And in the audience we see you as Joe Keller, not John Lithgow.

Well, that's the mystery of acting, isn't it? There's a tremendous amount of calculation, sort of blended with the spontaneity of the moment.

I'm going to let you in on a secret. I had the star role in my high school play, One Foot in Heaven, *and when it was over, our teacher Julia Garrett called me aside and said quietly, "You know, Bill, I think you ought to go into journalism." I took her advice, obviously, and never learned how an actor does what you do every night. How do you go to such a volatile interior space, time and time again?*

Technique is an enormous element of it, because I do it eight times a week. I did it last night. I'll do it about five hours from now. I have to be ready to do it, whether I feel like it or not. You simply find ways of just inducing the moment for yourself. It is a kind of sorcery, I guess, and the audience is in on it. I mean, that's the interesting transaction. It's not just what an actor does. It's the audience agreeing.

Do you have any idea of what Arthur Miller might have wanted us to think and see at that moment?

I think he wanted to really throttle people with emotion. He felt that it was important that the people onstage be stretched to an emotional extreme, to have them tortured and to have the audience tortured, to take everybody through this cathartic experience. It's wonderful to be a part of something that sort of reawakens Arthur Miller for you. This is a sixty-year-old play, and it's fantastic to perform it and have this kind of impact on an audience today, to resonate with so much that's on their minds. One tends to begin to take Arthur Miller for granted periodically. You need this restorative production every ten years or so to remind people that he's our great playwright.

There's a fascinating convergence on Broadway right now, a number of reviv-

als that are throwing a searchlight on human greed. David Mamet has two plays back in which he portrays the free enterprise system as a verbal con game. Horton Foote is here with Dividing the Estate, *about what happens when a family runs out of money. And then there's you in* All My Sons.

One of the reasons I wanted to do this, and why our kind of radical director from England, Simon McBurney, wanted to take it on, was how it spoke to our historical moment. *All My Sons* was written right after World War II and took up issues of death in war, war profiteering, accountability for mistakes made during wartime. These are our obsession right now, are they not? The father, Joe Keller—his sin was letting a moment pass when he should have stopped something bad from happening. And letting it pass in order that he should continue to prosper and thrive and benefit and profit from the war. That was his great sin. If nothing had gone wrong, if these engine parts had not malfunctioned, he would have won. And no one would have known about his sin. But twenty-one men died because of what he did. And he still pretends that it didn't happen. When it's revealed, he has to be held accountable.

Well, this is our era of accountability, is it not? Aren't you dying to know who let these various moments of our time pass? Who allowed some memo to be circulated that turned us into a nation that tortures? Or who allowed faulty intelligence to pass across the desk without saying, "no, no, no, no—this can't go any further than here, it's wrong"? Somewhere along the line, people are accountable. Arthur Miller, this enormously principled man with this gigantic social conscience, constructs a story that moves us so much because it involves this father and his own two sons. And he learns that he is responsible, not directly but indirectly, for the death of one of his sons by suicide. This is such a colossal moment of accounting for him. Miller has him fall on his own sword, metaphorically. It's the only way he can punish himself. It's somewhat redemptive but terribly, terribly sad and tragic. You see, Arthur Miller really makes demands on us. He says we have to be accountable.

What's the difference in doing All My Sons *and* 3rd Rock from the Sun?

Well, *3rd Rock* was very much a theater experience. It's what I loved about it. You would spend five days preparing a twenty-three-minute piece of comedy, and you'd perform it once for a live audience. It's your only chance to get it right. And you count on giving them a great show and making them laugh really hard. It was very, very exhilarating, but it was like sketch acting, like revue acting. Everything was so fast and so buoyant. *All My Sons*—any play like this—is a different experience. We're still discovering things after having done it eighty times. It's like polishing a jewel and getting it just right. And of course you take away all the trappings of television—the cameras and stagehands and everybody running in front of the actors.

Did the popular success of 3rd Rock *change how you thought of yourself when you went out on the street the next day?*

Oh, yes. It radically changes everything. You become such common currency, because you're in people's homes every week. Those people know me as zany, which is fine. I have to say, doing an episodic comedy was the one thing I was hesitant about, because I was afraid it would define me, make it difficult for me to play other roles. But I think I managed to escape that, just because, well, I had a big backlog of very different roles beforehand. And as soon as it ended, I had the good sense to go right back to the theater. I didn't even try to mess around with my public image. I just went back to the theater, where you can play very different parts and your audience for each of them is a tiny fraction of your television audience.

Do you have a favorite role out of all of those that you've done?

Well, there were many wonderful movie experiences: *Garp*, and I loved the *Twilight Zone* movie.

You played—

The man terrified of the monster on the wing of the plane. A great old classic *Twilight Zone* episode. But I think my favorite work has been on the stage: *M. Butterfly*. *The Changing Room*, which was my very first Broadway show. There were a couple of wonderful company productions I was in, like *Trelawney of the Wells*, and *Comedians*, and the two musicals I've done in the last few years, *Sweet Smell of Success* and *Dirty Rotten Scoundrels*. That was such an unbelievable lark. Every actor should have the thrill of starring in a Broadway musical comedy.

Your villain in Dirty Rotten Scoundrels *was so amazing—*

So much fun.

I thought I would not be able to forget him as I watched All My Sons, *but I was wrong. John Lithgow once again disappeared, taking the villain with him, and lo—Arthur Miller's Joe Keller was back.*

Bill, that's the great challenge—to try to completely deceive an audience yet again. To make them forget what they ever saw of you, because of what's happening right now.

Deception as a means of truth?

Yeah, that's right. That's what I do. I always say, "I lie for a living."

As coincidence would have it, that night after watching All My Sons, *in my library my eye fell on your book* The Poets' Corner. *I opened it up to Randall Jarrell's poem. I don't think there's enough appreciation for Jarrell in this country. He taught at my alma mater for a few years, at the University of Texas. A powerful war poet. That small poem in* The Poets' Corner *is one of your favorites, right?*

Oh, yes. When you think about the play *All My Sons*, it's like a symphony. Randall Jarrell writes chamber music compared to that. It's succinct, so I'll read it for you.

Give us the context. It's called—

"The Death of the Ball Turret Gunner." The ball turret was a little bulge near the back end of the fuselage of the old Flying Fortresses, the B-17s that were so important in World War II. They had machine guns, and you could spin around and shoot in all directions from that little ball turret. The ball turret gunner was absolutely the most vulnerable member of the crew of a B-17, because there he was—an inviting target, hanging right on the belly of the airplane.

THE DEATH OF THE BALL TURRET GUNNER

From my mother's sleep I fell into the State,
And I hunched in its belly till my wet fur froze.
Six miles from earth, loosed from its dream of life,
I woke to black flak and the nightmare fighters.
When I died they washed me out of the turret with a hose.

It's a very womb-like image, and you ask yourself, what does a young man think of when he's facing death? Probably his mother. It's just incredibly evocative of the deaths of these soldiers in the play.

This pull of the sentence, where did it come from for you?

My dad was a Shakespeare fanatic. He created Shakespeare festivals and produced them in Ohio when I was growing up. And he was also a great storyteller and a reader of stories to all of us kids. It was in our household where I did a huge amount of acting as a young kid. I was one of the princes in the tower. I was Mustardseed in *Midsummer Night's Dream*. As I was growing up, Shakespeare just washed over me like a warm bath. I didn't really intend to be an actor. I had other interests. I was much more interested in being an artist, but I went off to college and started acting, and I realized that I'd better give in to it. This is my destiny.

You include one of Shakespeare's poems in your book.

I actually read it at my father's memorial service. It's one of my favorite pieces of Shakespeare. It's a sustained poem, from *Cymbeline*. Well, some call it a song, and it's Shakespeare's great eulogy.

Fear No More the Heat o' the Sun

Fear no more the heat o' the sun,
  Nor the furious winter's rages;
Though thy worldly task hast done,
  Home art gone, and ta'en thy wages:
Golden lads and girls all must,
As chimney-sweepers, come to dust.

Fear no more the frown o' the great;
  Thou art past the tyrant's stroke:
Care no more to clothe and eat;
  To thee the reed is as the oak:
The scepter, learning, physic, must
All follow this, and come to dust.

Fear no more the lightning-flash,
  Nor the all-dreaded thunder-stone;
Fear not slander, censure rash;
  Thou hast finish'd joy and moan:

All lovers young, all lovers must
Consign to thee, and come to dust.

No exerciser harm thee!
  Nor no witchcraft charm thee!
Ghost unlaid forbear thee!
  Nothing will come near thee!
Quiet consummation have;
And renowned it be thy grave!

It's clearly the play of the language that holds you.

You have no idea. The interesting thing about that poem is, it's a colossal joke. That beautiful poem, which is spoken so deeply from the heart about mortality and the ephemeral nature of life—it's actually spoken by two brothers over the dead body of a young man who was their dear friend. Lo, it turns out not to be a young man but a woman dressed as a young man. And to top it off, the young woman is not dead. It's Shakespeare's crazy joke, to write this beautiful piece of poetry in which these two guys are completely oblivious.

Makes me wonder if in that great poets' corner in the sky, Shakespeare might be sitting next to Ogden Nash, comparing their views of life.

Boy, did Shakespeare love the twists and turns of language. The puns and the jokes and the ironies. Fantastic, and that's a fabulous example of it. You can't find a more moving piece of writing, and the fact that it's all a misdirect is just wonderful.

Your grandmother Ina Lithgow would have liked it.

Ah. Ina B. Lithgow, my father's mom. She lived to the age of ninety-five and used to recite long, long poems to us. I mean, really long. Epic poems by Longfellow and *The Wreck of the Hesperus* and *The Midnight Ride of Paul Revere*, and she knew them all by heart. In her eighties she could still remember them, start to finish, without missing a single syllable. I was astounded.

Is it true that you held forth with your first girlfriend with Walt Whitman?

You are intent on embarrassing! Yes, yes. I think, like many, many people—

including Bill Clinton, I might add—that I recited from *Leaves of Grass* to my first girlfriend. It was on a fabulously romantic summer travel trip to France, and oh! I was such an insufferable young aesthete. Can you imagine me, reading poetry, on the banks of the Loire?

Actually, I can. But why not Elizabeth Barrett Browning instead of Whitman? You have an Elizabeth Barrett Browning poem in here.

Why don't I read that, too?

Sure.

Talk about the ardor of language. This is "Sonnet 43," by Elizabeth Barrett Browning, which you will certainly recognize.

SONNET 43

How do I love thee? Let me count the ways.
I love thee to the depth and breadth and height
My soul can reach, when feeling out of sight
For the ends of being and ideal grace.
I love thee to the level of every day's
Most quiet need, by sun and candle-light.
I love thee freely, as men strive for right.
I love thee purely, as they turn from praise.
I love thee with the passion put to use
In my old griefs, and with my childhood's faith.
I love thee with a love I seemed to lose
With my lost saints! I love thee with the breath,
Smiles, tears, of all my life; and, if God choose,
I shall but love thee better after death.

Do you know people who still respond to such poetry?

Oh, I think that's the magic of archaic language. It takes us back in time. That's the beauty of Shakespeare—his turn of phrase in a language that's four hundred years old. And it's like music. I always feel that I'm an actor, Bill, I'm a performer. And an entertainer. Almost everything I do, in this respect, is using words. And there are these three aspects to a turn of phrase: the meaning, the emotion, and the music.

Arthur Miller will write a line: "Sure, he was my son. But I think to him, they were all my sons. And I guess they were. I guess they were."

That's very rough poetry, but in its way, it is poetic. It has meaning, music, and emotion. In Shakespeare it's a line: "Ay, but to die, and go we know not where; To lie in cold obstruction, and to rot." The language, as I say, is from four hundred years ago, but the music of that language and the emotion and the thought are all just as compelling today. It's just a very different kind of music. It's like listening to Erik Satie and Bach, you know.

What about the music in Ogden Nash?

It's comical music. Doggerel. And one of the reasons why I love Nash is—well, frankly, to the extent I write poetry at all, I write daffy doggerel for little children. But Ogden Nash is kind of my patron saint. His work is musical, all right, but it's musical the way Spike Jones is musical. There is Ogden Nash's comical poem:

No Doctors Today, Thank You

They tell me that euphoria is the feeling of feeling wonder-
    ful, well, today I feel euphorian,
Today I have the agility of a Greek god and the appetite of
    a Victorian.
Yes, today I may even go forth without my galoshes,
Today I am a swashbuckler, would anybody like me to
    buckle any washes?
This is my euphorian day,
I will ring welkins and before anybody answers I will run
    away.
I will tame me a caribou
And bedeck it with marabou.
I will pen me my memoirs.
Ah youth, youth! What euphorian days them was!
I wasn't much of a hand for the boudoirs,
I was generally to be found where the food was.
Does anybody want any flotsam?
I've gotsam.
Does anybody want any jetsam?
I can getsam.

I can play chopsticks on the Wurlitzer,
I can speak Portuguese like a Berlitzer.
I can don or doff my shoes without tying or untying the
    laces because I am wearing moccasins,
And I practically know the difference between serums and
    antitoccasins.
Kind people, don't think me purse-proud, don't set me
    down as vainglorious,
I'm just a little euphorious.

"Euphorious." What a word! You feel it even if you don't get it.

Right. He just loved music. He loved to—what should I say?—caricature language.

On the other side of the street, across from Nash in your book, there's a very short one that takes us somewhere else, by Gwendolyn Brooks.

Oh, yes.

> WE REAL COOL: THE POOL PLAYERS. SEVEN AT THE
> GOLDEN SHOVEL
>
> We real cool. We
> Left school. We
>
> Lurk late. We
> Strike straight. We
>
> Sing sin. We
> Thin gin. We
>
> Jazz June. We
> Die soon.

"We die soon." It's a very scary, very spare poem. Those last three words—"We die soon." They call to my mind a version of this poem in a *New Yorker* cartoon, of two inner-city kids sitting on a stoop. Little kids. One says to the other, "What are you going to be if you grow up?" Get that? "*If* you grow up."

You can startle people with something so emotional they are almost scared. Scaring them, you make them feel the hurt. All of us need that emotional exercise. I think that's what art is about. Certainly serious, dark art, as opposed to comic art, is to make you feel the pain.

Some of the shortest poems are the most powerful. Here's one of my favorites in your book: "To a Poor Old Woman" by William Carlos Williams.

I'll read it.

TO A POOR OLD WOMAN

munching a plum on
the street a paper bag
of them in her hand

They taste good to her
They taste good
to her. They taste
good to her

You can see it by
the way she gives herself
to the one half
sucked out in her hand

Comforted
a solace of ripe plums
seeming to fill the air
They taste good to her

Do you feel the pain and desolation of that? And yet she savors a plum in exactly the same way we savor a plum. We who don't experience anything near the pain she experiences.

Dylan Thomas told us that "too much poetry to-day is flat on the page, a black and white thing of words created by intelligences that no longer think it necessary for a poem to be read and understood by anything but eyes." So let's finish as you take one of his classics off the page.

Okay. This is a wonderful poem. I read this poem for a friend of mine, when his father passed away, at the memorial service. We all know it.

Do Not Go Gentle into That Good Night

Do not go gentle into that good night,
Old age should burn and rave at close of day;
Rage, rage against the dying of the light.

Though wise men at their end know dark is right,
Because their words had forked no lightning they
Do not go gentle into that good night.

Good men, the last wave by, crying how bright
Their frail deeds might have danced in a green bay,
Rage, rage against the dying of the light.

Wild men who caught and sang the sun in flight,
And learn, too late, they grieved it on its way,
Do not go gentle into that good night.

Grave men, near death, who see with blinding sight
Blind eyes could blaze like meteors and be gay,
Rage, rage against the dying of the light.

And you, my father, there on the sad height,
Curse, bless, me now with your fierce tears, I pray.
Do not go gentle into that good night.
Rage, rage against the dying of the light. ∾

WILLIAM GREIDER

*No one was less surprised by the "whoosh" that went out of the housing bubble, or
the clatter of Wall Street as the economy collapsed, than the journalist William
Greider. During forty years of covering politics and economics he has followed
the money like a bloodhound, reporting on how our system of checks and balances, of public safeguards against the might and will of organized wealth, was
being bought off. In chronicling the connections of wealth and power Greider
has tried to warn us of the inevitable consequences when moneyed interests are
allowed to dominate the government's decision making. His* Secrets of the
Temple: How the Federal Reserve Runs the Country *became a bestseller. So
did* Who Will Tell the People? The Betrayal of American Democracy *and*
The Soul of Capitalism: Opening Paths to a Moral Economy.

*No Robespierre radical, he once said that "we do not do guillotines. But there
are other less bloody rituals of humiliation, designed to reassure the populace
that order is restored, the Republic cleansed." Those "rituals"—the relief and
financial reform measures of FDR's first hundred days and the New Deal—
prevailed in the years following the Great Depression, bringing a measure of
stability to our financial system that was the basis of a widening prosperity for
a growing middle class. But recent years saw those reforms weakened to the
point of uselessness—in the face of chicanery and pressure from big business,
they snapped like the corroded beams of a bridge. The Glass-Steagall Act of*

1933, which erected a firewall between investment and consumer banks, was repealed, setting the stage for the subprime mortgage rampage, and Congress exempted national banks from state usury laws prohibiting exorbitant interest rates.

During our conversation, which took place in July 2008, after the collapse of Bear Stearns but before the complete meltdown that fall, Greider called for new laws to restore stability. Unfortunately, the reforms passed by Congress and signed by President Obama, while bringing some relief to consumers, are not likely to curtail the complex hoodwinkery that got the financial industry into trouble in the first place. Greider also said that in a time of economic pain our government will need to ask for sacrifices. It has not; the bailouts of banks and other financial institutions have in some respects only further spurred the avarice of the banking business. When the day of reckoning arrived, the emperors of Wall Street—as shameless as they were soulless—threw themselves on the mercy of the taxpayers they had so royally fleeced. But then they picked themselves up, dusted themselves off, and resumed business as usual.

—Bill Moyers

Where were the gatekeepers? Where were the watchdogs? Why did it take the Fed so long to put an end to predatory practices?

To make the story overly crude, Congress repealed the law against usury. It was done in 1980 by a Democratic Congress, a Democratic president. And of course, the Republicans all piled on and voted for it. That was the first stroke, only the first of many, in which they stripped away the regulatory laws from the financial system and from banking. That allowed the free market modernized gimmicks of one kind or another, all these things we're now reading about, to flourish. The gatekeepers said to the banking industry and to the financial industry, "We don't think federal control or regulation is good for you, so we're therefore liberating you to do your own thing."

So why did they do that in 1980?

Well, the driver then, and it was a powerful driver, was inflation. And through the '70s, for lots of reasons, inflation, which tends to undermine the value of financial wealth and money, was out of control. The Federal Reserve had lost control of it, not entirely its fault. But that set up a political climate that said, "The government is not working. Let's get the government out of the way."

And as framed by Ronald Reagan and other conservatives, that was very appealing. But I think it's fair to say most Democrats yielded to it against whatever their original instincts were because of political necessity. And then the third dimension, maybe the most important, was that you had this very powerful industrial sector, that is, banking and finance, that had pushed for years to get out from under the regulatory controls: limits on interest rates, the law against usury and against the merger of commercial banks with investment banks, which had been prohibited in the New Deal because it caused the disaster of 1929. The point I keep trying to make to people is that history learned the hard way that you need prudential controls on industries like banking because they're so central to everybody's well-being.

Left to their own devices, they go too far?

They will use their power to their own advantage, and that's what we're witnessing now, a kind of recklessness that was set free by political retreat. Some people were sincere; some of them were just on the make. But here's our great American tension. We want an economy that's dynamic, that's growing, puts more jobs out there for people to get, rising wages, all that good stuff. And at the same time, we want an economy that's stable. And that means no inflation, steady as you go, and so forth and so on.

This is the mortal condition. You're not going to escape that tension. Government is a powerful intervener that tries, ought to try, to balance those two desires. For many years, the Federal Reserve served that role and tried to strike a balance.

And then what happened?

During the last generation, twenty-five, thirty years ago, the Federal Reserve, the central bank that regulates money and credit, tipped hard in one direction, crudely in favor of capital and against labor. It not only hardened the value of money by suppressing inflation, but it participated very aggressively in the role of stripping away regulatory brakes on the financial system and banks, declined to enforce many of its own regulatory powers that exist in law. Meanwhile, it sort of kept a foot on the brake about economic growth and full employment and all those good things that might help working people by encouraging rising wages.

So at the same time the Fed was helping to keep wages down in order to keep inflation from escalating, its policies were nonetheless helping banks and investors to inflate the value of their assets beyond reality.

That's it. At one point, writing in *The Nation*, I somewhat playfully and wickedly referred to Alan Greenspan, the Federal Reserve chairman, as the "one-eyed chairman." He can see inflation in wages and goods and services and consumer prices, even when it doesn't exist, and he'll put his foot down on the brake. But he doesn't see the inflation in the financial system at all.

Inflation in the financial system, the value of financial assets, most obviously stock—rose fantastically over twenty, twenty-five years; two, three times the growth in the real underlying economy. Something's wrong there, right? How do these financial assets, which supposedly reflect the economy, suddenly become worth three times more?

With deregulation, with the help of the Fed, and with the success of the super bull market, everybody's animal spirits in the financial system became more animal. They went for it, and they said, "If you'll get this rule out of the way or you let us make this kind of weird little gimmicky paper innovation, we'll do even better."

And you had this force rising up, driving things higher in the stock market, while in many sectors of the economy, if not everywhere, people were saying, "Gee, this doesn't feel that good to us." Particularly working people.

You wrote about a fantasy that was sold, an illusion that led to the housing bubble. Whose interest was it to sell a fantasy?

The merchants of financial paper, to put it bluntly. The illusion was that you could dismantle or disregard traditional rules of proper banking and stewardship and that would definitely allow prices, profits, everything to go still higher, but could still somehow dissolve the risk not just for the society but for themselves. One example of that was what you heard about in the subprime mortgage thing. Who is holding this mortgage that's been lent to these people who we know are going to fail because their incomes just aren't sufficient? Well, it's kind of hard to say because this mortgage is designed as a securitized package of one thousand mortgages. And you sell it in the financial market to investors all over the world.

And then they sell it to somebody else, and it moves around, literally. So what you've done with this innovation is you've distanced the lender from the borrower. Each party—the guy who sold the mortgage, the bank, then the next guy who buys the bond—takes his returns up front, sells it on, and you strip away the responsibility for that lending. And that's a pretty good microcosm of what happened generally in the financial system.

I think you can get lost in the mechanics of how all this works. And it's sometimes pretty dizzying stuff. I think the bigger message is that what some of our old folks knew turns out still to be true. The process of lending, borrowing, investing, all of those things, requires a personal, hands-on knowledge of what you're doing and a level of integrity that, to put it bluntly, does not exist at this time in our financial system.

This is deeper than a politician rolling over for his campaign contributors, the guys who finance the Democratic Party or the Republican Party. They do that, too. But they were sold a fantasy, an illusion, which sounded wonderful, about how markets make better judgments than government and the public—and that liberating finance and business from prudential rules that society imposes upon them will produce a bigger, better economy and better returns for everyone.

All those fantasies have been wiped out. And if you think about it, as we go through the hard months ahead, America's going to have to take some pain, right? In one form or another. The government's going to have to probably ask for some sacrifices.

How do they do that when the American people have just seen the government rush in to bail out the biggest, most powerful institutions in the country—the financial investment houses and major banks? Restore the federal law against usury. That won't have too many details to it at first, but it'll be a general statement that the federal government is prohibiting the kind of outrageous predatory practices that have become general in this country, not just from banks but other financial firms. We're going to develop government laws that prohibit and penalize these institutions when they get caught doing it. Wealthy people, whether they're banks or individuals, ought not to be able to use their power, their wealth, to exploit people who don't have great wealth. That's not too complicated—and I'm not being utopian here. I'm just saying that you can reestablish legal, moral limits on the behavior of finance and their wealthy patrons. And if they don't want to observe those rules, then they need not apply for emergency loans at the Federal Reserve or the Treasury Department.

You have been writing for a long time that America's moving toward a corporate state. Can we exercise the self-correcting faculty that prevents us from hitting the iceberg out there?

The Federal Reserve, accompanied by the Treasury Department and the Congress, crossed a very dangerous line in their bailout. They essentially said, "We will put money on the table, taxpayers' money on the table, for any financial institution or business that is too big to fail." I regard that as profoundly dangerous for the American republic because once you cross that line and you have this special club that's privileged, that has benefits from government that nobody else can get, where do you stop it?

Both parties have been complicit in tipping the balance of power to capital, right?

I'm afraid so. If you go back over the last twenty, twenty-five years, it was always portrayed as a cause of conservative Republicans, even right-wing Republicans. And that was, of course, true. But I think a majority of the Democrats were in collusion virtually every step of the way, and sometimes they led the way.

So there's not much hope that our political democracy can produce economic democracy?

The short answer is, no. I've been in Washington as a citizen and resident for forty years, and I'm still occasionally shocked by its ignorance of the rest of the country. Some of that is willful, of course. But some of it is just that it's a very nice life in Washington. You get used to certain protective qualities.

We saw that recently with these political players who got good mortgages. How do they do that? Well, we know how they did it. And in any case, Washington doesn't yet see the depth of the problem. If you ask me, "Well, who's figured this out? Who understands, at least in general terms, where we are? The guys in Washington? The politicians and their governing policy advisors? Or the dimwitted public?" I would say the public. And I think there's a lot of evidence for that.

We have an opening in this crisis for a deep transformation in American politics. I don't say it happens this year, next year, or whether it's going to take a number of years. But we are in the shock of reality. People everywhere get it and see the blood in the streets. And you tell them how this worked and who did what to whom, and that's a basis for a new politics.

But it requires people—this is the hard part—to get out of their sort of passive resignation—"Well, we follow the Democrats" or "We follow the Republicans" or "We let this group or that group tell us how to think"— and engage among themselves in a much more serious role as citizens. And they have to be willing to punish the political powers, in smart ways or crude ways, however they can, first, to get a place in the debate. But second, to force the changing values of the system.

This may be wishful thinking, but I think in the next year, two years, five years, you're going to see both political parties floundering. We've told folks this lovely story for twenty, twenty-five years about the magic of the marketplace. Do we still want to kind of prop that up? That's where they are now. They're still trying to prop up the marketplace vision and make it work again. It's over. I think events will demonstrate that. So if they're not willing to change, then we need to change the politicians. And that's all a bloody process and doesn't happen quickly. But that's why I'm optimistic. ∾

Bill Greider returned to the Journal *in March 2009. He had published a new book,* Come Home, America: The Rise and Fall (and Redeeming Promise) of Our Country, *laying out the case for a fundamental restructuring of the economy and a return to values embodied in the social contract. "Just as World War II presented a chance to thoroughly reorder American life," he wrote, "this generation of Americans has the opportunity—the obligation—to envision a country very different from the one we have known for more than half a century."*

It was not to be. Secretary of the Treasury Timothy Geithner had just proposed expanding government authority to crack down on Wall Street's reckless behavior in an effort to prevent a future financial meltdown. For a brief spell it seemed there was real hope for the kind of reform Greider described in his book. But he saw in Geithner's proposals "a glass half full" and said only an aroused public could demand the change necessary. Citizens across the country were outraged that the bailout of the giant banks had left intact the very people whose excesses had brought on the financial debacle and whose profits and bonuses were again soaring. The public's rage, Greider wrote, "has great potential for restoring a functioning democracy. Timely intervention by the people could save the country from some truly bad ideas now circulating in Washington and on Wall Street."

In fact, Tea Party rallies did reflect some of the rage citizens were feeling toward crony capitalism, but mostly they were up in arms over President Obama's health care proposals and stimulus spending by the government. The financial regulation reforms eventually enacted offered some safeguards that Wall Street didn't like, but protected the status of a handful of the elite banks considered "too big to fail," meaning that they could repeat their excesses of the past, confident that taxpayers could again be sent the bill.

———

What's your take on these proposed reforms? What's missing?

I don't want to be a cynic, but it feels more to me like trying to restore the old order that failed. And I mean by that these big megabanks that had been liberated by deregulation to do as they pleased and the other rules that were undermined. I think this president's first priority seems to be to re-create those institutions, some of which are now insolvent, as healthy again. It's quite scary, because unless they set about to make much more fundamental changes, I fear we will, sure enough, get this back again.

Can ordinary citizens do anything about this? How do they break this grip that money has on the politicians?

They trust themselves. I read a wonderful book called *Many Minds, One Heart* by Wesley C. Hogan about how the civil rights movement and SNCC and others in the South, in Mississippi, the most treacherous, backward place you could go, brought the issue of racial equality there. And they said the organizers' first goal was to learn to listen to these people, poor blacks in Mississippi. The second goal was to convince themselves and these poor people to act like citizens even though they knew they weren't treated as citizens. And you think about that. That's kind of the mystery of democracy. People get power if they believe they're entitled to power.

Young people are part of my optimism. Smart kids want to be engaged in their times, see the injustices of their society. And they don't quite trust the great big existing organizations. And with some good reason, as you know. And particularly, they're not totally sold on the Democratic Party as the vessel of reform. They're telling Washington, "We're on to your silly ideas that Wall Street wants you to do about reform. We see through them. And we have some ideas of our own. And we're going to come talk to you, and if you decline to talk to us, we're going to come after you." That's the voice of democracy speaking, when people say that.

I hear that. But I also read your piece in The Washington Post *in which you wrote, "Obama told us to speak out. But is he listening?" Well, is he?*

I've been very enthusiastic about his opening as president. He did the stimulus package and a number of other things that are fulfilling his promise. But on this, he does seem absolutely committed to the restoration of the old order. There's no other way to say it. And the things Secretary Geithner is saying and others have been putting out all confirm that.

I think that's a huge mistake, financially, because I think their ideas are not going to work. And will, in fact, blow up in his face. Maybe a month from now. Or maybe six months, I don't know. But the handing out of government guarantees and capital to hedge funds and private equity funds—financial institutions founded on secrecy, by the way. They don't even pretend to be transparent. They're closed shops. He hands out that money, and then somewhere down the road people are going to learn that the so-called investors are reaping double-digit returns on this money with almost no risk at all to themselves. And whether that works or not, people will be outraged. And I think they should be. Outrage right now might just get the Congress to slow down a bit, calm down. We want reform, but we want it done right, and we want it done for the public interest, not for the old order.

The nature of democracy, authentically, is not simply supporting from the bleachers, and saying, "Gee, we hope you win the game." It's being on the field, engaged in whatever small or large way is possible, and expecting those elected representatives, including the president, to at least hear what you're saying, and rightly responding to it in some ways. That's the dynamic of a democratic society. Everybody knows in this country that this has been for some years, not exclusively but mainly, a top-down society. And you go into workplaces and hear the same things said as you hear about politics: "Well, I know what's wrong here, but they won't listen to me. I don't have any voice in the matter." Or investors, small investors, putting their money in mutual funds: "Well, they're not listening to me. Look who they're giving this money to." You know, you can go on and on. And that's what democracy would break.

One of your deep concerns about turning so much power over to the Fed is that it is cozy with the big institutions. And that the smaller, entrepreneurial organizations and businesses that do not have access to the inner circle are excluded.

President Obama, if the Democratic leaders in Congress follow along, will put the Democratic Party on the wrong side of history. What we ought to be seeking, the goal of reform and government aid, is creating a new financial and banking system of many more, thousands more, smaller, more diverse, regionally dispersed banks and investment firms. Not the other way around. What the administration's approach may be doing is consecrating "too big to fail," for starters, which, of course, everybody in government denied was the policy until the moment it arrived.

And secondly—and this will sound extreme to some people, but I came to it reluctantly—I fear what they're doing, not intentionally, but in their design, is ratifying the corporate state through the control of a rather small but powerful circle of financial institutions: the old, rather small, but very powerful circle of financial institutions. The old Wall Street banks, famous names, but also some industrial corporations that bought banks. Or General Electric, which is already half big financial capital, GE Capital. And that circle will be our new Wall Street club. Too big to fail. Yes, watched closely by the Federal Reserve and others in government, but also protected by them. And that's a really insidious departure, to admit that and put it into law. Then think of all those thousands of smaller banks. How are they going to perform against these behemoths that have an inside track to the government spigot? And for just ordinary enterprise in general? Before you even get to the citizens. How are citizens supposed to feel about that? My point is, in this situation, with the leading banks and corporations sort of at the trough, ahead of everybody else in Washington, they will have the means to monopolize democracy.

Some of my friends would say, "Hey, that already happened." The fact is, if the Congress goes down the road I see them going down on financial reform, they will institutionalize the corporate state in a way that will severely damage any possibility of restoring democracy. And I want people to grab their pitchforks, yes, and be unruly. Get in the streets. Be as noisy and as nonviolently provocative as you can be. Stop the politicians from going down that road. And, let me add, a lot of politicians need that to be able to stand up. Our president needs that to be able to stand up.

In your essay in The Washington Post *you describe President Obama as trapped between "the governing elites who decide things and the people who are governed." When does he finally have to choose sides?*

I think he has to choose as this story keeps unfolding, because I don't think it's going to change dramatically with these new plans announced. In fact, the anger will be stoked.

He did walk into a burning house.

That's true.

And his job is to put out the fire and rebuild the house.

Here's my take on the New Deal and the history of what actually happened. And it conveniently fits my deeper prejudices about the country and how progress is achieved in America. That is, people in the streets or churches or wherever found their voice and made it happen by agitating and informing the higher authorities. In the early '30s, Franklin Roosevelt had a set of things he thought he could do to right the ship of the Depression. He tried some of them. They didn't work very well. Meanwhile, organized labor and others were all over the country lighting bonfires for bigger changes. Social Security came out of that. Labor rights, the first attempt to give people the right to organize their own voices in a company, came out of that. A whole bunch of other reforms that we now take for granted. And Roosevelt didn't stand athwart and try to stop them. But he let them roll him. That's what I hope for now, that people of every stripe will stand up and say, "We love you, Mr. President, but you don't have it right yet. And we're going to bang on your door until you get it right." ∽

KAREN ARMSTRONG

Karen Armstrong's great passion, as a self-described "monotheistic free-lancer," is to get the world's three Abrahamic faiths—Islam, Judaism, and Christianity—to unite in practicing faith, hope, and charity; especially char-ity. Good luck to her. That's a tall order even here in the United States, just one province of her global mission, where there are enough spoilsports to rain on an ecumenical parade. Yet Armstrong is undeterred, as you might expect from a former nun who fled the convent and became a literary scholar, overcame epilepsy, fought depression, steeped herself in matters of religion, created tele-vision documentaries on the nature of faith, and published bestselling books, including A History of God, Islam, The Bible: A Biography, Buddha, and The Case for God.

Equally comfortable in church, synagogue, or mosque, Karen Armstrong has concluded that religion "isn't about believing things. It's about what you do. It's ethical alchemy. It's about behaving in a way that changes you." The proof of religion is in compassion; it is the seed, she believes, for nurturing toler-ance and peace among religions.

In 2008, the annual gathering of leaders in technology, entertainment, and design gave her their prestigious TED Prize, which comes not only with a $100,000 cash award but also, like the genie in Aladdin's lamp, grants the recipient a wish. Go to www.ted.com, and you can hear the speech in which

Armstrong made hers: "I wish that you would help with the creation, launch, and propagation of a Charter for Compassion—crafted by a group of inspirational thinkers from the three Abrahamic traditions of Judaism, Christianity, and Islam, and based on the fundamental principle of the Golden Rule."

One year later it was done: The Charter for Compassion was adopted in ceremonies around the world (read it at www.charterforcompassion.org). Signatories include the Dalai Lama, Archbishop Desmond Tutu, Prince Hassan of Jordan, Sir Richard Branson, and Rabbi David Saperstein, among many others, with and without rank.

The Golden Rule: "Do unto others as you would have them do unto you." Not as simple as it sounds. But as Karen Armstrong says, it's a start.

—*Bill Moyers*

——⌇⌇——

Tell us what you're up to with this movement.

My work has continually brought me back to the notion of compassion. Whichever religious tradition I study, I find that the heart of it is the idea of feeling with the other, experiencing with the other, compassion. And every single one of the major world religions has developed its own version of the Golden Rule. Don't do to others what you would not like them to do to you.

You see, the Greeks, too, may not have been religious in our sense, but they understood about compassion. The institution of tragedy put suffering onstage. And the leader of the chorus would ask the audience to weep for people, even like Heracles, who had been driven mad by a goddess and slew his own wife and children. And the Greeks did weep. They didn't just, like modern Western men, wipe a tear from the corner of their eye and gulp hard. They cried aloud because they felt that weeping together created a bond between human beings. You were learning to put yourself in the position of another and reach out, not only to acceptable people, people in your own group, but to your enemies, to people you wouldn't normally have any deep truck with at all.

So this is not just another call for another round of interfaith dialogue?

No, it's nothing to do with interfaith dialogue. Look, I'm not expecting the whole world to fall into a daze of compassion.

I don't think you have to worry about that.

But this is the beginning of something. We're writing a charter which we hope will be like the UN's Universal Declaration of Human Rights, two pages only, saying that compassion is far more important than belief. That it is the essence of religion. All the traditions teach that the practice of compassion and honoring the sacred in the other brings us into the presence of what we call God, Nirvana, or Tao. And people are remarkably uneducated about compassion these days. So we want to bring it back to the center of attention. But then, it's got to be incarnated into practical action.

Osama bin Laden and radical Islamists obviously won't sign on to this.

Of course not. But we have to understand that Osama bin Laden and the radical Islamists are largely motivated by politics. They may express themselves in a religious idiom.

As many of those suicide bombers did when diving into the World Trade Center.

They did. But their motivations, when you read Osama's declarations and the suicide videos of our own London bombers, are all political. Their grievances are political.

Were you there when London was bombed?

I was right in the middle of it.

What was your reaction?

I thought that this was virtually inevitable. This is a political matter. Tony Blair had put us right on the front line by joining with former President Bush in the occupation of Iraq. And we were all expecting this in London. There was no great surprise. I was actually in the British Library, right next to the King's Cross station, so it was a police zone. And we had to stay in there all day. We weren't allowed out. We didn't quite know what was happening.

Did this diminish or strengthen your resolve about compassion?

We've got to do better than this. Compassion doesn't mean feeling sorry for people. It doesn't mean pity. It means putting yourself in the position of the other, learning about the other. Learning what's motivating the other, learning about their grievances. So the Charter for Compassion was to re-call compassion from the sidelines, to which it's often relegated in religious discourse.

The scholar of religion Elaine Pagels told me many years ago, "There's practically no religion I know of that sees people in a way that affirms the others' choices."

Yes. And this is a great scandal. There used to be. Islam, for example—the Koran is a pluralistic document. It says that every rightly guided religion comes from God. And there must be no compulsion in religion. And it says that Muhammad has not come to cancel out the teachings of Jesus or Moses or Abraham. Now, Muslims have fallen into the trap that Jews, Christians, and others have done, of thinking that they are the one and only. This is ego. This is pure ego.

But it's inspired, is it not—even sanctified—by religion?

Well, no. The idea that everyone has to be Muslim is actually going against the explicit teaching of the Koran, in which God says to Muhammad, if we—using the royal *we*—had wanted the whole of mankind to be in one single religious community, we would have made that happen. But we did not so wish. This is not our desire. So you, Muhammad, leave them alone. And everybody, says the Koran, has their own *din*, their own religious tradi-tion, their own way of life.

Now, this is getting lost to the modern world. But that was also Muslim practice for the first one hundred years after the death of the Prophet, when conversion to Islam was actually frowned upon, because Jews and Christians and Zoroastrians and, later, Buddhists, had their own *din*, their own religion. And that was to be respected.

You're putting your finger on a real fault line, it seems to me. Metaphorically, the language of violence, which goes all the way back in these old stories, of-ten invokes God for the sanctification of violent acts. In your recent book The Bible: A Biography, *you quote, for example, from Joshua: "When Israel had finished killing all the inhabitants of Ai, in the open ground and where they followed them into the wilderness, and when all to a man had fallen by the edge of the sword, all Israel returned to Ai and slaughtered all its people. . . . All the people of Ai." And then in the Koran: "Allah hath sealed their hearing and their hearts, and on their eyes there is a covering. Theirs will be an awful doom." When you talk about the positive and affirmative side of even these texts, there is also a contrary side.*

Yes. These scriptures all have these difficult passages. There's far more of that kind of stuff in the Bible, both Old and New Testaments, than there is in the Koran. One of the things that I am going to call for in this Charter is for exegetes to look at these passages, see how they came into the tradition in the first place. What were the circumstances in which they appeared? What influence do they have on the tradition as a whole? And what do we do with them? How do we deal with them in this age? We need really to study them in depth.

By exegetes, you mean the scholars and students and interpreters of every faith?

Every faith. Yes. We must, first of all, study our own scriptures before we point a finger at other people.

You ask, "What would it mean to interpret the whole of the Bible as a commentary on the Golden Rule?" What's your answer to that question?

Well, this is one of the things that really intrigued me when I was researching this book. How frequently the early rabbis, for example, in the Talmudic period, shortly after the death of Jesus, insisted that any interpretation of scripture that read hatred or contempt for any single human being was illegitimate. Rabbi Hillel, the older contemporary of Jesus, said that anyone, when asked to sum up the whole of Jewish teaching while standing on one leg, should answer, "The Golden Rule. That which is hateful to you, do not do to your neighbor. That is the Torah. And everything else is only commentary. Now, go and study it." St. Augustine said that scripture teaches nothing but charity. And if you come to a passage like the one you just read, that seems to preach hatred, you've got to give it an allegorical or metaphorical interpretation. And make it speak of charity.

But of course, what some people do is to read for their own purposes what they call allegorical. And then read literally what they want to apply in their—

And of course, you have to understand that this tendency to read scripture in a literal manner is very recent. Nobody, for example, ever thought of interpreting the first chapter of Genesis as a literal account of the origins of life until the modern period. It's our scientific mind-set that makes us want to sort of read these texts for accurate information.

But as stories, they still have a very powerful effect. For example, the first murder in the oldest story grows out of a religious act. Cain and Abel are brothers. They're also rivals for God's favor. And out of jealousy, Cain kills Abel. And once that pattern is set, it is followed right through like a red thread from Ishmael and Isaac and Joseph and his brothers on down to Christians versus Muslims, Muslims versus Jews, Christians versus everybody.

I think these are difficult texts. We read these texts as though they're easy. Now, I see Genesis as deconstructing a neat idea of God.

What do you mean, deconstructing?

First, in chapter 1, God's sitting in the universe, center stage, totally powerful, totally benign, blessing everything, all that he has made. No favorites, impartial. Within two chapters, God's completely lost control of his creation. Then the impartial God turns out to be a God that has real favorites. And God the benign creator becomes God the destroyer, at the end of the Flood.

And by the end of Genesis, God has retired from the scene. Joseph and his brothers have to rely on their own insights and dreams, just as we do. You can't say what God is. That is, people often ask me, "Ms. Armstrong, do you or do you not believe in the God of the Bible?" And I always say, "Tell me what it is." I'll be fascinated to hear, because the Bible is highly contradictory. What it shows, I think, is that our experience of the divine is ambiguous, complex. We can misunderstand it. We can use it to create mayhem because of our own horrible sort of murderous tendencies. And there are no clear answers, no clear theology in the Bible.

But isn't the source of the trouble the fact that everyone interprets the text to fit his or her own bias?

But it shouldn't, because in the premodern world, you were expected to find new meaning in scripture. You have the beginning of the scientific revolution in Europe in the sixteenth century, and that starts changing everything. It's a much more literal approach to life. And the scientists, people like Newton, start to write theology, and the churches seize upon this and they start thinking that the Bible is literally and factually true.

But in the premodern world, what you see are the early Christian and Jewish commentators saying you must find new meaning in the Bible. And the rabbis would change the words of scripture to make a point to their pupils. Origen, the great Greek commentator on the Bible, said that it is absolutely impossible to take these texts literally. You simply cannot do so. And he said God has put these sort of conundrums and paradoxes in so that we are forced to seek a deeper meaning.

And the Koran is the same. The Koran says every single one of its verses is an *ayah*, a symbol or a parable. Because you can only talk about God analogically, in terms of signs and symbols. So you must go to the Bible and find new meaning, these early interpreters said. And the same was true of the Greeks. At the beginning of the rationalist tradition in Greece—Socrates, Plato, Aristotle—the people who commented on them didn't take down everything they did slavishly. They used it as a springboard to have new insights in the present. Rather as we might use weights at the gym to build up our strength. They used it as something to start them thinking. The rabbis used to say, "You may not leave a scripture or text until you have translated it into practical action for the community here and now."

Meaning . . . acts of kindness, acts of compassion.

Acts of compassion.

And acts of justice?

Yes. Absolutely.

We are all indebted to those Hebrew prophets for their powerful sense of social justice.

And the rabbis who came after them in the Talmudic age, and who created the Mishnah and said, "Now we have to move on." We've lost that confidence today. And that's what the Charter is trying to do—trying to nudge people into the hard work of being compassionate. People don't want to be compassionate. When I go around lecturing about this, I sometimes see the good faithful looking mutinous. They may know that they ought to be compassionate, but what's the fun of religion if you can't slam down other people? This is ego.

I'm glad you mentioned this, because I know many atheists and agnostics who are more faithful, if that's the right term, to the Golden Rule than a lot of believing religious people.

Yes. And I also know a number of atheists who have no time for the Golden Rule at all.

What is it that evokes the empathy and the commitment to people to put themselves in others' shoes?

Basically a sense of urgent need. If we don't manage to do better than this within our own communities, our own nations, and as regards other nations far away, then I think we are in for a very troublesome ride. We are not doing well at the moment. The three monotheisms—Judaism, Christianity, and Islam—have a besetting tendency. That is, idolatry taking a human idea, a human idea of God, a human doctrine, and making it absolute, putting it in the place of God. Of course, there have been secular idolatries, too. Nationalism was a great idolatry.

This is what we do. As Paul Tillich said, we are makers of idols. We are constantly creating these idols. Erecting a purely human ideal or a human value or a human idea to the supreme reality. Now, once you've made something essentially finite, once you've made it an absolute, it has then to destroy any other rival claimants. Because there can only be one absolute.

You wrote A History of God. *Who created God?*

Human beings created the idea of God. But the transcendent reality to which the idea of God nudges us is embedded in part of the human experience.

If we create God, then we can read into God our passions, jealousies, envies, animosities, aspirations.

Yes, and this is idolatry, when you are creating a God in your own image and likeness. When the Crusaders went into battle with the cry "God wills it" on their lips, they were projecting their own fear and loathing of these rival faiths onto other people. And we get a lot of secular people doing this, too.

The Stalinists, the Communists, the fascists—

And even nearer, here in the United States. There are people saying,

"We want to get rid of religion." There are radical Republicans slanging Democrats. We are a very agonistic society.

Agonistic?

Meaning competitive in our discourse. Let me say this. In our discourse, it is not enough for us in the Western democratic tradition simply to seek the truth. We also have to defeat and humiliate our opponents. And that happens in politics. It happens in the law courts. It happens in religious discourse. It happens in the media. It happens in academia.

Very different from Socrates, the founder of the rationalist tradition. When you had dialogues with Socrates, you came in thinking that you knew what you were talking about. Half an hour later, you realized you didn't know anything at all. And at that moment, says Socrates, your quest can begin. You can become a philosopher, a lover of wisdom, because you know you don't have wisdom, you seek it. And you had to go into a dialogue prepared to change, not to bludgeon your conversation partner into accepting your point of view. At every single point in a Socratic dialogue, you offer your opinion kindly to the other, and the other accepts it with kindness.

But you can't have a dialogue with people who don't want to have a dialogue.

No. But that doesn't mean we should give up altogether. Because I think so-called liberals can also be just as hard-line in their own way. Most fundamentalist movements, in every tradition that I've studied, in every fundamentalist movement in Judaism, Christianity, and Islam, have begun with what is perceived to be an assault by the liberal or secular establishment. Look at your Scopes trial. You have this absurd ban on teaching evolution in the public schools. And after the trial, the secular press does a number on the fundamentalists.

H.L. Mencken was ruthless in caricaturing them.

And they crept away. And we thought we'd seen the end of them. But of course, they were just regrouping. But before the Scopes trial, fundamentalists had often been on the left of the political spectrum. They were—many of them—prepared to work alongside socialists and alongside Social Gospel reformers in the slums of the newly developing industrialized cities. After the Scopes trial, they swung to the far right, where they remain. Before Scopes, fundamentalists tended to be literal in their interpretation of scripture. But creation science, so called, was the pursuit of a very tiny minority. After the Scopes trial they became more militant in their literal interpretation of scripture. And creation science became, and has remained, the flagship of their movement.

Does your notion of compassion embrace liberals, in the interest of harmony, accepting state schools teaching creationism alongside Darwin's notion of evolution?

You see, the assault by Richard Dawkins on creationism has resulted, for the first time, in a worry about Darwin in the Muslim world.

What do you mean?

There was no worry about Darwin in the Muslim world up until very recently. The Koran doesn't say how God created the world. The texts tell you this is an *ayah*—we don't know what happened in the beginning. And there was just no problem about not knowing. Now, because of the attacks on religion, it's headline news when British scientists slang creationism. And Darwin has now become an anathema as a result of that assault. So I think we've all just got to come off our high horses a bit to cool down the rhetoric. There must be an openness toward science, as St. Augustine pointed out years ago. He said if a religious text is found to contradict contemporary science, you must find a new interpretation for this text. You must allegorize it in some way. We need to get back to that. I don't want this to be going after the fundamentalists. I don't want this to be going after extremists. But I want this to just say, quietly, let us remember the primal duty of compassion.

Which is?

To feel with the other. To experience with the other. Do not do to others what you would not like them to do to you. If you don't like to be attacked, don't attack others. As Confucius—who was the first to propound the Golden Rule, five hundred years before Christ—said, you seek to establish yourself, then seek to establish others. If you don't like hearing your own traditions traduced, then have the discipline not to traduce the traditions of others. It's hard. People who say it's a simplistic idea, obviously, never tried to practice the Golden Rule, as Confucius said, "All day and every day." ∾

ROSS DOUTHAT

In the eight years George W. Bush and Dick Cheney reigned in Washington, conservatives made a mess of things. They bungled Iraq and deserted the fight against terrorists in Afghanistan, never getting their hands on Osama bin Laden, dead or alive. They sent spending into the stratosphere, rewarded the rich with huge tax cuts, and borrowed trillions from the future to pay for their indulgences. They botched Katrina and turned a wrecking crew loose on government agencies whose mission is to protect the environment, consumers, and the public interest. They used earmarks and contracts to fatten lobbyists on K Street as Tom DeLay and his congressional cronies honed a ruthless shakedown machine that turned the Conservative Revolution into a racket. More than fifty top administration officials were implicated in scandals that cost them their jobs. By 2008, as the discredited regime came to its demoralized end, principled Republicans were asking what went wrong, and how to redeem their future.

A member of the founding generation of modern conservatism, Mickey Edwards signed up with the movement when Barry Goldwater mobilized it in 1964. Edwards served sixteen years in Congress from Oklahoma, was one of three founding trustees of the Heritage Foundation, the conservative nerve center, and was elected chairman of the American Conservative Union. When

MICKEY EDWARDS

we spoke, he was turning heads with a new book, Reclaiming Conservatism: How a Great American Political Movement Got Lost—and How It Can Find Its Way Back.

On the other end of the generational spectrum, young conservatives were also offering thoughtful prescriptions for the recovery of their party. Ross Douthat was born in 1979, one year before Ronald Reagan was elected president. He and his colleague at The Atlantic Monthly, *Reihan Salam, wrote what the conservative columnist David Brooks called "the political book of the year,"* Grand New Party: How Republicans Can Win the Working Class and Save the American Dream.

Since then, events have altered the equation yet again. The collapse of the economy, although on Bush's watch, cast a shadow over the first years of Obama's presidency, giving Republican candidates ample ammo as unemployment remained high. On top of that, the GOP ignored the counsel of both Edwards and Douthat and sought recovery via the cognitive dissonance of the Tea Party movement. So keep in mind that our conversation took place in the middle of the 2008 presidential campaign, before Barack Obama's victory, before the financial meltdown, and after the 2006 midterms, when for the first time in decades, the Republicans turned both the House and Senate back to the Democrats. Ross Douthat has since become an op-ed columnist at The New York Times. *And Mickey Edwards is teaching courses on national security and American foreign policy at George Washington University in Washington, D.C.*

—Bill Moyers

—◦◦◦—

Republicans suffered only one sweeping defeat in the last thirty years. Why are you so upset?

EDWARDS: Republicans used to believe in a certain set of basic principles about divided powers, limited government. What happened is, with the Bush presidency, we have become the exact opposite of what we used to stand for. So we may win elections, but we are now standing for an all-powerful presidency, with limits on civil liberties. We've changed everything we believed in order to win elections.

DOUTHAT: In a sense, the GOP is a victim of its own success on a lot of fronts. Crime has fallen dramatically since the early 1990s. Marginal tax rates are vastly lower than they were when Ronald Reagan was running for president. The welfare system has been reformed. The Soviet Union obviously no longer exists. And so the GOP has sort of run out of things to say.

Sure, they've only lost one election, but if you look back to the Democratic Party in the early 1970s, a lot of Democrats after 1972, and then again after Reagan won in '80, would say, "Oh, well, we've only lost one election. We just need to regroup and come back." But there were deeper structural problems facing the Democratic Party. And that's what the GOP's facing today.

EDWARDS: It's not just a matter of Republicans losing an election or losing some by-elections. Our party is very unpopular. President Bush is very unpopular, and the party itself is very unpopular. Having a candidate like John McCain means that, running as a Republican, you have this giant weight around your neck.

How did this movement, which organized around Barry Goldwater, flowered with Ronald Reagan, and was consummated by George W. Bush, come to embody soaring spending, trillion-dollar deficits, an unpopular war, political corruption, moral decay, and an imperial presidency? How did that happen?

DOUTHAT: That's a mouthful right there.

EDWARDS: Sure is.

But it's true, right?

EDWARDS: Well, one of the things I talk about in my book, Bill, is how during the Gingrich years, some of the things were good. But there was a change in the dynamic for Republicans in Congress and winning power and holding power became the most important goal they had. It wasn't about what they had come there to stand for.

Party loyalty over principle?

EDWARDS: Party loyalty or loyalty to a person. Because what happens is, instead of the president becoming the head of a separate branch of government, all of a sudden you look at him as your team captain. So instead of keeping a check on him, what you do is you find a way to rally around him and help him.

And you said Newt Gingrich actually made the Republicans in Congress the handmaiden of the executive.

EDWARDS: Pretty much.

DOUTHAT: What's interesting about Gingrich is, in the short run, he was trying to change that. He was really the only figure on Capitol Hill in the last few decades who's tried to shift the center of political gravity in Washington back to Congress.

The problem was, the only way he could do it was by trying to rally the GOP around him and make it much more partisan, more like a parliamentary party, really, than a traditional House of Representatives–Senate party. And as a result, once the control of the White House flipped, once the GOP held all three branches, you did have this mentality that Mickey's describing, where Republicans in Congress were on the same team as George W. Bush. And they were going to go along with what whatever he was going do.

But we shouldn't underestimate the impact of 9/11. National traumas always produce overreactions, overconcentrations of executive power. They always produce power grabs in Washington. And if you look at what George W. Bush has done on this front, whether it's the detainee policy as it relates to prisoners in Guantánamo Bay or wiretapping citizens, some of it is an overreach. It also pales in comparison to what happened during World War I. Woodrow Wilson was imprisoning his political enemies. FDR was rounding up Japanese Americans and interning them. And even when you were getting started in politics, J. Edgar Hoover, the FBI, and Lyndon Johnson. So there is this long-term trend toward an imperial presidency. It is troubling. But I'm hopeful that some of it is just a temporary post-9/11 reaction.

EDWARDS: Justice Kennedy said, in the Guantánamo case, that the Constitution is not something to be set aside when it's convenient. And we have this tendency to do it. Every year as we do things like this, we lose a little more of our system of separated powers and checks and balances. And I'm not as sanguine as you are about the fact that we can resume the constitutional system as it was, which is how we protect our liberties.

DOUTHAT: But the challenge for conservatism, as a governing philosophy, is that it's a theory of limited government that's operating in a society and in a framework that was built by liberals. We have the New Deal. At least parts of the Great Society have endured to the present day. And this has always been the challenge for conservatives—that is, how do you govern as a party that's critical of the welfare state when most Americans want you to run the welfare state?

That's why the most successful conservative reforms over the last thirty years haven't been about abolishing government. They've been about taking programs that liberals built and reforming them. The problem is when you run out of things to do on that front. And I think that's one of the deeper problems of the Bush administration. Bush came to power in the late 1990s as a reaction against an overweening small-government fervor on the right.

If the most fundamental tenet of conservatism is small government, how do you explain the fact that Republicans keep expanding it when they are in power?

EDWARDS: I don't think the rationale of conservatism is small government. It's limited government, but that doesn't necessarily mean small. It means that there are areas where you cannot take government. There are areas where the rights of the people are paramount. In the old system, before America, you had rulers and their subjects, right? And the rulers told their subjects what to do. And our idea was that we're going to be citizens, not subjects. We're going to tell the government what to do and where government's not permitted to go. But within those areas the government can act. There's nothing that says it has to be a tiny government if the people themselves are willing to pay the taxes and support certain activities for the government within the Constitution. That's fine.

You've been very concerned about not just small government or limited government but about encroachments on personal liberty by President Bush, who has issued over eleven hundred signing statements, each one of them saying, "I may not respect this law that Congress has passed."

EDWARDS: Which he doesn't have the authority to do, but he's doing it. The problem with President Bush is not the eleven hundred signing statements saying, "I'll decide whether I'm going to obey that law or not." It's the designation of himself as head of the "unitary executive," as he and Vice President Cheney call it, saying that all of the members of all the agencies and departments cannot be told what to do by the Congress.

So it's not that there's one thing that he does, it's a whole pattern of basically saying, "I'm the decider. I'm the commander," or as Scalia put it, the nation's commander in chief, which I didn't know we had. That's not in the Constitution. That's the problem. It's the whole big picture of overreaching.

DOUTHAT: But I want to get back to your point about the size of government, Bill, because I think it's an interesting one. And it's something you hear a lot of complaints on the right about: "How has this happened? We came to power as a small-government movement and yet government has grown over the past thirty years under Republican administrations." However, the economy has also grown enormously. And, in fact, if you look at the government as a percentage of GDP, it's actually only inched up slightly.

Yes, but the economy grew faster under Bill Clinton and the Democrats than it has under George W. Bush.

DOUTHAT: It's true. But the thing about Clinton was that, in a sense—just as Nixon was, in theory, a conservative who often governed like a liberal—Clinton was a liberal who often governed like a conservative. He signed welfare reform. He said the era of big government is over. And I think conservatives really didn't often recognize it at the time. They decided it was more important to destroy him politically than to cooperate with him. And that ended up being a huge lost opportunity for the right.

You said the Republicans set out to destroy Bill Clinton and not to cooperate with him. And like Nixon, Newt Gingrich came to power not to defeat his enemies but to demonize and destroy them.

EDWARDS: If we hadn't gotten into party *über alles*, if we hadn't done that, when Bill Clinton said that we're making changes, the end of welfare as we know it or whatever, we conservatives would have declared victory. If our focus was on ideas and principles and a kind of governance, then it shouldn't have made any difference whether it was a Democratic president or a Republican president.

Instead Republicans impeached the president.

EDWARDS: It was nutty. It was totally nuts.

DOUTHAT: I agree. I do want to say, as a caveat, that there is an extent to which you practice what Pat Buchanan famously termed positive polarization, right? Which was what Nixon was trying to do. You deliberately divide the country because you assume you'll end up with the bigger half. That can be a poisonous force in American politics, but it can also be the way that you get things done. There's a tendency, especially among liberals after a long period of conservative dominance, to say, "Oh, well, it's terrible how Nixon divided the country. It's terrible how Gingrich divided the country." FDR divided the country, too. "They hate me and I welcome their hate," right? That's what he said.

Ross, you write that a party ideologically committed to a small government may be ill-equipped to run a large one.

DOUTHAT: Yes. And I think that's one of the lessons of the Bush years. The Bush administration came into power with the idea that they were going to be a center-right party that reformed the welfare state rather than abolish-ing it and sort of steered a middle course between the small-government purists on the right and liberals.

The problem is, because conservatives are naturally hostile or skeptical of government power, conservatives often don't think deeply enough about what they're actually going to do with government when they take power. And that's how you end up with a lot of the problems in the Bush years where you have people unqualified to run federal agencies being appointed. You have bills getting written up that are really good in theory, but then you look at the details, and they don't actually work.

The challenge for conservatives is to basically prove that liberal argu-ment wrong. Liberals say, "Well, because conservatives are fans of limited government, you can't trust conservatives to run the government we have." Conservatives need to prove them wrong, and they haven't.

How did conservatives come so far in one direction that we ended up with the Congress and the president trying to force Terri Schiavo's husband to keep her alive against his and, apparently, her will? Where do you draw the line on government if not there?

EDWARDS: There are areas that are not the government's business. The fed-eral government should not be overriding doctors. The situation in Oregon is that the voters there are saying that if a person is terminally ill, if more than one doctor has confirmed this person is dying and cannot recover, and that person says, "I want doctors to give me medications, not for them to administer it, but for me to administer it to myself, so I don't have to be in great pain and agony and die in anguish, over a long period of time." The voters said, "Yes, let them be given those medicines." Conservatives stepped in and said, "No, no, no. Our position is that we're the government. We will tell you how to live, and we're going to tell you how to die." That was a com-plete repudiation of everything that those of us who started this modern conservative movement believe in.

DOUTHAT: I agree, this is a real problem for conservatives. You start out with the principle of federalism and certain powers are left to the state. But then when you get control of the federal government, the temptation is to use that power to enact, in this case, conservative legislation about the end of life.

Was that impulse coming from the religious right or the political right?

DOUTHAT: Well, I don't think you can completely separate the two. And this isn't just true of the right. Religion has been a force in American politics going back to the nineteenth century, going back to William Jennings Bryan, going back to the civil rights movement. There is an idea among liberals and some conservatives that religious participation in politics, using religious arguments, is somehow illegitimate, that the separation of church and state means that you can't invoke religious arguments in public.

That's just not true to American political history. Now, it's true that if you only make religious arguments for a given position, if you say, "Abortion is wrong because the Bible tells me so; assisted suicide is wrong because only God has the right to take a life," you're actually not going to make much headway in American politics because we are a religiously pluralistic society. But that doesn't mean that there aren't reasonable arguments.

Mickey just made a very eloquent case for allowing assisted suicide, and I think it's persuasive in certain respects. But there is a case to be made that, in most of the cases where you allow assisted suicide, you're talking about people whose suicidal thoughts are, frankly, a species of depression, illnesses that are treatable. They aren't getting sufficient pain medication. This sets up openings to abuses by doctors, abuses by relatives, and so on. And, you know, the same goes with Terri Schiavo.

But do you agree with what happened then when conservatives brought the issue to Congress and the president flew back from Texas to sign legislation?

DOUTHAT: No, I don't. Because it's a violation of federalism. There are certain issues, especially some legal issues, that have to be left to the states. Here I agree with Mickey, this is a crucial conservative principle. If you look at the initial issue that sparked the rise of the religious right, it was *Roe v. Wade*. Now, what did *Roe v. Wade* do? It took the right to make abortion laws away from legislatures, away from the states, and said, "No, there's a right in the Constitution. You can't legislate about it." Now, if *Roe v. Wade* were overturned tomorrow, and I think this is something a lot of Americans don't understand, abortion wouldn't become illegal. All it would mean is that states and governments have the power or don't have the power to vote on it. And that's the conservative principle. That's where the antiabortion movement comes from. And that's what it was founded on. The danger is, then you take over the federal government and you want to use it to pursue your end, just like liberals do.

Let me explore this. Ross talked about how religion in the past has been invoked in the political arena. But when Martin Luther King called on all of us to follow a higher morality on civil rights, the Democrats then didn't say, "We're the party of God." And there is no question but that the Republican Party now presents itself as the party of God.

DOUTHAT: It's true that the Democrats at that moment didn't say, "We're the party of God." But actually, if you look back through American history, there are lots of moments when prominent figures, Democrats and Republicans alike, have said things along those lines. You look at Theodore Roosevelt's famous speech. He says, "We stand at Armageddon and we battle for the Lord." But I agree with you, Bill. I think that that kind of conflation of God's aims with the interest of a single political party is a real problem. I guess I just think it's more a problem for that party than for American democracy. When I hear Tom DeLay saying, "God's on our side," I think, well, this means the Republican Party's in trouble. It's becoming self-righteous. It's alienating the party from the broad religious diversity of the American people. I'm not really worried about the separation of church and state being breached. I think that separation is actually pretty strong. We're too pluralistic a society to ever have a theocracy. It's impossible to imagine.

Is it conservative to deny what science tells us about global warming?

DOUTHAT: No. But this happens again and again with modern conservatism, and it's a real problem. Conservatives assume that if you don't agree with the liberals on what we should do about global warming—let's say you oppose cap-and-trade regulations, or you oppose a carbon tax—you have to deny that global warming's happening at all. That's a mistake conservatives make time and time again. You see it on the stem cell issue. And I think, no, absolutely, there's nothing conservative about denying the scientific consensus on global warming. It doesn't mean, though, that conservatives should just leap to saying, "Oh, everything Al Gore says we ought to do about it is right."

Mickey, you've upset some of your longtime friends and colleagues by writing, "Conservatives today would have us believe they are the voice of American values. In fact, they are not even the voice of conservative values." Who are you talking about?

EDWARDS: Partly I'm talking about the Tom DeLays. I'm talking about our party coming in and saying, "We're going to tell you when you can die and how you can die. And we're going to come in and tell you that we're going to do electronic wiretapping of your conversations without a court warrant, despite the fact that the law says that a warrant is required."

When Ross mentioned *Roe v. Wade*—and what I'm going to say has no bearing on whether you're for or against abortion or *Roe v. Wade*—but this was a case of not understanding conservative values. Judge Robert Bork, when he was nominated for the Supreme Court, opposed *Roe v. Wade*, on the grounds that the Supreme Court had created a right of privacy that does not exist in the Constitution. I had breakfast with him with a small group. I said, "Did you really say that?" And he said, "Yes." I said, "So tell me, Judge Bork, you believe that the only rights the American people have are those that are spelled out in the Constitution?" And he said, "Yes."

Well, in fact it's the exact opposite. We're born with our rights. And the reason you have the Ninth and Tenth Amendments in the Bill of Rights, and the reason so many patriots like Patrick Henry opposed the Bill of Rights, was because they knew some idiot's going to come along in the twentieth century or twenty-first century and say that unless it's spelled out in here, it's a right the American people don't have. Well, Judge Bork was that idiot. That's what I mean when I say this is where we forget about values and we start thinking that the government has all the rights and we only have those that the government permits us to have. This turns American government on its head.

DOUTHAT: All right. But in defense of Judge Bork, there is a danger with our judicial branch because they have so much authority to interpret the Constitution that they can read rights that don't exist. Did Patrick Henry and the people writing the Constitution think that they were writing a document that protected the right to an abortion? It seems moderately unlikely to me.

So what is the core value that keeps both of you conservative?

EDWARDS: Look, I believe that the conservative movement—the one

Barry Goldwater believed in, that Ronald Reagan came out of—honors the idea of a constitutional system of self-government that protects the rights of the people. That is an incredibly important perspective on the relationship between government and the people. And I refuse to let people take it over who don't believe in it. I refuse to let a Tom DeLay or a Newt Gingrich or whomever turn that on its head.

But how did they take it over, Mickey? Given what you say about Goldwater and Reagan's belief in it?

EDWARDS: It happened out of frustration because Democrats controlled the Congress for so long. We conservatives were in the minority for a very long time.

Forty years.

EDWARDS: And I would say, Bill, the Democratic Party was pretty oppressive, would not let us offer amendments to bills, blocked our contributions at every turn. Conservatives finally reached a point of just so much anger about the way they were being cut out of the process that they came together, putting party loyalty and party control first. So I blame the Democrats for a lot of it. They created the monster and then we built on it.

Why do you remain a conservative, Ross? When I finished your book Grand New Party, *I thought you could be writing speeches for Barack Obama.*

DOUTHAT: Sure, there's language in the book that would sound pretty much right coming from Barack Obama's lips. I think what separates me from Barack Obama and the way I define conservatism starts with what Mickey's talking about. But I guess I have a more expansive definition. I think of American conservatism as the attitude and habit in politics that's dedicated toward defending American exceptionalism in all its forms.

Against?

DOUTHAT: Against the idea that we need to change America in pursuit of some abstract form of justice. Conservatism, broadly speaking, has been arranged against that tendency. And conservatism is for limited government, for a focus on the Constitution, and also for a defense of the particular habits and mores of American life. I think this separates me from Mickey and makes me more of a social conservative than he is in the sense that I think government does have a role to play in conserving those mores and institutions. One of the reasons we don't need the kind of strong central government you have in Europe is precisely because we've always been a nation of strong communities, of strong families, of churches that play a much more enormous role in the social fabric of American life than they do in Europe. Voluntary organizations, the same way. Charitable giving is much higher in the United States than in Europe. This is what American conservatism exists in an ideal form to defend.

If you go back to the 1970s and look at what conservatives wanted to do, they wanted a freer market. They wanted an end to the kind of wage and price controls that Nixon, imitating liberals, imposed. They wanted a reformed welfare system. They wanted a lower tax rate. Starting in the '70s and '80s they wanted a greater role for religion in public life. They wanted freer trade. A lot of what looks like conservative failure today is actually conservative success because so many conservative ideas have become the conventional wisdom.

Then what happened the last eight years that—

DOUTHAT: It's the same thing that happened to the Democratic Party in the late '60s and early '70s. You were there. I'm sure that there were people—

There were plenty of excesses.

DOUTHAT: Right. There were people then who saw those excesses and became conservatives. They were the neoconservatives, right? And there are some conservatives today who will look at their movement foundering and say, "We need to jump ship. We need to go write speeches for Barack Obama." I'm not going to do that for the same reason you didn't jump ship in the '70s. I think there's enough goodness in American conservatism that it's worth staying and fighting for. And America needs two healthy political movements.

EDWARDS: The Republican Party is not healthy. The Republican Party is not healthy at all. It's lost the confidence of the American people. It's lost the confidence of most Republicans. You'd be amazed, Bill, how many people I talk to every day who have been lifelong Republicans who just can't support the party anymore. One of the things that is harmful to John McCain is that people aren't looking at John McCain and asking, "Is he a good guy? Is he a bad guy?" He's got this Republican label around his neck. And I think our party is in quite serious trouble.

DOUTHAT: The Democrats are much healthier. And it's very likely that we're headed for a period of Democratic dominance, maybe four years.

Sure, there's a swelling of support for Obama and there was strong support for Clinton despite the Lewinsky affair. I'm not a practicing Democrat. I don't defend the Democratic Party. In fact, I look at the party in Congress and how beholden it is to wealthy interests, corporate interests. Democrats have lost their ties to working people.

DOUTHAT: A deeper problem for the Democrats is they're going to probably sweep into power this November. They already swept into power in Congress. They're going to have a large majority. But the question is, what do they do with it? When political movements take power, it helps to have a defined agenda.

This was why Ronald Reagan was so great. When Ronald Reagan was elected president in 1980, everybody knew it was a revolution because Reagan had been going around saying the same things for fifteen years. People knew what he stood for. The challenge for the Democrats is, yeah, there are some new ideas. There are some old ideas from back in the 1970s that they're rehabilitating. But when you watch the primary season, Barack Obama goes out and attacks free trade. And then when the general election comes, it's time to pivot and be for free trade. I think that the only good news for the Republicans right now in this moment of near Democratic triumph is that the Democrats are not positioned to establish a twenty-year majority.

EDWARDS: There's one other big problem for Democrats here. As I said, the Republican label is really hurting, and the Democratic label right now is very popular. But liberalism is not popular. In these by-elections this year, where Democrats were picking up seats that had been held a long time by Republicans, those were not liberal Democrats who were winning those seats. The country is not turning to the left. It's just turning against the Republicans.

DOUTHAT: Although to be fair, the Democratic majority that existed when you came of age, Bill, did depend on conservative Democrats. Sometimes having some ideological distinctions in your majority is a sign that you've got a really big majority.

The subtitle of your book is How Republicans Can Win the Working Class and Save the American Dream. *We share a concern that ordinary working people in this country are having real trouble making a living wage. The paucity of jobs that pay living wages is the great moral as well as economic crisis in America today, and neither party has fully addressed that. Conservatives won under Nixon with the "Silent Majority." Reagan won with "Reagan Democrats"—the working class that came over to the Republican Party. But I don't see what any of those people have gotten from the conservative revolution because they're worse off today in real wages, adjusted for inflation, than they were thirty years ago when you came to power.*

DOUTHAT: I'll push back on that argument a little bit. I think there are a lot of ways in which the working class is better off than they were in that era. I think just looking at wages is misleading because one of the things that's happened, thanks to free trade, thanks to policies that Republicans have championed, is prices. The cost of living has fallen dramatically across the board for Americans. If you look at the goods the poor and the working class buy versus the goods the rich buy, the goods that the poor and working class buy today are vastly cheaper than they used to be.

You're not saying that workers face wage stagnation?

DOUTHAT: No, workers do face wage stagnation. But those wages do, in fact, buy more goods than they used to buy. There are ways in which the working class is better off. But yes, on the big picture I agree with you. Republicans need a tax policy that helps people investing in America's future in another way, people struggling to raise families. So in the book we talk a lot about making the tax code more family-friendly, making it easier for people to have two kids, to have three kids, to put those kids through school.

Have working people benefited from these tax cuts to the rich? We have greater gaps between rich and poor today than we did in 1929.

EDWARDS: And a part of that is that our focus has changed. We used to be a party that prided itself on being the party of small business. We were for entrepreneurs, and we were for free enterprise, and more and more we seem to have become a party that idolizes big business, that supports big business in every way it can. Actually, if you go back to the Goldwater years, we were a party very much like what Ross is saying we need to become. And we got away from it.

It seems to me that both parties have contributed to the instability of working people today.

DOUTHAT: It's true. But I think one of the things that's changed in America over the past fifty years is you now have a mass upper class in a way you didn't before. It used to be you had the rich, you had the middle class, you had the working class, and you had the poor. Now there's been an explosion of wealth for highly educated Americans—Americans with college degrees, but especially with postgrad degrees—over the last thirty years. You see it especially in big cities on the coast. You see it in New York. You see it in Washington. You see it in Boston. And this has created a real constituency both for the Republicans and for the Democrats for policies pitched to these voters.

   Look at what Bill Clinton pushed. He would get up and give speeches about the need to make college affordable, right? And that's obviously a really important thing. But the way they went about making college affordable was by pushing for scholarships that went to upper-income families because that's a big constituency that likes getting merit-based scholarships, that likes getting financial aid to help them out. But that isn't where the American public education system actually ought to be focused.

If capitalism promotes inequality, as it does, shouldn't democracy try to strike a balance and promote fairness?

EDWARDS: Capitalism, in theory, does not promote inequality.

But in practice.

EDWARDS: What capitalism promotes is that if you are willing to invest your time and money to provide a service, a benefit, a product that is useful, you're going to get a reward for it, and that's going to cause you to do more. And you're going to create jobs. We have allowed the system to grow to where it has nothing to do with free trade. So we support people like Ivan Boesky and Boone Pickens and these predators . . .

Mickey, some of your conservative critics say you've gone soft.

EDWARDS: Right.

That your plans for reclaiming conservatism laid out in your book would take policy positions that John Edwards would love. You're against the war in Iraq and the Patriot Act. You would have the government protect abortion rights and the right of states to sanction gay marriage. You're suspicious of NAFTA and big business. And you're against the No Child Left Behind Act. One of my colleagues asked me, why isn't Mickey Edwards Obama's running mate? Because these are positions that would fit very comfortably on that side of the spectrum.

EDWARDS: Those are positions that for decades conservatives believed, conservatives championed. Keeping certain things out of the hands of the federal government, allowing people to make their own decisions, I haven't moved. I am where I was when we started out as conservatives. I've been a loyal Republican all my life, but my loyalty to my party does not transcend my loyalty to the principles that got me into politics in the first place.

DOUTHAT: And there's a tendency in American politics to say, well, if you're not for George W. Bush, you must be for Barack Obama.

EDWARDS: Absolutely.

DOUTHAT: No Child Left Behind, right? You brought that up. That's a good example. Why do you oppose No Child Left Behind? I assume it's because you think the federal government shouldn't be messing around with state education systems. Why do liberals oppose No Child Left Behind? Because it didn't spend enough money messing around with state education systems. So there's a huge diversity of political views that don't fall neatly into a "you're for Obama" or "you're for McCain" kind of camp.

EDWARDS: There is a line here. The people who are attacking me are post-Reagan people. I don't even know what they represent, but it is not conservatism.

They call themselves conservatives. Don't you think Rush Limbaugh considers himself the voice of conservatism?

EDWARDS: Well, I'm sure he considers himself the voice of everything. But look, the fact is the people who created the conservative movement, the people who were the Goldwater-Reagan people who wrote those platforms, insisted that the District of Columbia have a vote in Congress. In Arizona, Planned Parenthood gives an annual Barry Goldwater Award. Why? Because we believe in the free choice of people.

DOUTHAT: I'm certainly not part of the Republican power structure right now. Mickey and I disagree on a lot of stuff and represent kind of different visions for the Republican Party. But I think Rush Limbaugh would pretty much hate us both.

EDWARDS: Yes!

DOUTHAT: And that's a problem. But there is a tendency, too, among conservatives to pine for the golden age. When Ronald Reagan took power, after a couple of years people were already saying, "He's betraying conservatism," and—

EDWARDS: Let Reagan be Reagan, right?

DOUTHAT: Let Reagan be Reagan. The revolution is always being betrayed.

EDWARDS: I'm not longing for a golden age. I'm longing for adherence to the Constitution of the United States because when we talk about American exceptionalism, that's what it is. It's not our wealth. It's not our military. What makes us exceptional is our form of self-government, that keeps most of the major powers—whether to go to war, what our tax policies ought to be, how much we spend—keeps them in the hands of the people through their representatives.

What's the one thing that Republicans could do to win over the stagnating working class?

DOUTHAT: I think the biggest thing Republicans could do to win them over is to marry the language of family values—the pro-family party—to an agenda that goes beyond abortion and gay marriage. Being a pro-family party, being on the side of the American family, especially the working-class family, has to go beyond those. We have to look at health care. We have to look at the tax code. We have to look at all these areas that affect the well-being of American moms and dads and their kids.

It has to do the things that liberals have been talking about?

DOUTHAT: It doesn't have to do the things that liberals have been talking about, but it has to address the issues that liberals have been talking about in a conservative way. If you read our book, you won't find a lot of specific policy proposals that liberals embrace. This is why I'm not writing speeches for Barack Obama. He isn't going to sign up for the policy ideas that I support. But he is talking about the right issues.

Your book is subtitled Reclaiming Conservatism. *What's the most important thing conservatives can do to reclaim their philosophy?*

EDWARDS: We have to start standing for principle. We need to go back to "What kind of a government did we create?" You know, I came out of a very poor background, and I agree totally that we need to be addressing the concerns of the working class. But we have a system of government that keeps power in the hands of the people through their representatives. And we can't lose that. That's what we have to do. We have to stand for principle again instead of being a party that only stands for "How can we defeat Democrats?" ∾

GRACE LEE BOGGS

Grace Lee Boggs has lived in the same house in Detroit for more than half of her ninety-five years. She has seen that city, which had been the arsenal of democracy during World War II and had put America on wheels in the auto boom that followed, decline around her. Even before the riots of 1967—she calls them "a rebellion"—carmakers were merging and moving out of town to get close to new markets. Automation arrived and squeezed skilled workers out of a livelihood. The city's middle class headed for the suburbs; in the 1950s Detroit's population dropped by almost 200,000 people. Grace Lee Boggs was not among them; she would not be moved.

Despite the tumultuous changes around her, she remains a buoyant believer in grassroots democracy. In the last century, she has been a part of almost every major movement in the United States: labor, civil rights, black power, women's rights and environmental justice. Activists one-third her age have to run to keep up with her.

In 1992, she and her late husband—autoworker and organizer James Boggs—worked with other activists to found Detroit Summer, described as "a multicultural, intergenerational youth program to rebuild, redefine and respirit Detroit from the ground up." And in 2004, she helped organize the Beloved Communities Project, "an initiative begun to identify, explore and form a network of communities committed to and practicing the profound *pursuit of justice, radical inclusivity, democratic governance, health and wholeness, and social/individual transformation."*

Even as she has remained rooted in one neighborhood and one house, and writing an always spirited blog, she seems constantly on the road, speaking, cajoling, inspiring, prodding, and admonishing others to organize, organize, organize. Over her long life she has tried one radical idea after another, embracing some, discarding others, fashioning new ones of her own in her passion for a more humane and egalitarian America. Her passion springs from her own fascinating life story. She was born in Providence, Rhode Island, to immigrant Chinese. During the Roaring Twenties her father ran a popular Chinese restaurant on Broadway near Times Square, but to buy the land for their first house across the river in Queens, he had to put the deed in the name of an Irish contractor because Asians were prohibited to own land there. Every week Grace spent hours at the local library, winning a Regents scholarship to Barnard College and ultimately earning a doctorate in philosophy from Bryn Mawr. Quite a trip, considering that when she was born, the waiters in the family restaurant suggested that she be taken away and left on a hillside because "she's just a girl."

—Bill Moyers

———※———

And that's a true story—the waiters saying, "Dispose of her"?

Yes. I attribute some of my activism to being born female above a Chinese restaurant, where I quickly got the idea that a lot of things in this world needed to be changed.

Yet you came to identify, over the years, far more with the black American world than with the Chinese American world.

When I was growing up, Asians were so few and far between as to be almost invisible. The idea of an Asian American movement in this country was unthinkable.

What I'm trying to figure out is how it is that the daughter of a Chinese entrepreneur in New York City goes to Bryn Mawr at a very early age, gets her

Ph.D. in 1940, before the Second World War, becomes a Marxist theorist, an activist in the socialist movement, moves on to become a disciple of Martin Luther King, and having outlived all those theories and those characters and leaders, is still agitating for what she calls "democracy."

I had no idea what I was going to do after I got my degree in philosophy in 1940. But what I did know was at that time, if you were a Chinese American, even department stores wouldn't hire you. They'd come right out and say, "We don't hire Orientals." So the idea of my getting a job teaching in a university was really ridiculous. I went to Chicago and I got a job in the philosophy library there for $10 a week, and I found a little old Jewish woman right near the university who took pity on me and said I could stay in her basement rent-free. The only obstacle was that I had to face down a barricade of rats in order to get into her basement. And at that time, in the black communities, they were beginning to protest and struggle against rat-infested housing. I joined one of the tenants' organizations and thereby came in touch with the black community for the first time in my life.

One of your first heroes in that community was A. Philip Randolph, the charismatic labor leader who had won a long struggle to organize black railroad porters in the 1930s. With World War II going on, he was furious that blacks were being turned away from good-paying jobs in the booming defense plants. He took his argument to President Roosevelt, who was sympathetic but reluctant to act. Randolph told him that "power is the active principle of only the organized masses," and called for a huge march on Washington to shame the president. It worked. FDR backed down and signed an order banning discrimination in the defense industry. All over America blacks moved from the countryside into the cities to take up jobs, the first time in four hundred years that black men could bring home a regular paycheck. You watched all that unfold.

And when I saw what a movement could do, I said, "Boy, that's what I wanna do with my life." It was just amazing. I mean, how you have to take advantage of a crisis in the system and in the government and also press to meet the needs of the people who are struggling for dignity. Very tricky.

It does take moral force to bring on political change.

Too much of our emphasis on struggle has simply been confrontation and not enough recognition of how spiritual and moral force is involved in the people who are struggling.

Power never gives up anything voluntarily. People have to demand it.

Well, as Frederick Douglass said, "Power yields nothing without a struggle." But how one struggles, I think, is now a very challenging question.

You learned a lot from Jimmy Boggs, the man you married in 1954. He was a radical activist, organizer, and writer. You couldn't have been outwardly more different—he was a black man, an autoworker from Alabama, and you were a Chinese American college-educated philosopher. But the marriage lasted four decades until Jimmy died, right?

Yes. I owe a great deal of my rootedness to Jimmy, because he learned to write in a community where nobody could read and write. He picked cotton and then went to work in Detroit. He saw himself as having been part of one epoch, the agricultural epoch, then the industrial epoch, and now the postindustrial epoch. A very important part of what we need in this country is that sense that we have lived through so many stages and that we are entering into a new stage where we could create something completely different. Jimmy had that sense.

Help me understand what Jimmy meant when he wrote this letter to the philosopher Bertrand Russell: "Negroes in the United States still think they are struggling for democracy, when in fact, democracy is what they are struggling against."

Folks don't understand, for example, how the Democratic Party was a coalition of labor and liberals from the North, and racists like Senator Bilbo and Senator Eastland and all those Ku Klux Klanners down South. That was American democracy. People lived under awful conditions and that was called democracy. Fortunately, we broke through that in the '60s.

In the summer of 1967, you were living in Detroit when a police raid exploded into violence. You saw fires rage across the city, including in your own neighborhood. President Johnson called out the U.S. Army, and the nation watched on television, horrified as the city burned. The press called it a violent spasm of riots and lawlessness. But you saw something in those flames that many outsid-

ers missed. Your neighborhood was suffering the slow bleed of manufacturing jobs from the city. Twice as many blacks were out of work as whites. You have objected to descriptions of what happened as "a riot."

We in Detroit called it "the rebellion" because we understood there was a righteousness about the young people rising up.

Against?

Against both the police, which they considered an occupation army, and against what they sensed had become their expendability because of high tech. Black people had been valued, over hundreds of years, for their labor, and their labor was now being taken away from them.

And this question of work was at the heart of what happened in Detroit that summer?

I don't think that they were conscious of it. What I saw happen was that young people who recognized that working in the factory was what had allowed their parents to buy a house, to raise a family, to get married, to send their kids to school—that was eroding. They felt that no one cared anymore. What we tried to do is explain that a rebellion is righteous, because it's the protest by a people against injustice, but it's not enough. You have to go beyond rebellion. And it was amazing, a turning point in my life, because until that time, I had not made a distinction between a rebellion and revolution. And it forced us to begin thinking, what does a revolution mean? How does it relate to evolution?

That's when you began to take a closer look at the teachings of Martin Luther King Jr., right? He was wrestling with how to go beyond the civil rights movement to a profound transformation of society, and he came to New York's Riverside Church in the spring of 1967 to challenge inequality throughout America and to call for an end to America's war in Southeast Asia. But the war continued another seven years. His moral argument did not take hold with the powers that be.

I don't expect moral arguments to take hold with the powers that be. They are in their positions of power. They are part of the system. They are part of the problem.

Then do moral arguments have any force if they can be so heedlessly ignored?

Of course they do. I think because we depend too much on the government to do it, we're not looking sufficiently at what is happening at the grassroots in the country. We have not emphasized sufficiently the cultural revolution that we have to make among ourselves in order to force the government to do differently. Things do not start with governments.

But Martin Luther King was ignored on the war. In fact, the last few years of his life, as he was moving beyond the protest in the South, he was largely ignored, if not ridiculed, for his position on economic inequality. Many civil rights leaders, as you remember, Grace, condemned him for mixing foreign policy with civil rights. They said that's not what we should be about.

But see, he was talking about a radical revolution of values. And that radical revolution of values has not been pursued in the last forty years. The consumerism, materialism, has gotten worse. The militarism has continued, while people are just using their credit cards to get by. All that's been taking place. Would he have continued to challenge those? I think he would.

He said that the giant triplets of America were racism, consumerism or materialism, and militarism. And you're saying those haven't changed.

I'm saying that not only have those not changed, but people have isolated the struggles against each of these from the other. They have not seen that they're part of one whole, of a radical revolution of values that we all must undergo.

Whose failing is that?

I'm not sure I would use the word *failing*. I would say that people who have engaged in one struggle tend to be locked into that struggle.

When you look back, who do you think was closer to the truth, Karl Marx or Martin Luther King? The truth about human society.

King was an extraordinary thinker. He read Marx. He was serious about reading Marx. He was also serious about reading Hegel, about reading Gandhi, about Jesus Christ and Christianity. Marx belongs to a particular period. King was a man of our time.

Where is the movement today?

I believe that we are at the point now, in the United States, where a movement is beginning to emerge. I think that the calamity, the quagmire of the Iraq War, the outsourcing of jobs, the dropout of young people from the education system, the monstrous growth of the prison-industrial complex, the planetary emergency in which we are engulfed at the present moment—demand that instead of just complaining about these things, instead of just protesting about these things, we begin to look for, and hope for, another way of living. I see a movement beginning to emerge, because I see hope beginning to trump despair.

But where do you see signs of it?

I see signs in the various small groups that are emerging all over the place to try and regain our humanity in very practical ways. For example in Milwaukee, Wisconsin, Will Allen, who is a former basketball player, has purchased two acres of land, with five greenhouses on it, and is beginning to grow food, healthy food, for his community. And communities are growing up around that idea. That's a huge change in the way that we think of the city. I mean, the things we have to restore are so elemental. Not just food, and not just healthy food, but a different way of relating to time and history and to the earth.

And a garden does that for you?

Yes. A garden does all sorts of things. It helps young people to relate to the earth in a different way. It helps them to relate to their elders in a different way; it helps them to think of time in a different way.

How so?

Well, if we just press a button and you think that's the key to reality, you're in a hell of a mess as a human being.

Our economic system doesn't reflect the values you espouse—you know that. Outsourcing of jobs, the flight of capital, capital's grip on workers. The system isn't catching up with you.

Well, don't expect the system to catch up—the system is part of the system! What I think is that, not since the '30s have American people, ordinary Americans, faced such uncertainty with regard to the economic system. In the '30s, we confronted management and were able thereby to gain many advantages, particularly to gain a respect for the dignity of labor. That's no longer possible today because of the ability of corporations to fly all over the place and begin setting up all this outsourcing. So people are finding other ways to regain control over the way they make their living.

A lot of young people out there would agree with your analysis. And then they will say, "What can I do that's practical? How do I make the difference that Grace Lee Boggs is talking about?"

I would say do something local. Do something real, however, small. There was a time when we believed that if we just achieved political power it would solve all our problems. And I think what we learned from the experience of the Russian Revolution, all those revolutions, is that those who try to get power in the state become part of the state. They become locked into its practices. And we have to begin creating new practices. Right where we live.

Do you see any leaders who are advocating such change?

I don't see any leaders, and I think we have to rethink the concept of "leader." We need to embrace the idea that we are the leaders we've been looking for. ～

JAMES K. GALBRAITH

*Perhaps we'll never know how much Ayn Rand influenced Alan Greenspan all those years ago when they were close friends in New York City. She was, of course, one of the notable fantasists of the twentieth century, writing two famous books—*The Fountainhead *and* Atlas Shrugged—*based on the ideology of radical self-interest and an unblinking acceptance of unregulated capitalism. In the Gospel according to Rand, the business world was constantly beleaguered by evil forces practicing—gasp—altruism! Yes, the unselfish regard for the welfare of others was a menace to greed, and Rand would have none of it; she advocated the abolition of all government regulation except what might be needed to deal with crime.*

Greenspan has since downplayed her influence on him, but as chairman of the Federal Reserve for almost twenty years, he seemed quite the faithful disciple as he observed Wall Street's "irrational exuberance" with the detachment of a bored nanny on a park bench watching her young charges squabble over candy.

Then, after that "irrational exuberance" had brought down Wall Street, cratered the economy, and cost millions of Americans their homes, jobs, and pensions, Atlas—I mean, Greenspan—shrugged. On October 23, 2008, he confessed to Congress.

ALAN GREENSPAN: I made a mistake in presuming that the self-interests of organizations, specifically banks and others, were such as that they were best capable of protecting their own shareholders and their equity in the firms. . . .

CHAIRMAN HENRY WAXMAN: In other words, you found that your view of the world, your ideology, was not right, it was not working.

ALAN GREENSPAN: Absolutely. Precisely. You know, that's precisely the reason I was shocked, because I have been going for forty years or more with very considerable evidence that it was working exceptionally well.

Blindsided by reality, if Alan Greenspan had wanted to do penance and himself some good, he could have curled up with economist James K. Galbraith's book, The Predator State: How Conservatives Abandoned the Free Market and Why Liberals Should Too. *Galbraith served as executive director of the U.S. Congress's Joint Economic Committee. He now holds the Lloyd M. Bentsen Jr. Chair in Government/Business Relations at the LBJ School of Public Affairs at the University of Texas and directs the university's Inequality Project, which analyzes wages and earnings and patterns of industrial change around the world. Galbraith asks questions that seem never to have occurred either to Ayn Rand as she journeyed deep into fantasyland or to her many wide-eyed acolytes: "If conservatives no longer take free markets seriously, why should liberals? . . . Why not build a new economic policy based on what is really happening?"*

Or, as I theorized when we began our conversation, perhaps irrational exuberance had been overtaken by existential dread.

—Bill Moyers

⁓

Could the adrenaline of fear push us over the brink into panic so that we stop acting rationally or deliberately?

Fear is a factor. But we have an enormous advantage over our predecessors in 1929. We have the fact that the New Deal happened. And we have the institutions of the New Deal. Though they have been badly damaged in the last decade, they are still with us. We have deposit insurance. We have Social Security. We have a government that is capable of acting as the lender of last resort, which can borrow and spend as needed to deal with this crisis.

So here in the United States the capacity to handle the crisis exists. What we need is a government that's willing to use that capacity, that believes in it. And that's where the collapse of the old objectivism of Alan Greenspan is such a fundamental feature of the present situation, and very timely. With the collapse of that system of ideas, perhaps the way will be cleared for thinking afresh and clearly about the problems that we face and how to solve them.

We've seen a breakdown of an entire system. The consequence of deregulation, of failing supervision of the banking system, has been to cause a collapse of trust, a poisoning of the well.

Banks no longer trust each other because they no longer know whether their counterparties are solvent. Customers no longer trust the banking system. Banks no longer trust the people who would like to borrow from them for commercial purposes. This is a poisoned well. It is going to take a fair amount of time for it to be cleaned up.

What's the worst-case scenario you think about late at night?

Right now the thing that troubles me most is not the United States. The thing that troubles me most is that the same ideas of deregulation, of free markets, were applied in the construction of modern Europe. And the Europeans don't have the institutions of the New Deal, a central bank that can lend as necessary.

Mercifully, we have the institutions of government in this country that can act. The Europeans are winging it. They have to go against their charter of the Central Bank, against the Maastricht Treaty and its restrictions on government spending, government deficits. Their problem is a systemic problem. Our problem is a policy problem. We can solve our problem.

The other calamity is that people nearing retirement and the elderly have really been hit hard in their pension plans. What happens to them?

Well, you can't make people whole individually because everybody made different portfolio choices. Some were more in the stock market, some less. Those who were more in the stock market have been hurt harder. What you can do is protect the population as a whole. And we have a system for doing that. It's called Social Security.

Today, it supports about 40 percent of the American elderly population that basically has no other income. It's more than half of the retirement income of maybe 50 or 60 percent of that population. Social Security benefits, except for inflation adjustment, haven't been raised in a generation. We ought to think about replacing the losses to some degree in the aggregate that have occurred in the markets by raising Social Security benefits and particularly raising them for the poorest and most vulnerable.

But you and others have been calling for more spending because that's the only way you say to get capital into the system. Critics ask, where's that money going to come from?

The government has no problem with money. What we're learning, first of all, is that the dollar remains the anchor currency of the world. Uncle Sam's credit is excellent. Uncle Sam can borrow short-term for practically nothing these days. Everybody wants to have Treasury bills and bonds because they're safe. Uncle Sam can borrow for twenty years at 4.3 percent. That's the same rate that the United States could borrow at for twenty years in the last month of the Eisenhower administration. So from our point of view, we're actually well placed—I mean, the government of the United States—is well placed to take the lead in pulling the country and the world out of crisis.

The deficit isn't beyond sight. The deficits in the Bush administration in relation to the size of the economy were never all that large. They were certainly larger than they were under Clinton, but that was in part necessary because of the changed economic situation, the collapse of the dot-com bubble in 2000. The United States government's credit is good. The deficit is a financial number that people are going to have to get used to because there is no way in these circumstances of avoiding an increase in the deficit.

One of two things can happen. The government can take action and help stabilize the economy, in which case we will have more spending but also more employment. Or the government cannot take action and let the economy collapse, in which case we will have much less tax revenue. The deficit is going to be larger either way. There is no way of avoiding that. The only question is, do you work to have a good economy or do you accept a terrible economy?

What are the negative effects of a soaring deficit?

Well, the one thing I would have worried about is that we might not find lenders who are willing to provide funds to the U.S. government, that the Chinese or the Japanese might decide that they would rather be in some other currency and that we'd then have trouble with inflation. But that's not going to happen, because, as it turns out, the major alternative, the euro, simply isn't viable as a reserve asset for the rest of the world. It's the dollar or nothing. So the United States basically can finance itself to the extent necessary to deal with this crisis.

You call your book The Predator State. *Why that title?*

What I mean is the people who took over the government were not interested in reducing the government and having a small government, the conservative principle. They were interested in using these great institutions for private benefit, to place them in the control of their friends and to put them to the use of their clients. They wanted to privatize Social Security. They created a Medicare drug benefit in such a way as to create the maximum profit for pharmaceutical companies. They used trade agreements to extend patent protections for various interests or to promote the expansion of corporate agriculture's markets in the third world, a whole range of things that were basically political and clientelistic. That's the predator state.

You call it a "corporate republic." Which means that the purpose of government is to divert funds from the public sector to the private sector?

I think it's very clear. They also turned over the regulatory apparatus to the regulated industries, they turned over the henhouse to the foxes in every single case. And that is the source of the abandonment of environmental responsibility, the source of the collapse of consumer protection, and the source of the collapse of the financial system. They all trace back to a common root, which is the failure to maintain a public sector that works in the public interest, that provides discipline and standards, a framework within which the private sector can operate and compete. That's been abandoned.

What kind of regulation wouldn't punish entrepreneurial talent but protect the public interest?

Well, first of all, anyone who thought that voluntary regulation could work was either being dishonest or delusional. Voluntary regulation is regulation that, by its nature, you can evade. And what happens is that the people who are most intent on evading it, on not respecting the standards, come to take over the process. Their profits are better. And so they drive the complying firms and businesses to the wall. They outcompete them.

You need to have a mandatory system so that the firms that are more technologically progressive, which are safer, which are more compliant, which are prudent in the financial sector, which maintain credit standards, have a competitive chance. That's the first purpose of regulation. When it's done properly, it's a framework that favors the more efficient, the more progressive, the elements that are prepared to work within the guidelines set by a larger public purpose.

What kind of regulation do you think might be most effective?

Well, first of all, we need to clean up the mess that's there. The regulatory system, going forward, is going to have to treat banking like a utility, with limitations on growth, on rate of return, and on credit in such a way as to be much more transparent, to make it much easier to evaluate financial products that are traded. None of this over-the-counter, occult, too-complex-to-value stuff.

We need to end the offshore tax havens and other ways in which institutions have hidden from their responsibility to the country to pay their share of taxes. And we need to have a set of prudential standards that are reasonable and that basically can put the business of finance on a sustainable footing. It'll be a much less glamorous business going forward. But it will be more reliable for the country as a whole.

You are such an experienced economist in your own right that I hesitate to bring the spirit of your father to this table. He would have been one hundred last week. One of his classic books is The Great Crash of 1929. *Is the situation today comparable to what happened then?*

The situation today is very similar to the moment of panic and collapse that we saw in 1929, and for very similar reasons: an abandonment of the supervisory responsibility that should have been applied to keep the speculation and the fraud and the abuse from getting out of control. So there's going to be a major period of correction. But Dad, in writing this in 1954, talks about how memory fades and how, so long as people remembered '29, it wouldn't be repeated; eventually it would be forgotten, and the underlying speculative impulse would come back.

So the book, in addition to being a great read, is really prescient in a very balanced way. But I will say that we're not going to go back to 1929 because in 1929 we hadn't had Roosevelt. We hadn't had Kennedy and Johnson. We have had them now. So we have a body of history to work with.

There's a precedent, you're saying; there are tools there if people want to use them.

Not only precedent, there are institutions. There's a government structure. And if we use them, we can't avoid '29, but we can avoid 1930 and 1931, 1932, when output fell by a third, unemployment rose to 25 percent of the labor force, and a third or more of the banks in the country closed and people lost their savings. In fact, we are already in a position of moving to take steps to prevent that from happening. We need to recognize, though, that we can never go back to a system of this kind of buccaneering, finance-driven, Wall Street–led economy in which a group of people who are profoundly unqualified to run the country are, in fact, dictating policy from their perches in Manhattan.

What about the argument that it was actually the government's excesses and failures in the '80s and '90s that contributed to what began to happen in 2007 with the meltdown. That we must not criminalize business or raise taxes and dry up the economy.

First of all, I very much agree that it was failures of government that were responsible for this. It was the actual failure, the abandonment, the neglect of the supervisory and regulatory responsibility. That's at the root of this. Just as you cannot prosper without a private economy, you cannot prosper without an effective autonomous government capable of thinking for itself, capable of balancing things out, of standing for other interests, of standing for labor and consumers and for the public interest as a whole. If you don't have that, you're going to get these pyramids, these bubbles, these epidemics of fraud and abuse, and ultimately the collapse of trust and the collapse of the economy itself. That's what happened in the predator state.

You wrote that after World War II our American system wasn't imperial: "We spoke instead of community, of freedom, of common purposes and common values, and the world took us seriously because we had paid our dues." What's happened now?

It's clear that the world has lost its confidence in the responsible role of the United States. The invasion of Iraq is seen as reckless and self-serving rather than a necessary step to protect the mutual security.

In the financial sector, the world viewed us as a safe haven because they believed we had effective systems for legality, transparency, and security. That's taken a hard knock. But we are rescued for the moment by the fact that other people's systems turn out to be even worse.

How does this compare with what happened after the Great Crash in '29?

If you look at the trends in world trade and manufacturing, they're very similar. There's been a massive collapse that is comparable in scale to 1930. The overall economy hasn't come down nearly as much, and the reason for that is that we have the institutions that were created in the New Deal and the Great Society, institutions of the welfare state, Social Security. And, of course, there has been the influence of John Maynard Keynes, which gave us a very quick reaction in the form of the expansion bill and of the stimulus package. That also has kept the damage from being as large as it was from 1930 to '32.

What we're seeing today is distress of a different kind. The great wealth that the American middle class built up, over seventy years, largely in their homes, has been impaired—in many cases, wiped out. Their mortgages are worth more than the houses that they live in. Many millions more simply can't sell, can't move, can't change their circumstances, don't have a cushion.

My father was in his mid-twenties at the time of the Great Crash of 1929. That experience defined his life.

The same was true of my grandfather on my mother's side, who was a lawyer whose practice depended on the prosperity of the 1920s. My mother, who lived until last year, never really overcame the attitudes that were inculcated in her in the Great Depression. If something is not done to provide, particularly, young people, who are looking for work and cannot find it, with an opportunity to move on in life at this stage, it will mark them for the rest of their lives. I think there's no doubt about that.

The New York Times had a story just the other day about community colleges being so crowded right now that they're holding classes up until two o'clock in the morning. What does that say to us?

First of all, it says that people cannot find jobs. And second, they are looking to the educational system to provide them with something to do, and some way out of this dilemma. But until jobs are created, and in great numbers, there will not be places for those people to come out of the community college system and find useful work.

So what are our options?

We need to find another path for economic expansion. We need to set a strategic direction. Our problem now, our big social and environmental problem, is energy. It's climate change. It's the greenhouse gas emission issue. If we built a set of institutions that could deal with that problem effectively, you could employ a large part of the labor force for a generation. And you'd then make that profitable for private enterprise to get into in a serious way.

After all of the mergers, shakedowns, losses of the last year, you have five gargantuan financial institutions driving the system, right?

And they're highly profitable, and they are already paying, in some cases, extraordinary bonuses. And you have an enormous problem as the public sees very clearly that a very small number of people really have been kept afloat by public action. And yet there is no visible benefit to people who are looking for jobs or people who are looking to try and save their houses or to somehow get out of a catastrophic personal debt situation.

When President Obama came into office, people said, "This is a Rooseveltian moment. This is a moment to seize a crisis and do what FDR did."

Well, the public is way ahead of the political system. The public certainly wanted a Rooseveltian moment. The Congress, the Washington press corps, wanted a return to their familiar patterns of activity. In general, they're always more comfortable dealing with the issues they know than framing ideas. And so Obama's objective situation is much more like Herbert Hoover's than it is like Roosevelt's. When Roosevelt came in, in March 1933, there were machine gun nests on the rooftops of Washington for the inaugural parade, the banks were closed, everybody knew that you needed immediate action. Roosevelt's cabinet was sworn in on the first day. He had initiatives ready to go. This was not the situation that faced President Obama, by any stretch.

Suppose that your father were around in September '08, the time of the great collapse. Do you think he might have said, "Aha. Told you so?"

He did say, "I told you so," in *The Great Crash*. He talked about the conditions under which it would recur, and he said, "No one can doubt that the American people remain susceptible to the speculative mood—to the conviction that enterprise can be attended by unlimited rewards in which they, individually, were meant to share. A rising market can still bring the reality of riches. . . . The government preventatives and controls are ready. In the hands of a determined government their efficacy cannot be doubted. There are, however, a hundred reasons why a government will determine not to use them." And that's the point about the crisis. It could have been prevented. The people in authority two, three, five years ago knew how to prevent it. They chose not to act, because they were getting a political and an economic benefit out of the speculative explosion that was occurring.

You mean the people who could have prevented the dam from breaking were too busy fishing above it and reaping big rewards to want to fix the crack in it?

Sure. The Federal Reserve in particular knew that the dam was cracking. Alan Greenspan, I think, almost surely knew this, and chose to wait until it had washed away.

Why?

Because they were getting a superficially stronger economy out of it. The ownership society, all that was a scam, basically, designed to lure people who could never afford these mortgages into accepting them. And yes, I think they, any rational person, certainly people in the industry, knew that this was not going to last. There was a little industry code, I've learned: IBGYBG, "I'll be gone. You'll be gone."

But that's criminal fraud.

Oh, sure. There was a huge amount of it.

The perplexing question to me is whether or not you can reform a system that is so infiltrated by money from the people who are benefiting from what's going on, who have a vested interest, and use their money to promote that vested interest to make sure nothing changes.

I think you can. I think the law is powerful. I think you cannot legalize financial fraud. You cannot fully conceal the tracks of financial fraud. You have to put the resources in to uncover it. You have to prosecute it. You have to give appropriate punishments, but we have a system in this country for doing that. It is a question of making a decision to use the judicial resources that we have to clean up the system.

I think what you also have to do is aim to reduce the market power of these enormous, strategically, systemically dangerous institutions. And the way to do that is by reimposing some internal barriers, the Glass-Steagall separation of commercial and investment banking. By auditing and resolving the institutions that are really close to failure. Those institutions, if they're taken out of the picture, would permit smaller banks that did not get caught up in this dreadful business to grow into their market roles. And you would have a more competitive and healthier financial system.

Is our system so vulnerable that this is going to keep happening? After all, there was 1929, the savings and loan scandals in '89, the great collapse of '08.

It's clear that it's vulnerable and that this is a recurring problem. This is something that comes back after a few decades, because people forget, and because when the system succeeds, then you build up prosperous institutions and they start lobbying. They say, "Everything's fine. Things are going well." And they start lobbying for a relaxation of the rules. It's never going to go away, but you want to have these twenty-, thirty-, forty-year periods when you have relatively stable growth.

When you're focused on achieving a certain goal, you can eliminate poverty. You can deal with the environmental questions. You can, in fact, do this if you can sustain a course of policy for, let's say, a thirty- or forty-year period. And then you may have strong institutions that can carry you even further. Social Security, for example, is a nice example. It keeps the elderly population of the country largely out of poverty.

If I had one thing I could add to the health care debate, I would lower the age of eligibility of Medicare, say, to fifty-five. And the reason for that is that it would help workers who are only hanging on to their jobs because they don't want to lose their medical benefits to move out of the labor force. And there are a fair number of those, and it's a fairly heavy burden on the business sector. So what you want to do is to create jobs. We've lost seven million jobs. Many of those are older workers, and the jobs that you create, you want to give the first crack at those jobs to people who have started their careers. You want to get them into the workforce.

Young people.

Young people, sure. Let older people, you know, some of them, anyway, a fair number of them, pass to retirement comfortably, a little earlier than they otherwise would. I mean, you've got to think about every possible way to make getting through this crisis tolerable for the population. Recognizing that a year, even two years from now, we are not going to be through it. The official forecasts say we're not going to go back to 5 percent unemployment till 2014.

Didn't you recommend that anybody who wants a job should be able to get a job, paid $8 an hour or something like that?

I think it's a very sensible idea. Why not have a large Job Corps involving, among other things, neighborhood conservation efforts, or home health care?

Shades of the New Deal, right? But when you talk like that, you immediately bring chills to the deficit hawks, who say, "Wait a minute. We can't afford to do what we're doing now. We're putting it all on our grandchildren's credit card. How can Jamie Galbraith be arguing for more deficit spending now?"

With all respect to the deficit hawks, they don't understand the situation. And they don't know what they're talking about, in terms of federal finances. The United States is a large and powerful country. And it can, if it chooses, employ its workforce in a useful way. But the point I would make about jobs programs is that the alternative is not spending nothing. The alternative is keeping people on the dole, the term Roosevelt hated. And Lyndon Johnson. Keeping them on the dole is costly. But it's also debilitating to those people. And you don't get anything out of it, from the standpoint of the country. The obstacle here is not fiscal, federal finance. The federal government can finance what it wants to finance. It's, as I say, the most powerful financial entity in the world.

   The problem here is organizational. It's a matter of will. It's a matter of creating appropriate institutions that are in the public sector, and incentives in the private sector, to get certain jobs done. When you approach it with that frame of mind, we wouldn't be asking about the budget deficit, we'd be asking about the unemployment rate. We'd be asking about how we're doing meeting our energy and our environmental goals.

What is the one question you think all of us should be thinking about right now?

Where do we want to be in thirty years' time? How do we get there? It's not a question of how we return to full employment prosperity in five years, but how we solve the fundamental problems that we face in a way that gives us a generation of steady progress, and living standards that people can accept, that they'll live with, that they'll be happy with, while at the same time achieving sustainability and reestablishing the American position as a leading and responsible country in the world. So that we are developing the technologies and the practices that other countries will then adopt, something that we have done very effectively for a century, but which we are certainly not doing now.

It's a test. It's a test for the country as a whole, as to whether we have the capacity to state and pursue a truly public purpose. We've come through a generation where we have really denied the existence of a common good or a public purpose. And I think we've recognized that that path leads to collapse, the collapse that we've seen. And that the way out is to somehow reestablish for ourselves this vision of what we really could be. ⌒

DOUGLAS BLACKMON

It is curious to me that many conservatives, so deferential to tradition, rhetorically at least, can act as if tradition has no consequences. Slavery, for example—the tradition of extending property rights to include the ownership of other people's bodies and lives—lasted for well over two hundred years in America and wasn't abolished until a bloody civil war tore the country apart. Even then, slavery's evils persisted in other guises for another century until the civil rights movement finally aroused the public conscience.

The consequences of those three centuries of slavery and segregation were pervasive and palpable, and our government at last instituted affirmative action policies in an attempt to overcome the cruel effects of a long tradition. Much of the opposition to affirmative action was a continuation of the denial that enabled slavery to flourish so long in a society that had proclaimed "life, liberty, and the pursuit of happiness" as every citizen's inalienable right.

Denial was a blindfold slipped on and off as convenience required, a common practice where I grew up in deeply segregated east Texas in the 1940s and 1950s. In twelve years of public schooling I cannot remember one of the teachers I cherished describing slavery for what it was—if they mentioned the word at all. Nor did they or anyone else in town talk about that tortured period following the Civil War, when our town restored white supremacy, determined, with so many others across the South, to prevent emancipated slaves from realizing the freedom supposedly won when the Confederacy surrendered at Appomattox.

For decades to come, thousands of freed black Americans were arrested, often on trumped-up charges, and forced into labor as humiliating and painful as slavery. Such prolonged exploitation, which persisted right up until World War II, was like a hammer constantly raining blows on the limbs of its victims, who were then expected to get up and join America's fiercely competitive economy as if they merely had been in training for it at the local gym.

To read Douglas Blackmon's Pulitzer Prize–winning book Slavery by Another Name *and then have the opportunity to talk with him about it is to open the past, including the recent past, to the raw truth of an oppression whose scars persist today. Born in Leland, Mississippi, Blackmon is the Atlanta bureau chief of* The Wall Street Journal. *His team's articles on race, wealth, and other issues have been nominated by* The Journal *for Pulitzers four times. His reporting on U.S. Steel's use of forced African American labor in Alabama coal mines during the early twentieth century was included in the 2003 edition of* The Best Business Stories of the Year *and was the inspiration for his book, which will soon be the subject of a PBS documentary.*

—Bill Moyers

What you report is that no sooner did the slave owners, businessmen of the South, lose the Civil War than they turned around and, in complicity with state and local governments and industry, reinvented slavery by another name. And what was the result?

Well, by the time you got to the end of the nineteenth century, twenty-five or thirty years after the Civil War, the generation of slaves who'd been freed by the Emancipation Proclamation, and then the constitutional amendments that ended slavery legally, this generation of people experienced difficult, hard lives after the Civil War, but they had real freedom, in which they voted, they participated in government, they farmed. They carved out independent lives. But then, this terrible shadow began to fall back across black life in America that effectively reenslaved enormous numbers of people. And that was rooted in the Southern economy and in the way the American economy was addicted to slavery, addicted to forced labor, and the South could not resurrect itself. So there was this incredible economic imperative to bring back coerced labor. And they did, on a huge scale.

You said they did it by criminalizing black life.

Yes. Before the Civil War, there were Slave Codes, laws that governed the behavior of slaves. And that was the basis of laws, for instance, by which a slave had to have a written pass to leave the plantation and travel on an open road.

Well, immediately after the Civil War, all the southern states adopted a new set of laws that were then called Black Codes, and they essentially attempted to re-create the Slave Codes. This was such an obvious effort to re-create slavery that the Union military leadership still in the South overruled all of that. But that didn't work, and by the time you get to the end of Reconstruction, all the Southern legislatures have gone back and passed laws that aren't called Black Codes, but essentially criminalized a whole array of activities no poor black farmer could avoid.

Such as?

Vagrancy. You were breaking the law if you couldn't prove at any given moment that you were employed. Well, in a world in which there were no pay stubs, it was impossible to prove you were employed. The only way you could prove employment was if some man who owned land would vouch for you. None of these laws said it only applies to black people, but overwhelmingly, they were only enforced against black people. And many times, thousands of times I believe, young black men ended up being arrested and returned to the original farmer where they had worked in chains, not even as a free worker, but as a slave.

You write about how thousands of black men were arrested, charged with whatever, jailed, and then sold to plantations, railroads, mills, lumber camps, and factories in the deep South. And this went on right up to World War II?

It was everywhere in the South. These forced labor camps were all over the place. The records that still survive, buried in courthouses all over the South, make it abundantly clear that thousands and thousands of African Americans were arrested on completely specious claims, made-up stuff, purely because of this economic need and the ability of sheriffs and constables and others to make money off arresting them, providing them to these commercial enterprises, and being paid for that.

You have a photograph in the book I have not been able to get out of my mind. It's of an unnamed prisoner tied around a pickaxe for punishment in a Georgia labor camp. It was photographed sometime around 1932, which was only two years before I was born.

A journalist named John Spivak took an astonishing series of pictures in these forced labor camps in Georgia in the 1930s. He got access to the prison system of Georgia and these forced labor encampments, which were scattered all over the place. Some of them were way out in the deep woods. There were turpentine camps; some of them were mining camps. All incredibly harsh, brutal work. He got access to these as a journalist, in part, because the officials of Georgia had no particular shame in what was happening.

But what the picture also demonstrates was the level of violence and brutality, the venality of things that were done. This kind of physical torture went on, on a huge scale. People were whipped, starved, they went without clothing. Relatives reported that they would go looking for a lost family member, and they would arrive at a sawmill or a lumber camp where the men were working as slaves, naked, chained, whipped. It was just astonishing, the level of brutality.

You tell the story of a young man, a teenager, who spilled or poured coffee on the hog of the warden he was working for. He was stripped, stretched across a barrel, and flogged sixty-nine times with a leather strap. He died a week later. That's not a unique story in this book.

No, that was incredibly common. There were thousands and thousands of people who died under these circumstances over the span of the period that I write about. And over and over again, it was from disease and malnutrition, and from outright homicide and physical abuse.

You give voice to a young man long dead, whose voice would never have been heard had you not discovered, resurrected, and presented it. He's the chief character in this book. Green Cottenham.

Green Cottenham was born in the 1880s to a mother and father who had been slaves and who were emancipated at the end of the Civil War. Imagine a young man and a young woman who've just been freed from slavery, and now they have the opportunity to break away from the plantations where they'd been held and begin a new life. And so they do. They marry, they have many children. Green Cottenham is the last of them.

He's born just as this terrible curtain of hostility and oppression is beginning to really creep across all of black life in the South. And by the time he becomes an adult, in the first years of the twentieth century, the worst of the efforts to reenslave black Americans are in full power across the South. And in the North, the white allies of the freed slaves have abandoned them. Whites all across America have essentially reached this new consensus that slavery shouldn't be brought back, but if African Americans are returned to a state of absolute servility, that's okay.

Green Cottenham becomes an adult at exactly that moment, and then, in the spring of 1908, he's arrested standing outside a train station in a little town in Alabama. The officer who arrested him couldn't remember what the charge was by the time he brought him in front of the judge. So he's conveniently convicted of a different crime than the one he was originally picked up for. He ends up being sold three days later, with another group of black men, into a coal mine outside of Birmingham.

Slope Number 12 was a huge mine on the outskirts of Birmingham, part of a maze of mines. Birmingham is the fastest-growing city in the country; huge amounts of wealth and investment are pouring into the place. There's this need for forced labor. And the very men, the very entrepreneurs who, just before the Civil War, were experimenting with a kind of industrial slavery, using slaves in factories and foundries, had begun to realize, hey, this works just as well as slaves out on the farm.

Green Cottenham is one of the men, one of the many thousands of men who were sucked into the process, and then lived under these terribly brutalizing circumstances, this place that was filled with disease and malnutrition. And he dies there under terrible, terrible circumstances.

And you found the sunken graves five miles from downtown Birmingham?

All of these mines now are abandoned. Everything is overgrown. There are almost no signs of human activity, except that if you dig deep into the woods, grown over, you begin to see, if you get the light just right, hundreds and hundreds and hundreds of depressions where these bodies were buried.

You say that Atlanta, which used to proclaim itself the finest city in the South, was built on the broken backs of reenslaved black men.

That's right. When I started off writing the book, I began to realize the degree to which this form of enslavement had metastasized across the South, and that Atlanta was one of many places where the economy that created the modern city relied very significantly on this form of coerced labor. Some of the most prominent families and individuals in the creation of modern Atlanta, their fortunes originated from this practice. The most dramatic example was a brick factory on the outskirts of town that, at the turn of the century, was producing hundreds of thousands of bricks every day. The city of Atlanta bought millions and millions of those bricks. The factory was operated entirely with forced workers, and almost 100 percent black forced workers. There were even times that, on Sunday afternoons, a kind of old-fashioned slave auction would happen, where a white man who controlled black workers would go out to Chattahoochee Brick and horse-trade with the guards, trading one man for another, or two men.

And yet, slavery was illegal?

It had been illegal for forty years. And this is a really important thing to me. I was stunned when I realized that the city of Atlanta bought these millions and millions of bricks, and those are the bricks that paved the downtown streets of Atlanta. Those bricks are still there. They are the bricks that we stand on today.

Obviously, this economic machine that was built upon forced labor—these Black Codes, the way that black life was criminalized—put African Americans at a terrific economic disadvantage then and now.

Absolutely. The result of those laws—particularly of enforcing them with such brutality through this forced labor system—was that thousands of African Americans worked for years and years of their lives with no compensation whatsoever, no ability to buy property and enjoy the mechanisms of accumulating wealth in the way that white Americans did. This was a part of denying black Americans access to education, denying black

Americans access to basic infrastructure, like paved roads, the things that made it possible for white farmers to become successful.

And so, yes, this whole regime of abusive laws, the way that they were enforced, the physical intimidation and racial violence that went on, all of these were facets of the same coin that made it incredibly less likely that African Americans would emerge out of poverty in the way that millions of white Americans did at the same time.

How is it, you and I, both southerners, could grow up right after this era and be so unaware of what had just happened to our part of the country?

I think there are a lot of explanations for that. The biggest one is simply that this is a history that we haven't wanted to know as a country. We've engaged in a kind of collective amnesia about this, particularly the severity of it. And the official history of this time, the conventional history, tended to minimize the severity of the things that were done again and again and again, and to focus instead on false mythologies. Like the idea that freed slaves after emancipation became lawless and went wild, turned to thievery, that all sorts of crimes were being committed by African Americans right after the Civil War and during Reconstruction. But when you go back, as I did, and look at the arrest records from that period of time, there's just no foundation for that. There was hardly any crime at all. And huge numbers of people were being arrested on these specious charges so they could be forced back into labor.

Very often, those who raised these allegations, or wrote about them when I was growing up, were dismissed as Communists.

Anyone who tried to raise these sorts of questions was at risk of complete excoriation among other white southerners. But that's also what's remarkable about the present moment. One of the things I've discovered in the course of talking about the book with people is that there's an openness to a conversation about these things that didn't exist even ten or fifteen years ago.

Americans don't like to confront these pictures, these stories.

They don't. But over and over and over again I've encountered people who've read the book, who emailed me, or they come up to me after I talk about it somewhere, particularly African Americans, who know this story in their hearts. They may not know the facts. They may not know exactly the scale of things. But they know in their hearts that this is what happened. And so people come up to me and say, "Gosh, the story that my grandmother used to tell before she died twenty years ago, I never believed it. Because she would describe that she was still a slave in Georgia after World War II, or just before. And it never made sense to me. Now it does."

It is amazing that this was happening at a time when many of the African Americans retiring today were children.

Exactly. These are events unlike antebellum slavery. These connect directly to the lives and the shape and pattern and structure of our society today.

You can imagine why there might be so much anger in the black community among, let's say, African Americans who are my age, seventy-three, seventy-four, who were children at the time this was still going on.

Well, there's no way that anybody can read this book and come away still wondering why there is a sort of fundamental cultural suspicion among African Americans toward the judicial system, for instance. That suspicion is incredibly well founded. The judicial system, the law enforcement system of the South, primarily became an instrument of coercing people into labor and intimidating blacks away from their civil rights. That was its primary purpose, not the punishment of lawbreakers. And so, yes, these events build an unavoidable and irrefutable case for the kind of anger that still percolates among many, many African Americans today. ∼

SAM TANENHAUS

When I read Sam Tanenhaus's The Death of Conservatism, I wondered if he had spent his time and considerable talent on a premature autopsy. He had hardly finished writing it when the Tea Partiers burst onto the political scene, stirring new life on the right and prompting some to chuckle at the possibility that, like rumors of Mark Twain's demise, the obituary had been written before there was a corpse. Within a few months of this interview—which took place roughly one year after Barack Obama's victory and one year before the Republican resurgence in the recent midterm elections—conservatives were again in the ascendency. But Tanenhaus' book turns out to have been prescient about the nature of the insurgency. He distinguishes between the conservatism of Rush Limbaugh and Glenn Beck and the conservatism of Edmund Burke and William F. Buckley. Buckley, whose passing Tanenhaus grieves, could actually make a reasoned argument and hold forth at length on the corrective value of tradition, order, and authority as a restraint on the excesses of democracy. Conservatives of that bygone era feasted on ideas and first principles and welcomed debate; their successors wolf down raw meat laced with jalapeños.

Tanenhaus, editor of both The New York Times Book Review and that paper's "Week in Review" section, is a liberal who clearly respects a worthy adversary; he has practically made conservatism his reportorial beat. He wrote an acclaimed biography of Whittaker Chambers, the former Communist

and mainstream journalist who accused the State Department's Alger Hiss
of Soviet espionage. Chambers then became Bill Buckley's soul mate in the
founding days of Buckley's National Review. *Now Tanenhaus is working on a*
biography of Buckley himself, and wonders what that archer of quick wit and
rational debate would make of our nation's most recent surge of right-wing
agitation.

—*Bill Moyers*

———

If you're right about the decline and death of conservatism, who are all those
people showing up on television at rallies in Washington and across the
country?

I'm afraid they're radicals. Conservatism has been divided for a long time
between two strains, what I call realism and revanchism. We're seeing the
revanchist side.

Revanchism?

I mean a politics based on the idea that America has been taken away from
its true owners, and they have to restore and reclaim it. They have to con-
quer the territory that's been taken from them. *Revanchism* really comes
from the French word for "revenge." It's a politics of vengeance. And this
is a strong strain in modern conservatism. Like the nineteenth-century na-
tionalists who wanted to recover parts of their country that foreign nations
had invaded and occupied, these radical people on the right—and they include intellectuals and the kinds of personalities we're seeing on television
and radio, and also to some extent people marching in the streets—think
America has gotten away from them. Theirs is a politics of reclamation and
restoration: "Give it back to us."

What we sometimes forget is that in the last five presidential elections
Democats won pluralities in four of them. The only time the Republicans
have won, in recent memory, was when George Bush was reelected by the
narrowest margin in modern history for a sitting president. So what this
means is that, yes, what I think of as a radical form of conservatism is highly
organized. We're seeing it now—they are ideologically in lockstep. They
agree about almost everything, and they have an orthodoxy that governs

their worldview and their view of politics. They are able to make incursions. And when liberals, Democrats, and moderate Republicans are uncertain where to go, this group will be out in front, very organized, and will dominate our conversation.

What gives them such certainty? Your conservative hero of the eighteenth century, Edmund Burke, warned against extremism and dogmatic orthodoxy.

It's a very deep strain in our politics. Some of our great historians like Richard Hofstadter and Garry Wills have written about this. If you go back to the foundations of our republic, we have two documents, "creedal documents" they're sometimes called, more or less at war with one another. The Declaration of Independence says one thing and the Constitution says another.

The Declaration says—

That we will be an egalitarian society in which all rights will be available to one and all, and the Constitution creates a complex political system that stops that change from happening. So there's a clash right at the beginning. Now, what we've seen is that certain groups among us—and sometimes it's been the left—have been able to dominate the conversation and transform politics into a kind of theater. And that's what we're seeing now.

In your book, you call them insurrectionists. And you write that they're not simply in retreat, they're outmoded. They don't act like they think of themselves as outmoded.

They do and they don't. When I wrote that, I also say that the voices are louder than ever. Already we were hearing the furies on the right. Remember, there was a movement within the Republican Party, finally scotched, to actually rename the Democrats the "Democrat Socialist Party." So the noise is there. William Buckley had a wonderful expression. He said the pyrotechnicians and noisemakers have always been there on the right. I think we're hearing more of that than we are serious ideological, philosophical discussion about conservatism.

The news agenda today is driven by Fox News, talk radio, and the blogosphere. They are propagandists for the right. Why are they so powerful?

There's been a transformation of the conservative establishment. And this has been going on for some time. The foundations of modern conservatism, the great thinkers, were actually ex-Communists, many of them. Whittaker Chambers, the subject of my biography. The brilliant thinker James Burnham. A less-known but equally brilliant Willmoore Kendall, who was a mentor, oddly enough, to both William Buckley and Garry Wills. These were the original thinkers, and they were essentially philosophical in their outlook. Now, there are conservative intellectuals who we don't think of as conservative anymore—Fareed Zakaria, Francis Fukuyama, Andrew Sullivan, Michael Lind, the great Columbia professor Mark Lilla. They've all left the movement. So it's become dominated instead by very monotonic, theatrically impressive voices and faces.

What does it say that a tradition that begins with Edmund Burke, the great political thinker of his time, moves on over the decades to William Buckley and now embraces Rush Limbaugh as its icon?

Well, in my interpretation it means that the tradition is ideologically depleted. What we're seeing now and hearing are the noisemakers, in Buckley's phrase. There's a very important incident that occurred in 1965, when the John Birch Society, an organization these new groups resemble—the ones who are marching in Washington and holding tea parties, the very extremist revanchist groups that view politics in a conspiratorial way—decided during the peak of the Cold War struggle that Dwight Eisenhower was a Communist agent, and that 80 percent of the government was dominated by Communists, that Communists were in charge of American education, American health care, were fluoridating the water to weaken our brains. All of this happened, and at first Buckley and his fellow intellectuals at *National Review* indulged this. They said, "You know what? Their arguments are absurd, but they believe in the right things. They're anti-Communists. And they're helping our movement."

Actually, many of them helped Barry Goldwater get nominated in 1964. Then in 1965, Buckley said, "Enough." Buckley himself had matured politically. He'd run for mayor of New York. He'd seen how politics really worked. And he said, "We can't allow ourselves to be discredited by our own fringe." So in his own magazine he made a denunciation of the John Birch Society. More important, the columns he wrote denouncing what he called its "drivel" were circulated in advance to three of the leading conservative Republicans of the day—Ronald Reagan, Barry Goldwater, and

Senator John Tower of Texas. Tower read them on the floor of Congress into the *Congressional Record*. In other words, the intellectual and political leaders of the right drew a line. And that's what we may not see if we don't have that kind of leadership on the right now.

To what extent is race an irritant here? During the 1960s, when we were trying to enact the crucial civil rights bills, we were troubled by William Buckley's seeming embrace of white supremacy. It seems to me to have left something in the DNA of the modern conservative movement that is still there.

It is. And one of the few regrets Bill Buckley ever expressed was that his magazine had not supported the Civil Rights Act, although you may remember that in the late '70s, he did support a national holiday for Martin Luther King's birthday, when someone like John McCain did not. In the late '90s, I heard Buckley give a brilliant lecture in New York City in which he talked about the importance of religion in American civil life. And it was Martin Luther King who was the subject.

What changed him? Because he was writing favorably in the National Review *about the importance of preserving the white class structure.*

He actually did that a little bit earlier, in the '50s. Remember, in the early '60s, even a great thinker like Garry Wills, who was still a part of the *National Review*, supported the civil rights movement, but thought it might weaken the institutional structures of society if it became too fervent a protest. Now, what the Republican Party did was to make a very shrewd political calculation, a kind of Faustian bargain with the South. As you know, Lyndon Johnson thought, when he signed those bills into law, that Democrats might lose the "Solid South," as it had been called, for a generation or more.

And yes, the Republicans moved right in, and they did it on the basis of the states' rights argument. Now, however convincing or unconvincing that was, it's important to acknowledge that conservatives within the Republican Party thought that a hierarchical society and a kind of racial difference, established institutionally, was not so bad a thing. They were wrong. They were dead wrong. But that sense of animus is absolutely strong today. Look who some of the great protestors are against Barack Obama. Three of them come from South Carolina, the state that led the secession— Representative Joe Wilson, Senator Jim DeMint, and Governor Mark

Sanford. And there's no question that that side of the insurrectionist South remains in our politics.

When you heard Joe Wilson shout, "You lie," during President Obama's State of the Union address, did you think you were hearing the voice of conservatism today?

No. I thought, "This man needs to read his Edmund Burke." Edmund Burke gave us the phrase "civil society." Now, people can be confused about that. It doesn't mean we have to be nice to each other all the time. Bill Buckley was not nice to his political opponents. What it means is one has to recognize that we're all part of what should be a harmonious culture, and that we respect the political institutions that bind it together. Edmund Burke, in a very interesting passage in his great book *Reflections on the Revolution in France*, uses the words *government* and *society* almost interchangeably. He sees each reinforcing the other. It's our institutional patrimony.

When someone on the floor of Congress dishonors and disrespects the Office of the President, he's actually striking, however briefly, however slightingly, a blow against the institutions that our society is founded on. And I think Edmund Burke might have some trouble with that.

There's long been a fundamental contradiction at the heart of this coalition that we call "conservative." There is the Burkean conservatism that yearns for a sacred, ordered society, bound by tradition, that protects both rich and poor, and there is what has been called the "libertarian, robber baron, capitalist, cowboy America." That marriage was doomed to fail, right?

It was. First of all, this is absolutely right, in the terms of a classical conservatism. The figure I emphasize in my book is Benjamin Disraeli. The French Revolution concerned Edmund Burke, but half a century later what concerned Disraeli and other conservatives was the Industrial Revolution. That's what Dickens wrote his novels about—children, the very poor becoming virtual slaves in workhouses as the search for money, for capital, for capital accumulation, seemed to drown out all other values. Modern conservatism is partly anchored in that.

Yes, and you have to wonder, why isn't conservatism standing up against turbocapitalism?

One reason is that very early on in its history America reached a kind of pact, in the Jacksonian era, between the government on the one hand and private capital on the other. The notion that the government would actually subsidize capitalism in America, that's what the right doesn't often acknowledge. A lot of what we think of as the unleashed, unfettered market is, in fact, a government-supported market. Remember the famous debate between Dick Cheney and Joe Lieberman? Cheney said that his company, Halliburton, had made millions of dollars without any help from the government. Bill, it all came from the government! They were defense contracts. What's happened is the American ethos—the rugged individualism, the cowboy, the frontiersman, the robber baron, the great explorer, the conqueror of the continent—has been driven by the engine of the market. What brought them together, what we've seen on the right, is what I call a politics of organized cultural enmity.

Accusatory protest, you call it.

Accusatory protest, with liberals as the enemy. So if you are a free marketeer, or you're an evangelical, or a social conservative, or even an authoritarian conservative, you can all agree about one thing: you hate the liberals who are out to destroy us. That's a very useful form of political organization. I'm not sure it contributes much to our government and society, but it's politically useful to them, and we're seeing it again today.

It wasn't long ago that Karl Rove was saying this coalition was going to deliver a new Republican majority. It came apart in 2006–2008. Why?

I believe it had come apart earlier than that. I really think Bill Clinton's victory in 1992 sealed the end of serious conservative counterrevolution. We forget that election. It seems like an anomaly, but consider, Bill Clinton won more electoral votes than Barack Obama, despite the presence of one of the most successful third-party candidates, H. Ross Perot. But that's not the most important fact. The most important fact is that George H.W. Bush got a lower percentage of the popular vote in 1992 than Herbert Hoover got in 1932. That was really the end. But the right had been so institutionally successful that it controlled many of the levers, as you say. Then what happened in the year 2000? Well, the conservatives on the Supreme Court stopped the democratic process, put their guy into office. Then came September 11, and the right got its first full blank slate. They could do really whatever they wanted. Those were the eight years of the Bush administration, which, I think, was the end of ideological conservatism as a vital formative and contributive aspect of our politics.

Why?

Because it failed so badly. It wasn't conservative, it was radical. It's interesting. Many on the right say, "George Bush betrayed us." They weren't saying that in 2002 and 2003. Conservatives saw him as someone who would complete the Reagan revolution. I think a lot of it was Iraq. Now, I quote in the book a remarkably prescient thing from the thirty-one-year-old Benjamin Disraeli, who wrote in 1835 that you cannot export democracy, even then, to lands ruled by despotic priests. And he happened to mean Catholic, not Islamic, priests. But he said you actually have to have a civil society established in advance. He said that's why the United States had become a great republic so shortly after the Revolution. We had the law of English custom here. You see? So we were prepared to become a democracy.

There were conservatives who tried to make that argument before the war in Iraq—Francis Fukuyama, Fareed Zakaria. There were people in the Bush administration who tried to argue this, and they were marginalized or stripped of power. With the invasion of Iraq, what America saw was an ideological revanchism with all the knobs turned to the highest volume. The imperial presidency of Dick Cheney and all the rest. And we saw where it got us.

You say in The Death of Conservatism *that, even as the collapse of the financial system has driven us to the brink, "conservatives remain strangely apart, trapped in the irrelevant causes of another day, deaf to the actual conversation unfolding across the land." Yet it seems to me that they are driving the conversation today.*

Well, they have many mouths, Bill, but they don't have many ears. The great political philosopher Hannah Arendt once said, in one of her essays on Socrates, that the sign of a true statesman is the capacity to listen. And that doesn't simply mean to politely grow mute while your adversary talks. It means, in fact, to try to inhabit the thoughts and ideas of the other side. Barack Obama is perhaps a genius at this. For anyone who has not heard the audio version of *Dreams from My Father*, it's a revelation. He does all the voices. He does the white Kansas voices; he does the Kenyan voices. He has an extraordinary ear. There's an auditory side to politics. And that capacity to listen is what enables you to absorb the arguments made by the other side and to have a kind of debate with yourself. That's the way our deliberative process is supposed to work.

Right now, at this time of confusion and uncertainty, the ideological right is very good at shouting at us and rallying their troops. You know, one of the real contributions conservatism made in its peak years—as an intellectual movement in the 1950s and '60s—is that it repudiated the politics of public demonstration. It was the left that was marching in the streets, carrying guns, threatening to take the society down, or calling President Johnson a murderer. It was the conservatives who used political institutions and political campaigns, who rallied behind traditional candidates produced by the party apparatus. They revitalized the traditions and the instruments and vehicles of our democracy.

But now we've reached a point, quite like one Richard Hofstadter described some forty years ago, where ideologues don't trust politicians anymore. Remember during the big Tea Party march in Washington, many of the protestors or demonstrators insisted they were not demonstrating just against Barack Obama, but against all the politicians—that's why some Republicans wouldn't support it. This revanchist crowd believes in a cultural revolution. They think the system has been, some would say, hijacked. Of course, they wouldn't use that word. They would say it's been maneuvered, controlled, and that they can get their hands back on the levers. One important thing about the right in America is that it always considers itself a minority movement in an embattled position, no matter how many branches of government they dominate. What they believe in is what their early philosopher Willmoore Kendall called a politics of battle lines—of war.

What do you see as the paradox of conservatism today?

The paradox of conservatism is that it gives the signs, the overt signs, of energy and vitality, but as a philosophy, as a system of government, as a means of evaluating ourselves, our social responsibilities, our personal obligations and responsibilities, it has right now nothing to offer.

They disagree with you, obviously. They think you have issued a call for unilateral disarmament on their part—that brass knuckles and sharp elbows are essential to fighting for what one believes in, and therefore, you, Sam Tanenhaus, are calling for a unilateral disarmament.

Well, that's what Richard Hofstadter called the paranoid style, when it's living on the verge of apocalypse, when defeat is staring you in the face, and the only victories are total victories. Because even the slightest victory, if it's not complete, means the other side may come back and get you again. This is not serious, responsible argument. Much of my book is actually about the failures of liberalism in that noontime period of the 1960s. And many of the conservatives simply ignore that part of the argument.

What explains your long fascination with conservative ideas and the conservative movement?

Well, I think it has been the dominant political philosophy in our culture for some half a century. What particularly drew me first to Whittaker Chambers and then William Buckley is the idea that these were serious intellectuals who were also men of action. In their best periods, in the days when *National Review* and *Commentary* and *The Public Interest* were tremendously vital publications, conservatives were self-examining, developing new vocabularies and idioms, teaching us all how to think about politics and culture in a different way, with a different set of tools. They contributed enormously to who we were as Americans. Many liberals were not paying attention. Many liberals today don't know that a splendid thinker like Garry Wills was a product of the conservative movement. It's astonishing to them to learn it. They just assume, because they agree with him now, he was always a liberal. In fact, he remains a kind of conservative. This is the richness in the conservative philosophy that attracted me, and that I wanted to learn more about, to educate myself. ∿

MAXINE HONG KINGSTON

Once upon a time, according to a Chinese legend, there were three books of peace. They contained the wisdom human beings needed to live together peaceably, but were destroyed by fire. The wisdom within them perished.

When that legend reached Maxine Hong Kingston—one of many tales she heard growing up Chinese American in California—she set out to write a novel called The Fourth Book of Peace. *But as she was attending her father's funeral in 1991, fire engulfed the hills surrounding her Oakland neighborhood. She lost everything to the flames; all that was left of her manuscript was a block of ash.*

For a while she thought the fire also had consumed her imagination, but eventually, after much struggle, she began again. The result was The Fifth Book of Peace, *retelling the story she had begun to write, and adding an account of the fire, the loss of her work in progress, and her subsequent spiritual journey through myths and legends of the past. The book is written, as one reviewer describes it, "in a panoply of languages: American, Chinese, poetry, dreams, mythos, song, history, hallucination, meditation, tragedy."*

Such inventiveness helps explain how Kingston became a force in American letters with the publication of her first book, The Woman Warrior, *still a favorite in college writing and literature classes.* China Men, *her second novel, won the National Book Award, and was followed by* Tripmaster Monkey, *an-*

other almost magical blend of memory, meditation and imagination gleaned from her parents' stories of their native China and from Kingston's own life in California.

Throughout, she remained obsessed with the wisdom of peace extinguished by that legendary ancient fire. For the past fifteen years she has been searching for it in the memories of former warriors who came home from battle traumatized by what they had seen and done. More than five hundred veterans from five wars have participated in workshops at which Kingston and other writers help them turn their experiences into poems, novels, and essays. Some of their finest work has been published in Kingston's latest book, Veterans of War, Veterans of Peace. *She might well have called it* The Sixth Book of Peace.

—Bill Moyers

You describe the stories and poems of the veterans in this book as "immense in scope, and in heart, and—amazingly—full of life and laughter. They carried out our motto: Tell the truth."

Yes. We adopted that motto because these people come home from hell, and they have witnessed, committed, or been subjected to horrendous acts. Their first instinct is to keep it secret. They say to themselves, "I'll forget what happened. I'll not visit my experience on my children, my wife, my husband. I will not tell people about what happened." And holding it inside creates terrible illness and wrong. My task is to help them get it out: "Tell me exactly what happened. It's okay to talk about it."

Which is what Robert Golling, for one, did.

Yes. Robert's job was to escort home to Massachusetts the body of a young soldier, a comrade, and to help the family with the funeral arrangements and to give what comfort he could. The family invites him to stay overnight. Like them, he's Catholic. He even looks like the boy who was killed. So in a way the family was welcoming their son home.

Read me what Robert writes after that night in their dead son's bedroom.

Sure.

I thought, I can't stand here all night. I turned off the light. The street lamplight jumped in through the window, casting a cold edge on all the objects in the room. I looked around at each and every thing without thinking. Each in turn said nothing but waited for some careless touch of its owner. Atop the chest of drawers, a comb and brush still with hair, his daily missal, Catholic prayer book that looked just like mine, a baseball autographed by Ted Williams, ticket stubs.

Quietly, quickly, a peek in each drawer saw socks, underwear, and cigar boxes of childhood treasures. The bottom drawer held sweaters and a shoebox of baseball cards. To the left was a stack of comics. Should I look deeper beyond *Mad*? Nah, I thought. The *Playboys* would be in the closet, beneath something his mother wouldn't touch. I returned all the drawers to their original positions. I'd only touched with my eyes ever so slightly. A guest will look, will look to find the familiar, he will try to be at home. But still I felt strange. I couldn't put my finger on it. I can barely see it now, thirty-nine years later. It was like seeing a life that was not my life, but was my life. His life cut short, while mine was still in front of me. Michael was at rest, and I must sleep, too. Could I sleep in the chair? No! Slowly, I pulled back the covers further. I turned and sat slowly, very slowly. Trying not to disturb the sheets, I lay back, tucked my legs beneath the sheets. The sheets now cold around me, more goose bumps, alone, cold, I closed my eyes, not moving. I, too, lay at rest. Sleep would come sometime.

And then there's Sandy Scull, a lieutenant in Vietnam in the late 1960s. He wrote poetry before he went over. I guess he must have been like me—a poet since childhood. But when he came home there were no poems. He had a block. He said he lost his spirit, lost his imagination, and then, finally, he wrote a poem called "Sea Salt"—about coming home. He had suffered post-traumatic stress disorder; the body goes numb, his appetite left him, he felt alienated from his fellow citizens. And he wrote this poem:

SEA SALT

After the Vietnam War, I withdrew
to Nantucket: "faraway isle."
Hoping to glimpse the boy
before spirit fled the body.
Thirty-three miles of ocean exiling me
from a homeland offering little embrace.

Me and my dog, Christopher. Christ-love
disguised as loyal canine. We combed beaches.
Working for the island newspaper connected me.
Tides soothed with ebb and flow.
A rhythm I could trust. Even eat by.
I fish the last three hours of the east tide.
Buried my toes in the sand, searching
for the texture of littleneck clam

When water was warm, I sailed out solo.
Stripped then slid into the sound.
Looking up toward the surface light.
Christopher's gaze wavering with wind
and water between us. Breath bubbles
rose, bursting under his nose.

My body now embraced,
a ritual purification in salt.
Dismembered dreams floated closer.
Something dissolved in a solution
that held me. Breathing easier,
I could imagine again.

"Breathing easier"—a physical response that liberated his spiritual voice.

Yes, yes, "Breathing easier, I could imagine again." So the spirit's coming in—he's in-spirited, inspired. His soul returns through meditation, through poetry.

Several of these veterans speak of being "frozen in that moment." Listening to them, I keep seeing in my mind's eye the image of slowly melting glaciers of emotion, transformed into something else, something powerful and affirming.

And this healing happens when people are able to tell the truth, when they are able to find words for that human experience.

But it can take thirty, forty years.

Yes, it took thirty years before poetry came back to Sandy Scull. It took Odysseus twenty years to come home from Troy. People have to work hard to return from war. Several of the veterans in this book have been through therapy or became therapists themselves. One of them took a job for thirteen years as a night watchman on Alcatraz. In a way, I suppose it was his atonement for being in Vietnam.

Do you remember the young soldier who had seen his friend burned alive in the war and has never been able to attend a neighborhood barbecue without smelling human flesh?

Yes, that was the story of Hopper Martinez. It was his job to pick up the bodies of his friends. This story's called "Hopper's Last BBQ," and it's an incredible story of what happens to your senses from the devastation of war. He smelled the barbecued human flesh and he started to salivate. His whole body was turning against him. Hopper had to apply to the VA for his benefits, and instead of filling out an official form he decided just to write the story of what had happened to him.

Did he get some help from the officials on the basis of what he wrote?

Yes.

Not all of the writers at your workshops are veterans of combat. There's Pauline Laurent, who tells you what it was like to be twenty-two and pregnant and to get the news three days after Mother's Day in 1968 that her husband had been killed in Vietnam. She looks out the window and sees that ugly green army car with the words U.S. Army *printed on the side, parked in front of the house. And then she picks up the story:*

> The men continue to sit in the car. Hours seem to pass before they get out, straighten their uniforms, and head toward my door. . . .

"Good evening," they say, as they remove their hats. "We're looking for Pauline Querry."

"That's me."

They look at my protruding abdomen that holds my unborn child and then look at each other in silence that lingers too long.

"Was he wounded or killed? How bad is it?"

More silence. Finally they begin.

"We regret to inform you that your husband, Sergeant Howard E. Querry, was fatally wounded on the afternoon of May 10, by a penetrating missile wound to his right shoulder."

I'm dizzy. I can't think straight.

"Dead? Is he dead?"

They don't answer. They just reread their script as if practicing their lines for a performance they'll give someday.

"We regret to inform you . . ."

The room is spinning. I can't think, I can't hear anything. I'm going to faint. Alone . . . I must be alone to sort this out. Leave me alone.

Instead, I sit politely as they inform me of the details . . . funeral . . . remains . . . escort . . . military cemetery . . . medals.

Finally they gather their papers and leave. I politely show them to the door. My parents are hysterical. My dad weeps, my mom trembles. No sound is coming out—her whole body is shaking in upheaval.

After retrieving the dog, I stagger to my room and shut the door. I throw myself on the bed, gasping for air. My heart races and pounds. My unborn baby starts kicking and squirming. I hold my dog with one hand, my baby with the other, and I sob. I'm shattered, blown to pieces. It can't be true!

No medics come, no helicopters fly me away to an emergency room. I struggle to save myself but I cannot. I die.

Half an hour later, a ghost of my former self gets up off the bed and begins planning Howard's funeral.

> Mom calls relatives. People come over to console me. I
> just want to be alone. I just want to be alone.

I just want to say that it was a triumph of writing that Pauline was able even
to say her husband's name, Howard. She told us that she was a ghost of her
former self once she got up off the bed and started planning his funeral.
She said she had been shattered, blown to pieces, and that it was twenty-five
years before she began to think she could talk about that day when she had
learned of his death. When she came to the workshop and started writing,
she said it became easier to tap into the other hard days, like the one when
her daughter was born and there was no father at the hospital to celebrate,
and when her daughter married and there was no father to walk down the
aisle with her. She said writing became a container that kept saying, "Give
me more of your pain."

What is it about a story's power to change the psyche?

Oh, I am trying to come up with a good answer. I keep saying it's magic.
Story gives shape and form to chaos. A finely shaped story has the same
energy as sexual energy, or life energy. It's like the tide that Sandy Scull
wrote about. The ebbing and flowing of tide, of storms, goes through our
bodies, goes through our psyches, and there's "a ritual purification of salt.
Something dissolves in the solution." And story helps us communicate with
others. I know that the veterans are writing for themselves, but I always
hold up the standard of an ideal that the writer's job is to communicate,
and, I tell them, "No diary writing, no private writing." These are public
acts of communication. And you must tell the story so that you can give it
to another person. And when you read it aloud, there's mouth-to-ear trans-
mission, we are communicating, and we make connections with others and
build the community around us. These soldiers can come out of war alienated from everyone. From their families. From our country. From themselves. And this communication helps them rebuild a community and a
family around them.

*Tell me about Ted Sexauer, a medic. Two tours in Vietnam, one with a line
company of the 173rd Airborne. He writes that he became an accomplice to
murder.*

Well, he was one of the first people to join our group. His post-traumatic stress disorder was very strong, and he has worked for many years to get through the numbness—to feel again. He goes back to Vietnam twenty five-years after he was there and arrives in time for Têt, which is the celebration of the lunar New Year, and he wrote a few lines of a poem called "Poem for Têt." It's a very important poem about how the world can cure us.

POEM FOR TÊT
Lang Cô village, Viêt Nam
Lunar New Year, 31/1/1995

This is the poem
that will save my life
this the line that will cure me
this word, this, the word *word* the one

this   breath   the one I am

See, when we listen, we breathe in one another's words. So this poem is about breathing each other, communicating with one another. So you don't feel so isolated anymore. That's what Ted told us—he didn't feel so isolated anymore.

How do the veterans recently back from Iraq compare with those who you began to work with fifteen years ago—veterans of Korea, Vietnam, even veterans of the First Gulf War? Do you find differences in their stories?

No. Of course there are differences in where the war took place. Now, many of the stories in this book are from the Vietnam War, which we lost. It is still hard for the veterans to admit we lost a war. There's a sense of betrayal, of loss. So yeah, there is that sense of loss, that sense of betrayal. But the human consequences, the way that they think and feel, the trauma of what happened—they're the same from war to war.

Your own work with veterans was born out of trauma—one that nearly stole your own voice. Oakland was ravaged by fire—three thousand homes destroyed, twenty-five people killed. Your own father had just died, and you were finishing The Fourth Book of Peace.

Yes. 1991. I was coming back from funeral rituals for my father. And I turned on the radio, and I heard that the hills were on fire. And so I got there as quickly as I could, and I made my way up through the flames and over and under the fallen power lines because I was trying to save my book. I was trying to save *The Fourth Book of Peace*. The only copy of the manuscript was on my desk. And I got there and it was gone.

Everything?

The house, everything. The neighborhood, the forests. And I was standing in the middle of what looked like the land after Hiroshima was bombed, after Dresden, after Hue.

You were so traumatized that you couldn't write for a while.

I couldn't even read. I couldn't read. I mean, this happens to many people, in trauma after trauma. You can't read. And I couldn't write, either. But it was not being able to read that was very disturbing.

You have said: "In the shock of the loss, I changed.... But I wrote directly how I felt: there was no shape, just expressions of pain and loss. It was the way I wrote as a child: to huddle in a corner secretly, away from people, and make sounds, whimper, while writing." How did you come out of that corner?

I founded a community around me. I brought together veterans who have been through terrible war. We wrote together and created a new community from all that destruction.

So writing became for you again what it had, what it would become for these veterans.

Yes.

A way through the loss.

Yes. Or to understand loss and what our lives are like when we've been through devastation. When we have participated in events that are inhuman, how do we become human again? How do we re-create ourselves? I kept saying: Make something out of nothing.

You make it very clear that art, poetry, fiction can help us come to terms with trauma. It can help us to heal and all that, but it doesn't do anything to stop war in the first place. I mean, if a government is determined to go to war, there's almost no way to stop that government, right? You campaigned against the Vietnam War. When the United States was about to bomb and invade

Iraq, you were right there in front of the Bush White House—you and the other women in Code Pink, the feminist organization. And you were reading history and poems and hugging each other and singing.

And the dancers danced, and the drummers drummed . . .

And the bombs fell.

And, yes. We used all our tools of nonviolence. We used all our arts. And then, twenty days later, shock and awe. So of course the question is, it doesn't work? Nonviolence doesn't work. Art doesn't work. We did all of this, and we could not prevent the war. And four years later the war goes on.

Do you ever give up thinking you could make a difference?

Oh, yes. I give up. And I feel despair. "What's the use?" But when I am unhappy, and in despair, and everything hurts, I always go to the writing. I just start setting down those words. And I follow the path that those words take me. They will always take me somewhere, and by the time I get there, by the time I finish a poem, or finish a story, I am a different person. ➴

E.O. WILSON

When E.O. Wilson received the prestigious TED Prize award in 2007 (from notables in technology, entertainment, and design who gather every year to share ideas shaping the future), he made a plea on behalf of his "constituency . . . a million trillion insects and other small creatures." Without them, this world-renowned biologist told the audience, "the rest of life and humanity would mostly disappear . . . in just a few months." Specifically, Wilson called for an Encyclopedia of Life to be created for the Internet, with an ever-evolving page for every one of the 1.9 million known living species and those being discovered every day. Furthermore, he said, the Encyclopedia should be made available free to any and everyone, from trained biologists in the field or laboratory and curious first-graders in their classrooms. If such an ambitious proposal boggled the stratospheric IQs in the room, they didn't reveal it. To the contrary, they set about to fulfill the vision of this genius of modern science, one of the world's most influential theorists—"Darwin's natural heir," as he is often called. Within a year, the site was up and running, thanks to early support from the John D. and Catherine T. MacArthur Foundation and the Alfred P. Sloan Foundation. In the first six hours of operation, there were more than eleven million hits, overwhelming the computer servers. Check it out at www.eol.org, as I just did a few minutes before writing this, hopeful that I might find a photograph of the Megaloprepus caerulatus, the giant helicopter *damselfly, as preparation for a visit from our youngest granddaughter. Sure enough, there it was, right on my screen.*

The Encyclopedia of Life *owes its inspiration to Wilson's childhood in Alabama. Blinded in one eye by a fishing accident when he was a boy, he focused his attention on ants and other insects, beginning a lifelong exploration into "the little things that run the world." That boy grew up to be "the father of biodiversity" and win honors and acclaim galore, including two Pulitzer Prizes. He has now published his twenty-fifth book,* Anthill: A Novel. *Many of the characters are ants inhabiting large colonies and waging war in—where else?—rural Alabama. One more reminder of a child's curiosity that proved the beginning of wisdom.*

—Bill Moyers

⸻

You've wanted this Encyclopedia of Life *for a long time.*

It's always been a dream of mine, Bill, of classifying all the species and finding out what makes up the biosphere. We're maybe today about one-tenth through the discovery of species.

That's all we know today, 10 percent of the existing species?

Amazing, isn't it? We live on an unexplored planet.

I figured we had pretty well made the final census of everything that's alive on earth.

We have scarcely begun, but the Encyclopedia of Life allows you to go to your computer anywhere in the world and, on command, pull up ways to identify species if you have a plant or an insect you need to know about and find out everything that is known about it up to that time.

Sort of a YouTube of bugs, insects, and fungi, right?

A very distinguished scientist wrote me when I published an article on this several years ago saying that this was what we must do. And he said, literally, "Ed—what have you been smoking?"

What will it mean for my five grandchildren?

A lot. Consider how ignorant we are and what a difference it makes. We don't know the great majority of the kinds of creatures living in most ponds or patches of woods that you would pick even around here. When we're trying to stabilize the environment, trying to get sustainable development, trying to stop the ecosystem from collapsing in the face of global warming or whatever, we really need to know what's in each one of those habitats. It's like undertaking a medical examination but your doctor only knows ten percent of what's inside you, in all of the organs. We need to move ecology way ahead of where it is today to really change things.

I don't know anyone who has added more to our understanding of earth's ecology than you, Ed. As a thirteen-year-old boy, you discovered the very first fire ant colony in the United States. Right?

In Mobile, Alabama. We lived five blocks from the dock area, so I caught one of the first colonies when it was multiplying. It belongs to a group of species of ants that are potentially serious pests.

I think we both would probably still be living in the South if it weren't for those infernal fire ants.

That's right. They come from Uruguay and they just keep spreading. Down South we refer to them as a "far ain't." That's not dialect. It means they come from far away and they ain't going home. Well, there are thousands and thousands of these species, and some of them really aren't that funny.

You've discovered hundreds of new species of ants from the Pacific Islands to the Caribbean. That's a lot of anthills in one lifetime.

Every kid has a bug period, and I never grew out of mine. I just started as most kids do, you know, catching bugs and frogs in bottles and so on.

When your family moved north you carried your curiosity about nature with you. You settled in a place perfect for a budding naturalist.

Washington, D.C. And providentially, we lived within walking distance of Rock Creek Park and the National Zoo. So a child's interest in insects combined with the federal magnificence displaying the wonders of nature. And reading *National Geographic* was an inspiration to me. All those great pictures. They called beetles "the jewels of the jungle." Butterflies were the "magnificent insects of the world," and so on. I pored over that. And I said,

"How can I be anything other than a naturalist?" That's what I want to do all my life.

I would have thought that, growing up in Mobile, you might have become a devotee of, what was it? The Lord God bird?

Yes, if I had only known. The Lord God bird. Interesting name for that. That's the ivory-billed woodpecker, as you well know.

And people would say, "Lord God, what kind of bird is that?"

That's how it got the name.

It wasn't that common. There were some over in Louisiana near east Texas, where I grew up.

Yes, at the Singer Tract. That's where the last one was seen in 1944.

The last one?

It was a very sad story. The Singer Reserve had been cut over and the ivory-bills just went down. And then finally there was just one left. A little boy would go and watch it until one day a storm came over there, and then he couldn't see it anymore.

But why should we care if the woodpecker goes? We don't know how many species we've lost in the millennium.

No, but how many species going extinct or becoming very rare do you think it takes before you see something happening? We now know from experiments and theory that the more species you take out of an ecosystem—like a pond, patch of forest, marine shallow environments—the more you take out, the less stable it becomes. If you have a tsunami or a severe drought or you have a fire, the less likely that ecosystem, that body of species in that particular environment, is going to come back all the way. It becomes less stable with fewer species, and we also know it becomes less productive. In other words, it's not able to produce as many kilograms of new matter from photosynthesis and passage through the ecosystem. It's less productive. It sure is less interesting, though, isn't it? And more than that, we lose the services of these species, like pollination and water purification . . .

That we get from nature free of charge.

Here's an easy way to remember it. We get from nature, so long as we don't screw it up and destroy it, approximately the same amount of services, as far as you can measure them, in dollars as we ourselves produce each year. It's about $30 trillion a year. These creatures have built in them, in their genes and then in their physiology, an endless array of defenses, many of which we could use and have used, like producing antibiotics we never heard of using, chemicals that we never even dreamed existed. So we have already benefited immensely from wild species in that way. But let me get to the bottom line as far as I'm concerned. Isn't it morally wrong to destroy the rest of life, you know, in any way you look at it, considering what it's going to do to human spirit and aesthetics?

Are we destroying it?

Yes, we are. If we do not abate the various changes we're causing—climate, habitat destruction, the continuing pollution of major river systems and so on—we will, by the end of the century, lose or have right at the brink of extinction about half the species of plants and animals in the world, certainly on the land.

Hold on: half of what we have now will be gone by the end of the twenty-first century?

If we don't do something, yes.

You use the metaphor of a giant meteorite. You say we human beings are a giant meteorite, the biggest and most damaging the earth has ever known.

It now is pretty well established that 65 million years ago, the earth was struck by an unusually large meteorite, off the coast of what is now Yucatán. And even though it may have only been about ten kilometers across, when it struck the world its power caused gigantic tsunamis over a large part of the world. It rang the earth's surface like a bell. Volcanic eruptions occurred, clouds formed over the earth that knocked out the sun and greatly reduced photosynthesis. A majority of species of plants and animals died. And among the groups that died out finally and conclusively at that time were the dinosaurs. If we don't take care of the living environment, by the end of this century we're going to be getting pretty close to the impact of that big meteorite 65 million years ago.

How would that change life on earth?

Well, we'd just live in an impoverished environment. It'd be a lot tougher. We wouldn't have as many pollinators, we wouldn't have as many future crops and genes to feed ourselves. We wouldn't have the same kind of security given to us free in terms of water management. All sorts of things would happen in the most practical way. It should be a horror to people.

Are you telling me you actually think we could obliterate nature?

Yes. And did you know that there are people actually saying that'll be a good thing?

Why?

Because they think that it's the fate of humanity to go on humanizing the planet, turning this planet literally into Spaceship Earth. In other words—

Live in a synthetic ecosystem.

Yes, that's right. Or people who say, "Well, let's keep on going the way we're going. Let's use up the earth. And by that time, our smart scientists . . ." Trust me, I'm a scientist, none of us could be that smart. But they figure that by that time, maybe we can make it to the next planet, terraform it, you know? Turn it into an earthlike place and so forth. Dream on. This is crazy. This is the only planet we're ever going to have. This planet has taken hundreds of millions of years to create this beautiful natural environment we have that's taken care of us so well, that is, in fact, our greatest natural heritage. And we're throwing it away in a matter of a few decades.

But what is the serious response to the argument that, "Look, we human be-ings have always adapted to severe environmental change. Some come, some go. The Mayans are gone. The Sumerians are gone. The Aztecs are gone. Others have survived"?

Yes, but consider this. The common response is, "Well, evolution always provided new species." The problem with that is the birth rate of species is going down, because we're destroying the cradles in which new species are born, the natural environment. What difference does it make? Well, if humanity as a whole decided that it wants to live in a world where we give away this great heritage and all of this mystery and beauty and complexity that we haven't even begun to explore, I guess if that's what people want, that's what they're going to get. But I have more faith in human beings' intelligence and taste than that.

It can be argued that civilization was purchased by the subversion of nature.

It was, and that's why we destroyed so much already. When the agricultural revolution began, as you know, about ten thousand years ago, we went from a hunter-gatherer existence where we were more or less in balance—we weren't wiping out species at any great rate—to one in which we began to turn natural environments, particularly forests and the grasslands, into agricultural fields. That proceeded to an extent that it formed the economic basis for great human population growth and for the evolution of civilization. And who can say that that's not a good? It's just that it took a million years for humanity coming through these early stages struggling to survive in nature to finally learn how to displace nature. We did that ten thousand years ago, and we're continuing to displace it. Now we realize that we've got to put on the brakes and bring this to a halt. Otherwise we're going to be down many of the natural ecosystems in the world, the most beautiful ones. And we're not stopping. We're going to be through the whole bit of it in many parts of the world unless we do something. We're near the end of nature in many parts of the world.

The end of nature?

I mean the end of a large part of the rest of life on the planet.

Can't life survive without us?

Oh, it would do wonderfully well without us.

Nature was doing a pretty good job before we arrived, right?

Wonderfully well.

So where did this idea come from that we're the crown jewel of creation?

In one sense I sort of think we are. That is to say, we are the brain of the biosphere. We are the ones that finally, after 4.5 billion years of evolution, actually developed enough reasoning power to see what's happening, to understand the history that created us, and to realize almost too late what we're doing. We are something new under the sun and on the earth. We're the ones that can destroy the world. No other single species ever had anything like that power. And we also have the knowledge to avoid doing it. It's sort of a race to the finish line that we will develop the intelligence and the policies and the decency to bring it to a halt not just for life itself but for future generations before the juggernaut takes us over.

Give me your capsule analysis of why we are so rapidly escalating the destructive impact of our behavior. What's going on?

It's mainly that we're just the kind of reckless, ignorant, uncaring species we've been up till now that's doing the damage. We're still increasing in numbers. We're at 6.5 billion. However, we're slowing.

The prediction is that when we reach nine billion we'll begin to—

Yeah, we'll peak. Nine billion is 40 percent more than what we have now. I think we can handle that. That right now is a serious problem. It's not the big problem. The big problem is consumption. Rising per capita consumption around the world. So this is why the world has got to have a green revolution.

And that means—

I mean, let's keep on improving our quality of life, but let's figure out—and we've got the brains to do it—how to keep the economy growing and the quality of life improving with fewer and fewer materials and less and less fossil-based or nonrenewable sources of energy. It's as simple as that.

You're putting your hope in new technology?

I'm putting my hope primarily in human common sense. I like what Abba Eban once said during the 1967 Arab-Israeli war. He said when all else fails, men turn to reason. I think we are at the stage now that we are ready to turn to reason, especially if we can only persuade the leadership of the strongest and wealthiest country in the world to gain this understanding, then the technology will become relatively easy. That is, to go green and put less of what we call our ecological footprint onto the world. We'll ease up on the rest of the world and become sustainable and allow the rest of life to survive and come through. I like to call it the bottleneck. Come through the bottleneck we're in now. If we use our head, we'll come out the other end with the kind of improved lives that we all dream of and bring as much of the rest of life with us as possible. That's why I say what we're doing now, if we don't stop it, is the folly for which our descendants will least likely forgive us. Two hundred years from now, they'll say, "What did they think they were doing?"

Why do so many smart people remain passive in the face of the destruction of the conditions for survival?

I wish you would tell me.

I'm a journalist. I ask the questions, Ed. You're a scientist. You find out the answers.

If I knew, I would figure out better ways of persuasion.

What would the stewardship of the earth mean to each of us personally? If I said, "I'm going to take my share of the responsibility," what would that require of me? I think most people want to do something. They want to know what to do.

It can be just being locally active in saving a woodland along a nearby river or regionally allying yourself with a department of the environment, or one of the conservation organizations working locally to ensure that a certain biologically rich area or wetland is set aside as a park and a reserve rather than being turned over to developers. But let me tell you one that I think most might know. We desperately need leadership that works off of what we have learned through science, that has produced a consensus about what is happening to the earth's environment, including the living creation. Leadership that sees the potential in it and not just the need in it and gives, in this country especially, the kind of vision of a future that we can work toward as a people.

There is a bias at the moment against science—that it disrupts our religious belief or diminishes our economic growth—you know, the bias against climate science.

Both based upon misconceptions. A greening of America means new markets, new ways of developing resources, new technologies, new directions, new areas of education, training, and on. As far as the economy is concerned, that's a no-brainer. As far as religion is concerned, I have a very different view from what many scientists and environmentalists have of the religious community. I grew up as a Southern Baptist.

You answered the altar call. You were baptized.

I did. And I grew up in one of the reddest of the red states. I have the highest respect for folks who are called fundamentalists. I like them. I think they're highly intelligent, and a large percentage of them are highly educated. So it's always occurred to me that the schism between scientists, who are mostly liberal and nonbelievers, and the great majority of Americans, more than 75 percent of who could be called religious, to some extent might be an artifact.

What do you have in common with conservative Christians?

Actually, just about everything except certain beliefs about where it all came from and who's looking over us. I could go down and pick a pastor from some small country church along the byways of Alabama and I'll bet if we sat down and talked about our deepest beliefs together, we'd come up with more agreements on more things than disagreements. And then isn't that the American way? We could say, "Let's put that aside for a while and work together when we really have something we need to work together on."

Yes, but Ed, many of the Christians who read the Bible literally reject the conclusion of scientists that we've evolved from lower forms. They believe the earth is not our home. We're heaven-bound. Some of them believe the second coming of Jesus is imminent. You addressed your book The Creation: An Appeal to Save Life on Earth *to a Southern Baptist pastor. Why did you do that?*

Partly because that's my background, although I'm now a secular humanist, a thoroughgoing secularist. I understood and respected greatly the people of the culture I grew up in. But also, in addressing evangelicals instead of Unitarians, there was what I call the New York effect. If you can make it in New York, you can make it anywhere. In other words, if you can make it with Southern Baptists, you can make it anywhere. And the argument I make in *The Creation* is extremely simple. I said "Let us, in the service of a transcendent moral obligation and concern, put aside our differences for the time being and not fuss with each other over evolution. In other words, where it all came from. Let us agree, looking at the evidence, that it is disappearing. And let us, dare I use the word, gather at the river. Come together on common ground where we can exercise the extraordinary power we jointly have." I argue, and few people disagree with me, that science and religion are the two most powerful social forces in the world. Having them at odds with each other all the way up to the highest levels of government and the popular media all the time is not productive.

In your book, you ask both science and religion to set aside their differences about metaphysical issues.

Meet on the near side of metaphysics.

But can you ask religion to do that when it's concerned with the metaphysical, with unseen deities?

Sure you can. You know, I have a lot of physicist friends working on string theory who also are preoccupied with things they can't see or measure. The point here is yes, you can, and we've done it.

You say you're a secular humanist. What do you want me to hear when you say that? That term drives the Christian right into a frenzy.

A humanist is a person who believes that in matters ethical and in matters of aesthetic and central concern, we should put humanity as the first and final purpose of it all. We have just this one planet to live on. We are not being looked over. We are on our own, essentially. And we are responsible for ourselves and we better get together as a species and work it out and stop relying on supernatural powers. That's basically what humanism is.

What would you have us do to try to make a difference on the footprint we humans are leaving on this earth?

Let's go down one layer of thought from what we had earlier, and go to the deepest level. If we could change our worldview, it would be somewhat radical, but it would mean seeing ourselves as a biological species in a biological world. That we are a species exquisitely well adapted to this planet, and that we originated here, and that our peculiarities, including the ones that threaten our own existence, can be understood by the history of the way we originated in that living world. If we could just place ourselves realistically in that context and stop thinking of ourselves as semi-angels, that this is just a way station on our way up to an idealized existence, I think we would get pretty serious about peace and long-term security and saving the rest of life. Keeping our options open for the future. ❧

SIMON
JOHNSON

Wall Street's ability to come up with ever more ingenious and mysterious ways to extract a dollar—or rather, billions of them—without regard for the devastating impact their alchemy may have on people struggling to make a living is as breathtaking as a performance by magician David Copperfield.

In the fall of 2005, the banking giant Citigroup even conjured up a new word, plutonomy, to define an economic system where the privileged few make sure the rich get richer with the government as their enabler. Deciding that the time had come to publicly "bang the drum on plutonomy," the bank outlined an "equity strategy" in a document entitled "Revisiting Plutonomy: The Rich Getting Richer." Here are some excerpts:

> *Our thesis is that the rich are the dominant drivers of demand in many economies around the world.... These economies have seen the rich take an increasing share of income and wealth over the last 20 years, to the extent that the rich now dominate income, wealth and spending in these countries. Asset booms, a rising profit share and favorable treatment by market-friendly governments have allowed the rich to prosper and become a greater share of the economy in the plutonomy countries.... The top 10%, particularly the top 1% of the US—the*

*plutonomists in our parlance—have benefitted disproportion-
ately from the recent productivity surge in the US . . . [and]
from globalization and the productivity boom, at the relative
expense of labor.*

*The great collapse of '08 not only did little to dismantle those "dynamics of plu-
tonomy," it reinforced them. Even after the fall, which cost millions of people
their jobs, homes, and savings, the plutonomists—their own name for themselves, remember—are doing just fine; in some cases, even better, thanks to
the bailout of the big banks which meant record profits and record bonuses
for a few in the midst of widespread suffering. A recently released report from
the U.S. Survey of Consumer Finances confirms that the rich continue to get
wealthier and account for a disproportionate share of income and wealth. The
dynamics of plutonomy are still intact.*

*Why is this? Because over the past thirty years, the plutonomists have used
their vastly increased wealth to capture the American government. It hasn't
mattered which party was in power; Republicans and Democrats alike cheered
them on while dismantling, or refusing to enforce, safeguards that could have
protected ordinary citizens from the plunder.*

*Few have the know-how and experience to sort this out and make sense of
it for a lay audience. Simon Johnson does. I first discovered him while surf-
ing an early morning wave on the Internet and finding the website called
baselinescenario.com. It was founded by Johnson and his colleague James
Kwak, with whom he also wrote the bestselling book* 13 Bankers: The Wall
Street Takeover and the Next Financial Meltdown.

*Simon Johnson once served as chief economist of the International Monetary
Fund. He was schooled at Oxford, taught at the Fuqua School of Business at
Duke University, is the Ronald A. Kurtz Professor of Entrepreneurship at
MIT's Sloan School of Management, and serves on the editorial board of four
academic journals. Hardly a socialist pedigree! But Johnson has emerged from
the belly of the beast to become a formidable and oft-quoted chronicler of the
"plutonomy" that so shamelessly took title to our government.*

*Our conversation took place in February 2009, just a couple of weeks af-
ter Barack Obama became president and about six months into the financial
crisis. Johnson had just written a piece at baselinescenario headlined "High
Noon: Geithner v. the American Oligarchs," and I wanted to know more.*

—Bill Moyers

What are you signaling with that headline "Geithner v. the American Oligarchs"?

I'm signaling something a bit shocking to Americans, and to myself, actually. The situation we find ourselves in at this moment is very strongly reminiscent of the situations we've seen many times in other places, but places we don't like to think are similar to us: emerging markets—Russia, Indonesia, Thailand, Korea. Not comfortable comparisons. We somehow find ourselves in the grip of the same sort of crisis and the same sort of oligarchs as in those countries.

Oligarchy is an un-American term, as you know. It means a government by a small number of people. We don't like to think of ourselves that way.

I know people react a little negatively when we use this term *oligarchy* for the United States. It's a way of governing, as you say. It comes from a system tried in Greece and Athens from time to time, a very simple, straightforward idea from Aristotle. It's political power based on economic power. And it was actually an antithesis to democracy in that context. Exactly what you said: a small group with a lot of wealth and a lot of power. They pull the strings. They have the influence. They call the shots. It's disproportionate, it's unfair, it is very unproductive, and it undermines business in this society.

And it's the rise of the banks in economic terms that translates into political power. They then exercise that political power back into more deregulation, more opportunities to go out and take reckless risks and capture huge amounts of money.

The big banks became stronger as a result of the bailout. That may seem extraordinary, but it's really true. They're turning that increased economic clout into more political power. And they're using that political power to go out and take the same sort of risks that got us into disaster in September 2008.

Are you suggesting that the banking industry trumps the president, the Congress, the American government in a crisis like this financial catastrophe?

I hope they don't trump it. But the signs that I see—the body language, the words, the op-eds, the testimony, the way these bankers are treated by certain congressional committees—it makes me feel very worried. I have a feeling in my stomach that is what I had in other countries, much poorer countries, countries that were headed into really difficult economic situations. When there's a small group of people who got you into a disaster, and who are still powerful—made even more powerful by disaster—you know you need to come in and break that power. And you can't. You're stuck.

Both The Wall Street Journal *and* The New York Times *reported that Obama's top two political aides, Rahm Emanuel and David Axelrod, have pushed for tougher action against the banks. But they didn't prevail. Obama apparently sided with Geithner and the Treasury Department in using a velvet glove.*

What I read from that is an unnecessary and excessive deference to the experts, or the supposed experts. I live in Washington. I follow this very closely. The view is that you need to rely on the technocrats. And the technocrats are saying, "You must not be too tough on the banks; that will have adverse consequences for credit, for the economy, for unemployment." If that's what the technocrats are saying now, they're wrong. That is not the right way to deal with this crisis.

There are many fine professionals at Treasury with great experience who have spent their lives working on important issues related to the United States. What we face right now is not a typical U.S. issue. President Obama said we've never seen anything like this since the Great Depression. Well, that means nobody working on this has any firsthand experience. He also said we may face what we call a "lost decade." We've never seen that anywhere other than Japan in the 1990s. With all due respect to the officials at Treasury, they're not the ultimate authority. I don't think they're the right people.

The people you should be talking to are the people at the International Monetary Fund. They are saying the policy of being nice to the banks is a mistake. The powerful people in the country are the CEOs of these banks. They're the people who paid themselves the massive bonuses at the end of the last year. Now, those bonuses are not the essence of the problem, but they are a symptom of an arrogance, a feeling of invincibility, that tells you a lot about the culture of those organizations and the attitudes of the people who lead them.

Timothy Geithner hired a senior lobbyist from Goldman Sachs as his chief of staff. The deputy secretary of state was a vice president of government affairs at Citigroup. A managing director from Citigroup is now assistant to the president and deputy national security advisor for international economic affairs. One of his deputies also came from Citigroup. One member of the President's Economic Recovery Advisory Board comes from UBS, which is being investigated for helping rich clients evade taxes. Is this what you're talking about—this web of relationships?

Absolutely. I don't think you have enough time to go through the full list of people and all the positions they've taken. I'm sure these are good people. Don't get me wrong. These are fine, upstanding citizens who have a certain perspective and a certain kind of interest, and they see the world a certain way. And it's a web of interest, exactly as you say. That's exactly the right way to think about it. That web of interest is not my interest, or your interest, or the interest of the taxpayer. It's the interest, first and foremost, of the financial industry in this country.

Do you think the president understands how these guys play the game? Let me play you the recording of a conference posted on the Huffington Post. One of the top officials of Morgan Stanley is speaking to his colleagues. Here it is:

> JAMES GORMAN: *I'm going to turn to a topic that I suspect is near and dear to everybody's hearts, which is retention. There will be a retention award. Please do not call it a bonus, it is not a bonus; it is an award. . . . The award will be based on '08 full year production. . . . Clearly it would have been cheaper to do it off '09, but we think it's the right thing to do, and we've made that decision.*

What he's basically saying is: "Business as usual. Go about your daily lives. Get the bonuses. Rebrand them as awards." Bill, this is the arrogance of people who think they've won. They think it's over. They think we're going to pay out 10 or 20 percent of GDP to basically make them whole. It's astonishing.

Why wouldn't they believe it? Before I watched the eight CEOs testify before Congress at the House Financial Services Committee, I read a report that almost every member of that committee had received contributions from those banks last year. In a way that's like paying the cop on the beat not to arrest you.

I called up one of my friends on Capitol Hill after that testimony. I said, "What happened? This was your moment. Why did the members pull their punches like that?" And my friend said, "They know the bankers too well."

In 2008, the securities and investment industry made $146 million in campaign contributions. Commercial banks, another $34 million. American taxpayers don't have a flea's chance on a dog like that, do they?

It is a massive problem, obviously. The good news is there are people in the White House, the president himself, aware of this broader issue. Remember, throughout his campaign Obama was very good at getting small contributions and trying to minimize the impact of major donors like that. But at the same time, these people are throughout the system of government. They are very much at the forefront of the Treasury. Treasury is apparently calling the shots on their economic policies. This is a decisive moment. Either you break the power or we're stuck for a long time with this arrangement.

When Tim Geithner said earlier in the week [February 10, 2009] that the American people have lost faith in some financial institutions and the government, did it occur to you that this was the same man who was president of the New York Fed through much of this debacle?

I have no problem with poachers turning gamekeeper. If you know where the bodies are buried, maybe you can help us sort out the problem. And during the first three or four minutes of that hearing, what Timothy Geithner said was very good as a definition of the problem, and pointing the finger clearly at the bankers, and saying that the government had been slow to react, and, of course, that included himself when he was at the New York Federal Reserve in the run-up to the collapse. I liked that. And then he started to talk about the specifics. But when he said, in effect, that the compensation caps we've put in place, for the executives of these banks, are strong, I just fell out of my chair. That is not true. That is factually inaccurate.

It's deferred stock these guys are getting. It's not restricted. You can get as much stock as you want; as soon as you pay back the government, you can

cash out of that. That's one problem. Second, and I'm sorry to get technical, they can reset the stock option price. This is something you and your
viewers need to hear about. Just look for these words, okay? Follow them
through the press. When you get into trouble, when your company goes
down, and you have massive amounts of stock options that aren't worth
much anymore, because the stock price has gone down, you say, "Oh, well,
we're going to reset our option prices."

And basically it means that at the end of the day, these people are going
to walk away with tens if not hundreds of millions of dollars paid for basically by the insurance policy that you and I are providing. Think of it like
this: Our taxpayer money is ensuring their bonuses. We're making sure that
these banks survive. And eventually the economy will turn around. Things
will get better. The banks will be worth a lot of money. And they will cash
out. And we will be paying higher taxes—we and our children—so those
people could have those bonuses. That's not fair. It's not acceptable. It's not
even good economics.

We should certainly have a big say over critical matters like this. First of
all, it's our money that kept these banks in business. Not just the Treasury
recapitalization money, that's relatively small; it's the financial support provided by the Federal Reserve that has saved the day. Make no mistake about
it, if the Federal Reserve hadn't stepped in in late September 2008, in dramatic fashion, to prop up Goldman Sachs and others, they would be out
of business. It was our money that did that. The Federal Reserve acting on
behalf of the American taxpayer.

And second, the CEO of Goldman, Lloyd Blankfein, made mistakes
and led his company into deep trouble. Now other companies are in deeper
trouble. His company was in deep trouble and had to be rescued at that moment. We should change the leadership of these major banks.

*And, yet, as I said earlier, Secretary Geithner's chief of staff is the former lob-
byist for Goldman Sachs. How do they make a dispassionate judgment about
how to deal with Goldman Sachs when they're so intertwined with Goldman
Sachs's mind-set?*

I have no idea. It's a huge problem.

*So here's the trillion-dollar question that I take from your blog: can someone
like Timothy Geithner "really break with the vested elites" that got us into this*

much trouble? Have you seen any evidence that he's going to be tough with these guys?

I'm trying to be positive. I'm trying to be supportive. I like the administration. I voted for the president. The answer to your question is no. I haven't seen anything. But you know, perhaps next week I will. But right now, as we speak, I have a bad feeling in my stomach. My intuition, from crises—from situations that have improved, from situations that got worse—my intuition is that this is going to cost us a lot more money. And we are going down a long, dark, blind alley.

What you've written comes down to this: we must break the power of the banks and their lobbies. How do we do that?

I think it's quite straightforward, in technical or economic terms. At the same time I recognize it's very hard politically. What you need to do is the stress test that, actually, Secretary Geithner outlined in his speech on Tuesday [February 10, 2009].

Which is?

You go in and you check the bank's books, and you say, "Okay, using market prices and not pretend prices, not what you wish things are worth but what they are really worth, what are your assets really worth in the market today? And we also assess what will happen to the value of the things you own if there's a severe recession." It's a stress test, like the one you get when you go to see the cardiologist: they put you on a treadmill and make you run to see how your heart is going to behave under stress. Now we need to look at how the bank's balance sheets will look under stress. And then you say to them, "This is our assessment of the amount of capital you need to cover your losses, and to stay in business, and be able to make loans, through what appears to be a severe recession. This is the amount of capital you need. Now you have a month, or two, to raise this amount of capital privately."

This was done in Sweden, by the way, in the early 1990s. They did it with three big banks. One of the three was able to go to its shareholders, raise a lot more capital, and stay in business as a private bank, with the same shareholders. That's an option. Totally fine. However, the ones that can't raise the capital are in violation of the terms of their banking license, if you like.

We have no problem in this country shutting down small banks. In fact, the FDIC is world-class at shutting down and managing the handover of deposits for small banks, for example. They managed the closure of IndyMac beautifully. People didn't lose touch with their money for even a moment. But they can't do it to big banks, because they don't have the political power. Nobody has the political will to do it.

So you need to take an FDIC-type process. You scale it up. You say, "You haven't raised the capital privately. The government is taking over your bank. You guys are out of business. Your bonuses are wiped out. Your golden parachutes are gone." Why? Because the bank has failed. This is a government-supervised bankruptcy process. In the terminology of the business, it's called an intervention. The bank is "intervened." You don't go into Chapter 11 because that's too messy, too complicated. There's an intervention, you lose the right to operate as a bank. The FDIC takes you over.

I think we agree, everyone agrees, we don't want the government to run banks in this country. It's not gone well anywhere in the world. That's not what we're going to do. That's not what the Swedes did. That's not what the real banking experts are going to tell you to do. They're going to say, you set up the government intervention and make it work. It might take three months, it might take six months.

But there's a lot of private money out there—let's call it private equity—and these people would like to come in and buy these reprivatized banks. You would have to attach antitrust provisions to this, so the banks are broken up as part of this transaction. Senator Bernie Sanders of Vermont has a great saying. He says if any bank "is too big to fail, it is too big to exist." And he's exactly right. So in this transformation, you're bringing in private equity. To me, this is the right idea. You're using part of the powerful financial industry against another part. You're using private equity against the inbred insiders, big bankers. The new owners come in and do a lot of the restructuring. They're going to fire all of these managers. I can assure you of that. They're going to put in new risk management systems. They're going to have to make the banks smaller, and the taxpayer is going to retain a substantial equity interest. And as these banks recover, the value of our investment goes up. That's how we get upside participation.

You're not talking about nationalization.

I'm talking about a scaled-up FDIC intervention. I think we need the FDIC to be empowered with the political support to get this job done.

Splitting this one powerful interest group into competing factions and taking them on one by one?

That is the classic strategy for breaking up an oligarchy. Now, I do admit that once you've done that, you have to worry about the new oligarchs. That's why you're breaking up the banks. You don't want to just change the owners of banks that are too big to fail, because they'll be coming around in five years for another handout. The structure of our banking system, the concentration of power in big financial institutions, has to change. There's a lot of appeal to what FDR did in the Great Depression. I'd go back earlier than that, a hundred years, to Teddy Roosevelt, and think about trust-busting. We need to break up these big institutions for exactly the same reason that John D. Rockefeller's Standard Oil and other interests were broken up at the end of the nineteenth century. They were too powerful, economically and politically. That's where we are with the banks today. ✑

HOLLY SKLAR

The sturdy backbone of democratic capitalism is the confidence of workers that they are getting a fair shake. But American workers can no longer count on it. Although they are working harder, they receive less of the wealth produced by their labor. Their struggle to stay in the middle class or simply make a living wage accounts for much of the anxiety in the country. According to census data, in 2009 the income gap between the richest and poorest was the greatest on record.

More unequal than Germany, France, and Britain. More unequal, in fact, than Guyana, Nicaragua, and Venezuela. As the gap widens between the rich and everyone else, people lose faith in the essential fairness of the system and call into question its governance. In her book Raise the Floor: Wages and Policies That Work for All of Us, *Holly Sklar examines what it takes to make ends meet in America and how we can create a just economy to strengthen democracy. Sklar directs Business for Shared Prosperity, an organization of business executives and investors who are dedicated to our economy's long-term success. She also runs the Let Justice Roll Living Wage Campaign, a coalition of faith, community, and labor activists working to raise the minimum wage to a living wage at the state and federal level.*

—*Bill Moyers*

I read just the other day that a couple with two children has to work approximately three full-time minimum-wage jobs just to make ends meet.

That's right. And still they don't make ends meet. They're constantly trading off. They're going to food banks to feed their children. Do you know that we have people working in the food industry today who must go to food banks to help feed their children? People taking care of elderly folks can't save for their own retirement. Although they will be working their whole lives.

People working full-time can't earn enough money to make ends meet. How does this happen?

We have really shifted expectations in a terrible way. It used to be assumed that if you were working full-time, you would not only make ends meet, but you were heading toward the American dream, when it was possible for one full-time worker to support a family, you could have a home, you could have health care, you could send your kids through college, and you could save for your own retirement. Now we have many two-income households who can't even achieve what a single-income household could achieve before. We've been living the American dream in reverse.

Reverse?

In reverse. We have now gone back to the 1970s in terms of average wages, adjusting for inflation. The buying power of the minimum wage is lower than it was in the 1950s. Inequality of income and wealth is what it was in the 1920s. We are back at levels that we saw right before the Great Depression.

But the economy's been growing. Why aren't workers sharing in the prosperity that they've helped create?

That's exactly the problem. It used to be that when productivity went up, wages went up.

You work harder, you got more of the results.

More people got a fair day's pay for a fair day's work. You shared in the rise of worker productivity. Now almost all the rise in productivity is going to the very top of the upper class. We have had a vast redistribution of income and wealth in this country in the last three decades. As that redistribution of wealth and income has been going up to the very top, most people have been treading water or going under.

Is it true that about 60 percent of our workforce make their living from hourly wages? And about 80 percent of the workforce are production and non-supervisory workers?

When we refer to average workers, that's usually what we mean. It's just shocking what has happened to them. The people who have been driving this phenomenon, in corporations and in the government, have been saying we have to do this in order to make our country more competitive in the global economy.

We need to be leaner—

Exactly.

—and meaner.

Leaner and meaner, and they say we will all be better off in the long run because we will be more educated, more competitive and so on. Well, here's the problem. We haven't been making our country more competitive. We've been actually driving it into the ground. People at the top are like corporate raiders, raiding the whole country, milking it like a cash cow. That's what's been going on. So when you hear the expression "We're the richest country in the world," the truth is we're the most indebted country in the world. We have an infrastructure that was built by the tax dollars of prior generations and is now crumbling. We don't have a world-class infrastructure anymore. The infrastructure we built to recover from the Great Depression and after World War II is now crumbling. We're not even fixing that, much less building a world-class twenty-first-century infrastructure. And we are spending less on research and development. Our education system is sliding further and further behind. The idea that we're getting more competitive for the global economy is ridiculous, it's a myth.

Why aren't people in revolt over this?

Well, let's remember what happened in the 1980s. The two longest periods without a minimum-wage increase have both taken place since 1980. Early in the Reagan administration, PATCO, the air-traffic control union, went on strike. And President Reagan essentially said, "You're fired, good-bye." He broke the union. And this, in effect, was a real green light to union-busting.

BusinessWeek and other business magazines have written about this. A real wave of union-busting followed, and it became normal to replace striking workers, not even just temporarily while they were out on strike, but basically saying, "Your jobs are gone." The National Labor Relations Board lets companies get away with it, so one factor has been the sharp decline of union strength relative to the workforce.

There are plenty of studies that show that as unions increase their share of the economy, they bring other people who are not in unions up with them. They raise the wage standards for a lot of other people, too, right?

Absolutely. Now, another factor behind the decline is this: if everyone is afraid of losing their job, it's much harder to ask for higher wages. You fear your company will turn to outsourcing like many others have. You're caught in that grip.

How is it that our political system accepts this?

Accepts it, yes. That's exactly the problem. Jobs should keep you out of poverty, not keep you in it. But instead of a growing middle class, we have a growing class of people who are working jobs and making poverty wages in real terms. The politicians give a lot of lip service to helping middle-class families, but not much is done. Otherwise they would be making it easier for workers to unionize, respecting labor rights, raising the minimum wage.

Why is the minimum wage so important? Because it sets the floor. The biggest signal the government can send is to say that people should get a minimum wage that is a living wage. Franklin Roosevelt used to talk about a fair day's pay for a fair day's work. He instituted the minimum wage, among other things, in order to set the floor. When government basically allows the minimum wage to become not just a poverty wage but a desperately poor wage, it sends a big signal. It's okay for the minimum wage to be down there in quicksand dragging down wages above the minimum as well.

There is an argument that raising the minimum wage causes small businesses to lay people off and that it's best to let the market, not the government, determine matters like wages.

Bill, we shouldn't let the least that employers want to pay set the floor for wages, any more than we would set pollution policy by permitting the worst polluter to set the standard for the environment. No new employer should be able to stay in business based on the premise that they're keeping their employees in poverty. There's something basically wrong with your business model if you're keeping your employees in poverty. Also, raising minimum wages doesn't increase unemployment. It expands consumer purchasing power, decreases worker turnover, improves customer service. There are real benefits in raising wages.

The people earning minimum wage today are earning less than they would have forty years ago.

Oh, much less than they would have in terms of buying power.

And you write that those low-wage workers are actually subsidizing employers, stockholders, and consumers.

They are, because of what we talked about in terms of productivity. You are working, and you are creating value for the company, for the shareholder. Nowadays, a much bigger portion of that value is going to the very top of the corporation, to the top executives, to the owners, and to the shareholders. It's not being fairly shared with workers. Executives at big corporations have basically doubled their share of company revenues in the last decade. It's not that the pie has expanded so that if the rich are getting richer, that's okay because then everybody's improving. That's not the case. The rich are just taking more.

The rising tide is not lifting all the boats.

The rising tide's not lifting all boats. Little crumbs aren't trickling off the table. What's really happened is that so much is being ripped off at the top. It's a level of extreme, almost pathological greed, and it's not tolerated in any other of the democracies.

We have the greatest spread of inequality, I believe, of any industrialized country in the world.

And the highest rates of poverty. In other industrialized countries, they're making themselves more competitive in part by raising their level of math and science literacy. We've gone the other way. They've built out their infrastructure. They've been reenergizing their economy by greening energy. They have a much lower gap between CEOs at the top and the workers at the bottom. They just don't tolerate it.

What are the practical consequences of this inequality?

Well, one thing is that with so much wealth concentrated in so relatively few hands, we have a higher child mortality rate. We have lower life expectancies than many other industrialized countries in the world. A lot of Americans don't realize this. We don't have the highest life expectancy in the world. We're the only industrialized country without universal health care. We don't have the highest living standard. Those are the consequences of inequality.

Are we at some kind of breaking point?

We are at a breaking point. The question is, which way is it going to break? One of the reasons we're at a breaking point now is that people did so much to try and make up for the real fall in their real wages. They maxed out their work hours, they maxed out their credit cards, they maxed out their home equity loans. Many people took on large debt. Not to take a vacation, not to put their kids through college—although people of course go into debt for these reasons—but they were using it, in many cases, to just maintain a basic living standard. Make ends meet. Well, that's all maxed out now. The mortgage crisis cascading into the housing and the financial crises has carried us over the cliff. And people who had achieved not just a middle-class lifestyle but could save for retirement, help their kids make a down payment, put their kids or even their grandkids through college—that's all going to be gone for millions of people. And we have this growing workforce of poverty-wage workers and middle class in trouble. The question is, what are we going to do now that the illusion is gone?

We are at economic and environmental breaking points. We have to green the economy in order to survive as a country and in the world today. If you don't do it, it's a disaster for us and for the world. If you do it, it's a breaking point in the sense that it's actually going to be used to jump-start the economy in a good way.

What are some of the changes you and your colleagues think we could make?

Well, raise the minimum wage, for one. Raise the floor. Give a green light to fair wages. Provide universal health care.

Because?

Because people are dying preventable deaths. Because our present system is a giant redistribution of wealth and income with money pouring into the pharmaceutical companies, to highly paid insurance executives, and others. It's destroying a lot of small businesses in the sense that they want to give health care to their workers, but the cost is astronomical.

Your organization includes small-business people. What's your mission? What are you trying to do through Business for Shared Prosperity?

The mission is to say that we can change direction. We believe that what's really good for business is also good for workers, and good for communities, and good for the country. Instead of this low-road path we've been on—low wages for workers and lower taxes for the wealthy, reckless deregulation, irresponsible disinvestment in our infrastructure—we can go to a higher road, where we shore up the economy from below. And this is not only what's good for us today, it's what's good for us in the future, and it's exactly what will make us more healthy and competitive economically in the long run. ⌒

JANE
GOODALL

*When Jane Goodall walked into the building for this interview, faces lit up.
Our security chief told me she does animal rescue work after hours because of
Goodall. Our stage manager whispered into my ear, "She's been my hero for
decades." And the nine-year-old daughter of our video editor hurried into the
studio because she was writing a school report on Goodall (she got an A, by the
way). Everyone was aware of who Jane Goodall is and what she has done to
close the gap between the animal world and our own species.*

*Goodall herself evolved from a youthful enthusiast of animals—inspired by
her father's gift to her of a toy chimpanzee he named Jubilee—to the world's
leading observer of chimpanzees and a global activist for all of life on earth.
Through a chain of unintended consequences the young Goodall met the famous anthropologist Louis Leakey in Kenya, was hired as his secretary, and
then was sent into the forest as his primary researcher on chimps. Over many
years in the Gombe Stream National Park, she came to know her subjects as
individuals with distinct personalities, and with social and family lives shaped
by their emotions, as are our own. Her landmark studies diminished the distance between human and nonhuman, and her television specials were so popular it became easy to think all of us had grown up with her and the chimps.*

*She and I were born a few weeks apart in 1934, and I am in awe at the
pace she keeps, traveling more than three hundred days a year for the Jane*

Goodall Institute, challenging audiences to see themselves as caretakers of the natural world. Her Roots and Shoots program nurtures young people in 114 countries, teaching and encouraging them to improve and protect the environment. In a time of gloom and doom, as species disappear every day, development consumes more and more land, and global warming roils the climate, Jane Goodall insists that all is not yet lost. She makes the case in her book Hope for Animals and Their World, *and as the focus of a new documentary,* Jane's Journey.

—Bill Moyers

This life you're living now is such a contrast to the life of the Jane Goodall we first met many years ago, living virtually alone in the forest in the company of chimpanzees, sitting for hours quietly taking notes, observing. And now, three hundred days a year, you're on the road. You're speaking. You're lobbying. You're organizing. Why? What's driving you?

It actually all began in 1986. In the beginning of the year, I was in my dream world. I was out there with these amazing chimpanzees. I was in the forests I dreamed about as a child, I was doing some writing and a little bit of teaching once a year. And then this conference in Chicago brought together the people who were studying chimpanzees across Africa and a few who were working with captive chimps, noninvasively. We were together for four days and we had one session on conservation. And it was so shocking to see, right across the chimpanzees' range in Africa, forests going, human populations growing, the beginning of the bushmeat trade, the commercial hunting of wild animals for food, chimpanzees caught in snares, population plummeting from somewhere between 1 and 2 million at the turn of the last century to at that time, about 400,000. So I couldn't go back to that old, beautiful, wonderful life.

My team and I were just looking the other day at that great old classic—the National Geographic *special—which shows you meeting the chimps for the first time.*

Among the Wild Chimpanzees. That's still one of the best films. Hugo shot it, my first husband. I love that film.

Were the animals not affected by the presence of a camera crew?

Well, once they are used to you, they seem to pay very little attention. It's something which has surprised visiting scientists, who felt that the chimps' behavior must be compromised by our presence. But they accept you. And they by and large ignore you.

Do you miss them?

I miss being out in the forest. I do go back twice a year, not for very long. But a lot of those old friends, or nearly all, are gone. The very original ones have all gone. They can live over sixty years, but still. And, you know, we're now getting onto the great-grandchildren of the original chimps. And there's a research team following them, learning about them.

I've long wanted to ask you about the chimpanzee you loved best, David Greybeard. What was there about David Greybeard?

Well, first of all, he was the very first chimpanzee who let me come close, who lost his fear. And he helped introduce me to this magic world out in the forest. The other chimps would see David sitting there, not running away, and so gradually they'd think, "Well, she can't be so scary, after all." He had a wonderful, gentle disposition. He was really loved by other chimps; the low-ranking ones would go to him for protection. He wasn't terribly high-ranking, but he had a very high-ranking friend, Goliath. And there was just something about him. He had a very handsome face, his eyes wide apart, and this beautiful gray beard.

When you and David Greybeard were communing, what language were you speaking?

We didn't. I always tried not to use chimp language in the wild because we really do try and look through a window. And now we know how dangerous it is to transmit disease from us to them. So we keep further away, which is sad for me.

I ask the question because it seemed to me, watching the films, that there was some language being spoken, a means of communication without words that even communicated feelings.

Right in the early days there was this wonderful situation when I was following David Greybeard. I thought I'd lost him in a tangle of undergrowth, and I found him sitting as though he was waiting; maybe he was. He was on his own . . . I don't know. And I picked up this red palm nut and held it out on my palm. And he turned his face away. So I held my hand closer, and then he turned; he looked directly into my eyes. He reached out and took it. He didn't want it. He dropped it. But at the same time, he very gently squeezed my fingers, which is how one chimp reassures another. So, there was this communication: He understood that I was acting in good faith. He didn't want the nut, but he wanted to reassure me that he understood. So we understood each other without the use of words.

And where do you think this empathy comes from?

It's the bond between mother and child, which is really, for us and for chimps and other primates, the root of all the expressions of social behavior.

I know that you consider cruelty the worst human sin. You wrote, "Once we accept that a living creature has feelings and suffers pain, then if we knowingly and deliberately inflict suffering on that creature, we are equally guilty. Whether it be human or animal, we brutalize ourselves." But you learned from the chimpanzees that animals can be cruel, too.

Yes, but I think a chimpanzee doesn't have the intellectual ability, or I don't think it does, to deliberately inflict pain. You know, we can plan a torture, whether it's physical or mental. We plan it, and in cold blood we can execute it. The chimpanzee's brutality is always on the spur of the moment. It's some trigger in the environment that causes this craze, almost, of violence.

You saw gangs of males attacking single females. You saw cannibalism, including females who eat the newborn infants of females of their own community although there's other food available. You describe primal warfare among the chimps. Since you're looking at them to see what we can learn about us and about our evolution, what conclusion do you reach about their aggression?

Some people have reached the conclusion that war and violence are inevitable in ourselves. I reach the conclusion that we have brought aggressive tendencies with us through our long human evolutionary path. I mean, you can't look around the world and not realize that we can be, and often are, extremely brutal and aggressive. And equally, we have inherited tendencies of love, compassion, and altruism, because they're there in the chimp also. So we've brought those with us. It's like each one of us has this dark side and a more noble side. And I guess it's up to each one of us to push one down and develop the other.

You even wrote once that it was your study of chimpanzees that crystallized your own belief in the ultimate destiny toward which humans are still evolving. What is that ultimate destiny? And how did the chimps contribute to your understanding of it?

When you have the creature that's more like us than any other living being on the planet, that helps you to realize the differences, how we are different. We have this kind of language that's led to our intellectual development, that's led to refining of morals, and you know, the questions about the meaning of life and everything. So I think we're moving or should be moving toward some kind of spiritual evolution, where we understand without having to ask why.

But "why" is the fundamental question, isn't it? Isn't that one of the things that makes us human, that we can ask why?

Yes, but maybe we ask too often. Maybe we should sometimes be content, just being satisfied with the knowing, without saying, "Why do I know?"

Where does your own composure come from?

Possibly from months and months on my own in the wilderness. But I think I had it before.

I have an image of you in my mind, of a little girl in Bournemouth, England, reading relentlessly from Doctor Dolittle *and* Tarzan. *That's what you did.*

Absolutely. I've still got all the books. They're still there in my room.

And that's where your imagination was formed about Africa?

Yes.

Well, I read the Tarzan *books when I was growing up. You actually did something about what you read!*

Yes, it was a passion, and I had a wonderful mother. I attribute a lot of what

I've done and who I am to her wisdom, the way she brought me up. It was very supportive. She found the books she knew I would be interested in—animals, animals, animals. Everybody was laughing at me for dreaming of going to Africa. I was eleven, World War II was raging. We didn't have any money. We couldn't even afford a bicycle. My father was off fighting. And Africa was still thought of as the dark continent, filled with danger. And, you know, I was the wrong sex. I was a girl, and girls weren't supposed to dream that way then. I should have been dreaming of being a nurse or a secretary or something.

I was in love with Tarzan. I was so jealous of that other wimpy Jane. I knew I would have been a better mate for Tarzan myself. I was jealous!

You would have made a better mate for Tarzan than I would have made a Tarzan.

But my mother never laughed at my dreams. She would say, "If you really want something, if you work hard, if you take advantage of opportunity and if you never give up, you will find a way." See, how lucky I was. I'm now working so much with young people because I could kill myself trying to save chimps and forests, but if we're not raising new generations to be better stewards than we've been, then we might as well give up. So I can go to kids living in poverty in Tanzania or the inner-city Bronx, and tell them my story, and say, "Follow your dreams." And they write to me and say, "You taught us that because you did it, I can do it, too." And that is just right.

Roots & Shoots, your program of training young people to be active in conservation movements, began in Tanzania, didn't it?

Yes, it began with sixteen high school students in '91. And it emerged from Tanzania as a very new sort of thing. It's now in more than 120 countries and involves all ages, from preschool through university. And more and more adults are taking part, even in prisons, the staff of big corporations. It's basically choosing three kinds of projects to make the world better. One, for your own human community. Two, for animals, including domestic ones. And three, for the environment. There is a theme of learning to live in peace and harmony among ourselves, between cultures and religions and nations and between us and the natural world. Youth drive it. They choose the projects.

Are those young people the source of this hope for animals and their world that you write about?

They are a large part of it. I mean, isn't it great that high school students in some inner-city area will greet me as I walk in as though I were a pop star? That is so amazing, because they've got out of what I've done a message of hope. And the fact that our main message is, "You make a difference every day. You matter. Your life is important."

This is why they want to come to my lectures. And I've met many people who say, "Well, I was really depressed, and a friend said, 'You've got to go and hear Jane.'" And they come up in the book-signing line, which can be three hours long, and say, "I'm not as optimistic as you, but at least I now realize my life has more value than I thought, and I'm going to do my bit." That's what we need, isn't it?

You once said that you have the peace of the forest in you. What is that?

Being out there in the forest, all those months alone, there was a growing sense of this great spiritual power all around, something greater than me. So you could lie and look up at the stars and feel yourself tiny. And yet, somehow, having this extraordinary awareness that we have as human beings that we can encompass a vague sort of feeling of what the universe is. And all in this funny little brain here. So there has to be something more than just brain. It has to be something to do with spirit as well.

You had a very powerful experience in the spring of 1974, when you visited Notre Dame Cathedral in Paris.

It was a sort of low time in my life. And there I was. I went into the cathedral, and as I walked through the door, Bach's Toccata and Fugue in D Minor just suddenly filled the whole cathedral. And the sun was just coming through that rose window. It just was so powerful a feeling. You know, how could this amazing cathedral, all the people who built it, all the people who'd worshipped in it, all the brilliant minds that had been within it, how could that all be chance? It couldn't be chance.

But does the meaning come with the DNA, or is meaning something we create out of life? As you have created meaning with your life?

I don't think that whatever you're being faithful about really can be scientifically explained. I don't want to explain this whole life business through science. There's so much mystery. There's so much awe. I mean, what is it that makes the chimpanzees do these spectacular displays, rain dances? At least that's what I call them. They dance at the foot of this waterfall. And then sit in the spray and watch the water that's always coming and always going and always here. It's wonder. It's awe. And if they had the same kind of language that we have, I suspect that would turn into some kind of animistic religion.

You're a scientist who observes the world and reaches your observations. Spirituality can't be observed, it can be felt, and you reconcile those two in your own life.

But I also had my mother. And she said she never saw the conflict between religion and evolution. Louis Leakey, my great mentor who dug up early man, he felt the same. So I had this, and then, yes, it all came together in the forest. But you have to remember, I didn't start as a scientist. I wanted to be poet laureate, and I wanted to be a naturalist. That's how I began. I didn't have any desire to go and be a scientist. Louis Leakey channeled me there. I'm delighted he did. I love science. I love analyzing and making sense of all these observations. So it was the perfect rounding off of who I was into who I am.

There's a poem you wrote that I came across recently. I had not read it or heard it before. It seems autobiographical. I'd like to ask you to read it.

The Old Wisdom

When the night wind makes the pine trees creak
And the pale clouds glide across the dark sky,
Go out, my child, go out and seek
Your soul: the Eternal I.

For all the grasses rustling at your feet
And every flaming star that glitters high
Above you, close up and meet
In you: the Eternal I.

Yes, my child, go out into the world; walk slow
And silent, comprehending all, and by and by

Your soul, the Universe, will know
Itself: the Eternal I.

I want my grandchildren to read that one. By the way, I took one of my grand-sons up to the American Museum of Natural History, to their marvelous Hall of Biodiversity. And we read there that 99 percent of all the mammal and plant species that have existed since time immemorial have disappeared. I told him extinction is a part of life. It's a part of the history of the world. What's unique now?

Since the Industrial Revolution, our human impact on the planet, our greenhouse gas emissions, our reckless damage to the natural world, our continual growth of our populations, they have had a tremendously damaging effect, which has led to the sixth great extinction.

The exhibit at the museum shows that reportedly five times since time immemorial, we've had a speeding up of the extinction of species. And that now this is happening again. And that's why they refer to it as the sixth great extinction.

Yes. And it's happening faster than the others, and you only have to look around. About two months ago I was in Greenland, and I was standing with Inuit elders at the foot of a great cliff of ice which went right up to the ice cap that covers the top of the world. And hearing and seeing huge slabs of ice come crashing off and thundering down, looking at this water that emerged from the ice cliff, which before, even in summer, had never melted, the Inuits had tears in their eyes. Some of them hadn't been there since they were children. And they said, "This is our country crying out for help." I think it should give us a sense of responsibility. We're the ones who have set ourselves up as masters. We can change any environment to suit ourselves. So we'd better start thinking about the long-term consequences of those changes.

It may help that human beings can attach emotionally to animals. How do you explain that?

I suppose it comes from the time we domesticated wolves and got ourselves dogs. It's amazing. Like the scientific proof now that if you're sick, a dog can actually help you to heal, and so can a cat. So there is something in this bond, and it's again another window into the fact that we are part of the animal kingdom.

Is there any evidence that the animals, the chimps in particular, have this "spiritual awareness," this sense of other beyond themselves?

They understand the difference between "me" and "you," we're pretty sure. They're definitely aware of things going on around them. Over and above that, I don't know. I mean we, with our words, want to question, "Why am I here? What's the purpose of it all?" We call it a soul. So if I have a soul and you have a soul, then I think my chimp has a soul and my dog has a soul, too.

You even find mysticism in the whooping crane.

Well, I did, yes. I had the opportunity to visit those amazing birds. They're so ancient. It was in Wisconsin with Joe Duff of Operation Migration. We were flying up in an ultralight craft, which are used to teach the cranes a new migration route. The cranes normally learn from their parents. And they want to create a second migration route, in case the birds using the existing route are hit by bird flu or something. So some are being trained to fly from Wisconsin to Florida. I think it's the twelfth migration that's happening right now.

I went up in the ultralight for one of the training flights. Being up there was almost like being a bird up in the sky, open all around and looking down at the wetlands below. It was just so beautiful, training them this way. It's so impressive to meet people who say, "I won't give up. We will not let these amazing, beautiful birds disappear."

There's a report that somewhere around 17,300 species are actually endangered right now. That's what we're up against, right?

Absolutely. And wouldn't it be easy just to say, "Well, it's a trend. And it's just happening. The pendulum is swinging. We just better sit back and let it swing. And maybe one day it'll swing back." If everybody stopped, if everybody gave up, then I wouldn't like to think of the world that my great-great-grandchildren would be born into. The forests would go—they've been going so fast—the tropical rainforests and the woodlands as well. So there'd be huge areas of desert. The droughts which are already happening in Australia, in sub-Saharan Africa, would be worse. There would be very few wild animals. People would probably be living in some kind of bubble, a very artificial life. The water would all be polluted. The groundwater would be almost gone. I suppose we'd be desalinating the sea for our water. But I don't want to live in that sort of world.

About the time you started at what is now Gombe National Park—it was 1960—I was joining the Kennedy administration. I made many trips to Africa then, for the Peace Corps. When I've gone back over the years, as a journalist, it's been astonishing to me that what I used to see as green, verdant, rich countryside is now a desert.

It's this explosive overpopulation. There are two main causes of intense environmental destruction. One is absolute poverty, because what can you do except cut down some more trees and try to grow food. In the tropics, cut the tree cover down, and you soon get a desert. And that's happening all over the developing world. It's happened in the United States, the great Dust Bowl. Agricultural overuse. So poverty is one. And unsustainable lifestyles are another. And that's you and me and all the others like us.

Why don't we have the imagination to see what is happening but hasn't quite materialized as yet?

Well, I'll tell you. First of all, I have spent years watching chimpanzees. They are more like us than any other living creature. The brain is almost the same. The intellectual abilities are extraordinary. But even the brightest chimp, it doesn't make sense to compare intellectually with the average human, let alone an Einstein. It doesn't make sense.

Think of what we've done. Think of our technology. We've gone to the moon. We've got little robots running around Mars. I mean, it's extraordinary what we've done. So how come this most intellectual being, as far as we know, to ever have walked on this planet is destroying its only home? I think E.O. Wilson was the first to say that if everybody on the planet had the same standard of living as us, then we would need three new planets. Some people say four or five to supply sufficient nonrenewable natural resources. But we don't even have one new one; we've got this one. So do you think we've lost something called wisdom? We are not asking: "How does the decision we make today affect our people generations ahead?" Is there a disconnect between this incredibly clever brain and the human heart?

We started out talking about the chimps. What is it that you learned from them that might help us cope with this world?

One way is to help us be less arrogant and realize that we're part of it all. Some people say, "Well, you know, a few animals, what does it matter if they go extinct?" But I've been to places, as you have, where absolute crippling poverty as a result of environmental degradation is meaning that people are suffering horribly, too. And it's getting worse and worse. People are moving because their islands are going underwater. And, I mean, we should be able to understand the consequences of our selfish behavior by now. So we can learn from the chimp that we're different in these ways, and we should be able to do more to make change than they possibly could.

Do they seem concerned about or aware of their environment? The disappearing forest around them? The difficulty getting the food that they used to get rather easily?

They obviously know it's tough times, but I'm absolutely sure they don't know why. "Yeah, the forest was there yesterday and now it's not. I could wander there last year, but now I may get shot." I mean, they know there are changes, but they can't work out why.

They are endangered. You said there were about a million of them when you went to Africa in 1960.

Less than 300,000 now.

Almost two-thirds of them have disappeared in your lifetime.

Yes. And what's more, many of those remaining are stretched over twenty-one nations in Africa. Many are in tiny, isolated fragments of forest separated from others. They have no hope of surviving in the future because the gene pool's too small.

What do we lose if the last chimp goes?

We lose one window into learning about our long course of evolution. I've spent so long and looked into these minds that are fascinating, because they're so like us. And yet they're in another world. I think the magic is, I will never know what they're thinking. I can guess. And so it's like elephants and gorillas, and all the different animals that we are pushing toward extinction. Are our great-grandchildren going to look back and say, "How could they have done that? They did understand. There were lots of people out there telling them. How, why, did they go on not trying to do anything about it?"

When I told someone yesterday that I was talking with you, he said, "I just read that there are 3,200 tigers left in the world. And that their Asian habitat is disappearing very quickly." And he said, "But, you know, when the tigers are gone, will they be missed any more than the dodo is missed? What difference does it make?"

It's just that we don't know what difference it might make if some of these creatures that we're pushing to the edge disappear. You can take out a tiny insect from an ecosystem. Who cares? Well, it may turn out that some other creature depended on that tiny insect. So that will disappear. And goodness knows what effect that one had on something over there. So that will change. And so, in the end, you get what's been called ecological collapse.

Is there good news?

There's lots of good news. Can I start with Gombe?

Sure. That's where you yourself started.

When I got there, there were 150 chimps in three different communities living on the lakeshore. And from where I was, near Kigoma, you could go for miles along the lake, chimp habitat. You could climb up from the lake, look out, more chimp habitat. Few villages.

Then in the early '90s, I flew over in a plane. I knew there was deforestation. I had no idea it was virtually total. Just gone. So, this tiny little island of forest, 13.5 square miles, is surrounded by cultivated fields, eroded soil, landslides, horrible poverty. Too many people there for the land to support. How could we even think of saving the chimps with so much suffering? So that led to the Jane Goodall Institute's TACARE program [Lake Tanganyika Catchment Reforestation and Education].

And that program, over the years, has worked to improve the lives very holistically of the people in the twenty-four villages closest to Gombe. Everything from different farming methods, helping them with water projects, and such. Especially important have been microcredit programs for women. A group of five women take out a tiny loan, each one for a different project, or sometimes all together. It's got to be environmentally sustainable. So, maybe buying a few chickens, selling the eggs, raising chicks, selling some more. Pay back. Then you can take out a slightly bigger loan. So all these women have been empowered, because they now have something that's theirs. They haven't had a handout.

The real encouragement is that as soon as their lives began to improve, they began to allow trees to come back. As a result, they have set aside the land the government requires them to put into conservation in such a way as to make a buffer between the Gombe chimps and the villagers. And so, other small remnant groups and Gombe chimps will be able to interact again.

In other words, as people's incomes increase the quality of life increases, and they're more interested in preserving what is around. They understand more clearly what's at stake with the environment on which their local economy depends.

Exactly. They understand saving the watershed. They understand that you can't destroy the trees along the edge of a stream or the water level will decrease. They've seen it happen, and they completely understand. The trees and the water and the environment and their future wealth and happiness are all mixed together. And you must have had the same experience as me, traveling around the world. And realizing, you know, Africa's problems aren't just generated within Africa. They're generated outside. They've been generated through hundreds of years of colonial exploitation.

And there's something else that always irritates me. There's a saying, "We haven't inherited this planet from our parents, we've borrowed it from our children." When you borrow, you plan to pay back. We've been stealing and stealing and stealing. And it's about time we got together and started paying back. ᴖ

JAMES CONE

Students walking to school that September morning in 2006 looked up to see three nooses hanging from a tree. For the black children, the scene was both infuriating and frightening. Days earlier they had asked school authorities for permission to sit under that same tree, a spot traditionally used only by white students.

Now, the hangman's halter dangled from its limbs—three of them, grotesque reminders of a horrific past when innocent black people would be seized by white mobs, tortured, and lynched. Yet school authorities in the little Louisiana town of Jena didn't seem to take the nooses seriously, and when black students protested, they were told by a local district attorney to knock it off or "I can make your life disappear with the stroke of a pen."

That entire school year of 2006–7 trembled with tension, rage, fistfights, catcalls, arson, and eventually, after they beat a white male schoolmate, the arrest of half a dozen African American high school students for attempted second-degree murder. The black students became known as the Jena Six. After a public outcry, charges were reduced.

No doubt triggered by the media's continuing coverage of the turmoil in Jena, nooses, real or depicted, began to show up elsewhere in the country; not many, just enough to shake our complacency about a "postracial" society. Just enough to invoke memories of Billie Holiday's signature song, "Strange Fruit":

Southern trees bear a strange fruit
Blood on the leaves and blood at the root
Black body swinging in the southern breeze
Strange fruit hanging from the poplar trees.

James Cone grew up in the shadow of the lynching tree, in the little town of Fordyce, Arkansas. He went on to a life of teaching and scholarship, and in 1969, his book Black Theology and Black Power *established him as the founding figure of black liberation theology, the interpretation of Christianity through the experience of black people. As the Charles A. Briggs Distinguished Professor of Systematic Theology at the Union Theological Seminary in the City of New York, he has used the lynching tree as a metaphor for race in America, telling his students that "the lynched black victim"—falsely accused and put to death—"experienced the same fate as the crucified Christ." In a remarkable coincidence, as the students in Jena came upon the nooses swaying in the tree, James Cone was preparing a lecture that he would soon deliver on the subject at Harvard Divinity School: "Strange Fruit: The Cross and the Lynching Tree." You can view it at www.hds.harvard.edu/news/events _online/ingersoll_2006.html.*

—Bill Moyers

—◦◦◦—

I know you're familiar with that old Billie Holiday song "Strange Fruit." It has traces deep in our DNA, doesn't it?

Yes, it's deep. Because lynching is so deep. And that song is about lynching. It's about black bodies hanging on trees. And, oh, that's deep in the American experience, particularly after the Civil War. Lynching wasn't a part of slavery, because black people were worth too much. After slavery it was used to put fear and terror in the hearts of black people so that they would be forced to obey and stay out in the fields and work and not loiter—and to remember that whites controlled the South even though they had lost the war. That's when lynching started. They wanted to remind black people that whites were in charge. Some of the same reasons why the Romans crucified people in the first century.

It worked.

Yes, it worked to a certain degree, but only in the sense that it reminded black people—and white people—that whites actually had the political, social, and economic control. Of course they didn't have control of their humanity. See, that's what religion is about. Religion is a search for meaning when you don't have it in this world. So while whites might have controlled the black people physically and politically and economically, they did not control their spirit. That's why the black churches were very powerful forces in the African American community—always have been. Religion has been that one place where you have an imagination that no one can control. As long as you know that you are a human being, then God is the reality that enables you to know that nobody can take that away from you.

Even though you're living under the shadow of the lynching tree.

Even though you're living under the shadow of the lynching tree. Because religion is a spirit not defined by what people can do to your body. They can kill your body, but they can't kill your soul. We were always told that. There is a spirit deep in you that nobody can take away from you because God gave it to you. Now, if you know you have a humanity that nobody can take away from you, they may lock you up, they may lynch you, but they don't win.

You and I grew up about a hundred miles or so apart. My home was in east Texas; you were in southwestern Arkansas. Did people where you lived talk about lynching very much?

Yes, my mother and father did. Not so much publicly, but all the time at home. They told us stories about lynching. I think that was true for many black families.

I don't remember whites in my deeply segregated hometown talking about it. But when my father died, I found in his effects a yellowed newspaper clipping from the town where he was born and lived the first years of his life. It was a photograph of a lynching near his farm. Several thousand people had come to watch this man lynched. That was not too long before I was born.

Spectacle lynchings were especially prominent just after the Civil War and in the beginning of the twentieth century. They didn't stop until the late 1930s.

Here's a recent story from the suburbs of New York City. A noose is found in the locker room of the village police department. The deputy chief of police is black. And then you've got what's been happening in Jena, Louisiana. Do you think people understand what the symbol represents? Do they know what actually happened to human beings when that noose was placed around a neck?

Well, you don't have to know all about the Holocaust to understand what a swastika is. You don't have to understand all about the history of lynching to know what a noose is. That symbol is in American culture. As you say, it's in the DNA. It's white America's original sin, and it's deep. I think you know that for a long time, people didn't want to talk about slavery, all 246 years of it. Then came a hundred years of legal segregation and lynching after the Civil War.

But you don't get away from that experience by not talking about it. That's too deep. Germany is not going to get away from the Holocaust by not talking about it. It's too deep. So America must face up that we have this ugly thing in our history. We are one community, and you can't escape our history. Black people and white people know we're one community and there's a tussle in this land we can't get out of. It's a history of violence—246 years of slavery. Black people built this country. White people know that. Then, after slavery, segregation, and lynching, we still helped build this country. We're one people, and violence is a recurring experience in our relationship.

Like the Jews and the Arabs, right?

That's right. And you can't let each other go. I don't care what you do. And that's why those nooses in the news create that kind of response.

Even so, we don't like talking about lynching.

Yeah, it's ugly. "Black bodies hanging on trees." That's ugly. And Billie Holiday can make you feel like you're at the foot of that tree. People don't like to talk about stuff that's really deep and ugly.

James Allen wrote a book in which he talked about the terrible beauty of the lynching tree.

Well, that's my phrase. It comes from Reinhold Niebuhr.

The theologian Reinhold Niebuhr. You teach Niebuhr today at Union Theological Seminary, where he taught for thirty-two years. He's one of the most influential thinkers of the twentieth century. Still relevant today?

Oh, without question. Especially his perspective on humanity. Niebuhr has a profound understanding of the human being. He sees the human being as a creature who is finite but also free. It's that freedom that makes us anxious because the good and the bad in us are always mixed together. America's never clean. And if we could understand that our society isn't innocent, we might be able to play a more creative role in the world today. Niebuhr could help America see that.

If you were asked to recommend one of Niebuhr's books to read, which would it be?

The Irony of American History. The core of it is, let's get over America's "innocence." Help America to see itself through the eyes of people from the bottom. America likes to think of itself as innocent, and we are not. No human being, no society, is innocent. That would be the book I would recommend. I would also recommend *Beyond Tragedy.* Niebuhr tells us that Christianity takes us through and beyond tragedy by way of the cross to victory in the cross.

Go on.

Meaning that the cross is victory out of defeat.

And the lynching tree?

And the lynching tree is transcendent of defeat. That's why the cross and the lynching tree belong together. That's why I have to talk about the lynching tree, because Christians can't understand what's going on at the cross until they see it through the image of a lynching tree with black bodies hanging there. Because the Christian gospel is a transvaluation of values. Something you cannot anticipate in this world, in this history. But it empowers the powerless. What do I mean by power in the powerless? That's what God is. Power in the powerless.

That's of little comfort to the victims of lynchings. They're dead.

Their mothers and fathers aren't dead. Their brothers and sisters aren't dead. I'm alive. And I'm here to give voice to those who did die. And all of us do that. That's why we can't forget it.

I went online and watched the video version of your speech at Harvard where you talked about "strange fruit," the cross, and the lynching tree. I must say that audience didn't seem very comfortable with that linkage.

No, they did not. I said it at a divinity school. Mostly whites were there. But blacks felt comfortable with it. They understand the connection because it gives them a perspective on the lynching that empowers rather than silences them. You know, Bill, people who have never been lynched by another group usually find it difficult to understand why it is blacks want whites to remember lynching atrocities. "Why bring that up?" they ask. "Isn't it best forgotten?"

I say, absolutely not! The lynching tree is a metaphor for race in America, a symbol of America's crucifixion of black people. See, whites feel a little uncomfortable because they are part of the history of the people who did the lynching. I would much rather be a part of the history of the lynching victims than a part of the history of the ones who did it. That's the kind of transcendent perspective that empowers people to resist. That's why Martin Luther King Jr. knew he was going to win even when he seemed to be losing.

You think that's what he meant when he said, "I've seen the Promised Land"?

Yes.

And "I'm going to go up to the mountain"?

Yes.

He said that in Memphis, his last speech. The next day he was dead. Murdered.

That's right.

And you think he had in mind the symbol of the cross, as you were talking about it? Victory snatched from defeat?

Oh, without question. The cross was the most dominant symbol in King's understanding of the gospel and in his life. And the more difficult it became—and it did become difficult—the more difficult it became, the more he knew he was going to be killed, the more he turned to the cross.

I'm sure you appreciate the fact that my audience includes a lot of people who understand that language, who are of the Christian faith. But many people listening are people for whom the cross makes no sense.

Yes, right.

The Roman Empire puts a man on the cross, kills him, and the next thing you know, a religion is growing up from a dead body. So for those people, how do you put into popular language—beyond the dogma, beyond creed, beyond, if you will, the Christian story—the essence of what you are talking about when you talk about "strange fruit"?

See, the cross is my story. It's the story of black people. That's the only way I can talk about it. When people ask me to tell my story, that's what I tell. Now, my story may not be your story. I've been all over the world: India, Sri Lanka, Africa. I've been all over the place where people did not have the cross as their dominant symbol. But they wanted to hear my story. When I tell my story, that's what I tell.

But then I want people to tell me their story. Religion is always the search for meaning for people who are weak and powerless. And religion in that sense connects me with people all over the world. I want to hear the stories because I know God is not without witness. All over the world. And God speaks in many tongues. I know where God is present when I see little people, "the least of these," affirming their humanity in situations where they have few resources to do that. That power is what I mean by the cross.

And you say, "The cross and the lynching tree interpret each other. Both were public spectacles, usually reserved for hardened criminals, rebellious slaves, rebels against the Roman state and falsely accused militant blacks who were often called 'black beasts' and 'monsters in human form.'" Exactly how do the cross and the lynching tree interpret each other?

It keeps the lynchers from having the last word. The lynching tree interprets the cross. It keeps the cross out of the hands of those who are dominant. Nobody who is lynching anybody can understand the cross. That's why it's so important to place the cross and the lynching tree together. Because the cross, or the crucifixion, was analogous to a first-century lynching. In fact, many biblical scholars, when they want to describe what was happening to Jesus, say, "It was a lynching." And all I want to suggest is, if American Christians say they want to identify with that cross, they have to see the cross as a lynching. Anytime your empathy, your solidarity is with the little people, you're with the cross. If you identify with the lynchers, then no, you can't understand what's happening.

That's what resistance means for helpless people. Power in the powerless is not something that we are accustomed to listening to and understanding in America. It's not a part of our historical experience. America always wants to think we're going to win everything. Well, black people have a history in which we didn't win, so our resistance is a resistance against the odds. That's why we can understand the cross.

How should we respond to these recent events with the nooses?

They ought to encourage us to connect, blacks and whites. They ought to remind us of the community we do not have. Instead of separating us from each other, they should bring us together. Listen, there were whites in all of the marches in Jena. There are always whites there, witnessing for justice. That's a sign of hope.

Jena's one thing because of the tradition and history of the South. But how do you explain the presence of these nooses anonymously in the New York suburbs, for example, not far from where we're sitting right now?

Well, racism and white supremacy were not confined to the South. It was all over America. It's just expressed in different ways. It existed here in the North, but it wasn't acknowledged.

There's a recent book called Lynchings in the West: 1850–1935, *photographs from Ken Gonzales-Day. He went searching for California's lynching trees. And he found three hundred lynching trees out there. The Far West!*

Yes! Yes! Lynching happened all over. Pennsylvania, New York, California. All over America lynching happened. Now, it was more prominent in the South, places like Mississippi and Georgia. The terror was deeply embedded there. But it was a part of America. And that's why Malcolm X said, "Mississippi is America." You know, it's not separate. Now, Malcolm X came from the North, and his voice was a lot more militant than King's, who came from the South. Malcolm was trying to get people to listen to something that they didn't want to listen to. King knew the difference. His truth was obvious. Malcolm's truth was not so obvious.

The truth that . . . ?

That white supremacy is as present in New York City as it is in Jackson, Mississippi. That's the truth. And when America can see itself historically—

it wasn't just the South that did the lynching, it was part of American culture—then we can figure out how we can start to overcome that legacy. You can't overcome something if you never acknowledged its presence.

Do you acknowledge the presence of crucifixion and lynching today?

Yes, I do.

Where?

It's in the prisons, especially. But it's all over. Again, crucifixion and lynchings are symbols of the power of domination. They are symbols of the destruction of people's humanity. Black people are 12 percent of the U.S. population and nearly 50 percent of the prison population; that's a form of lynching—legal lynching. So there are a lot more ways to lynch a people than just hanging them on the tree. A lynching is trying to control the population. It is striking terror in the population so as to control it. That's what the ghetto does. It crams people into living spaces where they will self-destruct, kill each other, fight each other, shoot each other because they have no place to breathe, no place for recreation, no place for an articulation and expression of their humanity. The ghetto becomes, just like prisons, a metaphor for lynching, if lynching is understood as one group forcing a kind of inhumanity upon another group.

Do you believe God is love?

Yes, I believe God is love.

I would have a hard time believing God is love if I were a black man. Those bodies swinging on the tree. Where was God during the 246 years of slavery? Where was God during the era of lynching in this country?

See, you are looking at it from the perspective of those who win. You have to see it from the perspective of those who have no power. For them, God is love because it's that power in your life that lets you know you can resist the definitions that other people are placing on you. And you sort of say, "Sure, nobody knows the trouble I've seen; nobody knows my sorrow. Sure, there is slavery. Sure, there is lynching, segregation. But glory, hallelujah, there is a humanity and a spirit that nobody can kill." And as long as you know that, you will resist. That was the power of the civil rights movement. That was the power of those who kept marching even though the odds were against them. How do you keep going when you don't have the battle tanks, when you don't have the guns, when you don't have the military power? When you have nothing? How do you keep going? How do you know that you are a human being? You know because there's a power that transcends all of that.

What do you mean when you say God is love?

God is that power, that power that enables you to resist. You love that! You love the power that empowers you even in a situation in which you have no political power. You have to love God. Now, what is trouble is loving white people. Now, that's tough. It's not God we're having trouble loving. Loving white people—now, that's difficult.

Have you forgiven whites for lynching your ancestors?

Well, it's not a question of forgiveness except in this sense. You see, when whites ask me about that, then I want to know why they're asking. First I want to talk about what you're going to do in order to make sense out of the world to make me want to do that—to forgive. I don't think my forgiveness of you depends on what you do, but I am curious why you ask me that.

I ask it because I'm not sure I could give it.

That's because when you have a power and a reality in your experience that transcends both you and me, then it's not just what you can do or what I can do. It is what the power in us can do. That presence of a spirit that is greater enables you to do the unthinkable because you know you're connected with the scoundrel even though he might have lynched you or lynched your brother. You are going to fight him about that. He's a bad brother. But he's still a brother.

That's hard to grasp, actually. But that's what you're about, it seems to me. You said in your Harvard speech that you hoped, by linking the cross and the lynching tree, to begin a conversation in America about race. What would you like us to be talking about?

I'd like for us, first, to talk to each other. And I'd like to talk about what it would mean to be one community, one people. Really one people.

And what would that mean?

It would mean that we would talk about the lynching tree. We would talk about slavery. We would talk about the good and the bad all mixed up there. We would begin to see ourselves as a family. Martin Luther King called it the "beloved community." That's what he was struggling for.

Okay, what can people do to try to help bring about this beloved community?

First is to believe that it can happen. Don't lose hope. If people lose hope, they give up in despair. Black people were enslaved for 246 years. But they didn't lose hope.

Why?

They didn't lose hope because there was a power and a reality in their experience that helped them to know that they were a part of this human race just like everybody else, and they fought for that.

All right, I have hope. What's next?

The next step is to connect with people who also have hope: blacks, whites, Hispanics, all different ages, all different kinds of people. You have to connect and organize with people who have hope.

What do you mean, organize?

You organize to make the world the way it ought to be. And that is the beloved community. You have to have some witness to that, even if it's a small witness by just you and me.

You don't have to be angels to do that. If men were angels, our founding fathers said, we wouldn't need government.

No, we're not angels. But where there are two or three gathered, as it says in the scripture, there is hope. There is possibility. And you don't want to lose that. That's why I keep teaching.

Speaking of race, there's so much talk today about blackness. People are arguing about whether Barack Obama is black enough or not.

Well, everybody should be aware of their heritage. Blackness is a powerful, powerful symbol in America. Because we were taught to be ashamed of being black. And in a society in which you are taught to be ashamed, the only recourse is to affirm it. You shouldn't be bashful about talking about it, because to be bashful about talking about it is, in some sense, to be ashamed of it, at least from the perspective of those who are black and who don't have the kind of position that Condoleezza Rice or Barack Obama would have. What these people are saying is, express some identity with our history and our culture. It's okay to identify with the larger culture, because we are one community. But that should not entitle one to just forget about one's own particular culture of blackness.

Is Obama "black enough"?

I'm not sure I'm black enough for a lot of people. I think what is relevant here is that people are reaching out to Barack Obama, wanting him to address some of the issues that are particularly important to them. He has addressed one or two, but from the perspective of the people who are asking the question, at least, not black enough to affirm the fact that he really is as much for black people as he is for everyone else. The problem here is that whites make it difficult for black people to be black and also for them to support him. It's because we haven't been talking about that lynching tree. We haven't been talking about slavery, the ugly side of our country. So if Barack Obama comes out and says, "I'm black and I'm proud of it," well, whites would get nervous. And they would be careful about whether they would vote for him. He has a narrow, narrow road on which to walk. Because he won't be elected if he doesn't get the white vote. It's hard to get the white vote if you express a kind of affirmative identity with black people. You get caught between a rock and a hard place. You see, white people are proud of their cultural history. When you talk about Thomas Jefferson and George Washington, you're talking about slaveholders. But you don't say that.

Why don't we say that?

Because America likes to be innocent. It likes to be the exception. That's why it's hard for Barack Obama or Secretary of State Condoleezza Rice to talk about blackness; if they talked about blackness in the real, true sense, it would be uncomfortable. But America can't be what America ought to be until America can look at itself, the good, the bad, and the ugly, and keep working on making ourselves what we ought to be. We're not the country we can be. ∽

DAVID BOIES

This had to be one of the most unusual and intriguing legal teams in American judicial history. Two courtroom titans who had battled each other all the way to the Supreme Court in Bush v. Gore were back, this time on the same side, defending same-sex marriage.

David Boies was no surprise. Long a champion of progressive causes, he had been the Justice Department's special counsel in its successful antitrust suit against Microsoft. But Ted Olson? An icon of the right, an influential legal advisor in the Reagan administration, he had triumphed in 2000 when the conservative majority on the Supreme Court decided the contested election for George W. Bush, who later asked Olson to be his solicitor general. Now he was breaking with his own crowd to champion a cause they abhorred.

On Election Day in 2008, as Barack Obama was collecting California's fifty-five electoral votes on his way to the White House, voters in that state, by a margin of 52 to 48 percent, approved Proposition 8, which ordered the state constitution to define marriage as the union between one man and one woman, effectively prohibiting gay and lesbian marriage. A year later the California Supreme Court upheld the amendment's constitutionality. Olson and Boies then filed a legal challenge on behalf of two same-sex couples—two men, two women—who had been denied the right to marry.

Thanks to activists who reenacted the hearings online, I could follow the

TED OLSON

arguments as if they were a courtroom drama on TV, and I found them so fascinating I asked Olson and Boies to join me on the Journal even before the federal judge had handed down a ruling. That ruling came down on August 4, 2010, when U.S. District Judge Vaughn Walker agreed with Boies and Olson and overturned Proposition 8. Pending appeal, his decision remains on hold, and it seems clear that Boies and Olson will eventually be back before the Supreme Court of the United States—an ideological odd couple, allies instead of foes.

—Bill Moyers

❧

Many people in this partisan and polarized country have been hoping to see conservatives and liberals unite on at least one principle that they could agree upon. But just about everyone I have talked to was surprised to see the two of you show up in the same court arguing for gay marriage. What do you have in common on this?

BOIES: I think one of the things we have in common on this issue is respect for the rule of law, respect for civil rights, respect for the Constitution. This is not a liberal or conservative issue. It's not a Republican or Democratic issue. Conservatives and liberals alike need the Constitution. Conservatives and liberals alike want to keep the government out of regulating our personal conduct, want to keep the government out of the bedroom.

Both conservatives and liberals have an interest in seeing the rule of law applied to everybody. So although sometimes people say that they're surprised to see the two of us together, I don't really think they ought to be, because I think this is something that both conservatives and liberals ought to unite behind.

But everyone knows conservatives in this country have been clear that they are opposed to gay marriage. And the strong base of the Republican Party, the religious right, is adamant about this. Your own friend, your good friend, former judge Robert Bork, has called same-sex marriage a judicial sin. He said he can't even bear to talk to you about this case. Now, if he should say, "Come over and let's have a drink and talk about it," what would you do to justify the position you have taken?

OLSON: I think the more people hear what David and I have to say, the more people will understand. That's one of the wonderful things about the fact that we have come together, because people will ask the question that you've just asked: "Why are you doing this? What is your explanation?" It gives us a chance to explain the damage that's being done by discrimination, and the great burden that would be lifted if we finally stop.

But might not Judge Bork counter that you've joined with this liberal elitist here to find in the Constitution another "new" right that really isn't there?

OLSON: We're not advocating any recognition of a new right. The constitutional right to marry has been recognized by the Supreme Court over and over again. We're talking about whether two individuals should be treated equally, under the equal protection clause of the Constitution, the same thing that the Supreme Court did in 1967, when it recognized the constitutional rights of people of different races to marry.

In 1967, seventeen states prohibited persons of a different race from marrying one another. The Supreme Court didn't create a new right—the right was the right to marry. The Supreme Court unanimously said discrimination on the basis of race in that instance was unconstitutional.

The voters in California spoke very clearly, 52 to 48 percent. The referendum said, "Only marriage between a man and a woman is valid or recognized in California." And you're telling the majority of those voters they're wrong?

BOIES: If you didn't tell the majority of the voters that, under the Constitution, they were wrong sometimes, you wouldn't need a constitution. The whole point of the Bill of Rights and the Fourteenth Amendment is to say, "This is a democracy. But it's also a democracy in which we protect minority rights." The whole point of a constitution is to say there are certain things that a majority cannot do, whether it's 52 percent or 62 percent or 72 percent or 82 percent of the people.

They can't say, for example, that blacks and whites can't go to school together—even though most of the people might have thought that. They can't say that women aren't allowed to vote, or aren't allowed to work, or earn equal rights or equal wages—even though a majority of people might vote that way in some places.

There are certain rights that are so fundamental that the Constitution guarantees them to every citizen regardless of what a temporary majority may or may not vote for. What Ted said is very important. Nobody's asking to create a new constitutional right here. This is a constitutional right that has already been well recognized by the Supreme Court.

What your opponents are saying is that you're extending that fundamental right to same-sex partners, and there's nothing in the Constitution that refers to sexual orientation of any kind.

BOIES: What the Constitution says is that every citizen gets equal protection of the law. It doesn't just say heterosexuals.

So this is the Fourteenth Amendment you're invoking.

BOIES: The Fourteenth Amendment. And remember, the Fourteenth Amendment was passed just after we got rid of slavery, which prohibited slaves from getting married. And one of the things that happened when slavery was abolished was that large numbers of African Americans rushed to get married, because they viewed this as one of the most important human relationships. And they viewed the recognition, the sanctioning of that relationship, as critical to their ability to live together as a family.

The same thing is happening with gays and lesbians in our society today.

We're saying to these people, "You are somehow less than human. We're not going to give you all of humanity's rights." Because remember, if we recognize them as human, if we recognize them as full citizens, the Constitution guarantees that they have equal protection of the laws. They have the same rights as any heterosexual.

You're both comfortable invalidating seven million votes in California?

OLSON: Well, this happens when the voters decide to violate someone's constitutional rights. We have a constitution and we have an independent judiciary for the very protection of minorities. Majorities don't need to seek protection from the courts. The original Constitution didn't have the Bill of Rights attached to it. And the framers of our Constitution had a big debate and people said, "Well, we're not going to ratify that constitution unless you attach a Bill of Rights, which protects individual liberty, individual freedom, the right to speak, the right to assemble," and those sorts of things.

Over our history, voters get passionate about certain things, and they may not like certain minorities. Minorities are disfavored. Blacks have been denied the right to vote. California prohibited the Chinese from having any kind of business in California or getting married. Those kind of votes are not acceptable if they violate fundamental constitutional rights.

You're going up not only against the voters of California, the majority, you're going up against the Congress of the United States. In the 1990s, Congress passed the Defense of Marriage Act, which actually defined marriage as "a legal union between one man and one woman," and even declared that states need not recognize the same-sex marriages of another state. President Bill Clinton signed this.

BOIES: But remember, that happens every time the Supreme Court declares a law unconstitutional. In a case that Ted argued, the Supreme Court just declared certain restrictions on the ability of corporations to participate in political contests unconstitutional [*Citizens United v. FEC*]. They were overruling the will of the democratically elected Congress of the United States. The power to hold laws unconstitutional was given to an independent judiciary for the specific purpose of protecting minority rights against majority abuses.

OLSON: Fifty years ago the Congress and the President of the United States made it illegal for someone who is gay or lesbian to have a job working for the federal government. Many states made it a crime for a homosexual to be in a bar and have a drink. We all remember the '50s, when civil rights were taken away from people because they were suspected of being a member of a "subversive" organization.

And we frequently go to the courts and, Bill, it often happens that the measures that are passed almost unanimously in Congress, because Congress gets carried away, are overturned by the Supreme Court. And you go back to members of Congress and you say, "What happened there?" And they'll say, "Well, we knew it was unconstitutional. We expected the courts to take care of that. We wanted to get reelected. The courts are the ones that come back and help us."

At what point does the Supreme Court take on public opinion? Roughly forty states have laws banning gay marriage. Isn't it risky to ask the court to invalidate that much public opinion before the public is really ready for it?

BOIES: When the Supreme Court held that it was unconstitutional to prevent interracial marriages, 64 percent or more of the population of the United States, about two-thirds of the population, believed interracial marriages were wrong. That's a much higher percentage than opposes gay and lesbian marriage in this country today.

If you look at where this country's going, if you look at the polls, the vast majority of people are moving in this direction already. Certainly all the young people.

As you both know, some leading gay groups were opposed to what you have done. They argued that the country was not politically ready for this kind of judicial decision. And they said they need more time to win over the public opinion, state by state, that if you go to the Supreme Court and lose, you will actually set back the cause of equality in marriage for years. Why did you go against the wishes of so many in the gay community who didn't want you to do this?

OLSON: When people said, "Maybe you should be waiting. Maybe you should wait until there's more popular support," our answer to that was, "Well, when is that going to happen? How long do you want people to wait?

How long do you want people to be deprived of their constitutional rights in California?"

You've clearly read Martin Luther King Jr.'s "Letter from a Birmingham Jail."

OLSON: People told Martin Luther King, "Don't do it. The people aren't ready." And Martin Luther King responded, "I can't wait. I'm not going to make people wait." And when people told Martin Luther King, "You may lose," he said that battles for civil rights are won ultimately by people fighting for civil rights.

And one more thing. The Supreme Court had made the decision in *Loving v. Virginia* in 1967, striking down the laws of seventeen states that prohibited interracial marriage. Now it's, what, forty years later? The public sometimes follows the opinions of the Supreme Court, reads the opinion and says, "My gosh, thank goodness for the Supreme Court. We realize how wrong that was."

In 1973, when the court ruled in favor of women's reproductive rights, many people weren't ready for it. There was a huge backlash. And today women's reproductive rights are threatened because the political movement that grew up after Roe v. Wade *has become so powerful.*

BOIES: Well, I don't think they're any more threatened now than they would have been if you hadn't had *Roe v. Wade*. You have to sometimes fight these battles over and over again. But that's no reason not to fight them and try to win them when you can.

What did you tell the gay activists who came to you?

BOIES: For one thing, the gay activists who came and talked to me were not nearly as impassioned as you suggest. They recognized that there were two sides to the question. They were concerned. And I think a lot of those concerns have been alleviated as they've seen the record that we've built. I think a lot of the people who were dubious about this case have now come to Ted and have come to me and said, "We're glad you brought this case."

There are still some people who are very worried about what the Supreme Court will do. And I sympathize with that. These are people who have dedicated their lives to promoting gay and lesbian rights. And they are people you need to listen to. But one of the things that I've always said to them is this case is going to be brought. You can't keep people from litigating.

And if it's going to be brought, you want it brought by people who know how to try cases, who know how to argue cases on appeal, who are going to have the resources and the commitment to try it right. I think anybody who saw the case that we made in California last month can see that we've built a record there; you cannot look at it and come away believing that Proposition 8 is constitutional. And that record took a lot of work.

We brought in experts from all over the world, the leading experts, leading scientific experts in psychology and sociology and history and political science and anthropology. We canvassed all the scientific studies. We made a presentation that would have been very difficult for a lot of lawyers to have made. So if you're going to have this case go up to the Supreme Court, we think it ought to go up with the absolute best record.

Tell me about the two couples that you are representing.

BOIES: We put them on the stand, all four of them, right at the beginning of the trial. And you could not listen to these people and not be moved by their stories. You could not listen to these people and not be moved by their love for each other, by their desire to be married, by the harm, the pain that they were being caused by not being able to do what we take for granted, which is to marry the person we love.

OLSON: The lesbian couple is raising four boys. They've been together for many, many years. The gay male couple has been together in a loving relationship for a long period of time. They put a real face on the discrimination. And they talked about how much it mattered to them that their loving relationship and their role in the community and their ability to go to work and pick up their children at school and all of those things are threatened and demeaned because people won't recognize that they are in the same kind of relationship as their next-door neighbor.

We're hurting them enormously and hurting ourselves by treating a class of our citizens as different and less worthy of respect. It is not American. It's not a part of our culture. It's damaging to America to take a class of our citizens, who are every bit as much contributors to our society, and say, "Your relationship is not recognized. It's a second-class citizenship." If you believe in the sanctity of marriage, if you believe in family values, why in the world would you want to exclude a whole class of citizens from that?

You've always had respect for your adversary in the courtroom. And this opponent was one of your friends, Charles Cooper. You served with him in the Reagan Justice Department. What was the most effective argument he made against you?

OLSON: I have great respect for him. He's a very fine lawyer. He had a very fine group of lawyers and they were doing their best, but I didn't find any of their arguments effective. I have said from the beginning of this case, I've yet to hear an argument that persuades me or even comes close to persuading me that we should treat our gay and lesbian colleagues differently and deny them equality.

But what was a very eye-opening event, during one of the early proceedings, the judge asked my opponent, "What harm to the institution of heterosexual marriage would occur if gays and lesbians were allowed to marry?"

This went back and forth and back and forth. The judge kept wanting an answer. And my opponent, finally, had to answer it truthfully. He paused and said, "I don't know. I don't know." That to me sums up the other side. Allowing the two couples or others like them to engage in a relationship with their partner where they can be treated as equal members of society doesn't hurt your marriage or my marriage or David's marriage or any other heterosexual marriage. People are not going to say, "I don't want to get married anymore if those same-sex people can get married." That's not going to happen.

Yet your opponents kept coming back to the argument that the central reason for Proposition 8 is its role "in regulating naturally procreative relationships between men and women to provide for the nurture and upbringing of the next generation."

OLSON: We have never in this country required the ability or desire to procreate as a condition for getting married. People who are seventy, eighty, ninety years old may get married. People who have no interest in having children can get married.

The Supreme Court has said that the right to get married is a fundamental individual right. And our opponents say, "Well, the state has an interest in procreation and that's why we allow people to get married." No one's stopping heterosexual people from getting married and having all the children they want. It is simply allowing people who have abiding affection for one another to live a civil life. The same way you are.

One of the opposing lawyers credited the two of you with putting on a spectacular show, but he said your evidence was irrelevant: "The best thing for a child is to have both a mother and a father. A same-sex couple couldn't offer the same benefits as a mother and a father," he said. "That's the case."

BOIES: As to whether a heterosexual couple raises better children than a same-sex couple, all the evidence is to the contrary. The scientific evidence, and this has been studied over and over again, shows that what's important is to have a loving, stable, two-parent family. And that can be a heterosexual couple. It can be a gay couple. It can be a lesbian couple.

OLSON: The world's leading expert about the welfare of children, from Cambridge, testified that children do as well in a same-sex environment, where both of their parents are the same sex, as with opposite-sex parents. And it's important to recognize that California recognizes the right of same-sex couples to live together, to have children, to adopt children, or conceive children in various ways that are available these days. There are 37,000 children in California with same-sex couples. And the evidence shows that those children are doing fine, just fine. Compare an opposite-sex couple in which there's an abusive father with a same-sex loving couple. The quality of a parent is not based upon gender or sexual orientation. It is in the quality of one's heart.

When the court first ruled that gay marriage was permissible in California, 18,000 gay and lesbian couples got married. Then Proposition 8 comes along and declares gay marriage unconstitutional. What happens to those 18,000 who married in that interim?

BOIES: They're still valid. And one of the things that makes the equal protection argument so strong for California is that California has this absurd classification system right now. If you are a gay or lesbian couple who got married, one of those 18,000, your marriage is valid. In addition, if you were a gay or lesbian couple that got married in another state where it was

valid and moved to California during that period, that marriage is also recognized. But if you're one of the other gay and lesbian couples who didn't
get married, you can't get married now. And if you happen to be one of the
people who did get married in that window and you get divorced, you can't
get remarried. Because of Proposition 8.

OLSON: So you have various different classes of persons. People who can't
get married. People who can get married. People who are married. People
who are married but can't get remarried. People who got married in another
state who may remain married. So, California's got what we call a crazy-
quilt system of laws that treat people differently in different categories.

*I'm sure you know you're up against some very powerful religious sentiment on
this. The Southern Baptist Convention, with millions of members, the largest
Protestant denomination in America, describes homosexuality as an abomination. The Catholic Church calls homosexual activity gravely immoral.*

*Archbishop Joseph Kurtz of the U.S. Conference of Catholic Bishops says,
"The difference between man and woman allows them to make the fundamentally unique commitment of marriage, ordered to love and the creation and
nurturing of new life. Because of the unique nature and responsibilities of this
relationship, it deserves the protection and promotion of the state."*

OLSON: We respect people's individual religious convictions. They're entitled to those convictions under that same Constitution that protects the
free exercise of religion. But this point of view is based upon the idea that
intimate sexual conduct between persons of the same sex is evil, it's a sin, it's
wrong, it's unnatural. Well, the Supreme Court of the United States just a
few years ago struck down laws that violated the fundamental rights of individuals to have intimate sexual relationships with one another.

*This was Lawrence v. Texas. The Court said that sodomy is not unconsti-
tutional.*

BOIES: That's right.

So is the religious doctrine wrong?

BOIES: You can't say the religious doctrine is wrong. Religious doctrine is
a doctrine of belief. And I don't think either Ted or I or anybody would say
that the archbishop or the Southern Baptists don't have the right to believe

whatever they believe. And our Constitution, the First Amendment, guarantees them that right of freedom of conscience and freedom of religious beliefs.

But that same First Amendment, in the antiestablishment clause of that amendment, says that they cannot impose those religious beliefs on other people. No one is saying that the Southern Baptist Church or the Catholic Church or any other church ought to marry people who they don't want to marry. However, what we are saying is that no religious group, no matter how numerous, should be able to pass a law that says the state will only sanction marriages that we religiously approve. That's the separation between church and state that our Constitution has always guaranteed.

Couldn't you have avoided all of this if you had just said, "Well, gay people, lesbians, have the same legal rights in civil unions." And you wouldn't have stirred up this crowd.

OLSON: Well, yes, they'd get stirred up anyway. But if the American people would just listen to what the plaintiffs and the other experts said in this case, they would understand so much more about the damage that's done by people who say, "You can live together. You may have children. We sort of think it's okay for your relationship to exist, but you can't call yourselves married. And your relationship doesn't count. And you don't count." You know, that is demeaning. And if the American people see that, they'll see the difference.

BOIES: One of the reasons we put the individual plaintiffs on the stand was for the judge and, hopefully, for the appellate court to see the human face of this discrimination. To see the cost, the pain that this kind of discrimination causes. Americans believe in liberty. We believe in equality. It's baked into our soul. The only way that we have engaged in the kind of discrimination that we have, historically, is by somehow overlooking the humanity of the people that we discriminate against. We did that with African Americans. We did that with Asians. We did that with American Indians. We did that with women. We're doing it with gays and lesbians today. We somehow put out of our mind the fact that we're discriminating against another human being by characterizing them as somehow not like us. Not equal to us. Not fully human. Not a full citizen. And that's what is so pernicious about this campaign.

This is the first time that state laws banning gay marriage have been challenged in a federal court. No matter who wins, no matter how the judge in San Francisco comes down, it's likely this will be appealed all the way to the Supreme Court, right?

BOIES: Yes.

OLSON: Yes.

If you go to the Supreme Court, Ted, you're going to run smack up against some of your best friends. You mentioned that 2003 case, when the court outlawed Texas laws against sodomy. As you know, Justice Scalia issued a strong, some say virulent, dissent. And he said that this decision effectively decrees the end of all morals legislation and would lead to sanctioning same-sex marriages.

He went on to accuse his colleagues on the court of aligning themselves with the "homosexual agenda." Let me read you this. This is from Justice Scalia. "Many Americans do not want persons who openly engage in homosexual conduct as partners in their business, as scoutmasters for their children, as teachers in their children's schools, or as boarders in their home. They view this as protecting themselves and their families from a lifestyle that they believe to be immoral and destructive." If you get to the Court, how are you going to deal with your friend Justice Scalia?

OLSON: Well, let me say that I have enormous respect for all of the members of the United States Supreme Court and I've had wonderful relationships in one way or another with all of them. My friends are not on one side or the other. Second, Justice Scalia writes beautifully. And he has passionate, powerful views. But he lost. And he went on to say in that very opinion, "If we decide this case that way, what's to prevent same-sex marriage from being held to be a constitutional right?" Well, he's right.

And once you make that decision in that case, and you put it together with the marriage cases, that's the end of it, as far as that's concerned. We hope to persuade everyone on that Court. And part of what you just read was that some people don't want a homosexual to be a teacher in a school. Well, today, I don't think hardly anyone would agree that you could make a law that said a person whose sexual orientation is homosexual can't teach in a public school.

There was a ballot proposition in California in the '70s—you might remember this—that would have restricted the rights of homosexuals to be teachers in schools. And it was going to pass. It was a major amendment to the California law. And Ronald Reagan came out and said that's unwise. That will hurt people. That will cause people, teachers, good teachers, to be persecuted. And it went down to defeat.

You know that some of your friends and longtime colleagues, including Charles Cooper, are saying that Ted Olson has turned to the very kind of judicial activism that he's always lamented and opposed. Do you understand that they're saying that?

OLSON: I know they're saying this. Some of them to my face. And my answer is, it isn't judicial activism for the Supreme Court to recognize an associational right, a liberty right, and a privacy right for two people who love one another to be married. I don't think it's judicial activism to treat our citizens equally, and to require that equality under the law be accorded to all of our citizens. There are a lot of people in this country who have a sexual orientation that is different than ours, and if we treat them differently, we're hurting them, no one can question that. We're hurting them. We're saying that they're different. If you're going to be a citizen, take the time to read the transcript of this trial and what the experts had to say and what the plaintiffs had to say. And then come to me and tell me that I'm wrong.

BOIES: I think that conservatives, just like liberals, rely on the Supreme Court to protect the rule of law, to protect our liberties, to look at a law and decide whether or not it fits within the Constitution. And I think when you're thinking about judicial activism the point that's really important here is that this is not a new right. Nobody is saying, "Go find in the Constitution the right to get married." Everybody, a unanimous Supreme Court, says there's a fundamental right to get married.

The question is whether you can discriminate against certain people based on their sexual orientation. And the issue of prohibiting discrimination has never, in my view, been looked on as a test of judicial activism. That's not liberal, that's not conservative. That's not Republican or Democrat. That's simply an American constitutional civil right. ⁓

WENDELL POTTER

One of the most dramatic moments in the fight for health care reform came early in the summer of 2009 when a bespectacled onetime journalist with a slight southern accent, so faint only kindred Tennessee ears might have detected it, looked up at a row of senatorial faces and began:

> *My name is Wendell Potter, and for twenty years I worked as a senior executive at health insurance companies, and I saw how they confuse their customers and dump the sick—all so they can satisfy their Wall Street investors.*

In those two sentences Wendell Potter, most recently a senior vice president of CIGNA, the country's fourth-largest health insurance company, had broken the industry's code of silence on the lethal consequences of corporate spin in the pursuit of profits over patient care.

And he was just getting started. He went on to describe how the industry spent billions of dollars to spread disinformation, buy influence, skirt regulations, and mislead consumers. He knew the tactics firsthand; as a consummate insider earning a six-figure income, he sat on policy committees, crafted executive messages, and cajoled the press. Just two years earlier he had defended CIGNA during a public relations nightmare as protestors forced the company to reverse its decision not to pay for a liver transplant for seventeen-year-old Nataline Sarkisyan, who died two hours after CIGNA relented.

Who can say exactly when enough's enough? When a person reaches the tipping point and blows the whistle on his own circle, his own colleagues and work? Potter still can't say, although he carries with him to this day pictures he took while visiting a rural health "fair" in Wise, Virginia, where hundreds of people stood in the mist and rain waiting to be treated in stalls built for live-stock. He quit CIGNA in 2008 and one year later went public, warning the Senate Commerce Committee that the industry was mounting "duplicitous and well-financed PR and lobbying campaigns," a charm offensive to shape the health care debate "in a way that benefits Wall Street far more than average Americans."

The mainstream press carried little of his testimony. I missed it myself. Then John Stauber called. The founder of the public interest organization Center for Media and Democracy, a pioneer in exposing corporate disinformation, he urged me to take a serious look at Potter. "Are you sure he's for real?" I asked. "Grill him yourself," Stauber answered. So I did, with my editorial team: five uninterrupted hours in private, followed by a week of forensic research into his answers and background. We were convinced. Still, when we began the inter-view, I decided to test him again. . . .

—*Bill Moyers*

You left CIGNA after working there fifteen years.

I did.

Were you pushed out?

I was not. It was my decision to leave, and my decision to leave when I did.

Were you passed over for a promotion?

Absolutely not. No.

Had you been well paid and rewarded by the company?

Very well paid. And over the years I had many job opportunities, many bo-nuses, salary increases. And in fact, there was no further place for me to go in the company. I was head of corporate communications, and that was the ultimate PR job.

Did you like your boss and the people you worked with?

I did, and still do. I still respect them.

And they gave you a terrific party when you left?

They sure did, yes.

Why are you speaking out now?

I didn't intend to, until it became really clear to me that the industry is resorting to the same tactics they've used over the years, and particularly back in the early '90s, when they were leading the effort to kill the Clinton plan.

During the fifteen years you were there, did you go to them and say, "I think we're on the wrong side. I think we're fighting the wrong people here"?

I didn't, because for most of the time I was there, I felt that what we were doing was the right thing, and that I was playing on an honorable team. I just didn't really get it all that much until toward the end of my tenure at CIGNA.

What did you see?

I began to question what I was doing as the industry shifted from selling primarily managed care plans to what they refer to as consumer-driven plans. Those are really plans with very high deductibles, meaning that they're shifting a lot of the cost of health care from employers and insurers—insurance companies—to individuals. As a result, a lot of people can't even afford to make their co-payments when they go get care. But the turning point for me was a trip back home to Tennessee. That's when I began to see exactly what is happening to so many Americans.

When was this?

July of 2007.

You were still working for CIGNA?

I was. I went home to visit relatives. And I picked up the local newspaper and I saw that a health care expedition was being held a few miles up the road, in Wise, Virginia. And I was intrigued. I borrowed my dad's car and drove fifty miles up the road to the Wise County Fairground. I had my camera and took some pictures. It was a very cloudy, misty day; it rained some. As I walked through the fairground gates, I didn't know what to expect. I assumed it would be health booths set up for people to get their blood pressure checked, things like that.

But what I saw were doctors providing health care in animal stalls, or in tents they had erected. There was no privacy. In some of my pictures people are being treated on gurneys on rain-soaked pavement. And there were long lines of people, standing and sitting, waiting to get care. People had driven from South Carolina, Georgia, Kentucky, Tennessee—all over the region—because they had heard about this by word of mouth. I thought, these could have been people I'd grown up with, people down the road from me, people I had known.

How did you react?

It was absolutely stunning. It was like being hit by lightning. It was almost like, what country am I in? It just didn't seem possible that I was in the United States.

Skeptics are going to say, "How can Wendell Potter sit here and say he was only now finding out that there were a lot of Americans who didn't have adequate insurance and needed health care? He'd been working in the industry for over fifteen years!"

And that was my problem. I had been in the industry and I'd risen up in the ranks. And I had a great job. And I had a terrific office in a high-rise building in Philadelphia. I was insulated. I saw the data. I knew that 47 million people were uninsured, but I didn't put faces with that number.

Just a few weeks later though, I was back at corporate headquarters in Philadelphia, and flying to meetings on the company jet. And I thought, what a great way to travel. You're sitting in a luxurious corporate jet, leather seats, very spacious. You're served lunch by a flight attendant who brings it on a gold-rimmed plate. And she handed me gold-plated silverware to eat it with. And then I remembered the people I had seen in Wise County.

But for years you had seen premiums rising. People purged from the rolls, people who couldn't afford the health care that CIGNA and other companies were offering. And this is the first time you came face-to-face with it?

It was, Bill. Certainly I knew people and talked to people who were uninsured. But when you're in the executive offices, when you're getting prepared for a call with a financial analyst, going over the numbers—you don't think about individual people. You think about the numbers, and whether or not you're going to meet Wall Street's expectations. That's what you think about at corporate headquarters. And it helps to think that way, it helps you do your job, if you don't really think about real human beings.

Did you go back to corporate headquarters and tell them what you had seen?

I went back to corporate headquarters. I was trying to process what I had seen, trying to figure out what I should do. I did tell many of them about the experience in Virginia. I showed them some pictures I took while I was down there. But I didn't know exactly what I should do. You know, I had bills of my own. How do I step away from this? What do I do?

One day I was reading President Kennedy's book *Profiles in Courage*. In the foreword, his brother Robert Kennedy said that one of the president's favorite quotes was from Dante: "The hottest places in Hell are reserved for those who, in a time of great moral crisis, maintain their neutrality." And when I read that, I said, "Oh, jeez, I'm headed for that hottest place in Hell, unless I say something."

I'm looking at your résumé, describing what you did at CIGNA. It says: "With the chief medical officer and his staff, Potter developed rapid response mechanisms for handling media inquiries pertaining to complaints." It goes on, "This was highly successful in keeping most of such inquiries from becoming news stories, at a time when managed care horror stories abounded." You knew there were horror stories out there.

I did. I did.

You put these techniques to work representing CIGNA during the Nataline Sarkisyan case, right?

That's right.

And that was a public relations nightmare, you called it.

It was. It was the most difficult of the high-profile cases. A family or a patient goes to the news media and complains about having some coverage denied that a doctor had recommended. In this case, Nataline Sarkisyan's doctors at UCLA had recommended that she have a liver transplant. But when the coverage request was reviewed at CIGNA, the decision was made to deny it. The family had sought some help from the California Nurses Association and was very successful in getting media attention like nothing I had ever seen before. Protestors gathered outside the office there shouting, "Shame on CIGNA! Shame on CIGNA!" I'll tell you, that got our attention in the corporate offices.

You were also involved in the campaign by the industry to discredit Michael Moore and his film Sicko *in 2007. Moore went to several countries around the world and reported that their health care systems were better than our health care system, in particular, Canada and England. What did you think when you saw that film?*

I thought he hit the nail on the head with his movie. But from the moment that the industry learned that Michael Moore was taking on the subject, people inside our industry were really concerned.

What were they afraid of?

They were afraid that people would believe Michael Moore.

We obtained a copy of the game plan that was adopted by the industry's trade association, AHIP [America's Health Insurance Plans]. And it spells out the industry strategies in gold letters. Part of that strategy, according to this document, was: "Highlight horror stories of government-run systems." What was that about?

The industry has always tried to make Americans think that government-run systems are the worst thing that could possibly happen to them, that you're heading down the slippery slope toward socialism just to think about them. So they have used scare tactics for years and years and years to keep that from happening. Their biggest concern was that a broader program of coverage like our Medicare program could potentially reduce profits.

The industry document also advises: "Position Sicko *as a threat to Democrats' larger agenda." What does that mean?*

That means that part of the effort to discredit this film was to use lobbyists and their own staff to go onto Capitol Hill and say to members of Congress: "Look, you don't want to believe this movie, you don't want to talk about it, you don't want to endorse it. And if you do any of these things, we can make it tough for you."

How?

By running ads against you in your home district when you're up for reelection, by refusing to ever again contribute to your campaigns and giving the money instead to your competitor.

And here it reads: "Build awareness among centrist Democratic policy organizations, including the Democratic Leadership Council."

Absolutely.

The Democratic Leadership Council is the front group for the corporate wing of the Democratic Party. Now, the industry document also says, "Message to Democratic insiders. Embracing Moore is a one-way ticket back to minority party status."

Yes.

They radicalized Moore, in an effort to discredit his message.

Absolutely. By the way, when we did media training for our people, we would always have Moore referred to as "the Hollywood entertainer" or "Hollywood moviemaker Michael Moore."

Why?

People think of Hollywood as entertainment—you know, that's moviemaking, not real documentary. They didn't want you to think that it was a documentary with some truth in it. They would want you to see this as just some fantasy that a Hollywood filmmaker had come up with. That was part of the strategy.

And you would actually hear politicians mouth the talking points that had been circulated by the industry to discredit Michael Moore. And you would hear ordinary people repeating those lines?

Absolutely.

Your plan worked.

It worked beautifully.

The impact of the film was blunted?

The film was blunted.

Did you think the film contained a great truth?

Absolutely.

What was it?

That we shouldn't fear government involvement in our health care system. That there is an appropriate role for government, and it's been proven in the countries that were in that movie. You know, Bill, we have more people who are uninsured in this country than the entire population of Canada. We have huge numbers of people who are also just a layoff away from joining the ranks of the uninsured, or being purged by their insurance company, and winding up there. And another thing is that the opponents of reform are those who are saying that we need to be careful about what we do here, because we don't want the government to take away your choice of a health plan. It's more likely that your employer and your insurer are going to switch you from a plan you're in now to one that you don't want. You might be in the plan you like now. But chances are, pretty soon, you're going to be enrolled in one of these high-deductible plans in which you're going to find that much more of the cost is being shifted to you than you ever imagined.

Here's a memo from the Republican strategist Frank Luntz. He's the fellow who wrote the script for opponents of health care reform. "First," he says, "you have to pretend to support it. Then use phrases like 'government takeover,' 'delayed care is denied care,' 'the consequences of rationing,' 'bureaucrats, not doctors, prescribing medicine.'" Those are among the talking points in a memo from Frank Luntz for the opponents of health care reform in this debate, including the politicians puppeting messages from the industry.

Yes, they are ideologically aligned with the industry. They want to believe that the free market system can and should work in this country, like it does in other industries. But I don't think they understand what that actually means, and the consequences to Americans. So they parrot those comments without realizing what the real situation is.

I was watching MSNBC one afternoon. And I saw Congressman Zach Wamp from Tennessee. He's from just down the road from where I grew up, in Chattanooga. And he was asked a question about health care reform. It was just a day or two after the president's first health care reform summit, and he was one of the Republicans being interviewed. He was actually saying that the health care problem is not as bad as we think—that half of the uninsured are that way because they want to go naked.

He used the word *naked*. That's an industry term for those who presumably choose not to buy insurance because they don't want to pay the premiums. It was an absolutely ridiculous comment. And it's a specific example of a member of Congress buying what the insurance industry is peddling.

Why is the industry so powerful on both sides of the aisle?

Money and relationships, plus ideology. The industry can hire and does hire many different lobbying firms. They hire firms that are predominantly Republican or predominantly Democrat, and maybe both, because they need to reach influential members of Congress like Max Baucus. There are people who used to work for Max Baucus who are in lobbying firms or on the staff of companies like CIGNA or the industry association itself.

The Washington Post recently reported that when Max Baucus' staff met with a group of lobbyists, two of them had once served as his chief of staff.

That's the way it works.

They leave the government. They go to work for the industry. Now they come back with insider status.

Oh, they do, they do. And these lobbyists' ability to raise money for these politicians is very important as well. Many of the big lobbyists contributed a lot of money themselves. One of the lobbyists for one of the big health insurance companies is Heather Podesta, of the Podesta Group. She's married to Tony Podesta, the brother of John Podesta, who was Clinton's White House chief of staff—Democrats. That's how Washington works. Hiring the right lobbyists gets your foot in the door, and you get your message across in ways average Americans can't.

You've seen it become harder and harder for ordinary citizens to be heard, right?

Absolutely. It's the way the American system has evolved, the political system. And it offends me that the special interests, who are so profitable and so powerful, are able to influence public policy in the way that they have. The insurance industry has been one of the most successful in beating back any legislation that would hinder or affect the profitability of the companies.

Why is public insurance, the public option, so fiercely opposed by the industry?

The industry doesn't want to have any competitor. In fact, over the course of the last few years, the industry has been shrinking the number of competitors through acquisitions and mergers. It's as simple as that. They don't want any more competition, period. And they certainly don't want it from a government plan that might be operating more efficiently than they are. Our Medicare program, as you know, is a government-run program that has administrative expenses that are like 3 percent or so compared to the industry. The insurance companies spend about 20 cents of every premium dollar on overhead—administrative expense or profit.

You told Congress the industry has hijacked our health care system and turned it into a giant ATM for Wall Street. You said, "I saw how they confuse their customers and dump the sick, all so they can satisfy their Wall Street investors." Talk about how they satisfy their Wall Street investors.

There's a measure of profitability that investors look to, and it's called a medical loss ratio. It's unique to the health insurance industry. By medical loss ratio, I mean how much of a premium dollar is used by the insurance company to actually pay medical claims. And that has been shrinking over the years as the industry has become more and more dominated by for-profit insurance companies. Back in the early '90s when the Clinton health plan was being debated, 95 cents out of every dollar, on average, was used by the insurance companies to pay claims. Last year, it was down to just slightly above 80 percent.

Of course investors want that to keep shrinking. If they see that a company has not done what they think meets their expectations with the medical loss ratio, they'll punish that company. Investors will start leaving in droves. I've seen a company's stock price fall 20 percent in a single day when it did not meet Wall Street's expectations with this medical loss ratio. Say a company's medical loss ratio was 77.9 percent in one quarter, and the next quarter it was 78.2 percent. That seems like a small movement. But investors will think that's ridiculous, horrible—

That they're spending more money for medical claims and less money on profits.

Exactly. In their eyes this company has not done a good job of managing medical expenses. It has not denied enough claims. It has not kicked enough people off the rolls. And that's what happens, Bill. It's what these companies do to make sure that they satisfy Wall Street's expectations with the medical loss ratio.

And what do they do to keep diminishing the medical loss ratio?

Rescission is one thing, denying claims is another. They also purge employer accounts. Say a small business has an employee who suddenly has to have a lot of treatment or is in an accident. Medical bills pile up. When that business's coverage is up for renewal—and it typically is up for renewal once a year—the underwriters will jack up the rates, jack up the premiums, knowing the employer will have no alternative but to leave. And that happens all the time. Dumping employer groups from the rolls. Because the more of the premiums that go to pay my health claims, my medical coverage, the less money the company makes.

And the more profit those companies make by not paying claims—

A big chunk of it goes into shareholders' pockets. The return on their investment. It goes into the exorbitant salaries that a lot of the executives make. It goes into sales, marketing, and underwriting expenses. All these administrative functions. Overhead.

At a recent hearing on Capitol Hill three insurance executives were asked if they would end the practice of rescission—canceling policies for sick enrollees. They refused. Why did they refuse?

Well, they knew Wall Street was listening. They were signaling Wall Street that we're going to continue business as usual.

You know, I've been around a long time. And I have to say that I just don't get this. I just don't understand how the corporations can oppose a plan that gives unhealthy people a chance to be covered. Especially since they don't want to cover those people themselves.

But the simple fact is they are out to enhance their profits. Enhance shareholder value. That's number one. They may be in the health care business, but it is a business—and their primary motivation is to reward their shareholders. And keep in mind that most of the shareholders are large, institutional investors and hedge funds. We're not talking about mom-and-pop investors.

You wrote a column with the headline "Obama's False Friends of Health Reform." And you use as a prime example a man named Ron Williams, who is at the top of the list of insurance executives in terms of compensation. Who is Ron Williams, and why do you invoke him as the example of what Wall Street expects and wants from the insurance companies?

Williams was recruited by Aetna from WellPoint. Aetna had gone on a buying binge. I said earlier there's been an enormous amount of consolidation in the health insurance industry over the last several years. Aetna bought a lot of competitors and reached 21 million members. But investors began to see that a lot of the businesses that it had bought were not all that profitable. So Aetna was in a pickle. Their stock price started to drop. And they brought in Ron Williams, and one of the first things he did was a revamp of the IT system—

The information technology system.

Exactly, so that the company could better determine which accounts were not profitable or only marginally profitable. With that new system they were able to identify the accounts that they wanted to get rid of. Over the course of a very few years, they shed eight million members. Many of them no doubt wound up in the ranks of the uninsured.

And what happened to Aetna's stock?

It went up. And so did Ron Williams's compensation.

What an irony. We hear the companies and their trade groups talking about how we don't want a public option that would put a bureaucrat between a patient and his doctor. But you've just described a situation in which a CEO actually comes between a doctor and the patient.

It's true. That same thing happened in the Nataline Sarkisyan case. Corporate bureaucrats made the decision. They came between the patient and the doctor.

Any company is in business to make a profit, right? Can we object when an insurance company wants to increase its profits?

It's a very serious question. I just think the people who believe our health care system should operate according to the free market fail to realize that we're really talking about human beings here. And it just doesn't work as well as they would like it to for a lot of human beings. I'm a capitalist, Bill. I think it's wonderful that companies can earn a profit. But when you do it in such a way that you are adding to the number of people who are uninsured and can't get health care, then we have to change it.

Do you believe that health reform that includes a public plan can actually rid our system of the financial incentive on the part of the insurance industry to provide less for more?

It would help. Would it rid it? No, I don't think it would, because the for-profit structure dominates in America. But the public plan would do a lot to keep the insurers honest, because they would have to offer a standard benefit plan. They would have to operate more efficiently, as does the Medicare program. There would need to be a level playing field so the public option wouldn't be at an unfair advantage to the private insurance companies. But because it could be administered more efficiently than the private insurers, they would have to operate more efficiently. And that 20 cents in that medical loss ratio we talked about earlier just might narrow. That's what they don't want. They don't want competition.

As this debate unfolds, what will be the industry's strategy?

To keep scaring us. To make us afraid that if we get a public option—something like Medicare—the American people will be forced to stand in line for health care. Well, I just wish they would go with me down to Wise, Virginia. They would see all those people already standing in line waiting for health care. ∾

Benjamin Barber

My four-year-old granddaughter Sara and I were watching television—PBS, naturally—when it was time for Word Girl, the animated superheroine (and fifth grader) who fights evil with the vocabulary of a budding acolyte of Will Shortz, the crossword genius. In this episode, Word Girl is up against the villainous Mr. Big, who floods the market with a new product called The Thing, which of course everyone in Preposterocity has to have because . . . well, because it's "The Thing" to have. No one knows or seems to care what it is or does, but the commercials are irresistible, and viewers are seduced into believing they can't live without it. Enter Word Girl:

WORD GIRL: Everyone stop, you're being tricked. The Thing doesn't do anything.

FIRST PERSON: Yes, it does. It does so much stuff.

SECOND PERSON: The commercial says I needed one for my boat!

WORD GIRL: You don't have a boat!

SECOND PERSON (TO HER MATE): Hon, we need a boat for our Thing.

WORD GIRL: You don't need a Thing!

SECOND PERSON: But the commercial says . . . !

Whoa! Time for political theorist Benjamin Barber, who in real life knows a thing (no pun intended) or two about the culture Word Girl is challenging. After 9/11, Barber's book on the conflict between consumer capitalism and religious fundamentalism, Jihad vs. McWorld, *rocketed onto the international bestseller list. He then scrutinized the global economy for* Consumed: How Markets Corrupt Children, Infantilize Adults, and Swallow Citizens Whole. *In it, Barber argues that modern capitalism is producing too many goods we don't need and too few of those we do. In an age when "the needy are without income and the well-heeled are without needs," he writes, a consumerist society can only be sustained by constantly rekindling childish tastes in grown-ups, creating "rejuveniles" with a permanent mentality of "Gimme!" and "I want it now!"*

Not only is childhood perverted by this "ethos of infantilization," but democracy is deprived of responsible grown-ups capable of functioning as mature citizens, generating, as Publishers Weekly *noted, "a 'civic schizophrenia' where everybody wants service but nobody wants to serve." Corporations determine our political choices, Barber writes, citing studies that babies as young as six months can form mental images of corporate logos that are then established as brand loyalty by the age of two. It's a complex and controversial argument, but not one that would surprise Preposterocity's Mr. Big. Benjamin Barber knows it well.*

—*Bill Moyers*

—◦◦◦—

You are blunt about it: Capitalism's in trouble. Why?

Because things are flying off the shelves that we don't want or need or even understand what they are, but we go on buying them. Because to stay in business capitalism needs us to buy things way beyond the scope of our needs and wants. That's the bottom line. Capitalism is no longer manufacturing goods to meet real needs and human wants. It's manufacturing needs to sell us all the goods it's got to produce.

But on the Friday after Thanksgiving we go to the mall. "Black Friday"—the mall is packed with stuff you say we don't need.

And do we need to shop at 4:00 A.M.? I keep looking for signs saying, "Please open the stores at 4:00 A.M. so I can go shopping at 4:00 A.M." I don't see any. That's the stores' idea. That's the marketers' idea. That's the idea to create this hysteria about purchasing. About buying and selling.

But Ben, nobody is forcing them to do that. People are out there looking for bargains. You like a good bargain, don't you?

I love a good bargain when it's for something I need and something I want. But here's the thing. We live in a world where there are real needs and real wants, and capitalism should be addressing those real needs and those real wants.

Example?

Give you a fine example. Here in the United States, the cola companies couldn't sell enough cola. So they figured out how to persuade people to buy water from a bottle instead of getting it free from a tap. More than $10 billion a year in bottled water. In the third world there are literally billions without potable water, without drinkable, clean water. Now, why shouldn't capitalism figure out how to clean the water out there and get people something they need and make a buck off it? Because that's what capitalism does. It makes a profit off taking some chances and meeting real human needs. Instead it's convincing Americans and Europeans that they shouldn't drink pure, clean tap water but instead pay two bucks a bottle for it.

Third world people have no money. Why would a company go where people don't have money and try to sell them something?

In capitalism you don't expect a profit right away. You make an investment. You create jobs, you create products, you create productivity. That's the way it works. That's the way we in the West created our prosperity. But we don't have the patience any longer to do it in the third world. We don't want to bring them into the marketplace. We'd rather exploit a finished marketplace. But you're right. Here's the paradox: those with the dough don't have any needs, those with the needs don't have any dough. And so capitalism has to decide: needs or dough. And their decision has been to go for the dough, regardless of the needs.

The trouble is, we're looking the wrong way. It's not what's wrong with American consumers, it's what's wrong with American capitalism, American advertisers, American marketers. It's what I call push capitalism. It's supply side. They've got to sell all this stuff, and they have to figure out how to get us to want it. So they take adults and they infantilize them. Dumb them down. They get us to want things. And then they start targeting children. Because it's not enough just to sell to the adults. You've got to sell to that wonderful demographic—first it's twelve-to-eighteen-year-olds, then it's the 'tweens, the ten-to-twelve-year-olds, then it's the toddlers.

Infantilize? There's that word again.

What I mean is that part of being grown-up is getting ahold of yourself and saying, "I've got to be a gatekeeper for my kid. I want to live in a pluralistic world where, yes, I shop, but I also pray and play and do art and make love and do lots of different things. And shopping's just one part of that." As an adult, we know that. But if you live in a capitalist society that needs to sell us all the time, they've got to turn that prudent, thoughtful adult back into a child who says, "Gimme, gimme, gimme. I want, I want, I want." Just like the kid in the candy store.

But isn't all of this part of what keeps the hamster running?

It is. But part of the problem here is that the capitalist companies have figured out that the best way to do their job is to privatize profit but socialize risk. The banks that have just screwed up so big, not one of them is going to go under because they'll be bailed out by the feds. 'Cause the feds, the federal government, will say we can't afford to let this gigantic multibillion-dollar bank go under. Now, the whole point of profit is to reward risk. But what we've done today is socialize risk. You and I, and all of your listeners out there, pay when companies like subprime market mortgage companies and the banks go bad. We pay for it.

The other day I heard a commercial by a big bank—a multinational bank— that said, in effect, "Okay, we're coming into the season where you want a lot of things, and you don't have any money. What do you do? You call us. Whatever you want, we'll make it happen."

Yes. And this is after the crisis and crash. This is not before. This is after.

So what's at stake? What's at stake in this for democracy?

There are two things at stake here. First of all, capitalism itself is at stake, because capitalism cannot stay indefinitely in business trying to manufacture needs for people in the middle class and the developed world who have most of what they need. It has to figure out how to address the real needs of people. And it's not just in the third world. We have real needs here for alternative energy. And I would want to reward corporations that invest in alternative energy. Not just biofuels and so on, but that also look at geothermal, that look at wind, that look at tidal. Tidal is an amazing new field where you use the motions of the tides. It's expensive, difficult right now. But that's what you get the profits for, by investing in that. So there are lots of things we can do. With global warming, sea levels at coastlines around this country are rising. We need housing that can withstand flooding. Big thing: you could make a lot of money figuring out how to build inexpensive housing that withstands hurricanes, withstands flooding. Very few people are doing it. That's the way capitalism ought to be working.

So capitalism itself is in trouble. But, second of all, capitalism has put democracy at risk. Because capitalism has tried to persuade us that being a private consumer is enough, that a citizen is nothing more than a consumer. That voting means spreading your dollars around your private prejudices, your private preferences. Not reaching public judgments. Not finding common ground. Not making decisions about the social consequences of private judgments, but just making the private judgments. And letting consequences fall where they will.

We were in Vermont one Thanksgiving. In this little town there's a town square, there's a police station, there's a fire station. There's a city hall, a school just a block off the town square. There are the shops around the square. It reminded me of Marshall, Texas, where I grew up.

Any one of those towns is an exemplar of the variety and diversity of American life. Now compare that town to a mall. You walk through the mall, nothing there but shops. You could walk for miles and think that the whole world is constituted by retail shopping and nothing else.

But there are jobs there. People are working there. And people say, "Barber,

Moyers, get with it. This is the twenty-first century, not the first half of the twentieth century." The world has changed.

Yes, but there are jobs in the drugs industry. There are jobs in the penitentiaries. You know, you could say, "Gee, the prison expansions are good. More jobs for guards." Sure, anything provides jobs. The question is, at what price? Where do we want the jobs to be? Do we want our jobs to be in education? Do we want our jobs to be in the arts? Do we want our jobs to be in general services? Do we want our jobs to be in health care? Or do we want our jobs to be in selling gadgets, selling salt/sugar laden food that makes half the country obese? Where do we want the jobs? And, again, that's a social decision. The market puts the jobs wherever the marketers push them. What we need to do as citizens is say, "Where do we want the jobs to be? What kinds of jobs do we want our young people to have?"

So there's a role for possible intervention?

Shhh, say that very quietly.

Wherever he is, Milton Friedman is whirling.

Well, wherever Milton Friedman is right now, he's at the soul of the Republican Party and the Democratic Party. And the reality is, here there is a powerful role for small "d" democratic parties, for citizens, for participatory institutions. They include our townships. They include our PTAs. They include our NGOs and our philanthropies. There's a whole civil society that is a whole lot more than just the government, where we act not as private consumers or selfish individuals but as neighbors. We act as citizens. We act as friends to establish the social character of the world we live in. You know, as a consumer, everyone loves Walmart. So do I. Lots of goods, cheap prices. But it has social consequences that, as consumers, we don't think about. We know it means low wages, it means low wages without pensions. It means wage earners who don't have proper health care. But worse than that, it means the destruction of mom-and-pop stores. The destruction of local retail. The destruction of those very little shops that are at the heart of America's villages and towns.

The free market economists say that's creative destruction, the heart of capitalism.

But you know what? Democracy has a simple rule. The social conscience of citizens trumps the consumer. But with Milton Friedman's help, we've inverted that. Now the consumer trumps the citizen. And we're getting a society that manifests the trumping by the consumer of civics, which means a selfish, privatized, and ultimately corrupt society. Who really wants their own children to grow up in that society?

How is it—and this is not original to me—how is it that when politics permeates everything we call it totalitarianism, when religion permeates everything we call it theocracy, but when commerce pervades everything, we call it liberty?

Well, that is the central paradox of our times. As Americans, I would think we understand that, above all, democracy means pluralism. If everything's religion, we rightly distrust it. If everything's politics, even "good" politics, we rightly distrust it. But when everything's marketing and everything's retail and everything's shopping, we somehow think that enhances our freedom. Well, it doesn't. It has the same corrupting effect on the fundamental diversity and variety that are our lives, that make us human, that make us happy. And, in that sense, focusing on shopping and the fulfillment of private consumer desires actually undermines our happiness.

Many people will tell you choice is joy.

And they are right. But the question is, what kind of choice? You go to Los Angeles today, you can rent or buy two hundred different kinds of automobile. And then, in those automobiles, you can sit, no matter which one you're in, for five hours not moving on the freeway system there. The one choice you don't have is genuine, efficient, cheap, accessible, public transportation. There's nothing as a consumer you can do to get it. Because the choice for public transportation is a social choice. A civic choice.

I can't go out and buy a subway for my private use.

Exactly. You can't do that. And no choice that's available to you allows you to do that. So many of our choices today are trivial. We feel that we're expanding and enhancing our choice, but the big choices—a green environment, a safe city for our kids, good education—simply are not available through private consumer choices. That's the problem with vouchers for schools. You know, we think that with vouchers we can all find a good school. But if education itself is going under and is not supported as a social good, no amount of private choice is going to give any of our kids in public or private schools appropriate education.

We are now spending more than we are saving. We have become a true significant debtor nation. What does that mean in the long run?

It means a couple of things. And, by the way, this is a devastating economic fact. Here the economists will agree with me, a political scientist and a political theorist, it's no good for a country to do that. A country that stops saving becomes a debtor nation in every way. That's why we're in hock to China and the others who own dollars. That's why the dollar has collapsed abroad. But it also means that we are no longer in a position to create the forms of industry, capitalism, and social consciousness that come from saving. Saving is how we invest in the future. Saving means that we're putting money aside, deferring our own gratification, to create a future that our children can be part of. When we spend it all on ourselves and then more than we have, we put ourselves and, more importantly, we put the future itself in hock. We're really selling our kids and grandkids when we do that.

How do we encourage capitalism to do what it does best, to meet real human needs?

There are three things we can do. First of all we, as consumers, have to be tougher. We are the gatekeepers for our kids and our families. We have to take a stand. Again I ask anyone out there, "Who needs to go out at 2:00 A.M. to go shopping?" For God's sake, wait till Monday afternoon. Second thing, capitalism has to begin to earn the profits to which it has a right by taking real risks on behalf of addressing real needs. There's a company in Denmark that's gotten very rich very fast making something called the LifeStraw. It's a thing about nine inches long containing about nine filters that filter out all the contaminants and germs that you find in third world cesspool water. You can buy one of these for a couple bucks, and a woman in the third world and her family can drink through it for eighteen months, and it doesn't matter what water they have available. The LifeStraw cleanses that water. A little firm in Denmark that makes it is making out like a "capitalist bandit," we'd say, but properly so. They're being rewarded for taking a risk.

Inventing something that is needed. Folks working in alternative energy, some of them are also going to make real money. And that's a good thing. That's what they ought to be doing.

Creative capitalism and tough consumers. Third?

And, number three, we've got to retrieve our citizenship. A cliché perhaps but our toughest task. We can't buy the line that government is our enemy and the market is our friend. We used to say government can do everything, the market can do nothing. That was a mistake. But now we seem to say the market can do everything and government can do nothing. But government is us. Government is our institutions. Government is how we make social and public choices working together to forge common ground. So, number three, toughest of all, we've got to retrieve our citizenship. ∼

MARGARET FLOWERS

"Make me an offer I can't refuse," President Obama said when he talked about health care reform during his 2010 State of the Union address. "If anyone from either party has a better approach that will bring down premiums, bring down the deficit, cover the uninsured, strengthen Medicare for seniors, and stop insurance company abuses, let me know . . . I'm eager to see it."

Dr. Margaret Flowers took him at his word. The very next day she was outside the White House with a letter urging the president to revive the idea of single-payer health care—Medicare for all. The Secret Service turned her away, but she didn't give up. She followed President Obama to Baltimore, where he once again made his offer to hear ideas on health reform.

Once again, Dr. Flowers tried to deliver her letter. This time, she and her colleague Dr. Carol Paris refused to move when security told them to, because they didn't want to be excluded, marginalized, and ignored. They were arrested, and when I saw the pictures of them being led away, I recalled the famous words attributed to another Margaret, the anthropologist Margaret Mead: "Never doubt that a small group of thoughtful, committed individuals can change the world; indeed, it's the only thing that ever has."

Margaret Flowers is a pediatrician from Maryland who worked at a rural hospital and in private practice. She is now advocating full-time for single-payer health insurance, working on Capitol Hill for the organization

Physicians for a National Health Program. Channeling Glenn Beck, I think
I may have startled her with my first question. . . .

—*Bill Moyers*

———◈———

Are you a Communist?

No.

A socialist?

No.

A paid agitator?

No, I don't get paid for what I do.

Do you advocate the violent overthrow of the United States government?

No, I really want our country to be the best it can be.

So why did you get yourself arrested?

Because what I'm advocating is in the best interests of the people instead of
the corporations that are funding the political campaigns.

Why do you say single-payer is the best? What did you learn when you were
practicing that made you such a passionate advocate for single-payer?

I went into medicine because I really do care about taking care of my patients. I chose pediatrics because I feel that if you give children a great start,
a healthy start, they can carry that through the rest of their lives. And I really believed that medicine was about taking care of patients. I learned otherwise, that it was more about fighting with insurance companies and being
pushed to see more and more patients. When I looked at what was going on
and at what works in other places and what has worked here, what models
have worked here, I saw that if we have a Medicare-for-all system, doctors
can practice medicine again, the art that we train to practice.

What do you mean by "Medicare-for-all"?

With a Medicare-type system the administration is very simple. Medicare is very quick at reimbursing you. They don't have a profit to make. Furthermore, the Medicare system allows patients to choose the doctor they want to go to. They don't have an insurance company saying who's in network and who's not in network. So it's universal, full choice, allowing doctors to practice medicine and patients to choose their care.

Why weren't you able to do the medicine you wanted to do because of our present health care system?

It started when I was working in the rural hospital. When we admitted a patient to the hospital, the first person who would come to visit us was someone from utilization review, which is the group that interfaces with the insurance company. And they would say, "You have this many days to make this patient better. This is how many days they've been authorized for." And we often found that it didn't match the number of days that we felt the patient needed to be in the hospital. So the system puts the physician in the really uncomfortable position of debating whether you send a child home before they're ready. Do you ask the family to bear the extra cost? We usually ended up asking the hospital to just write off the rest of the stay, if we didn't feel that a patient was ready to go home. And then in private practice, it's the same kind of thing. You see a patient. You determine the best treatment, and then the insurance company says, "No, they can't have that test" or "They can't have that medicine." It didn't make medical sense. It wasn't based on the patient's need. It was based on what the insurance companies could get away with.

My own doctors have told me that they are constantly lobbied by industry representatives trying to sell them something that increases the profit of the industry, whether or not the doctor thinks it's the right thing for patients. Was that your experience as well?

Completely, yes. You have representatives coming into your office all the time, wanting to bring you lunch, gifts, tell you how great their product is. And there's no really independent body that can tell you whether what they're saying is true or not. When you're practicing and so busy, it's hard to figure that out. My friends who work in the military health system or the VA love what they do because that system actually provides them nonbiased information on what things are best for their patients.

Nonbiased information?

It's an independent review that's not done by the company that's profiting from selling a certain device or medication. It's a board that looks at the various products and really compares them and tells you which is better and which isn't.

Was there a moment when, as a pediatrician, you said, "I can't keep doing this. I've got to change this system before I can really practice medicine"? Was there a eureka moment?

There was. It happened when our office manager sat down with us in our practice and said, "Okay, if we want to keep in business, this is what you need to do. You can only see one well child a day, and the rest of the patients have to all be sick patients that you can churn through this many patients each hour." And—

They gave you a quota?

Basically. And that is the model that many primary care practices use.

One of my doctors teasingly said to me the other day, "I've got seven minutes for you now."

Right. And if your patient happens to bring up something else that's bothering them, you have to ask them to reschedule and come back to talk about that other thing, which means they have to take more time from work and continue to carry that worry with them while they're waiting for the next appointment. That just wasn't why I went into medicine. I like the relationship that I have with patients. I want to take care of them. And when you build that relationship with your patient and you get to know them, you can provide the best care for them. You can't with the way things are right now.

You didn't go into medicine to get arrested three times in less than nine months, either. And yet there you are in the video, being handcuffed and led away

Yes, I never really dreamed that this was a path that I would go down. I mean, I'm a mother. I try to be a good citizen in my community. But it came to a point where this was the only way that we could be heard. We were being completely excluded, and when we tried the traditional avenues of being heard, we were just pushed aside.

I remember. When you and several others stood up in protest during the Senate hearings on health care in May 2009, Senator Max Baucus, the chairman, had you put in handcuffs and taken away.

They did. They did. And it was terrifying. I had never been arrested before. But I knew at that moment. I looked around the room, and I looked at the people who were sitting at the table, both the senators and the people from industry who had been invited to testify, and in my mind, I juxtaposed that with the stories and the people that I've met, and the doctors I've talked to, and I felt as if I were there on behalf of them. And I would do what I needed to do. And that I was ready for that.

At the moment, it seemed like there might be momentum behind this single-payer Medicare-for-all movement. What happened?

Good question. That was a big step for us, taking civil disobedience action. And when we did that, the powers that be actually did start inviting us in to have a seat at the table. Senator Kennedy's committee contacted us. And I was the first person to testify in the Health, Education, Labor, and Pension Committee hearing. I sat next to the CEO of Aetna, which was a very interesting experience. And then when we went over to the House and spoke to the leadership there, they said, "We want your voice to be heard here." So we actually thought we were starting to get our foot in the door. And then we had some good amendments that were introduced. They would have substituted a national single-payer system for the legislation that was moving through Congress. And then we saw all that fall apart. What we learned is there was a lot of control coming from the White House. They wanted to pass something. And they were concerned that if the single-payer voice was in the discussion, or if it was in any way associated with certain legislation, it would hurt their ability to pass that legislation. So they put the kibosh on us.

The White House?

Yes, it really came down from the top.

Why were they able to get away with this? Several polls suggest that 60 percent or more of your fellow doctors support a single-payer option, Medicare for all. How can elected representatives refuse to hear and negotiate with that many people, so many doctors who care about this?

They weren't listening to us. The industry has so many lobbyists talking to the staffers and the legislators. This summer [2009] we actually brought doctors and nurses to Capitol Hill, to meet with legislators and staff and tell them what makes good sense from a health standpoint. When we tried to reach the White House to be included there—we requested meetings with the president on numerous occasions—they just said no. They wouldn't allow us in.

When you stood outside the White House last week, wanting to give your letter to the president, did you really think the "leader of the free world" was going to respond to a petition from a single individual standing outside his gate?

I did make the point that I was representing the majority of the public and the majority of physicians.

How could you make that claim?

Because numerous polls have shown that the majority of the American public wants a national health system. When the poll actually describes what it is, a system where everybody pays in and everybody can get the care that they need, people want it, they support it. You know, I supported President Obama. I even worked the polls on Election Day, and I knocked on doors to get people out. I guess I was naive.

Had you taken him seriously when, before his campaign, he was an advocate for single-payer?

Yes. We knew that he understood what single-payer was. In the debates he said that he understood health care was a human right. I know that he didn't campaign on single-payer or anything like it. But we felt that if we built the grassroots movement and showed that this is what the American people want, that he would actually, in some ways, include us. The exact opposite happened. The whole process was very tightly scripted. And very exclusive. He didn't want us causing any trouble.

One of the front groups for the health industry ran a full-page ad in The Washington Post *this week, taking credit for killing off any public option that might include a version of single-payer in the health care reform. The ad said: "In last week's address to the nation, he [the president] pulled the plug on the Public Option. After nearly a year as the centerpiece of his health care reform*

*plans, amazingly he didn't utter a word about it and hoped no one would no-
tice." Whose side do you think the president was on in the health care reform
process the last nine months?*

This whole process was dominated by fear of the industry. I believe he was
really on the side of the industries that profit from the current situation.

What did they fear?

These industries have such power and so much money to buy influence over
members of Congress. If the politicians come out in favor of a Medicare-
for-all approach, the industry instantly runs ads against them or even candidates against them. They fear not being reelected.

*If the president had sent a staff person out to invite you in for coffee last week,
what would you have told him?*

I would have told him that the American people were expecting more from
him, that there's been such a huge amount of suffering in this country and
so many preventable deaths. And that it's completely unacceptable that we
are the only industrialized nation that allows this to happen. And that it
doesn't have to be this way. America's already spending more than any other
country on health care, so it's not an issue of whether we have the money.
We have the resources to have one of the top health systems in the world.
And why wasn't this debate about what is best for the people? In terms of
our economic recovery this is vital, because our whole health system is a
drag on the economy. So why is the president excluding us? Why isn't he letting us be at the table, when this makes complete sense from the standpoint
of public health policy and economic health policy?

*He didn't invite you in for coffee. He didn't hear you say what you just told me.
You tried to give him the letter. And when you learned that he was going to
speak in Baltimore the next week, you were waiting there.*

It felt like another opportunity, yes.

When you were arrested last Friday, were you taken to police headquarters?

I was, with Dr. Paris.

Handcuffed?

We were.

You were interviewed independently by the Secret Service?

Yes. They wanted to make sure that we didn't have a psychiatric history or we wished the president any harm.

What did you tell them?

That no, we don't wish him any harm. In fact, if we passed a Medicare-for-all system, it would be a huge win, not just for the American people but for this administration. If you look at Tommy Douglas in Canada, the father of their health system, he was voted their national hero.

I watched the video of your arrest. I think I heard you say to somebody: "Would you please call my husband?" Is it true he didn't know you were out there and were going to get arrested?

It's true.

Did somebody call him?

Actually, his brother called him because he saw it on the news. And he said, "Do you know where your wife is right now?" And my husband said, "No." I have to tell you that Dr. Paris and I weren't sure what was going to happen that morning. We just knew that we would go down there with our banner and our letter and that hopefully we could get our message across and that hopefully they would call a staffer to take our letter. Instead, they kept telling us to move on, to go across the street, and there came a point when we looked at each other and without speaking we just knew that we were not going across the street.

Why did you decide not to comply with their request to go across the street?

Because it's too important. Our message is too important. We can't continue to be excluded anymore. We're losing doctors from practice. People are suffering who don't need to suffer. There's so much preventable death. This is unacceptable.

But you were stymied last May. You were frozen out of the months of discussion that followed, when the White House was striking deals with the health industry and the drug industry. You were out in the cold, literally and figuratively. They won't listen. Do you really believe this is going to make any difference?

It has to. And whether or not it does, I have to do this, because if we don't push for this, nobody is going to push for this. And we're going to do everything we can to build this movement and to push our country in a direction that puts us at least on par with the other industrialized nations.

So what happens now to your movement?

Our movement is growing. We'll keep on growing until we get Medicare for all. We're completely committed to doing this, and to keep moving forward on the national and the state level. One way or another, we're going to get there.

Looking back over the last year, what have you learned about our political process?

I didn't realize how broken it was. I knew that there were powerful special interests influencing the process. But I didn't realize the degree, the depths to which they affect our political process. ∽

PHILIPPE SANDS

It took an outsider to hold up a mirror to the culture of cruelty spawned by our government after 9/11. The international lawyer Philippe Sands, long a friend of America, was dumbfounded at how the Bush administration had abandoned the principles of Abraham Lincoln, who in the middle of the Civil War told his generals that "military necessity does not admit of cruelty . . . nor of torture to extort confessions."

Philippe Sands, QC (Queen's Counsel), is known in top legal circles for his investigation of torture cases under such infamous dictators as Chile's Augusto Pinochet and Liberia's Charles Taylor. He directs the Centre on International Courts and Tribunals in London, where he closely studied the British fight against terrorists of the IRA and concluded that "coercion doesn't work . . . it extended the conflict with the IRA probably by between 15 and 20 years." His reputation gained him access to the key officials in Washington who helped to develop the Bush-Cheney policy of "enhanced interrogation methods," the official code for the use of cruelty in the pursuit of confession.

The administration fought tooth and nail to keep secret the internal debates behind that policy, no doubt because many of the participants feared they could one day face prosecution for war crimes if their actions turn out to have been illegal. Some of them, however, agreed to meet with Sands. What he learned became the core of his book Torture Team. I met him when he was asked to *testify before the House of Representatives Judiciary Committee, which had finally begun hearings into the culture of cruelty.*

—*Bill Moyers*

———✦———

Let me go right to the story of the suicide bomber in Baghdad who drove his bombing vehicle into an Iraqi police station. He had been held at Guantánamo for over three years. Pentagon records say that he had told people he wanted to kill as many Americans as he possibly could. Why give someone like that the benefit of the doubt?

We give people the benefit of the doubt because that's the nature of our system. We believe fundamentally in democratic values. We don't assume guilt, we assume innocence. There are people at Guantánamo who pose a threat, undoubtedly. But there are also a great many more people who don't pose a threat. And in those circumstances, I think using this as an example to somehow come down on the merits of the Guantánamo system is not a sensible thing to do. I think Guantánamo has been a problem, as Abu Ghraib has been a problem, because it has undermined America's claim to moral authority in facing up to the very real challenge of terrorism. Locking them up and throwing away the key is only going to exacerbate the problem. And it's a problem that we faced in Britain, for example, in relationship to the IRA back in the 1970s and the 1980s. That's not the way to go.

What's your evidence for saying that the British experience in fighting the terrorists of the IRA actually extended the conflict fifteen to twenty years?

The story's a simple one. Back in '71, '72, the British moved as the United States has done, to aggressive techniques of interrogation. They used pretty much the same techniques: hooding, standing, humiliation, degradation. They were ruled to be illegal in 1978 by the European Court on Human Rights. But there was a bigger problem, even beyond their illegality, in my view. And that was this: what the use of those techniques did was to really enrage part of the Catholic community, who felt that IRA detainees alleged to be terrorists were being abused. It turned people who were perhaps unhappy with the situation into being deeply and violently unhappy with the situation. And if you speak to British politicians who were involved in that period, and the British military, what they'll tell you is that there is a feeling that the use of those types of techniques extended the conflict.

Did you learn that people will say anything to stop the torture?

I think it's self-evident that that is what happened. If you speak to interrogators, they will tell you that aggressive techniques of interrogation don't work. They don't produce meaningful information. Just the other day, I was listening to a very interesting tape of John McCain. He explained how, when he was a POW in Vietnam, in the end he had signed a confession owning up to crimes against children and women in North Vietnam. This was basically because he had reached a point at which he simply couldn't bear it anymore, and he wanted the pain to stop. And the only thing he could do was to tell them what he thought they wanted to know. That's what interrogators will tell you: abuse produces information that the detainee thinks you want to know, and nothing more than that. It's not reliable.

In my book *Torture Team* I have homed in on the interrogation of one man, Detainee 063 [Mohammed al-Qahtani, the alleged "twentieth hijacker" of 9/11]. The administration has publicly declared they got a mass of information out of him that related to all sorts of extraordinarily important things to protect the Americans. I spoke to the people who were involved in his actual interrogation and the head of his exploitation team. That's not what they told me. If the evidence I had been given had been different, then I would possibly have reached a different conclusion. Not as to the legality or the utility of torture, but what do we do in the face of evidence that it works? But there isn't evidence that it works. The British experience is that it doesn't work. The Spanish experience is that it doesn't work. The Egyptian experience is that it doesn't work, in the sense of producing meaningful information that is going to protect a country. Sure, it produces information. But as John McCain said in his interview in 1997, it produces the wrong information. Because someone who's subject to that sort of pain and suffering is going to do anything they can to stop it from happening. And they will tell the person who is abusing them what the person wants to hear, and nothing more and nothing less.

You spent a long time and made a lot of trips and talked to a lot of people to do this book. What was driving you?

I was fascinated by a simple question. How could lawyers at the upper echelons of the administration, trained at Harvard Law School and other distinguished institutions, have approved torture? In what circumstances could that happen? And it combined with a real sense of injustice that the truth of the story had not come out. I was really catalyzed by a press conference I read about in June 2004, as the administration struggled to contain the disaster of Abu Ghraib. The administration spun a story, and the story was this: The desire for aggressive interrogation came from the bottom up. People on the front line, people at Guantánamo and elsewhere, told us they needed to move to new techniques. Who are we at the top to say no? It struck me as counterintuitive, because I know the American military. I've got friends in the American military, and they are deeply committed to the rules of the Geneva Conventions and other international rules, and don't go about the abandonment of President Lincoln's disposition that in no circumstances is cruelty to be used.

So what I decided to do was I took the famous memorandum signed by Donald Rumsfeld in December 2002, where he writes on the bottom, "I stand for 8–10 hours a day. Why is standing limited to 4 hours?" and I tracked back the entire decision-making process, identified the ten or twelve people I needed to meet. And one by one, tracked them down, went and found them, spoke to them, and I'm truly grateful to them. Once I'd had my first conversation, with Diane Beaver, who was the lawyer down at Guantánamo, I was then able to get right up to the very top. And one by one, I followed from Diane Beaver's boss, Mike Dunleavy, who's the head of interrogations, through General Hill, who is the head of Southern Command in Miami, up through General Myers, the Joint Chiefs of Staff, up to Doug Feith, the head of policy at the Pentagon, and then right up to the main man in my book, Jim Haynes. Jim Haynes was Mr. Rumsfeld's lawyer, and wrote the infamous, iconic "Why is standing limited to four hours" memo. And he went to Harvard Law School. I just couldn't understand how someone so well trained could authorize abusive interrogation like that.

I had two meetings with him. The fact of the meetings was on the record, the content of those meetings was off the record. But the concluding chapter of the book takes into account everything he said to me. I think you'll agree that they're fascinating characters and you'll see that with some of them I developed a real empathy, actually, in ways that surprised me.

Take Diane Beaver. She had been the person down at the bottom who'd signed off on aggressive interrogation. I didn't like her legal advice at all. I thought it was really bad and wrong. And I was rather uncomplimentary, perhaps even rude about it, in my last book *Lawless World*, in 2005. Then I met her. And she explained to me the circumstances in which she found herself. I don't think it justifies what happened. But she described to me the pressure she felt herself under, with the anniversary of 9/11 coming up: this man, Detainee 063, al-Qahtani, present and caught. Tremendous pressure coming from the upper echelons of the administration. She described to me a visit that the administration has never talked about in which the three most important lawyers in the administration—Mr. Gonzales, the president's lawyer; Mr. Addington, the vice president's lawyer; and Mr. Haynes, Secretary Rumsfeld's lawyer—came down to Guantánamo at the end of September, talked to them about interrogations and other issues, watched an interrogation, and left with the message, do whatever needs to be done. Now, put yourself in Diane Beaver's situation. You're getting a signal from the main men at the top of the administration: do whatever needs to be done. That takes the lid off and opens the door.

Was there a single architect of the decision, the person who said, "Take the gloves off"?

There was one lawyer in particular who everyone kept referring to as being, if you like, the brains. I'm slow to use that word for such an awful series of events. But the driving force behind it was said to be David Addington. Diane Beaver and Mike Dunleavy, who was her boss, the head of interrogation at Guantánamo, told me that when they came down, it was obvious that Addington was the main person. He was the leader of the team. I think they were very anxious around him, with his big booming voice, his big beard. I think that the finger of responsibility in the end will most likely go to the vice president. But Mr. Rumsfeld was deeply involved. And, of course, the president has indicated that he signed off on everything.*

You subtitle the book Rumsfeld's Memo and the Betrayal of American Values. *Tell me briefly about that memo and why it betrayed American values.*

---

*As of November 2010, President Bush confirmed in his memoir, *Decision Points*, that he had signed off on aggressive techniques of interrogation, including waterboarding.

The memo appears to be the very first time that the upper echelons of the military or the administration abandoned President Lincoln's famous disposition of 1863: the U.S. military doesn't do cruelty.

And that's the basis, isn't it, for the military handbook that soldiers use to follow, to try to stay within the rules of the game?

It's the U.S. Army field manual, and it's the bible for the military. And the military, of course, has on occasion fallen into error, and there have been previous examples of abuse.

There were prison camps in the Civil War that were abominable.

Absolutely. No one is saying it hasn't happened before. But apparently what hasn't happened before is the abandonment of the rules against cruelty. And the Geneva Conventions were set aside, as Doug Feith told me, precisely in order to clear the slate and allow aggressive interrogation.

And Rumsfeld's memo was the catalyst for this?

Well, the timing was that the Geneva Conventions were set aside in February 2002 by decision of the president, at the insistence of Doug Feith and a small group, including some lawyers. And the memo by Donald Rumsfeld then came in December 2002, after they had identified Mohammed al-Qahtani. By removing Geneva, that memo became possible.

Why does it abandon American values? It abandons American values, because the military in this country has a very fine tradition, as we've been discussing, of not doing cruelty. It's a proud tradition, borne on issues of principle, but also of pragmatism. No country is more exposed internationally than the United States. I've listened, for example, to Justice Antonin Scalia saying, if the president wants to authorize torture, there's nothing in our Constitution which stops it. Now, pause for a moment. That is such a foolish thing to say. If the United States president can do that, then why can't the Iranian president do that, or the British prime minister do that, or the Egyptian president do that? You open the door in that way to all sorts of abuses, and you expose the American military to real dangers, which is why the backlash began with the U.S. military.

And you say, from there, it slipped into a culture of cruelty?

It slipped into a culture of cruelty. It was put very pithily for me by a clinical psychologist, Mike Gelles, who is with the Naval Criminal Investigative Service, spending time down at Guantánamo, who described to me how once you open the door to a little bit of cruelty, people will believe that more cruelty is a good thing. And once the dogs are unleashed, it's impossible to put them back on. And that's the basis for the belief amongst a lot of people in the military that the interrogation techniques basically slipped from Guantánamo to Iraq and to Abu Ghraib. That's why the administration had to resist the argument and the claim that this came from the top.

For a long time, the story was that it went up the chain from Bagram in Afghanistan to Abu Ghraib and then to Guantánamo. But you're saying it started in Washington and went down?

It started with a few bad eggs. I don't think the bad eggs are at the bottom, I think the bad eggs are at the top, and what they did was open a door which allowed the migration of abuse, of cruelty and torture, to other parts of the world in ways that I think the United States will be struggling to contain for many years to come.

And the backlash came from the military?

I think it's a really complex story. It's more like a thriller, actually. You've got different camps who are struggling down at Guantánamo. And I think it would be wrong in any way to give the sense that there was unanimity to move toward abuse or that there was even strong support toward moving toward abuse. There was a strong body of belief down at Guantánamo amongst the military community, amongst the military lawyers, with the FBI, with the Naval Criminal Investigative Service, that this is a bad thing. Abuse doesn't work, abuse undermines authority, abuse undermines morale. We are going to stop it. Initially, they weren't successful. But once the abuse began, a backlash followed. And the folks down at Guantánamo identified a man in Washington who was the general counsel of the navy, a man by the name of Alberto Mora, who truly is a heroic individual, in my view, who intervened very courageously, directly with Jim Haynes, and said, "This must stop. If it doesn't stop, I'm going to reduce this into writing, and I'm going to cause a big fuss." And eventually, it did stop. But only after fifty-four days of abusive interrogation of Mohammed al-Qahtani, and not before the door had been opened, and the dogs had slipped their leash. The Geneva

Conventions were plainly violated in relation to this man. And in our system, if a man violates the law and commits a crime, he is punishable.

So who violated the law?

I think it goes to the top. And I think that the lawyers contributed to the violation of the law and face exposure. But I'm not on a witch hunt. I'm not saying that there should be a campaign of investigation and prosecution and sentencing, and conviction. What I'm saying is let's start by sorting out the facts. Once the facts have been sorted out, let's see exactly what they say, and it will be for others to decide what needs to be done. But until that's done, you can't close on the past and you can't move forward.

But David Rivkin, former White House lawyer, said at the Judiciary Committee hearing, "I think it would be madness to prosecute anybody, given the facts involved." He said, "The effort to go after the lawyers borders, to put it mildly, on madness. These lawyers were not in any chain of command. They had no theoretical or practical ability to direct actions of anyone who engaged in abusive conduct."

He's just wrong. The lawyers were deeply involved in the decision-making process. John Yoo at the Department of Justice prepared a legal memorandum which abandons American and international definitions of torture and reintroduces a new definition that has never been passed by any legislature, that is totally unacceptable. What was he doing there? Was he really giving legal advice? No, he wasn't. He was rubber-stamping a policy decision. This is not careful, independent legal advice. What was Jim Haynes doing when he recommended to Donald Rumsfeld the authorization for the approval of fifteen techniques of interrogation? He was saying to the secretary of defense, "I'm your lawyer. I'm telling you this is fine. You can do it." If he hadn't done that, Mr. Rumsfeld would not have signed the piece of paper that Jim Haynes wrote. Jim Haynes is directly involved in the decision-making process. And the lawyers, as such, play an absolutely key role. Now, at the end of the day, they're not the most important people. The most important people are the people whose signatures are actually appended. They are the politicians who actually decided the issue. But in this case, without the lawyers, they would never have had a piece of paper to sign.

Do you think that people such as David Addington and John Yoo and Jim

Haynes, and the other lawyers you've mentioned who advised and were on the torture team, should ultimately be held responsible in court for what they did in government at this period of time?

If they were complicit in the commission of a crime, then they should be investigated, and if the facts show that there is a sufficient basis for proceeding to a prosecution, then they should be prosecuted. Lawyers are gatekeepers to legality and constitutionality. If the lawyers become complicit in a common plan to get around the law, to allow abuse, then yes, they should be liable.

Many Americans say, "I don't want to hear about this." It's like being diagnosed with cancer. You don't really want to hear the terrible news. This is something that was done in a particular period of intense fear and uncertainty. We had been attacked, thousands of people killed right here in New York. And I just want the government to take care of it. I don't want to hear about the cruelty, the torture, the enhanced interrogation techniques. Do you understand why they would say that?

I do understand that. And here's what I'd say. I would want the government to take care of it in a way that is going to protect me over the long term. If it is indeed the case that those pictures from Abu Ghraib and Guantánamo are going to make it more difficult to protect the American public, I want to sort it out, remove that obstacle to protecting the American public, and ensure that it doesn't happen again in the future. And, as necessary, make sure that those who erred in putting in policies that allow that to happen face appropriate responsibility. You know, Bill, what has really agitated me the most about this is that it's not just that a crime was committed. It's that there's been a failure to take responsibility. There's been a cover-up from the top in terms of pointing the finger to people who should not take blame for what has happened.

Soldiers on the front lines who are doing their best in difficult circumstances to protect the United States should not be blamed for what was decided at the top. But there's an even bigger issue at a very personal level. It's not about legality, about criminality. It's about taking individual responsibility. If people like Doug Feith and Jim Haynes had said to me, "Look, Philippe. September the 11th came. The anniversary was coming. We were getting information that there were going to be more attacks. We had people that we were told had information that we need to do something about. And we therefore felt, in those circumstances, it was right to use all means appropriate and necessary to get the information. But with the benefit of hindsight, we realize we fell into error, we made a mistake. We accept responsibility for that. We will learn from those mistakes. We'll make damn sure it doesn't happen again." I didn't get that at all. There was not a hint of recognition that anything had gone wrong, nor a hint of recognition of individual responsibility. When you read my account along with Doug Feith's and others, you will see the sort of weaseling out of individual responsibility, the total and abject failure to accept involvement. Read Doug Feith's book on how to fight the so-called war on terror, and it's as though the man had no involvement in the decisions relating to the interrogation of detainees. And yet, as I describe in the book, the man was deeply involved in the decision making from step one. So it's about individual responsibility. And there's been an abject failure on that account.

Do you think torture's still going on?

I'd have to say my own view is that there has not been systematic torture at Guantánamo. I think it was isolated to two or three cases. I think the Guantánamo facility violates international law in many other ways and is wrong in many other ways, but I don't think that there was systemic torture at Guantánamo. I think there was probably far more systemic torture in Afghanistan, at Bagram and in Kandahar, but not in the military. And I think the military has now stopped. But it's important not to forget that although the military has apparently stopped, there remains the other side, the dark side, as Vice President Dick Cheney called it, the CIA. President Bush has vetoed legislation which would prohibit the CIA from using the very techniques of interrogation that are the subject of this book. And I think that has disturbed a lot of people.

But truth has consequences. In that congressional hearing, Representative Steve King of Iowa said to you, you're hurting the war on terror. You and all the critics, all the journalists, all the people who are trying to stir up this debate, and expose what happened in the inner workings of the administration.

I think he has no sense of history. He's revealing his lack of understanding in other contexts, where similar analogous situations have arisen. I come back to my own experience in Britain. I was a kid growing up in London when the streets of London were being bombed by the IRA. For a period during the 1970s, the view was, "Let's hit them hard. Let's hit them very hard." And it soon became clear that that is not a technique that works. Over time, Prime Ministers John Major and Tony Blair tried a different approach. And the different approach is, you understand what's at the root cause of the conflict. You talk to these people, sometimes secretly.

You try to reconcile errors that have been made. And that is a crucial part of bringing closure to a painful past. It happened in South Africa. It happened in Chile. It's happened in many other countries around the world. So I directly contradict the views of Representative King. Until you begin to come to terms with the past, and accept that if errors were made, that they were made, and who has responsibility for them—not necessarily in a prosecutorial way, but in some appropriate way—without that, you can't move on.

A noted Arab scholar said that if you walk the streets of Cairo today, stop at the bookstalls, stop at the bookstores, you see, looking out at you everywhere, photographs of Abu Ghraib and Guantánamo. That this torture, these enhanced interrogation techniques, this cruelty, has seized the imagination of the Arab world. And that long after all of us have gone, including the torture team, the next generation of Arabs will live with those images. What's your own sense of that?

I travel in the Arab world, and it's sad but true. The image of the United States today is that it's a country that has given us Guantánamo and Abu Ghraib. Now, that is not the America that I know. I've spent a lot of time here, you know. I'm married to an American. My kids were born in the United States. I know what the true America is. And for me, this is a distressing story, because it has allowed those who want to undermine the United States a very easy target for doing it. It's even worse than that, Bill. In a globalized world with the Internet, the legal advice that has been written by people like John Yoo at the Department of Justice and the memos written by Jim Haynes that were put on the desk of Donald Rumsfeld have gone all over the world. They've been studied all over the world. Other governments are able to rely upon them, and to say equally, "Look, this is what the United States does. If the Unites States does it, we can do it." It has undermined the United States' ability to tackle corruption, abuse, human rights violations in other countries, in a massive way. And it will take fifteen or twenty years to repair the damage. That's why, irrespective of whichever next president happens to hold that high office, there will be a recognition of a need to move on. And moving on means recognizing that errors were made.

I think we're all going to be wrestling with this. And I think we have a responsibility to wrestle with it in a constructive way precisely because we do face real global challenges. And the threat of terror is real. And the importance of putting the spotlight on the past is to make us learn for the future and to make sure it doesn't happen again.

Working on this book, I learned an important lesson, which is that you can't always deal with materials as they appear in newspapers or in documents. You need to take the trouble to go and spend many, many hours with people, talk to them, get to know them, understand what motivated them, understand that these are not people who wanted to do bad things. These are people who found themselves in a very difficult situation, under intense pressure from the top. I think once you've spoken to people, you begin to get a clearer picture. And I hope I have accurately conveyed the conversations in a fair and balanced way. There are people I like, there are people I didn't like. There are people whose views I shared, there are people whose views I didn't share. But I thought it was terribly important to lay out in the book the range of views that were expressed, and often not even to comment on them, but to let people's views inform the reader, and the reader can then form a view as to whether they agree or disagree. I have put the other side of the argument against my own argument. And there will be many, I'm sure, who will disagree with me. That's fine. Because that's what our societies are about, debating these important issues. I know what I think, though. What happened was wrong, and it needs to be sorted out. ∽

HOWARD ZINN

Tears welled up in Howard Zinn's eyes as he talked about Genora Dollinger, the twenty-three-year-old organizer who rallied women to "stand beside your husbands and your brothers and your uncles and your sweethearts" who occupied a General Motors factory in Flint, Michigan, in 1937 and refused to leave. Sure enough, when the police moved against the strikers, Dollinger's summons brought waves of women into the battle zone. Zinn and the actor Matt Damon, who as a kid was the historian's next-door neighbor, turned Dollinger's story into one of the most compelling sequences in their History Channel special, The People Speak. The TV show was based on Howard Zinn's work, including his most famous book, A People's History of the United States, the epic story of heroic, everyday men and women who stood up to organized power.

The book was inspired, in no small part, by his own experiences growing up in a working-class immigrant family in Brooklyn, New York. Zinn worked in the shipyards there before joining the U.S. Army Air Corps and becoming a B-17 bombardier. On his final mission in 1945, to take out an isolated German garrison in the French seaside town of Royan, the Eighth Air Force used napalm for the first time, killing hundreds of civilians. He returned to Royan twenty years later to study the effects of the raid and concluded there had been no military necessity for the bombing; everyone knew the war was *almost over (it ended three weeks later) and the attack made no contribution to the outcome.*

    Zinn's grief over having been a cog in a deadly machine no doubt confirmed his belief in small acts of rebellion. After the war, he came home to work at a warehouse loading trucks while enrolling as a twenty-seven-year-old freshman at New York University. In the years that followed, he ran afoul of the FBI when he was anonymously—and wrongly, he said—accused of Communist proclivities, was fired as chairman of the history and social sciences department at Spelman College in Atlanta in 1963 because of his civil rights activities, and spent the remainder of his long teaching career as a professor of political science at Boston University. Zinn passed into popular lore in 1997 when the film Good Will Hunting *was released. The title character, played by Matt Damon, praises* A People's History of the United States*—"a real* history book*"—and urges Robin Williams's character to read it.*

    After I screened Zinn and Damon's The People Speak, *eighty-seven-year-old Howard Zinn came to New York for this interview. He died five weeks later. One of his longtime friends and colleagues wrote that "shifting historical focus from the wealthy and powerful to the ordinary person was perhaps his greatest act of rebellion and incitement."*

—Bill Moyers

———※———

History and Hollywood: is this the beginning of a new career for you?

I hope not. But I am happy it is a way of reaching a larger audience with the ideas that were in the book. The idea of people involved in history, people actively making history, people agitating and demonstrating, pushing the leaders of the country into change in a way that leaders themselves are not likely to initiate.

What do these characters from the past have to say to us today?

What they have to say to us today is, think for yourself. Don't believe what the people up there tell you. Live your own life. Think your own ideas. And don't depend on saviors. Don't depend on the founding fathers, on Andrew Jackson, on Theodore Roosevelt, on Lyndon Johnson, on Obama. Don't depend on our leaders to do what needs to be done, because whenever the government has done anything to bring about change, it's done so only because it's been pushed and prodded by social movements, by ordinary people organizing. Lincoln was pushed by the antislavery movement, Johnson and Kennedy were pushed by the southern black movement, and maybe Obama today will be pushed by people who have such high hopes in him and who want to see him fulfill those hopes.

Traditional history creates passivity because it gives you the people at the top and it makes you think that all you have to do is go to the polls every four years and elect somebody who's going to do the trick for you. We want people to understand that that's not going to happen. People have to do it themselves.

One of my favorite sequences is when we meet Genora Dollinger.

She was a woman who got involved in the sit-down strikes of the 1930s, those very dramatic moments when workers occupied the factories of General Motors and wouldn't leave, and therefore left the corporations helpless. This was a time when strikes all over the country galvanized people and pushed for the reforms that we finally got from the New Deal. And Genora Dollinger represents the women who are very often overlooked in these struggles, women so instrumental in supporting the workers, their men, their sweethearts. And Genora Dollinger just inspires people with her words.

She was only twenty-three when she organized.

Amazing. Yes.

> GENORA DOLLINGER (PLAYED BY MARISA TOMEI): Workers overturned police cars to make barricades. They ran to pick up the firebombs thrown at them and hurl them back at the police. . . . The men wanted to me to get out of the way. You know, the old "protect the women and children" business. . . . I told them, "Get away from me." . . . The lights went on in my head. I thought, "I've never used a loudspeaker to address a large crowd of people, but I've got to tell them that there are women down here." . . . I called to them, "Cowards! Cowards! Shooting into the bellies of unarmed men and firing at the mothers of children." Then

everything became quiet. . . . I thought, "The women can break this up." So I appealed to the women in the crowd, "Break through those police lines and come down here and stand beside your husbands and your brothers and your uncles and your sweethearts." . . . I could barely see one woman struggling to come forward. A cop had grabbed her by the back of her coat. She just pulled out of that coat and started walking down to the battle zone. As soon as that happened there were other women and men who followed . . . that was the end of the battle. When those spectators came into the center of the battle and the police retreated, there was a big roar of victory.

What do you think when you hear those words?

First, I must say this, Bill. When my daughter heard Marisa Tomei shout to the police, "Cowards! Cowards!" she said a chill went through her, she was so moved. I've seen this so many times, and each time I am moved because what it tells me is that just ordinary people, you know, people who are not famous, if they get together, if they persist, if they defy the authorities, they can defeat the largest corporation in the world.

When I was last at the National Portrait Gallery in London, I was struck all over again by how the portraits there were of wealthy people who could afford to hire an artist. It's like Egypt, where you see the pyramids and the tombs and realize that only the rich could afford to consider their legacy and have the leisure time to do what they want. We know almost nothing about the ordinary people of the time.

Exactly. I remember when I was going to high school and learning, it was such a thrilling story to read about the Transcontinental Railroad. You know, the golden spike and all of that. But I wasn't told that this railroad was built by Chinese and Irish workers who worked by the thousands. Long hours, many of them died of sickness, overworked, and so on. I wasn't told about these working people. That's what I tried to do in *A People's History of the United States*, to bring back into the forefront the people who created what was called the economic miracle of the United States.

One of the producers of this film was Matt Damon. And I understand that when he was in the fifth grade, he took a copy of your book in to his teacher on Columbus Day and said, "What is this? We're here to celebrate this great event, but two years after Columbus discovered America, a hundred thousand Indians were dead, according to Howard Zinn. What's going on?" Is that a true story?

Not all stories are true, but this is true. Matt Damon, when he was ten years old, was given a copy of my book by his mother. They were next-door neighbors of ours, in the Boston area, in Newton. And Matt says that he and his brother, Kyle, would wake up sometimes in the middle of the night and see the light on in my study, where I was writing this book. So they were in on it from the beginning.

What about people today, doing what Genora Dollinger and others did in the past?

I think there are people like that today, but very often they're ignored in the media. Or they appear for a day on the pages of *The New York Times* or *The Washington Post*, then disappear. There are those people recently who sat in at this plant in Chicago that was going to be closed by the Bank of America, and these people sat in and refused to leave. I mean, that was a modern-day incarnation of what the sit-down strike was in the 1930s. There are people today who are fighting evictions, fighting foreclosures. There are people all over the country who are really conscience-stricken about what's going on. But the press is not covering them very well.

Several people in the program have talked about populism. How do you think of populism?

The word *populism* came into being in the late 1800s—1880, 1890—when great corporations dominated the country, the railroads and the banks. These farmers got together and they organized in the North and South, and they formed the Populist movement. It was a great people's movement. They sent orators around the country, and they published thousands of pamphlets. It was a high moment for American democracy.

Well, if populism is thriving today, it seems to be thriving on the right. Sarah Palin, for example, and the Tea Parties. One conservative writer in The Weekly Standard *even said that Sarah Palin could be the William Jennings Bryan of this new conservative era because she is giving voice to millions of people who feel angry at what the government is doing, who feel that they're being cheated out of a prosperous way of life by forces beyond their control. What do you think about that idea?*

Well, I guess William Jennings Bryan would turn over in his grave if he heard that. William Jennings Bryan was antiwar, and she is not antiwar, she is very militaristic. But it's true that she represents a certain angry part of the population. And I think it's true that when people feel beleaguered and overlooked, they will turn to whoever seems to represent them. Some of them will turn to her, some of them will turn to the right-wingers, and you might say that's how fascism develops in countries, because they play upon the anger and the frustration of people. But on the other hand, that anger, that frustration, can also lead to people's movements that are progressive. You can go the way of the Populists, of the labor movement of the '30s, of the civil rights movement, or the women's movement to bring about change in this country.

You mentioned the women's movement, and there's another remarkable moment in your film of Susan B. Anthony. She's on trial for trying to vote when she and other women didn't have the right.

> JUDGE HUNT (PLAYED BY JOSH BROLIN): The sentence of the Court is that you pay a fine of one hundred dollars and the costs of the prosecution.

> SUSAN B. ANTHONY (PLAYED BY CHRISTINA KIRK): May it please Your Honor, I will never pay a dollar of your unjust penalty. All the stock in trade I possess is a debt of $10,000, incurred by publishing my paper—*The Revolution*—the sole object of which was to educate all women to do precisely as I have done, rebel against your man-made, unjust, unconstitutional forms of law, which tax, fine, imprison, and hang women, while denying them the right of representation in the government; and I will work on with might and main to pay every dollar of that honest debt, but not a penny shall go to this unjust claim. And I shall earnestly and persistently continue to urge all women to the practical recognition of the old revolutionary maxim, "Resistance to tyranny is obedience to God."

I think what that says to people today is you must stick up for your principles, even if it means breaking the law. Civil disobedience. It's what Thoreau urged, it's what Martin Luther King Jr. urged. It's what was done during the civil rights movement and the Vietnam War. Susan B. Anthony thought it was right for her to try to register to vote. And yeah, people should defy the rules if they think they're doing the right thing.

You have said that if President Obama were listening to Martin Luther King Jr., he'd be making some different decisions.

Well, first of all, he'd be taking our troops out of Iraq and Afghanistan, and he'd be saying we are no longer going to be a war-making country. We're not going to be a military country. We're going to take our immense resources, our wealth, and we're going to use them for the benefit of people. Remember, Martin Luther King started a Poor People's Campaign just before he was assassinated. And if Obama paid attention to the working people of this country, then he would be doing much, much more than he is doing now.

Those of us who were around then remember that 1967 speech Martin Luther King gave here in New York at the Riverside Church, a year before his assassination. He said, "True compassion is more than flinging a coin to a beggar. . . . It comes to see that an edifice which produces beggars needs restructuring." I mean, that's pretty fundamental, right? Change the system?

King had a much more fundamental critique of our economic system, certainly more fundamental than Obama has because a fundamental critique of our economic system would not simply give hundreds of billions of dollars to the bankers and a little bit to the people below. A fundamental change in our system would really create a greater equalization of wealth, including free medical care, not the kind of half-baked health reforms that are debated in Congress.

This is one reason you are seen as a threat to people at the top, because your message, like King's message, goes to a fundamental rearrangement of power in America.

Yes, that is very troublesome for people at the top. They're willing to let people think about mild reforms, and little changes, and incremental changes, but they don't want people to think that we could actually transform this country into a peaceful country, that we no longer have to be a super military power. They don't want to think that way because it's profitable for certain interests in this country to carry on war, to have the military in a hundred countries, to have a $600 billion military budget. That makes a lot of money for certain people, but it leaves the rest of the country behind.

Let's hear the words of a labor person, a member of the Industrial Workers of the World, the IWW—the Wobblies.

> IWW MEMBER (PLAYED BY VIGGO MORTENSEN): If you were a bum without a blanket; if you had left your wife and kids when you went west for a job, and had never located them since; if your job had never kept you long enough in a place to qualify you to vote; if you slept in a lousy, sour bunkhouse, and ate food just as rotten as they could give you and get by with it; if deputy sheriffs shot your cooking cans full of holes and spilled your grub on the ground; if your wages were lowered on you when the bosses thought they had you down; . . . if every person who represented law and order and the nation beat you up, railroaded you to jail, and the good Christian people cheered and told them to go to it, how in the hell do you expect a man to be patriotic? This war is a businessman's war, and we don't see why we should go out and get shot in order to save the lovely state of affairs which we now enjoy.

They refused to go along with World War I, and he's explaining why they won't. Basically, he's speaking to poor people in all wars. He's saying, "It's a businessman's war." War is a businessman's war. It always is. The ordinary guys have nothing to gain from this war.

How do you explain the absence of protest in the streets today? The passivity in response to the fact that Obama has now doubled the number of troops in Afghanistan over the number George W. Bush had there.

I don't think people are apathetic about it. I believe most people in this country do not want us to be in Afghanistan. But they're not doing anything about it, you're right. We're not seeing protests in the street. And I think one of the reasons is that the major media, television, and newspapers have not played their role in educating the public about what is going on.

There was a poll showing that a bare majority of Americans support sending more troops to Afghanistan.

You have to remember this—it is not easy for people to oppose sending troops to Afghanistan, especially once they have been sent and once the decision has been made. It's not easy for people to oppose what the president is saying, and what the media are saying, what both major parties are working for. So the very fact that even close to a majority of the people are opposed to sending troops to Afghanistan tells me that many more people are opposed. I have a fundamental faith in the basic decency and even, yes, the wisdom of people, once they make their way through the deceptions that are thrown at them. And we've seen this historically. People learn.

I was struck in your television special by what the labor leader Cesar Chavez had to say about organizing his fellow farmworkers.

> CESAR CHAVEZ (PLAYED BY MARTÍN ESPADA): I'm not very different from anyone else who has ever tried to accomplish something with his life. My motivation comes . . . from watching what my mother and father went through when I was growing up; from what we experienced as migrant farmworkers in California. . . .
>
> It grew from anger and rage—emotions I felt forty years ago when people of my color were denied the right to see a movie or eat at a restaurant in many parts of California. It grew from the frustration and humiliation I felt as a boy who couldn't understand how the growers could abuse and exploit farmworkers when there were so many of us and so few of them. . . .
>
> I began to realize what other minority people had discovered: that the only answer—the only hope—was in organizing. . . .
>
> Like the other immigrant groups, the day will come when we win the economic and political rewards which are in keeping with our numbers in society. The day will come when the politicians do the right thing by our people out of

political necessity and not out of charity or idealism. That day may not come this year. That day may not come during this decade. But it will come, someday!

Do you believe it will come?

I do. I can't give you a date, but I have confidence in the future. You know why? You have to be patient. Farmworkers were at one point in as helpless a position as the labor movement is today. But as Cesar Chavez said, we learned that you have to organize. And it takes time, it takes patience, it takes persistence. I mean, think of how long black people in the South waited.

More than two centuries, and then another century after the Civil War.

I don't think we'll have to wait a hundred years.

So populism and people power aren't really a left or right issue. It's more "us versus them"—bottom versus top?

It's democracy. You know, democracy doesn't come from the top. It comes from the bottom. Democracy is not what governments do. It's what people do. Too often, we go to junior high school and they sort of teach us that democracy is three branches of government. You know, it's not the three branches of government.

I'd like to end with a woman in your film who showed us the power of a single voice, speaking for democracy. Born into slavery, largely uneducated, she spoke out for the rights of people who didn't have any. She was an unforgettable truth-teller.

SOJOURNER TRUTH (PLAYED BY KERRY WASHING-TON): That man over there says that women need to be helped into carriages, and lifted over ditches, and to have the best place everywhere. Nobody ever helps me into carriages, or over mud-puddles, or gives me any best place! And ain't I a woman? Look at me! . . . I have ploughed and planted, and gathered into barns, and no man could head me! And ain't I a woman? I could work as much and eat as much as a man— when I could get it—and bear the lash as well! And ain't I a woman? I have borne thirteen children, and seen most sold off into slavery, and when I cried out with my mother's grief, none but Jesus heard me! And ain't I a woman? . . .

Then that little man in the back there, he says women can't have as much rights as men, 'cause Christ wasn't a woman! Where did your Christ come from? Where did your Christ come from? From God and a woman! Man had nothing to do with Him.

If the first woman God ever made was strong enough to turn the world upside down all alone, these women together ought to be able to turn it back, and get it right side up again! And now they is asking to do it, the men better let them.

Why did you include that excerpt?

Because it's so empowering. Because here is this woman who was a slave, oppressed on all sides, and she's defiant. She represents the voice of people who have been overlooked. She represents a voice that is rebellious and, yes, troublesome to the powers that be. ～

MICHELLE ALEXANDER

In the spring of 1968, Martin Luther King Jr. was exhausted and depressed. Under fire from politicians, the media, and even fellow leaders in the civil rights movement for his stand against the Vietnam War, he came to Memphis, Tennessee, three times in support of striking garbagemen. More than a thousand African American sanitation workers had walked off the job after two co-workers had been crushed to death by a garbage truck's compactor. They were fed up at being treated with contempt—white supervisors called them "boy"—as they performed a filthy and unrewarding job, so poorly paid that 40 percent of them were on welfare. Their picket signs read simply: "I _AM_ A MAN."

Opposition and violence met the strike; King led one march that ended in tear gas and gunfire. He came back one more time to try to put things right and made the famous speech that would prove prophetic:

> I just want to do God's will. And He's allowed me to go up to the mountain. And I've looked over. And I've seen the promised land. I may not get there with you. But I want you to know tonight, that we, as a people, will get to the promised land. And I'm happy, tonight. I'm not worried about anything. I'm not fearing any man.

The next night, April 4, he was assassinated. In the wake of his death, mil-

BRYAN STEVENSON

lions mourned as riots burned across the country. Twelve days later, the strike was settled, the garbagemen's union was recognized, and the city of Memphis begrudgingly agreed to increase their pay, at first by ten cents an hour and later by an extra nickel.

That paltry sum would also be prophetic. After all these years, unemployment among African Americans is nearly double that of whites, according to the National Urban League. Black men and women make 62 cents for every dollar earned by whites. Less than half of black and Hispanic families own homes, and they are three times more likely to live below the poverty line. The nonpartisan organization United for a Fair Economy reports, "The Great Recession has pulled the plug on communities of color, draining jobs and homes at alarming rates while exacerbating persistent inequalities of wealth and income."

On the forty-second anniversary of King's murder I asked two leading advocates of justice to discuss the state of his vision for economic justice. Bryan Stevenson lives in Alabama, where he founded the Equal Justice Initiative to advocate for the poor and people of color. He also teaches clinical law at New York University and is a recipient of the MacArthur Fellowship for his efforts to end the death penalty. Michelle Alexander once directed the civil rights clinics at Stanford Law School and now teaches law at Ohio State University. When we spoke, she had just published a widely acclaimed book, The New Jim

Crow: Mass Incarceration in the Age of Colorblindness. *Both are immersed in Martin Luther King's legacy.*

—Bill Moyers

———⟿———

Let's begin with some speculation. Martin Luther King would be eighty-one. How do you think he would react to the state of America today?

STEVENSON: I think he would be heartbroken. In 1966, Dr. King went to Wilcox County, Alabama, one of the counties in the Black Belt. Dr. King became very close to the poor there, and really organized and inspired people to confront poverty. And they participated in marches and demonstrations. They had all largely been evicted from lands where they'd been sharecroppers and tenant farmers. If you go to Wilcox County today, virtually nothing has changed. Nothing. Today, 27 percent unemployment. Half of all black families have household incomes under $10,000 a year. Dr. King would be heartbroken that in 2010 there would be forty million people in this country who live below the federal poverty level.

Blacks and whites?

STEVENSON: Blacks and whites.

And Hispanics and others.

STEVENSON: And others. I think he would be devastated by that, because we've also had this explosion of great wealth. It's this proximity of poverty next to wealth. I think it would be sad to him to see how wealth has caused many people, people of color and others, to abandon the poor, to give up on this dream of economic justice. It would, I think, force him to confront these larger psychological dynamics. What was so powerful to me about his work in Memphis was not only that he was pushing for economic justice, but he was also pushing for the kind of liberation that every person who's been excluded and marginalized and subordinated by poverty has to want.

The kind of recognition that you're as good as the people who have more than you. That sign that those sanitation workers were wearing—"I AM A MAN"—was almost more provocative than the fact that they were seeking higher wages, because if these are men, we have to deal with them as men. That challenges everything. I continue to believe that in this country the opposite of poverty is not wealth. The opposite of poverty is justice. I think there are structures and systems that have created poverty and made poverty so permanent that until we think in a more just way about how to deal with it, we're never going to make the progress that Dr. King envisioned.

But surely he would have been thrilled on Election Night 2008, with the election of the first African American president in our history.

ALEXANDER: Yes. But individual black achievement today masks a disturbing, underlying racial reality. To a significant extent, affirmative action—seeing African Americans go to Harvard and Yale, become CEOs and corporate lawyers—causes us all to marvel what a long way we have come.

But as Bryan just indicated, much of the data indicates that African Americans today, as a group, are not much better off than they were back in 1968 when Martin Luther King delivered the "Other America" speech, talking about how there are two Americas in the United States. One where people have great opportunities and can dream big dreams, and another where people are mired in poverty and stuck in a permanent second-class status. Those two Americas still exist today. The existence of Barack Obama and people of color scattered in positions of power and high places creates an illusion of much more progress than has actually been made in recent years.

You describe in your book how thrilled you were on Election Night as the returns came in. And then you walked out of the Election Night party, and . . . ?

ALEXANDER: On Election Night, I was filled with hope and enthusiasm. Like much of America. And as I left the Election Night party, along with hundreds of others folks, there in the gutter was an African American man handcuffed behind his back, on his knees in the gutter, and he was surrounded by police officers who were talking and joking, completely oblivious to him, to his human existence.

And as people poured out of the party, people glanced over briefly, took a look at him, and then went on their way with their celebrations, and I thought to myself, "What does the election of Barack Obama mean for him? In what way are those folks who are truly at the bottom of the well in America, in what way have they benefited?" The difficult reality that we have to come to terms with is that not much has changed or will change for the folks at the bottom of the well until we as a nation awaken, awaken to their humanity.

STEVENSON: One of the great problems for the communities where I work is that people actually still feel pained by the absence of any truth about the real cost of Jim Crow, about the real cost of segregation, about the real cost of decades of racial subordination.

Jim Crow was that long and awful period when African Americans were forced into segregation and second- and third-class citizenship.

STEVENSON: And humiliated every day. You could not drink the same water. You could not go to the same bathrooms. You had to get off the sidewalk when a person who was white came by. You were absolutely branded as inferior. That went on for decades. And we've never been told the truth about what that did to these communities.

Other countries that have confronted historic problems of racism and gross ethnic conflict have recognized that to overcome that, there has to be a period of truth and reconciliation. In South Africa, they had to go through truth and reconciliation. In Rwanda, there had to be truth and reconciliation. In this country, we've never had truth and we've never had reconciliation. And so the day-to-day reality for the people I work with is one that's still hurt, angry, broken.

After 9/11—the terrorist attacks—older people come up to me, and they say, "Mr. Stevenson, I grew up with terrorism. We had to worry about being bombed. We had to worry about being lynched. We had to live in communities close to each other because the threat of violence was constant. My uncle was nearly lynched. My aunt had to leave Alabama and go to Kentucky or Ohio or the North because they were afraid she was going to be lynched after speaking out and taking a stand." That reality still lingers with them. So that they experience the things that we talk about on TV very differently. There is a quite powerful psychic injury that comes with being told day in and day out, "You're not as good. You're not as worthy. You're less than. You're subordinate."

When Lyndon Johnson signed the Civil Rights Act in 1964, the Voting Rights

Act in 1965, he thought a woman would be president before an African American. Here, just forty years later, an African American is president. Does that pull some of the sting out of the hurt?

STEVENSON: It does. But I don't think it changes the fundamental dynamics. Let's not be confused about the election of Barack Obama. In my state of Alabama, Barack Obama got 10 percent of the white vote. He got 13 percent of the white vote under the age of thirty. Those are very discouraging statistics. John Kerry got twice that in '04 when he lost.

What do those statistics tell you?

STEVENSON: They say to me that we still live in a society where there is incredible race consciousness. My state of Alabama is a state where in 2004 we tried to get rid of segregation language in the state constitution, and a majority of people in Alabama voted to keep that language, and we're supposed to just carry on, as if somehow that doesn't matter. These very stark racial divisions and realities are very dominant. There's a very strong reaction among whites against the Obama election in the Deep South. In many places, the number of incidents of hate crimes, and of complaints by black teachers and others, has increased. So I don't want us to think that the election stands alone. For every action there's a reaction, and the reaction is quite worrisome to many people of color in the Deep South.

You call your book The New Jim Crow. *What's the parallel between the old Jim Crow that Bryan has just described and the new Jim Crow that you describe in your book?*

ALEXANDER: Well, just a couple decades after the collapse of the old Jim Crow system, a new system of racial control emerged in the United States. Today, people of color are targeted by law enforcement for relatively minor, nonviolent, often drug-related offenses. Those are the types of crimes that occur all the time on college campuses, where drug use is open and notorious, that occur in middle-class suburban communities without much notice.

People of color are targeted, often at very young ages, for relatively minor offenses. Arrested, branded felons, and then ushered into a parallel social universe, in which they can be denied the right to vote; they're automatically excluded from juries, and legally discriminated against in many of the ways in which African Americans were discriminated against during the Jim Crow era. So when I say that we have a new racial caste system, what I mean is that we have a system of laws, policies, and practices in the United States today that operate to lock people of color, particularly poor people of color, living in ghetto communities, in an inferior second-class status for life.

Now, most people think the drug war was declared in response to rising drug crime or crime rates, but that is not the case. The current drug war was officially declared by President Ronald Reagan in 1982, a couple years before crack hit the streets and became a media sensation. The drug war was part of the Republican Party's grand strategy, now known as the "southern strategy," to use racially coded political appeals on issues of crime and welfare in order to appeal to poor and working-class white voters who were resentful of and disaffected by many of the gains of the civil rights movement—folks who were upset by busing, desegregation, and affirmative action. The Republican Party strategists openly talked about the need to use racially coded political appeals on crime and welfare in order to get those voters who used to be part of the Democratic New Deal coalition to defect to the Republican Party.

You quote President Richard Nixon's White House chief of staff, H.R. Haldeman: "The whole problem is really the blacks. The key is to devise a system that recognizes this while not appearing to." But wasn't there also an issue of punishing criminals and stopping crime?

STEVENSON: I think that's where you have to really focus on what's a crime, what's a threat to public safety, and what's something else. We've always had a commitment to stopping crime. People convicted and charged with violent crimes were always people who were going to be arrested and prosecuted. What's interesting is that over the last thirty-five years, there haven't been tremendous fluctuations in the violent crime rate in this country.

At the same time, we've gone from 300,000 people in jails and prison in 1972 to 2.3 million people in jails and prisons today, with nearly 5 million people on probation and parole. Most of that is explained by this so-called war on drugs. The point can't be overstated that when we talk about challenging drug use, we're not talking about challenging drug use throughout society. Because this is actually one crime area where there aren't huge differences between black use and white use for illegal drugs. It's about the same.

Black people are 13 percent of the population of this country. They're about 14 percent of the drug users. However they end up being about 60 percent of the people sent to prison. You have to focus on these policies and the targeting. I think that what's meant by these policies is that we didn't have to incarcerate people for ten, twenty, thirty, forty years for drug use. We didn't have to do that. We made choices around that.

And now the consequences are devastating. I think they're not only devastating from a political perspective, but I think—this is the way I think it relates to Jim Crow as well—it's also been devastating within communities of color. Right now, for black men in the United States, there's a 32 percent chance you're going to jail or prison.

In poor communities and minority communities, urban communities, rural communities, it could be 60 percent or 70 percent. Well, what does that do? You're born, you're a ten-year-old kid, there's a 70 percent chance that you're going to go to jail and prison. What does that do to you? And the heartbreaking thing for me when I work in communities like that is I see kids who are thirteen and fourteen who expect that they're going to go to prison.

And they tell me. "Mr. Stevenson, don't tell me about staying in school. I've got to go out here and get mine before I'm dead at eighteen or twenty-one or I'm sent to prison for the rest of my life." This culture of despair is a function of this so-called war on drugs, that is also like Jim Crow, because it has actually diminished the aspirations and hopes of people of color in ways that actually contribute to these cycles of violence and destruction and hopelessness.

ALEXANDER: The enemy in this war is not drugs. The enemy has been defined in racial terms. Now, if we were to look for drugs as aggressively in suburban middle-class white communities as we do in ghetto communities, we would have those kinds of stunning figures in middle-class white communities as well. And as Bryan indicated, the rates of drug use are about the same among all racial groups. But also, and what many people don't realize, is that the rates of drug sales are about the same among people of all different races.

This defies our racial stereotypes. When we think of a drug dealer, we think of a black kid standing on a street corner with his pants hanging down, right? Well, drug dealing certainly happens in the ghetto, but it happens everywhere else in America as well. A white kid in Nebraska doesn't get his marijuana or his meth by driving to the 'hood to get it. No, he gets it from a friend, a classmate, a co-worker who lives down the road.

Why is it that the burden, then, falls hardest on the people you've described— young black men in the inner cities?

ALEXANDER: There are a number of reasons. First, the enemy was defined politically as black and brown. For political reasons. It was part of the Republican Party's effort to prove they were getting tough on them, the people that many poor and working-class whites had come to believe were taking their jobs and disrupting their lives through the social upheaval brought by the civil rights movement. The Reagan administration actually hired staff whose job it was to publicize crack babies, crack dealers in inner-city communities, in the hope that these images would build public support for the drug war and persuade Congress to devote millions of more dollars to the war.

This converted the war from a rhetorical one into a literal one. It was part of a larger political strategy. And once the media became saturated and our public consciousness began to associate drug use and drug crime with African Americans, it's no surprise that law enforcement efforts became concentrated in communities defined by race as well.

STEVENSON: The reality is that, in poor communities, the police do raids all the time. I've worked in communities where the SWAT team comes and they put up a screen fence around the public housing project. They do searches. They stop people coming in and out. There are these presumptions of criminality that follow young men of color.

When they're someplace others think they don't belong, they're stopped and they're targeted. And so, because you don't have the resources actually to create privacy and security, you're much more vulnerable to prosecution. As Michelle said, middle-class communities, elite schools in this country would not tolerate drug raids from federal law enforcement officers and police even if there's illegal drug use.

There is this way in which resources and economic status actually make you more vulnerable to criminal arrest and prosecution. It becomes a self-fulfilling story. So that when I walk down the street in the wrong kinds of clothes, if I'm in the "wrong place," there's a presumption that I'm up to something criminal.

And that means that a police officer being very rational, not necessarily being overtly racist, has an interest in me and a concern about me that he's going to follow up on. And a lot of these things are not willful or intentional. But we have so embraced this image, this notion, this narrative about black criminality and drug use and all that sort of thing, we almost unconsciously accept that, yes, that person looks like a drug dealer.

In your book, you used the metaphor of the birdcage to describe what Bryan is talking about. Talk about that.

ALEXANDER: Academics have a tendency to use terms like "structural racism" to explain how people of color are trapped kind of at the bottom. But one way of thinking about these forms of structural disadvantage is to think about it as a birdcage. Not every wire of the cage needs to be intentionally designed to keep the bird trapped, right? Now, the rules and laws that exist today, the drug laws and the ways in which they're enforced, all of the forms of discrimination that people who have been branded felons now face, all the forms of legal discrimination against them are wires of the cage that serve to keep people of color trapped in an inferior, second-class status. As Bryan suggested, not every law or policy has to be adopted with discriminatory intent in order for it to function as part of a larger, and in this case literal, cage for black people.

There are people who are going to disagree with you, of course. And they're going to say, "Look, there was a great deal of concern back in the '60s and early '70s with law and order. 'Lock them up' became a way to deal with crime." And they will say today that prisons actually work because as the prison population goes up, the crime rate has been dropping.

STEVENSON: But that would not be accurate. That is, we had huge prison growth between 1984 and 1991, and the crime rate actually increased. It's interesting. The states that have had the lowest rates of incarceration growth have actually had the greatest rates of reduction of crime. So I don't know that we can simply say that, yes, because we have this huge prison population there's been a decrease in crime.

No one disputes that there are things that threaten public safety. Violent crimes have to be managed with some intervention. But what we're talking about here is a huge increase in the prison population, say, for marijuana possession, around things like using illegal drugs. Most of these crimes are not violent crimes. My state has a three-strikes law where you can be sentenced to life imprisonment without parole for four felony convictions.

I represented a man who stole a bicycle worth $16 after being convicted of public urination, stealing a transistor radio, and stealing a hand tool from a hardware store. He got life without parole. A Vietnam vet I represented had three marijuana possession convictions. The fourth conviction, he got life without parole. These cases do not reflect the debate about law and order. I don't think it's about that. It's more about control and this kind of use of the politics of fear and anger as a way of empowering some and disempowering others.

Are most of those people who get life imprisonment African Americans?

STEVENSON: Yes. About two-thirds of the people in our state prison system are people of color. There are complexities to this, and I don't want to understate the complexities. We have a criminal justice system that's very wealth-sensitive. Our system treats you better if you're rich and guilty than if you're poor and innocent.

Poor people brought into the criminal justice system, who don't have the means for good legal representation, who don't have the resources to protect themselves, who can't afford to pay the fees for getting into drug court and avoiding jails and prisons, are going to fare worse than people who do have those resources. That's a function of the criminal justice system. But now we see these incredibly troubling race effects. The federal government has created a sentencing scheme for crack cocaine versus powder cocaine that has been devastating to people of color. We sentence a hundred times to one.

And Bill Clinton signed that law, by the way. It's not just Republicans whose fingerprints are on this.

STEVENSON: That's exactly right. In 1996, President Clinton signed a provision in the Welfare Reform Act that bans people with drug convictions from public housing and public benefits and food stamps. Women with children have been devastated by that, and that was a policy signed by a

Democratic president. What I mean by failure, though, and our failure, our inability to recognize it, is that we now know that this has been horrific. In my state, 31 percent of the black male population has permanently lost the right to vote as a result of felony convictions. Yet we are unwilling to talk about that, even as we celebrate the Selma-to-Montgomery march, even as we talk about the Voting Rights Act as this great period in American revelation around race consciousness. The projection is that in a few years we're actually going to have a higher level of disenfranchisement among African American men than existed at the time of the Voting Rights Act. Most politicians wouldn't concede that having a third of the black male population in prison is a bad thing. And that's what I mean by failure.

Your passion is the abolition of capital punishment. Although each case is horrendous in its own right, relatively few people are affected by capital punishment. Why is it that capital punishment has become so symbolic of what you see as the crisis in American justice and American life?

STEVENSON: Several things. It shapes all criminal justice policy. It's only in a country where you have the death penalty that you can have life without parole for somebody who writes bad checks and for somebody else who steals a bicycle. It shapes the way we think about punishment. We've gotten very comfortable with really harsh and excessive sentences. And I think the death penalty permits that. We've had 130 people in this country who've been exonerated, proved innocent, who were on death row. For every eight people who have been executed, we've identified one innocent person. If we will tolerate that kind of error rate in the death penalty context, it reveals a whole lot about the rest of our criminal justice system and about the rest of our society.

There was a death penalty case that went to the Supreme Court, McCleskey v. Kemp. *You used this as an example of our tolerance of failure.*

STEVENSON: The case involved an African American who was accused of killing a white police officer in Atlanta, Georgia. And the history is that in 1972, in *Furman v. Georgia*, the Supreme Court said that the death penalty is arbitrary, in part because it is so racially biased. They noted that 87 percent of the people executed in this country for rape were black men convicted of raping white women. But they didn't say it's cruel and unusual punishment. So the Court says, "We're not going to presume bias and discrimination in the death penalty until you prove it to us." *McCleskey* comes back in 1987 and says, "Here's the evidence, here's your proof." And I think the devastating thing about the opinion is that they said that these kinds of disparities based on race are inevitable.

Inevitable?

STEVENSON: Inevitable. I'm a product of *Brown v. Board of Education.* Grew up in a community where black kids couldn't go to the public schools. I remember when the lawyers came into our community and made the public schools accessible to me. I wouldn't be sitting here talking to you but for that intervention. And the difference between *Brown* and *McCleskey* can't really be defined or explained by jurisprudence. It's defined and explained by this hopelessness that we have projected onto this community.

ALEXANDER: *McClesky v. Kemp* has immunized the criminal justice system from judicial scrutiny for racial bias. It has made it virtually impossible to challenge any aspect of the criminal justice process for racial bias in the absence of proof of intentional discrimination—conscious, deliberate bias. Now, that's the very type of evidence that is nearly impossible to come by today, when people know not to say, "The reason I stopped him was because he was black. The reason I sought the death penalty was because he was black." People know better than to say that they are recommending higher sentences or harsher punishment for someone because of their race.

So evidence of conscious, intentional bias is almost impossible to come by in the absence of some kind of admission. But the U.S. Supreme Court has said that the courthouse doors are closed to claims of racial bias in the absence of that kind of evidence, which has really immunized the entire criminal justice system from judicial and to a large extent public scrutiny of the severe racial disparities and forms of racial discrimination that go on every day, unchecked by our courts and our legal process.

STEVENSON: I argue cases at the Supreme Court. And every time I go there, I have this little ritual. I stand outside the Court. I read where it says, "Equal justice under law." I have to believe that to make sense of what I do. And this decision essentially said, "There will be no equal justice under law."

It seems to me your book boils down to this: mass imprisonment, mass incarcer-

ation constitutes a racial caste system, and the entrance to this new caste system can be found at the prison gate. Is that what you mean by that metaphor?

ALEXANDER: Absolutely. The entrance into this new caste system can be found at the prison gate, because that is when you are branded. Once you are branded a felon, your life as you knew it before is over. All the forms of discrimination that are illegal for the rest of the country now can be practiced against you with impunity.

I think it's important to recognize, though, that there are white people who have been harmed by the drug war. There are white families, particularly poor white families, that have been shattered by the incarceration of loved ones. The drug war was declared with black folks in mind, and mass incarceration as we know it would not exist but for the racialization of crime in the media and in our political discourse. But just because African Americans have been the target of this war doesn't mean that people of all colors haven't suffered as a result.

We may have the opportunity to see how racial caste systems can harm people of all colors, that truly few benefit from the imposition of these vast systems of control.

Two progressive groups, the Economic Policy Institute and the Urban League, say that structural inequality cannot be confronted if we practice "identity politics." And these progressive groups are asking for universalism. What does that mean to you?

ALEXANDER: Well, universal policies are policies that apply to everyone. And obviously, health care and education are examples of the type of thing. Quality education, quality health care, the types of things we would want to be available to everyone. But not everyone is similarly situated. Which means that we need to take into account unique, lived experiences of particular communities and particular groups, which in our country are still often defined by race.

All poor communities and all poor groups are not the same, right?

ALEXANDER: That's right. So having a blanket approach to all communities as though they were all similarly situated is doomed to failure. We have to take into account the unique experiences. We need to be race-conscious, conscious of the ways in which communities that are still segregated by race may experience educational inequity, may experience the underfunding of their schools in ways that are different from communities that are located in other areas. We have to take into account that difference in order to treat everyone fairly.

But can you target racial differences, as Michelle just said, without a racist backlash?

STEVENSON: I don't think we can overcome our racist past without recognizing the consequences of decades of segregation, without recognizing the consequences of terrorizing a group of people based on their race. And I think we can actually find some reconciliation if we tell the truth about those histories and we deal with them in a structured, sensible way.

I actually think we can undermine this tension, this tendency toward backlash, if we just deal with these things. For example, in my state, we still have segregated school systems. Even in integrated school systems, there's a black homecoming queen and a white homecoming queen. Sometimes there's a black prom and a white prom. Dealing with that, I think we can challenge some of the thinking behind that without backlash. It just means we have to kind of move forward.

Some politicians, African American politicians, are urging that we give a pass to President Obama because, as the first African American president, he can't really be expected to take on racially targeted issues. That is, he can't appear to be president of black people. He has to be president of all people. Do you agree with that?

ALEXANDER: What I think is important is for us to have a president who cares about all people. And what it means to care about someone who lives in a racially segregated ghetto is to be responsive to their unique concerns, their unique challenges. So if we're going to care about all people and treat all people fairly, we're going to have to extend certain types of help and support to some groups of people that may not be needed for others. So it's not about having a black agenda and a white agenda, a brown agenda. It's about having an agenda that genuinely extends care, compassion, and concern to all people.

And jobs, right?

ALEXANDER: Especially jobs today. Yes.

STEVENSON: I think sometimes when we say "American agenda," we don't mean, we don't include, people of color. We don't include poor people. I expect every president to care about poverty in this country. If we have forty million people living in poverty, I think every president has to deal with that. And you don't get a pass just because you're African American or because of anything. We need for President Obama to have a real American agenda.

If we have mass incarceration, that's an American problem. Every president needs to be concerned about the fact that we incarcerate more people than any other country in the world. If we want to be the home of the brave and the land of the free, we've got to think about what that means and what that says. If we violate people's rights because they're poor, because they're people of color, if we incarcerate them wrongly, if we condemn them unfairly, then that implicates who we are. And I don't think that in any way is a black agenda issue or poor people agenda issue. It's an American issue.

ALEXANDER: It's critically important for us to recognize that throughout our nation's history, poor and working-class whites have been pitted against people of color, triggering the rise of successive new systems of control, even slavery. You know, many people don't realize that before we had an all-black system of slavery, there was a system of bond labor that included both whites and blacks working right alongside each other on plantations. When blacks and whites joined together and challenged the plantation elite—and there were slave uprisings or bond laborer uprisings—the way in which plantation owners were able to split the workforce and gain control over their workers was by proposing an all-black system of slavery. Which led the white folks to believe that they had received some kind of benefit. And they no longer were willing to engage in struggles with fellow black laborers, with whom they had once joined in struggle. And so we had an all-black system of slavery in part because plantation owners wanted to prevent poor whites and blacks from joining together to seek economic justice.

STEVENSON: There's a tremendous effort right now to antagonize and polarize black and white poor communities and direct that anger toward new immigrants and people in this country who are undocumented. That has to be challenged and resisted.

In poor communities, rural poor communities, the issues are different sometimes than in urban communities. We have huge problems with transportation. We will not solve the economic problem until we do something about the transportation problem. In my community, you know, people working minimum-wage jobs have to drive seventy miles to get to work. When the gas prices go up, it no longer becomes sensible for them to work. They have to quit their jobs, because it actually costs them more to get to work and work eight hours and get home than what they earn. We have to think about that. We have to think about urban communities, where there are these horrific housing conditions that feed violence and drugs and all of these other conditions, we've got to talk about it in that way. But the basic commitment is universal. That is, we've got to recognize that poor people in America have to be addressed. We can't keep ignoring them. If we keep ignoring the poor, we not only undermine Dr. King's vision, we corrupt our values. You judge the character of a society not by how you treat the rich and the privileged and the celebrated. You judge the character of a society by how you treat the poor, the condemned, the incarcerated. And I think this is an American challenge that Dr. King understood. And that's what's universal for me.

ALEXANDER: We need to go back and pick up where Martin Luther King left off, with the poor people's movement, when he dreamed of joining poor and working-class whites, blacks, Latinos, Asians, Native Americans in a mass movement for human rights in the United States. King said it is high time we switch our focus from a civil rights movement and begin building a human rights movement. Shortly before he died, he said the gains of the past several years have been easy compared to the work that lies ahead.

Gaining the right to vote, earning the right to sit at the same lunch counter—these cost people relatively little. But the changes that lie ahead, which require a restructuring of our nation's economy and ensuring that every person has their basic human rights—the right to work, the right to education, the right to health care—honored, no matter what their race or ethnicity, these challenges require a movement even larger than the one that he inspired. So we need to go back to the movement-building work that Martin Luther King believed in so strongly at the time of his death.

What would a commitment to economic justice, equality of opportunity for all, look like?

STEVENSON: I think we can take the incarceration question and turn it on its head. In some states we're spending $45,000 a year to keep a nineteen-year-old in prison for the next thirty years for drug possession—$45,000 a year. What could we do if we spent half that amount of money on that nineteen-year-old when he's five or six or seven or eight?

Economic justice would say, let's not wait until we've arrested them at eighteen and nineteen and spend $45,000 a year on them. Let's spend half of that a year, between five and eighteen, and see if we can avoid incarceration, see what kind of opportunities we can create. See what kind of society we can create if we invest in the lives of these children who are living in the margins. Let's see what kind of America we can create if we invest in deconstructing the systems that have created poverty. Reinvesting in jobs. Reinvesting in the politics of hope. We talk about it, but we don't make it real unless we deal with the most hopeless, marginalized, subordinated communities in our society.

Does President Obama get it?

STEVENSON: I think that elected politicians, at this point in our history, have a very difficult time confronting the politics of fear and anger, I really do. I think it's very hard. President Clinton used crime to reinforce support among conservatives and moderates. He went back to Arkansas to preside over the execution of Ricky Ray Rector even though that man was brain-damaged, and it was a horrible thing.

Mr. Clinton signed the Antiterrorism and Effective Death Penalty Act of 1996. He used tough-on-crime rhetoric throughout that administration. That was certainly embraced by his successors. And we're hearing some of that from this administration. We haven't seen the kind of commitment to this issue that many of us had hoped for. So I think it's very difficult for majoritarian politicians who have used the politics of fear and crime to create support to turn against that.

Your book is the least sentimental of any I've read in a long time. You're really tough on the new Jim Crow.

ALEXANDER: Absolutely. The mass incarceration of people of color in the

United States is the most pressing racial justice issue of our time. It is a tragedy of proportions as great as Jim Crow was in its time. And you're right. I pull no punches in the book. But I do have great hope. And I devote the last chapter of the book to talking about why we must and we can build a new movement not just to end mass incarceration, but the history of racial caste in America. ∽

THOMAS CAHILL

*Thomas Cahill roams history looking for little-known individuals who, at pivotal moments in the rise of civilizations, changed the course of events. The iconic figures of the past rarely appear in his books. Cahill told me, "I'm not really interested in Alexander the Great or Napoleon. Every once in a while there's a general or a politician in one of my books. But he doesn't stay around very long." Instead, you meet in the pages of his bestselling books people you may never have heard of—men and women who helped turn the hinges of history and then were largely swallowed up by the shadows of the past. Cahill discovered them among the monks of the Middle Ages (*How the Irish Saved Civilization*), in the synagogues of ancient Judaism (*The Gift of the Jews*), in the golden age of Greece (*Sailing the Wine-Dark Sea*), and in the rise of Christianity (*Desire of the Everlasting Hills*), as well as in his book *Mysteries of the Middle Ages.*

At first, his most recent volume seems to be a puzzling detour from his excavations of the past and his curiosity about what makes a civilization. But only at first. In A Saint on Death Row: The Story of Dominique Green, *Cahill is taking the measure of civilization not as a pageant of events and personalities but through the story of one man's life and death in a society riven by conflicted notions of justice.*

Dominique Green was eighteen years old in 1992 when he was convicted of a fatal shooting during a Houston convenience store robbery. He admitted taking part but insisted that he did not pull the trigger. The victim's own wife believed Green did not deserve to die. "All of us have forgiven Dominique for what happened and want to give him another chance," she wrote to Governor Mark Perry and the Board of Pardons and Paroles. They turned a deaf ear, hardly surprising in Texas. That state leads the way in executions, with four times more than any other state in America.

While he was on death row, Green learned of Italy's strong opposition to the death penalty (the Roman Colosseum lights up whenever a death sentence is commuted anywhere in the world). He wrote to an Italian newspaper asking for help, and his petition came to the attention of Sant'Egidio, a Catholic lay organization, whose members work globally against capital punishment. Their headquarters are in the same neighborhood along the Tiber River as the home where Thomas Cahill lives when he's in Rome. Soon they joined forces on Green's behalf, and Cahill arranged for his friend Archbishop Desmond Tutu of South Africa to visit the Texas prison where the condemned young man was waiting to die. Tutu emerged from their two-hour meeting to plead for Green's life, calling the death penalty "an absurdity that brutalizes society."

It was to no avail. Green, now thirty, was executed by lethal injection at 7:59 P.M. on October 26, 2004. Thomas Cahill was determined that the story would not end there.

—Bill Moyers

—◦◦◦—

Talk about where Dominique Green came from and where he wound up.

He came from an alcoholic, drug-using household. He was sexually abused several times. He was put in juvenile homes. Just about everything that could be done to him—that anyone could imagine being done to a child—was done to him. When it says in the Old Testament that the sins of the fathers will be visited on the children into the third and fourth generation, I think that's correct, that these terrible things that go on in families go from one generation to another to another. That's how Dominique wound up on death row.

What happened on the night of the killing that he was accused of committing?

He and some other kids were robbing people in a number of different situations.

And there are people who swear he pulled the trigger that killed the man whom he was then convicted of murdering.

Right. But what actually happened was—and this is an example of how badly they do it in Texas—there were four kids. One of them was white. He was not charged with anything. Ever. And you cannot interview him to this day.

Why?

You can't find him, but he exists. I know his name. And the other three were black. Dominique was the youngest. And it looks to me that two others turned against him to get lighter sentences. They decided that he would take the rap. He was certainly guilty of robbery. I don't think he was guilty of murder. But even if he was, that's not what I see in this. What I see in this is that we, as a country, are actually sacrificing children to an evil God, to the God of whatever this justice is that we trumpet. Instead of doing something for Dominique Green—a kid who grew up without the aid of civilization—we condemn him to death, and first to the torture of eleven years on death row.

There was a trial. Dominique had very bad representation. The judge he came before was the same judge who in a slightly earlier appeal had been asked to reverse a decision because the defendant's lawyer had slept throughout the trial. And the judge, in his decision, said, "The Constitution gives you the right to a lawyer. It doesn't say whether he has to be awake or not." Throughout the country, but especially in the state of Texas, there is a kind of collusion among lawyers—whether they're prosecutors or defenders—and judges, and an awful lot of horrible things happen in order to get as many people executed as possible.

Some people there see it as a matter of crime and punishment.

There are no millionaires on death row, nor will there ever be. Almost everyone on death row is poor. And do you really think that no millionaire ever committed a capital crime? I'm saying that there are certain people in our society who we are willing to offer up, and not others. The ones we offer up have no power. We're not killing Dominique Green because he committed murder. We're killing Dominique Green because we want to kill somebody.

People ask, "What would Tom Cahill write if someone in his family had been killed by a Dominique Green?"

I understand very much the feeling of somebody who has lost a person through murder. But however difficult it may be, the only way you are going to gain closure is to let go of your hatred. Holding on to it is never going to get you out of it. It's never going to get you out of the bind, the knot that you're in. The widow of Andrew Lastrapes, the man who was killed in the incident for which Dominique was executed, said to me, "Of course I forgive Dominique. And I forgive them all." And I said, "How do you do that?" And she said, "Isn't that what we're supposed to do?" She's an extremely bright but simple woman, and she had no doubts about where her values lay. That doesn't mean that I would be able to say that, if such a thing had just happened to me. I understand very much the rage. I'm full of rages myself.

Most democratic societies have given up capital punishment. There's a new movement internationally to ban it.

That's true. When someone is executed in this country, you rarely see the name in *The New York Times*—maybe on a back page. But our executions are front-page news throughout Italy.

Why is that?

Because they consider it to be a terrible injustice that people are still being executed. A country can't join the European Union if it executes people.

Have you seen those photographs of the Iranians hoisting prisoners up on a crane while thousands of men and women shout, "God is great—God is great"?

Yes, and it wasn't all that long ago that we did things like that. Now we execute in private, out of the public square. But, it wasn't all that long ago that we were executing publicly, and people would come. It was a big deal. They'd bring a picnic lunch and sit there with their children and watch some guy be strung up.

The Taliban does it. Al-Qaeda does it. The IRA in Ireland did it. Bin Laden says that chopping off heads is a justified form of punishment. What does it say that violent death becomes a policy option, that in the name of life, we take life?

I think that there are many things within the human soul or within the human character that we ignore. There's a tendency to violence in all of us. There's even, I believe, a prehistoric desire for human sacrifice. We see it in all ancient cultures. I refer to it in my book *How the Irish Saved Civilization*. Before Christianity, the Irish sacrificed children and prisoners of war. The Jews seemed to have been doing it in the time of Genesis. The near sacrifice of Isaac is an example of the Jews finally rejecting human sacrifice.

What does the death penalty tell you as you survey civilization over the ages?

Well, getting rid of it is a very new phenomenon. It wasn't very long ago that all societies had the death penalty. Of course, a historian really wants a few hundred years to elapse before he makes a statement about the importance of anything. But I think the death penalty is among the touchstones right now of where different societies are going. The crueler societies—China, Saudi Arabia, the United States—support the death penalty. The more generous societies in Western Europe do not.

And yet that's the continent that was ravaged by one war after another for so long.

They finally learned something—thanks especially to what happened in the World War I and World War II, in which Europeans behaved abominably. Maybe they learned that it was time not to do that sort of thing anymore. And that's basically what at the end of the seventeenth century the original Anabaptists were doing. The people who became the Quakers, the Mennonites—people like that—were the first against capital punishment. They were the very first people to try to reform prisons so that they would not simply be places where other people were punished. They were to be put in penitentiaries, where they could repent.

Penitentiaries—penitence.

Yes!

You say repentance happened in the story of Dominique Green.

Oh, yes, very much. And a man who goes up and down death row seeking to forgive and be forgiven is not somebody we have to be afraid of.

And you really believe, as you've been quoted as saying, that Dominique Green turned that prison cell on death row into a zone of peace?

Well, you see in somebody's body, in their face and their eyes, in the way they move—you see what they're about. This was a young man who was deeply at peace with himself, who embraced you with his language since he couldn't get through the glass partition when you visited him.

What struck you?

Instead of talking about himself—the poor conditions he had to live in, the other inmates, the past, the looming execution—he wanted desperately to talk about books and writing. He had become a great reader in the eleven years that he had been in prison. The book that he had read most recently and that he really cared deeply about was Desmond Tutu's *No Future Without Forgiveness*, which is Archbishop Tutu's book about the Truth and Reconciliation Commission in South Africa. But what also came out was that even though they're all in solitary confinement and you would think they can't communicate with one another, they manage. Human beings are incredibly resourceful in situations like this, and Dominique was able to send that book up and down that death row after he had read it.

Tutu's book—handed from cell to cell?

Yes, and most of the inmates on death row agreed that they had to ask forgiveness from the people they had hurt and to forgive those who had hurt them, insofar as they could. There was this tremendous—you'd have to call it a conversion. That's certainly what it sounds like to me, all these guys on death row that nobody cares about, asking forgiveness on the basis of a book.

Did Dominique Green ever get to communicate that to the family of the victim in that crime?

The victim, a man named Andrew Lastrapes, was still in his thirties when he was killed. He had two small children—two sons—who became friends of Dominique in his last days. You don't have an awful lot of things to give away on death row. Dominique gave Tutu's book to one of the sons of Andrew Lastrapes. And the other son received a rosary that Dominique kept around his neck. And each bead on that rosary was a reminder of one of the people on death row who had been executed before Dominique and who had helped Dominique to become the person he became.

And you truly believe he was a changed man after eleven years there? He had been nineteen years old when he was arrested for the killing.

That cell in that prison became the means of his transformation. Yes, I believe it. I saw it.

You heard about Dominique Green from the community of Sant'Egidio in the Trastevere district of Rome, where you and your wife, Susan, live when you're not in New York. That's the community dedicated to bringing an end to capital punishment around the world, right?

Yes.

As I understand it, you and they were able to honor Dominique Green's request that he be cremated and that the ashes be placed in that ancient church in Rome, Santa Maria in Trastevere, not far from your home there.

Yes. Well, he couldn't be buried within the Basilica of Santa Maria itself, because of secular laws affecting interment within those churches. But he has been interred in a beautiful anteroom within the Piazza of Santa Maria. That's where he is. He didn't want to be buried in Texas.

We were in Rome in the spring, and walked from that piazza to the Colosseum. That's when I learned that because of Italy's opposition to the death penalty, the Colosseum is lit up when a death sentence is commuted somewhere in the world or when a country abolishes the death penalty. That's quite something to think about, given that once upon a time the Colosseum was where the lions used to tear human beings to shreds. Now what used to be a cockpit of cruelty is also one of the world's great tourist attractions.

Yes, well, it says something that, again, we don't want to look at. The Colosseum is the single largest monument to human cruelty in the world, and now it's on the new list of the seven wonders of the world.

Help me understand that psychology.

Why have there been so many movies about Romans sitting in the Colosseum turning thumbs up, thumbs down? We get a kick out of it. The real evil in the world, it seems to me, is cruelty. To me the word *evil* equals *cruelty*. It's human cruelty that is evil. We all have to deal with that. We all have a tendency to cruelty that we're not willing to acknowledge inside of us. It's there.

You write in the beginning of your book on Christianity, Desire of the Everlasting Hills: *"The history of the world, like the history of its hills, is written in blood." Has there ever been any period when that wasn't so?*

It's hard to find in Greco-Roman civilization. But you find it, for instance, in the communities set up by Francis of Assisi. You find it among the Quakers. Now, none of those people have been able to transform whole societies. But they did create a moment—what I would think of as a Shangri-la moment.

What do they share in common?

They were people able to recognize what human cruelty is about and renounce it. It doesn't really matter whether they said explicitly, "I renounce human cruelty." What was important is that they began to treat one another more kindly. Francis of Assisi said that the best thing you can do to any other person is to say to him or her, "May the Lord give you peace." And that's how we should go about our business: "May the Lord give you peace." That already puts you in a completely different mind-set. And Francis said to do that with everybody. Leper, heretic, Muslim: "May the Lord give you peace."

You've studied history enough to know that what works for the individual in a small realm of relationships isn't a rule the nation-state can live by.

I don't think real civilization ever occurs because of anything that a nation-state does. It occurs because of movements within the nation-state that are led by one individual or a series of individuals. Desmond Tutu is an excellent example of that. And in fact, I'll tell you something that I've never told anybody before. In each of the books that I've written, when I come upon a great historical figure that I'm trying to understand and deal with, I try to think of someone I know now who is like that person. And my model for St. Patrick is Desmond Tutu. I think he would be surprised to hear that, but Tutu in South Africa, and his wife, Leah, and their four children—

they were all in danger of being assassinated for opposing apartheid. Those six people were constantly in danger of death by hatred. Nelson Mandela is always credited with so much, and I don't mean to take anything away from him. But during his twenty-seven years in prison he wasn't on the scene. It was Desmond Tutu who was on the scene. It was Tutu who would stand up to those horrible South African guards and say, "You don't know what you're talking about. Our God is a God of resurrection. You're not going to do us in." This little guy, five feet four, standing up to the forces of cruelty and evil. Amazing.

So it's the individual who acts?

And his wife and his children—and Stephen Biko and all the others. It wasn't just one man. But Tutu embodied their courage.

Taking on this book about Dominique Green seems way off your beaten path. For years you've been working on your series on the hinges of history.

What I'm really interested in is what makes for civilization and what does not. How did we become the people we are? And why do we think the way we do, and feel the way we do, and perceive the way we do? Underneath this curiosity, I am looking for what's good about us. What do we do that's good? I started with *How the Irish Saved Civilization*—which is not the beginning of Western history by any means—for a reason. It was the simplest story that I had to tell. And it was about this guy named Patrick who had been a Roman citizen on the island of Britain who was kidnapped at the age of sixteen and taken to Ireland and made into a slave for six years before he escaped. Then in middle age he returned to Ireland—a rough, rough place, not a place anybody would willingly return to—and brought the gospels with him. He became the evangelist to the Irish. It was an act of great generosity to spend the last thirty years of his life there, among these very crazy people who practiced human sacrifice, who had no problem with slavery in its most awful form, who believed in really dark gods. In that great act of generosity he also realized that though he was never going to make them Romans or Athenians, he had to teach them to read and write. So he taught them to read and write from these simple lives of the saints who were the early Roman martyrs.

And it was all the terrible things that the Romans had done to the early Christians—they were eaten by lions, they had their eyes plucked out, they were slowly eviscerated; remember, St. Lawrence was burned on a griddle first on one side and then on the other side. The Irish loved this kind of stuff, thought it was just dandy. Loved these stories. And the only thing that made them sad was that Christianity came into Ireland without any martyrs. The Irish just kind of rolled over and accepted the new faith because they said it made more sense than what they had been doing. It was so much more. It was so superior to the old ways. But because Patrick taught them to read and write, they ended up setting themselves the task in the sixth, seventh, and eighth centuries of saving Western literature. The whole of the Western library was in danger of extinction at that time because the Germanic barbarians had invaded the Roman Empire, and within a century almost no one could read or write. Literacy itself was gone.

Civilization can be swept away.

If there are no books, there's no Western civilization, that's for sure. The Germanic barbarians thought that the only thing books were good for was kindling. They had no other use for it. So you have these very simple Irish people who had been great warriors and crazy kidnappers and all that sort of stuff, now sitting down and copying out Plato, which they couldn't understand but thought was important. They had learned the alphabet, and dammit, they were going to do this difficult thing. And that's one thing the Irish did like; they liked things that were difficult. So they copied out all of Latin and Greek literature. And they added to it in the margins. Now, they couldn't understand Plato very well, and it was kind of hard for the scribe to copy page after page of Plato without understanding it very well. He started doodling in the margins. And that's the beginning of the great decorated books like the Book of Kells. You have all these funny little medieval people peeping through in the margins. The copier would sometimes put in little comments or jokes or a little poem that had been part of the repertoire of the wandering bards, so that Irish becomes the first vernacular literature to be copied out and written down.

You start that book on the Irish with a chapter on the fall of Rome. What do you think about analogies between the fall of the Roman Empire and the fall of America?

I would say in some ways yes and in some ways no. History never repeats itself. That's one thing you can say about it. It never happens again exactly the same way. There are tremendous differences. But we can look into the past and learn things. For instance, why did Rome fall? Because of things interior and exterior. The interior reasons included less and less just taxation; more and more it was the poor and the middle class that bore the burden of taxation. The wealthy and very wealthy pretended to pay but actually didn't. We are in a very similar situation.

Then the big external thing was all of these Germanic barbarians who we think of as marauders, pillagers, and plunderers. But you know, they were on the wrong side of the river, and they knew it. They wanted farms and vineyards like the Romans had. They thought it looked great. They wanted to cross the river. What were they? They were immigrants—not at all unlike the situation today at the borders of our country and the borders of Europe. And the Romans couldn't make that border guard strong enough and those walls high enough to keep out the barbarians. If people really want to get in, they're going to find a way in.

I'm intrigued by your thoughts on the evolution of tolerance, especially among Christians, who so often seem to have so little of it for their own factions.

Well, as you know, in the sixteenth and seventeenth centuries both Protestants and Catholics eliminated one another to their heart's content. They liked nothing better than a bonfire and putting somebody in the middle of it. And that was happening on both sides. Somebody has said that at one point in papal Rome, there were more heads on the bridge that led out of the Vatican than there were melons in the market. But you could have said that about Geneva. You could have said that about London. Other places. Finally people began to ask, "Is this the only way? Does the religion of the monarch have to be the religion of all his subjects? Is that really necessary?"

And the answer was no. You begin to have enlightened monarchs who say no. There were setbacks, but finally you get the United States of America, the first country on earth to build tolerance into the very framework of government.

Well, unless you were an indigenous American, or a slave, an African brought over in the hold of a slave ship.

Or unless you were an Irish immigrant in the late nineteenth century. Yes, there are plenty of exceptions, plenty of times where it doesn't work. And yet it's a new idea that the government would refuse to play the old game of "whose religion was true." America fostered a generously agnostic view of religious truth.

Yes, you may believe as you like, and I may believe as I like, and we don't impose our beliefs on each other. Could that change? Could we go backwards?

It may be changing somewhat in the face of militant Islam. I think we are going to have to find a way of dealing with Islam that is better than the way that we have constructed so far.

And they with us.

Absolutely, absolutely, but we already have gone through that process. It was called the Enlightenment. And the result of the Enlightenment was the American Constitution. That was the process by which we said, "Do we really have to keep killing one another?" Now, the Muslims have not gone through that, and the Sunnis and the Shiites still think that they have to keep killing one another. And God knows that the Wahhabis and any number of other sects hate one another with far greater ferocity than they hate us. Religious history shows you over and over again that you hate most of all the people that are closest to you but just a little bit different. Protestants and Catholics throughout the sixteenth and seventeenth centuries, for example. If you were a Martian coming to earth, you would have said, "What are they arguing about? They seem to believe the same things, more or less. What's the problem here? Why do millions of people have to die?" Jonathan Swift said it was really about how you set an egg on the table. Some people did it one way and some people did it another. And that was enough reason to kill. It more or less does come down to that. There are still plenty of people who feel that way. But we have essentially gotten beyond that. It would be a dreadful tragedy if we fell back into it.

Do you think that what's going on now between the Shiites and the Sunnis in Iraq is comparable to what went on between the Catholics and the Protestants in the sixteenth century?

It's so much a parallel, it's amazing. If you're not Muslim, you look at them and say: "What are they arguing about? What's the big difference between them?" Well, I can tell you what some of the differences are. And you would begin to lose interest. Anyone would if they weren't Muslim. And the same thing about the differences between Catholics and Protestants. I remember once giving a talk in a church. A guy stood up and said, "Do you believe we are saved by faith alone?" And I said, "Well, I believe we're saved by faith. But I believe with Paul the Apostle that we're saved by faith, hope, and charity, and the greatest of these is love or charity." He walked out. From his standpoint I had given the wrong answer, and he wanted me to know that I had nothing to say that he wanted to hear.

Suppose Thomas Cahill is reincarnated a thousand years from now and decides to resume writing the Hinges of History *series. What would be, as of now, the defining characteristic of the American society you would write about in the twentieth and twenty-first century?*

That all societies have a dream and a nightmare. And our nightmare has been our racism. We practically committed genocide on the people who already were here, the Native Americans. We enslaved another race of people, the Africans. And then we dropped the atom bomb on Asians. We would have never dropped that bomb in Europe, in my view. That's the nightmare of America.

The dream of America is enunciated by the great speech by Martin Luther King. The dream is that there is no country on earth that has tried to embrace all the people that we have tried to embrace. All you have to do is walk through New York City to see that, or any of our cities and not a few of our countrysides. We could be called the most racist. Or we could be called the least. We are both. And it always remains a tension and a question as to which side of us, the good side or the bad side, will win out in the end. ∽

SHELBY STEELE

No one saw Barack Obama's quandary more clearly than Shelby Steele. Like Obama, he was born to a black father and a white mother, and early on faced the challenge—and sometime ordeal—of living with a complex identity. Unlike Obama, Steele moved to the right, a self-described black conservative who opposed affirmative action and called on African Americans to renounce using victimization as a means toward advancement by stoking white guilt; better, wrote Steele, that blacks replace "set-asides and entitlements" with "a culture of excellence and achievement."

Now a black politician had emerged who seemed tailored to Steele's dream, a candidate who "is interesting for not fitting into old racial conventions. Not only does [Obama] stand in stark contrast to a black leadership with which Americans of all races have grown exhausted—the likes of Al Sharpton, Jesse Jackson, and Julian Bond—he embodies something that no other presidential candidate can: the idealism that race is but a negligible human difference."

Nonetheless, Steele titled his book about the candidate A Bound Man, and subtitled it Why We Are Excited About Obama and Why He Can't Win. It appeared late in 2007, months before Obama clinched his party's nomination. Steele described the Democrat as "caught between two classic postures that blacks have always used to make their way in the white American mainstream: bargaining and challenging."

But even before the endgame, and the misread tea leaves of his book's subtitle notwithstanding, Steele thought Obama might negotiate a third way, break the old molds, and cast himself "as the perfect antidote to America's corrosive racial politics." It was an intriguing analysis from a notable conservative, a senior fellow at Stanford University's Hoover Institution who was presented the National Humanities Award by President George W. Bush in 2004 and who won the National Book Critics Circle Award with his bestseller The Content of Our Character: A New Vision of Race in America.

—*Bill Moyers*

———

The subtitle of your book is Why We Are Excited About Obama. *Are you rooting for him?*

I can't say that. You know, our politics are probably different. But I'm proud of him. And I'm happy to see him out there. He's already made an important contribution to American politics.

But you go on to say why he can't win. That would seem to suggest you don't think he can become president.

Part of the infatuation with Obama is because he's something of an invisible man. He's kind of a projection screen. And you sort of see the better side of yourself when you look at Obama, more than you actually see Barack Obama.

You say that his supporters want him not to do something but to be something. What do you think they want him to be?

I think, to be very blunt about it, in a lot of that support is a desire for convergence of a black skin with the United States presidency, with power on that level. The idea is that to have a black in that office leading a largely white country would be redemptive for America, would indicate that we truly have moved away from that shameful racist past that we had.

That's perfectly logical, isn't it? And desirable?

Yes, it is. I want it.

You say in this book that white people like Barack Obama a little too much for the comfort of many blacks. Why?

Well, the black American identity, certainly black American politics, is grounded in what I call "challenging." They look at white America and say, "We're going to presume that you're a racist until you prove otherwise." You keep whites on the hook, you keep the leverage, you keep the pressure. Here's a guy who's what I call a "bargainer," who's giving whites the benefit of the doubt.

Give me a simple definition of what you call a "bargainer." And a simple definition of what you call a "challenger."

A bargainer is a black who enters the white American mainstream by saying to whites, in effect, in some code form, "I'm going to give you the benefit of the doubt. I'm not going to rub the shame of American history in your face if you will not hold my race against me." Whites then respond with enormous gratitude, and bargainers are usually extremely popular people. Oprah Winfrey, Bill Cosby, Sidney Poitier back in the '60s and so forth. They give whites this benefit of the doubt. You can be with these people and not feel that you're going to be charged with racism at any instant, so they tend to be very successful, very popular. On the other hand, say challengers, "I presume that this institution, this society is racist until it proves otherwise by giving me some concrete form of racial preference"—affirmative action, diversity programs, opportunities of one kind or another. And so there is a much more concrete bargaining with the challengers. Go into any American institution today and they're all used to dealing with challengers. They all have a whole system of things that they can give to challengers, who then will offer absolution. We'll say, "This institution is vetted now. It's not racist anymore."

One of the worst things that can happen to you in this country is to be charged with being racially biased.

You never get over it. In your obituary, it'll be the first line. And there's almost no redemption. The good side of that is that it makes the point of how intense this society is in its desire to overcome racism and its past.

On the other hand, the bad side of it is that it has become a form of cruelty. All you're doing is terrifying whites. We've underestimated the power of this. Our institutions live under this threat of being stigmatized as racist, and they're almost panicked over it. Whites know to never tell blacks what you really think and what you really feel because you risk being seen as a racist. And the result is that, to a degree, we as blacks live in a bubble. Nobody tells us the truth. Nobody tells us what they would do if they were in our situation. Nobody really helps us. They use us, they buy their own innocence with us, but they never tell us the truth. And we need to be told the truth very often. America is a great society, a great country, the world's greatest society in many ways. Those same values will work for blacks. They will help us join the mainstream, become a part of it. But whites can't say that because then they seem to be judgmental. They're seen as racist. And so no one says it to us.

Some whites think that Obama is a way out of all of that, that he will bring an American redemption. And whites are very happy for that bargain and show gratitude and even affection for bargainers. Oprah Winfrey is the classic bargainer who also has a kind of magic about her. That I think again reflects the aspirations of white America.

But she never challenges white America.

No. She makes you feel that this aspiration is possible, that it's real. White American women love Oprah. She makes them feel that way.

Bill Cosby did that.

But he made a big mistake, Bill Cosby. The last few years he has been saying what he thinks. One of the ironclad rules for bargainers is they can never tell you what they actually think and feel. They can never reveal their deep abiding convictions, because the minute they do that, they're no longer an empty projection screen. They become an individual, and whites begin to say, "Well, I didn't know you felt that way. I didn't know you believed that." And the aura dissipates. If Barack Obama starts to say, "I really think there's a value to racial preferences even though it conflicts with equality under the law," that's a little too revealing of who he might really be.

So you're saying he cannot serve the aspirations of one race without antagonizing the other?

That's right. They're two different agendas. And so his answer is to remain invisible as much as possible.

What do you mean invisible? Because he's all over television.

But if you listen to his speeches—change, hope—it's kind of an empty mantra. What change? Change from what to what? What direction do you want to take the country? What do you mean by hope? There's never any specificity because specificity is dangerous to a bargainer.

You also say he has a nuanced view of whites, and that that's a problem for some blacks. Why is it a problem to have a nuanced view of other people? I think that's what we all should have.

Well, then we've let whites off the hook. If you want to make blacks angry, start letting whites off the hook. Start saying that they're not all inherently racist. The fact that we can charge them with racism and have some degree of credibility is black power. So when somebody like Obama comes along, in their eyes he is undermining the power of his own people by having an open mind toward whites, saying, "I'm going to presume you're not racist. I'm going to believe in the better part of you." And so he flatters whites in that sense. Boy, you know, Al Sharpton doesn't do that.

You point out that the first thing that Barack Obama usually tells you about himself is that he was born to a white mother and a black father. Isn't that part of his political appeal, that he transcends both black and white?

The fact that he has a white mother signals to white Americans that he has to give them the benefit of the doubt. He knows in the most intimate way that not all whites are racist, that you have to go individual by individual. Instinctively, white Americans perceive that in him and feel comfortable.

You had a white mother.

I had a white mother and a black father as well. I'm older than Obama, grew up in segregation, and certainly had a different experience than he did. Here's a kid being raised in an apartment in Hawaii by a white mother and two white grandparents, with no connection either to his father as a father or to a racial identity. One of the themes, I think, that comes out of his first book, *Dreams from My Father*, is almost an obsession with establishing himself as an authentic black, of achieving a sense of belonging. I empathize with that. I went through a bit of that myself.

You say that children of interracial unions often live under a degree of suspicion. Why?

I can remember in the '60s, if your mother was white, your mother was the enemy.

And you were collaborating with the enemy.

By birth, you were collaborating. At the very least, there was a sense that you're going to have to prove yourself a little more than the rest of us.

Was there a moment you claimed blackness as your identity, that you definitively made that choice?

This is, I think, a difference in my case than Obama's. Growing up in segregation, you didn't get the choice. The "one drop" rule applied: one drop of black blood and you're black. That's what kept the wall between whites and blacks. So I was raised with absolutely no ambiguity about that.

Where?

On the South Side of Chicago.

Where Obama eventually became an organizer. But he was raised in Hawaii and Indonesia, because his mother moved there. You think that environment made a different choice for him.

It probably gave him a much more intense need to belong than I had. On the other hand, that background accounts for this fine, successful, highly educated, polished young man that we see running for president today.

I've read Dreams from My Father, *and it was very powerful. He's just a child, four-thirty in the morning, his mother gets him out of bed out there in Hawaii or in Indonesia, and she makes him study, she makes him read.*

She made him who he was. That's right.

His biography seems to be his platform.

But then he turns around and says that maybe things are so desperate for blacks that they don't need this model, that they can rely on black nationalism and blackness. Maybe it will give them—he uses the word—an "insularity" out of which they can feel proud. Well, which is it? Is it your mama or is it black nationalism who's responsible for you being here? I want to know. What evidence do you have that black nationalism works? You know that what your mother did works. Why don't you give her credit? Why don't you build a politics out of that?

Who did it for you?

My mother and my father. Period. I went to wretched segregated schools that were abusive. And then I saw something else. I saw my mother organize that little community and shut that school down and boycott that school. So I saw that there's a place for collective action. It can work. They made it a better school. I'm here solely because of my mother and my father.

Describe what whites see in Obama.

Barack Obama is the first black American to bring bargaining into the political arena. Barack Obama is saying, I'm going to treat you as though you're not a racist. And I'm going to simply ask you to treat me as though I'm not black. Treat me just as an individual. Well, it's a nice bargain. But boy, does it make blacks nervous. Our blackness is our power—we think. I don't think it is. But that's the delusion, I think.

What is your power?

I think our power is the same as it is for anybody, any other group—the collective energies, the imagination of the individuals within the group. We're no better than what our individuals achieve. Identity should be the result of effort and achievement. It's not an agent. It's not going to bring you there.

But you can't escape a part of your identity, because it is about, as you say, blood and color.

You can't escape it. And I certainly don't want to escape it. I am black and happy to be so. But my identity is not my master. I'm my master. And I resent this, you know, civil rights leadership telling me what I should think and what issues I should support this way or that way. In black America, identity has become almost totalitarian.

That's a very strong word. What do you mean?

That you subscribe to the idea that the essence of blackness is grounded in grievance. And if you vary from that, you are letting whites off the hook.

And we're going to call you a sellout. We're going to call you an Uncle Tom.

At the same time you write, "When someone tells me that I am not really black, I hear their words as . . . a little attempted murder." What are they killing in you?

They're taking away something that is sacred to me—I look at the history of my people, and coming from that kind of oppression, it's glorious. In just the last century, we've created a literature that is on a par with the literature of many nations. We transformed music all over the world. This, from this relatively small group of truly oppressed people. So I'm proud of that. And you get a little sense of superiority.

Well deserved, I think.

Yes.

So how is it that to be, as you say, a "true" black involves, and I'm quoting you, "a slight corruption . . . a little habit of self-betrayal"? Explain that to me so that I can understand how you feel about it.

In order to be black, if I'm going to fit myself into the current identity, I'm going to have to betray impulses, desires, certain aspirations in myself as an individual in order to squeeze myself into this identity, which is, again, grounded in grievance. Maybe I, as an individual, don't believe that's the biggest problem that I face. But I've got to pretend that it's the biggest problem that I face in order to stay inside the group. Stay inside the church, as we say. And I'm going to be a backslider if I start to say grievance is really not the central thing.

You say in your book that to be black means you have to wear a mask. Do you wear a mask?

All of this work that you see here came about because I got exhausted with the pressure from whites and blacks to wear a mask.

What kind of mask were you expected to wear?

I was in academia, I was expected to be a challenger: "You should have a chip on your shoulder. You should be angry. If you're not, you're going to take the pressure off this institution and we'll lose. That chip on your shoulder is our power as a minority group." Well, I just got completely fed up with that, and again, the self-betrayal that it continued to force me into. I began to understand, it was going to be me or the group. And I was going to have a life or I was just going to be a kind of surrogate for blackness. And it was very difficult—I was scared to death, because I knew the price that that one would pay for that.

And that price is?

I don't want to overdramatize this or seem to be playing the violin. But you enter a kind of exile where the group identifies you as someone who is a threat. And part of being black is despising or having contempt for people like me, for people who refuse to wear the mask.

I can understand that in the context of the '60s, black power, the '70s, and in the '80s with the Reagan revolution—anyone like you who supported the Reagans, the conservative movement in this country, was called an Uncle Tom. But today, it seems to me—and I may be naive about this—that Obama is the result of a transformation of race in this country, so that you're no longer penalized for being a black conservative.

Oh, boy.

Am I wrong?

I think so. It's no accident that 92 percent of blacks vote Democratic in every presidential election no matter what. The black identity is with liberal politics and the Democratic Party. If you're not a Democrat, you're not altogether black.

That's why you say that for Obama, liberalism is blackness?

Yes.

I don't get that.

Because liberalism is what he has to offer blacks, saying, "See, I still believe in challenging." He talks in the rhetoric of the civil rights movement and protests, and often does a pretty good imitation of Dr. King. He's putting on his challenging mask in order to capture the affection of black America, but he has to touch that very lightly or white America will say, "We like you precisely because you don't do that. You don't challenge." And so he has to touch it very lightly. I've had whites come up to me and say, "I don't know if you ever have any contact with Obama, but I saw him in the paper the other day with Al Sharpton. He shouldn't do that." They didn't consciously know why they were saying that.

Sharpton is a challenger.

Barack Obama is the anti–Al Sharpton. Al Sharpton is probably his best ally among whites.

Because when they see Sharpton, they think Obama is a great relief.

He relieves the anxiety of being white. That's what Obama does, and that's why he gets so much affection.

I know so many white politicians who have made their way by accommodation—to corporate contributions, to wealth, to the constituency.

It's the very nature of politics, which may be why Obama is such a good politician.

And you say he's not a revolutionary. He's not a reformer.

Well, look at his background. He felt he didn't belong. He had to accommodate on the black side, yet he knew very well how to, in a sense, manipulate whites. He knew them better than he knew blacks in many ways. That became a kind of talent, this bargaining became a talent.

He does have a talent for politics.

And he understands white people. When he was a teenager, he realized that one thing whites love is a black who's not angry. So he knew that when he was a kid.

You write that the black identity Obama longs for means that "you must join a politics that keeps alive the idea of white obligation to blacks." You think that's Obama's mission, to keep alive the white obligation to blacks?

I think that that's what he tells blacks. I think that when he speaks as he did in Selma, as he did in Harlem not too long ago, he puts on the challenger's mask.

When he spoke at Selma, he used that inflection of the southern dialect that you don't hear in the rest of his speeches.

Barack Obama is John F. Kennedy. Sometimes he's Martin Luther King. Sometimes he's Stokely Carmichael in 1968. He has these different masks that are tailored to the audience that he's in front of. And he does it with such facility that you cannot help but wonder, who's the real voice?

Ten years from now, how do you see race relations in this country? Are we going to deepen the American dream?

I think so. I think that these paradigms I'm talking about exhaust themselves. We just get tired of them. Masking is something that comes inevitably to minority groups, who use it to survive. It was a survival mechanism in slavery and segregation, and we're still using it. We're still entering the mainstream using it. We will get tired of that. Our children will and their children will be even more tired of it, will understand, I think, that the challenge of the collective is to produce individuals.

I understand that. I'm tired of asking black people questions about race. I'd like to know what you think about Schwarzenegger. I'd like to know what you think about economics. I'd like to know what you think about money and politics.

And I want to talk about those things, too.

But aren't we being naive in a culture that is still racially divided—that race is always on the table, but it's also under the table?

Yes. It still plagues us. I don't care what Obama's politics end up being, liberal or conservative. I would love nothing more than to see him break through and into "This is my experience. These are my values. I know these work because they worked in my life. They are responsible for me being here where I am today." ∼

ROBERT KAISER

Within hours of his arrest, charged with fraudulently separating investors from billions of their dollars, the grandiose Texas banker Robert Allen Stanford received an electronic valentine that read, "I love you and believe in you," and urged Stanford to be in touch "if you want my ear/voice." It was signed "Pete"—as in Representative Pete Sessions, a fellow Texan who is also chairman of the National Republican Congressional Committee. Never intended for public consumption, the email, like the proverbial grain of sand, reveals a universe—in this case, the cosmos of corruption that has replaced representative democracy.

Sessions was one of dozens of politicians onto whose outstretched palms Stanford slathered his largesse. "Sir Allen"—he was knighted by the governor-general of Antigua, the center of his offshore banking enterprise—bankrolled junkets for them to his private fiefdom on the Caribbean island, where his personal chef served up lobster and caviar while they enjoyed the bonhomie of faithful retainers in the presence of financial royalty.

Never mind that as early as 1999 the State Department reported that Stanford had created "one of the most attractive financial centers in the Caribbean for money launderers." Here was an equal-opportunity inducer whose generosity made sure politicians didn't ask embarrassing questions. His money flowed to George W. Bush's inaugural committee, the Democratic

Senatorial Campaign Committee, key members of the Senate Banking Committee, and to the Republican leader in the House of Representatives, Tom DeLay, who flew the friendly skies sixteen times in a Stanford jet, including—I am not making this up—a trip to Houston for DeLay's arraignment on his own money-laundering charges. In addition to campaign contributions, Stanford also spent at least $5 million on a small army of lobbyists in Washington whose mission was to ensure that no legislative and regulatory measures would expose his offshore hijinks. (As I write this, Stanford has been judged mentally incompetent to stand trial in federal court.)

Coincidentally, the Stanford story broke as I was reading Robert G. Kaiser's book So Damn Much Money *for a second time. A native Washingtonian, no one understands better how money works its will in the labyrinth of government and politics than Kaiser. Over the past forty-five years he has held just about every position on* The Washington Post's *masthead, from foreign correspondent in Saigon and Moscow to national editor and managing editor. This, his seventh book, documents how the lobby industry "has helped moneyed interests protect their status and privileges, undermined government regulation . . . and turned our elected officials into chronic money-chasers."*

All, as Representative Pete Sessions might put it, for love.

—*Bill Moyers*

———— ❧ ————

*Where did you get the title—*So Damn Much Money*?*

From Bob Strauss—Robert Strauss, former chairman of the Democratic National Committee, who started out as a fixer in Dallas, Texas, and ended up as a fixer in Washington. A remarkable character. I went to Strauss, and said, "Explain to me why the lobbying business has boomed so, in the thirty-five years that you've been in it." He thought about it for a minute, and he said, "You know, there's just so damn much money in it."

He got his share of it, didn't he?

Sure. You know from your own reporting over the years that money has become so important in politics now. The cost of a campaign has gotten so high, and the compulsion on the part of incumbents to get reelected, to raise that money, is the single biggest gift the lobbyists get. The lobbyists see that the politicians need that money. They know how to help them raise it. And they know how to exploit the gratitude that comes after they've raised it.

Let's take one of the subjects you write about—"sweeteners." You say that after the House defeated the huge bailout bill for banks in the fall of 2008 it was saved by "sweeteners."

"Sweeteners" is a wonderful Washington term. It means a provision that helps somebody in a congressman's or a senator's constituency. In this case, as you remember, the House voted down the bailout bill the first time. The stock market plummeted as it was happening. They had to go back to the drawing board, and with sweeteners, they got the break they needed. They came back and passed the bailout, Bill, thanks to those sweeteners.

And when you say a break, you're talking about $100 million to stock car race-tracks, $192 million to the Puerto Rican rum industry, $478 million for moviemakers who shoot their films in the USA. And you say that did the trick?

Yes. You have referred to the bailout as the lobbyist enrichment act, and it is that, in a way. When the government spends so much money, we have to be ready to see the potential recipients of that money troop to town and look for their share.

Your book throws a lot of light on how and why, over the last thirty, forty years, policies in Washington have favored the rich over the poor.

Yes. One of my favorite statistics is that since the 1970s, working-class incomes in this country have been stagnant. In that same period we've seen skyrocketing incomes at the top. And this is part of the story. It's not a secret. There's a terrific quote about it from Bob Dole, former U.S. senator and Republican candidate for president, where he reminds everyone that poor people don't contribute to campaigns. So much of the story of the last thirty years is right in that phrase. We've watched the cost of these elections climb every two years, like clockwork. In 2008 it cost $25 million to run for the Senate in North Carolina.

They have to get that money somewhere, and it comes from corporations, lobbies, wealthy individuals, as we see with Sir Allen Stanford.

Exactly.

You build your book around a fellow named Gerald Cassidy, once a liberal Democrat, who back in 1972 worked for Senator George McGovern, the Democratic candidate for president. For a spell, Cassidy was the single biggest lobbyist in Washington. At one time he even hired the notorious Jack Abramoff. Cassidy once did legal aid work for poor people. How did he grow up to become this lobbying superstar?

He's a classic American type to me. I call him the Jay Gatsby of modern Washington. He's a self-invented man. And just as you say, he went to work for migrant workers in Florida as a young lawyer. He still today would call himself a liberal Democrat. He gives more money to Democrats, by far, than Republicans. And he thinks of himself as doing good work when he can. But more important to him was to get rich. And, boy, he's gotten really rich. He's worth more than $100 million, partly because he's a good investor, but mostly because he's a great lobbyist and a very shrewd businessman. The Cassidy story is wonderfully illustrative of how Washington became a venue, in my time and your time, for the great American pastime, which is not baseball, but making money.

And his first clients were not "greedy" but—

Colleges and universities. Another wonderful story, really. Cassidy and his original partner invented the modern earmark. One of their first clients was Jean Mayer, the president of Tufts University and a famous nutritionist. These two guys in the lobbying firm had worked with Mayer on nutrition issues when McGovern chaired a hunger committee in the Senate. They were friends. Mayer says, "I got an idea, come and talk to me. My congressman here wants to help Tufts University." Well, his congressman was Tip O'Neill, then the majority leader.

Who in time became Speaker of the House.

With O'Neill's help, they figured out how to get $26 million for Tufts to build a center on human nutrition research.

Not a bad thing.

Not a bad thing in and of itself. I argue that this was the first modern earmark. Then they got a veterinary school for Tufts. Then a medical library for Tufts. Boston College, across town, heard about this and hired Cassidy. Then Boston University wanted to get on board. John Silber, the new president of BU, hired Cassidy. And suddenly this little lobbying firm had a big new business—academic earmarks.

Getting money designated for specific university projects?

Exactly. And as you say, what's wrong with that? Well, what's wrong is that, yes, Tufts wanted to build a nutrition research center. But nobody asked if Princeton had a better idea, or if the University of Texas had a better idea. The fix was in for Tufts. That's the essence of the earmark system. The congressman gets the credit, because the fix is in. The lobbyist gets the money, because he got the fix in. It's a wonderful circle, but it doesn't create a fair, competitive, open system.

And Cassidy became so successful doing this for universities that corporations begin to say, "Hey, look what that guy is doing. He could do that for us."

Yes.

What was his expertise?

The system. How it worked. How the appropriations system works. It's a very technical system. You have to pass two bills, traditionally. You have to pass an authorization bill, to authorize spending on such and such. And then you have to pass the appropriation to pay for such-and-such. It's a tricky, complex system. It takes a couple years, often, to get one of these earmarks through. Cassidy's method was to master the technicalities, literally to teach members of Congress how to do it.

So many congressional staff graduate from working for members of Congress to working for the lobbyists downtown.

That's one of the biggest changes in Washington in my time. There was a famous case in the late '70s. You may remember Jim O'Hara. Good congressman from Michigan, liberal Democrat. Ran for the Senate and lost. Came back to town. He had five or six children and no job. So he went to work for one of the biggest lobbying firms in town. And I remember this vividly; it was said to be a scandal—"Jim O'Hara's become a lobbyist! Gee, that doesn't look very good."

Well, that was then. Today we've got 185 or more former members of the

House and Senate registered as lobbyists. It's absolutely routine, happens all the time. And nobody's eyebrows go up the way yours just did. It's all legal.

And the results?

It creates a system of self-dealing, cashing in your experience and your contacts from public service for your and your client's private gains, which bothers me as a citizen. It wasn't meant to be that way.

I was amazed by the extent to which Cassidy talked to you for your book and told you so many secrets.

I think he was encouraged by his associate Jody Powell. Powell was Jimmy Carter's White House press secretary, whom Cassidy hired years ago to set up a public relations firm within his lobbying operation. Jody advised Cassidy, "This Kaiser guy is so determined to do this, he's going to do it whether we cooperate with him or not. I can't promise how good it'll be. But I know one thing, it'll be worse if we don't cooperate than if we do." Jody's told me that's what he told Cassidy, and I'm sure that was the key thing.

So Cassidy decided to talk. Once he decided to talk, he got into it. And you've seen this over the years. People in Washington who think that they're big players, important people, but have never had much attention—I'm sure most of your viewers have never heard of Gerald Cassidy—well, Cassidy liked the idea, clearly, of getting this attention from a reporter from *The Washington Post*. He liked telling his story. He's very proud, understandably, of his accomplishments. He came from a really painful, booze-sodden Irish childhood in Brooklyn. He was the first member of his family to go to college, the first to go to law school. He's done extremely well, accumulated all this money. He didn't mind the world knowing how well he'd done. And talking to me was the way to make that known.

And how well he has done! You have some photographs in your book that are quite revealing. His home is 165 acres—

On the Eastern Shore of Maryland. It's quite remarkable.

An $8 million estate.

There's a photograph in there of him turkey hunting with his friend Jody Powell. He made Powell rich, too.

And there's the photograph of Jack Abramoff. There's a moment in your book when Cassidy goes to Abramoff and hires him.

Cassidy's firm, as I said, was number one on the lobbying revenue table, the macho way these guys have measured themselves for many years. And just at the moment that Abramoff was fired in 2003 by his previous Florida law firm, the new revenue table was published showing that Cassidy had fallen into second place. I'm sure that at that moment he thought, "I've got to do something to get back in first place. This guy Abramoff is obviously a hell of a rainmaker. He brings in a lot of money. I'm going to see if I can make contact with him." They were completely different. Abramoff is a right-wing Republican. Cassidy is a liberal Democrat. They had no acquaintances in common to speak of, no past in common to speak of.

What did they have in common?

The appetite for big bucks. It was a natural marriage. They made a deal quickly, and Cassidy drove right through flashing red lights. It was really a silly mistake he made. But he was called on it—it's a wonderful Washington story—by someone he called his old friend, Senator Dan Inouye of Hawaii, also a Democrat. In my reporting, I asked Inouye repeatedly, "Is Cassidy your friend?" He would never say the word *friend*. He'd say, "Well, I've known him for a long time. We've worked together on a lot of things." Bill, believe me, in the Washington context, they were friends. Cassidy had even hired Inouye's closest aide for many years—a guy called Henry Giugni—to be a vice president of Cassidy & Associates. This is another gimmick in town for getting the attention of members of Congress you want to influence: you hire their aides. Henry Giugni helped make Cassidy even richer by bringing in a lot of new clients. Inouye was a member of the Indian Affairs Committee, which was investigating Abramoff. When he realized what was coming down, Inouye called Cassidy to tell him how bad it was going to be, and he told Cassidy, "You got to get rid of this guy [Abramoff] right now." And Cassidy did.

Another example of Washington operators refusing to pass judgment on each other until one of them breaks the law. What accounts for it?

The falling away of taboos, the changing standards in Washington. The "everybody does it" syndrome. All this has made moral judgments really difficult in our nation's capital. People shy away from saying, "That's just wrong."

There's a revealing story involving Mississippi Senator John Stennis. It's a real signal of what was happening. In the early 1980s, John Stennis is running for his seventh term in the Senate. He's never spent more than $5,000 on a campaign before. You knew Stennis, although I imagine a lot of your viewers don't remember him. He was a vicious racist, a bad guy on the race issue, but on other things a very serious, very smart man. And interestingly, the first chairman of an Ethics Committee in the Senate. He actually believed in ethics.

He was in trouble in Mississippi because a young guy called Haley Barbour, then thirty-four years old [now governor of Mississippi after years of lucrative lobbying in Washington] was running against him. It was the first time Stennis had a serious opponent, and his friends in the Senate were scared, Russell Long of Louisiana and Lloyd Bentsen of Texas, particularly. They actually hired a political consultant for Stennis, something he would never have dreamed of, and they sent this guy down to Mississippi to check out the situation. He's a charming southerner named Ray Strother. And he comes back and explains to Stennis that it's going to be an ugly campaign; this Barbour is going to make a lot of TV commercials accusing Stennis of being too old and too feeble to run for another term. Strother says, "We're going to have to respond to him. We're going to have to make our own TV commercials. It's going to cost $2 or $3 million."

Stennis was shocked. He said, "How could I raise so much money?" And Ray started to explain, "You're going to go to the defense contractors, the companies you've helped as the chairman of the Armed Services Committee for so long, and you're going to ask them for contributions." And Stennis utters this memorable line, which I love. He looks at Strother and says, "Young man? Would that be proper?" And then he answers it himself: "No, it wouldn't be proper. I hold life-and-death power over those companies. I will not solicit their money." But he did. He did, and they got the money. The commercials were made, and Stennis won the election. I think that was 1982. And I think that's when we lost the war in

Washington. From then on, "Would that be proper?" became a question we don't hear very often.

What about the argument that with Roosevelt's New Deal, when Washington began throwing money at so many problems, it became a fact of life that there was money to be made by connecting people who wanted money to people who were spending it—giving lobbyists their opening?

There's no avoiding this. And it's also important for a couple of journalists like us to acknowledge that lobbying is protected in the same First Amendment to the Constitution that you and I like for its journalistic implications. The right to petition the government for the redress of grievances is right there in the First Amendment. And that's lobbying. And it's true that big government means big spending, means big opportunities, means business for lobbyists. It's inevitable. I see no way to stop it. But it can be much more transparent than it's been. We should be able to see what people are doing much more clearly than we've been able to do so far. There are reforms that are possible. But we're never going to make "pure Christian gentlemen" out of these people. It doesn't happen that way.

Can the process be tamed?

Obviously, public financing of elections would have the most dramatic impact. It's very hard to imagine how that would come to pass.

It has in some states. Maine and Arizona, for example.

Exactly. Our new secretary of homeland security, the former governor of Arizona, has talked very articulately about what a difference it made to her to be able to run for reelection using public funding. She didn't feel indebted to anybody, and that's a liberating thing.

I have an idea that would be fun, and I think could be very significant. If you required every official in the government to report, on the Internet, at the end of the business day, every day: "Here are the lobbyists I met with today. And here's what we talked about." Just a daily file of real transparency. That could have a huge impact.

Do you think Obama gets this—understands the game?

He does, remarkably well. In a recent piece for *The Washington Post* I credit him for being a good cultural anthropologist. He only spent two years in the Senate before he started to run for president. But he did figure it out. He's the one who said, "Politics has become a business, not a mission."

So there is hope for renewing democracy?

Well, I'm a believer. I'm an optimistic person. But boy, it won't be easy. ∽

BARBARA EHRENREICH

When the predators of high finance spot their prey, they can move with a terrible swiftness. In 2007, Wall Street Journal *reporter Ianthe Jeanne Dugan described how the private equity firm Blackstone Group swooped down on a travel reservation company in Colorado, bought it, laid off 841 employees, and recouped their entire investment in just seven months, one of the quickest returns on capital ever for such a deal.*

Blackstone made a killing while ordinary workers were left to sift through the debris of their devastated lives. They sold their homes to make ends meet, lost their health insurance, took part-time jobs making sandwiches and coffee. That fall, Blackstone's chief executive, Stephen Schwarzman, reportedly worth billions of dollars, rented a luxurious resort in Montego Bay, Jamaica, to celebrate the marriage of his son. The bill reportedly came to $50,000, plus thousands more to sleep 130 guests. Add to that drinks on the beach, dancers and a steel band, marshmallows around the fire, and the following day an opulent wedding banquet with champagne, jazz band, and a fireworks display that alone cost $12,500. Earlier in the year Schwarzman had rented out the Park Avenue Armory in New York (his thirty-five-room apartment couldn't hold the five hundred guests) to celebrate his sixtieth birthday. Cost: $3 million.

So? It's his money, isn't it? Yes, but consider this: the stratospheric income of private-equity partners is taxed at only 15 percent. That's less than the rate paid by the struggling middle class. When Congress considered raising the rate paid on their Midas-like compensation, these financial titans sent their lobbyist mercenaries swarming over Washington and brought the "debate" to an end in less time than it had taken Schwarzman to fire 841 workers.

Our ruling class had won another round in a fight that Barbara Ehrenreich has been documenting for years. After studying theoretical physics at Reed College and earning a doctorate from Rockefeller University, Ehrenreich joined a small nonprofit in the late 1960s, advocating for better health care for the poor. She began researching and writing investigative stories for the organization's monthly bulletin, and went on to journalistic prominence with articles and essays for Ms., Mother Jones, The Atlantic Monthly, *and* Harper's, *among others.*

Ehrenreich reports on inequality in America by stepping into the real-life shoes of the people who experience it. For her bestselling book Nickel and Dimed: On (Not) Getting By in America, *she worked as a waitress, cleaning woman, and a Walmart sales clerk, testing what it's like to live on $7 an hour. (Damned near impossible.) She went undercover again, looking for a white-collar job and writing about it in* Bait and Switch: The (Futile) Pursuit of the American Dream. *She saw so many professional people falling to the bottom rung of jobs that she launched an organization—unitedprofessionals.org—to fight back against the war on the middle class "that is undermining so many lives."*

—Bill Moyers

⚬⚬⚬

Now even The Economist *magazine agrees with you: "A growing body of evidence suggests that the meritocratic ideal is in trouble in America. Income inequality is going to levels not seen since the Gilded Age. . . . America is increasingly looking like Imperial Britain, with . . . a gap widening between the people who make the decisions and shape the culture and the vast majority of ordinary working stiffs." The Economist says we're becoming a European-style "class-based society."*

Well, I would say, not a European style, but a third world style. We are the most class-divided of the industrialized countries, the most polarized, in a different rank from France or Germany or Britain, where there's actually more social mobility. What we're coming to resemble is something more like Brazil, which has always had its wealthy, and then has extremely poor people.

The first book of yours I read was Fear of Falling: The Inner Life of the Middle Class. *And that was before the safety net was fraying. The loss of pensions, the loss of insurance, the loss of upward mobility—how do you measure the pain of the middle class in America today?*

Some of the things are hard to get an exact fix on. Take the woman working part-time making sandwiches—probably in the $7-to-$9-or-less-an-hour range of pay. Now, she's counted as employed, so her pain is not going to show up in the unemployment statistics. White-collar people are driven out of their jobs, churned out of their jobs by reorganizations, mergers, by buy-outs. After a few months, they'll take something, but it will usually be at a lot less pay than they got. The majority of people who get laid off come out at a lot lower pay. But if they get anything, they're counted as employed.

How do these women—the maids, the waitresses—how do they keep going, day in and day out? You met so many of them when you were gathering material for Nickel and Dimed.

You begin not to see a lot of alternatives when you are just faced with expenses, when you have to keep moving to keep a roof over your head or to feed your children. I would keep thinking, "Hmmm, I should look for another job." You know, the typical middle-class thing, like, "Well, I should look for something better." And then I began to figure out, if you're paid very little, it could be a disaster to change jobs, because you might have to go one, two, three weeks without any paycheck at all. And that's not doable.

There was one woman who said something to me that was so poignant, it's painful to repeat. Speaking of her hopes for the future, she said, "My big wish would be to have a job, where if I missed work one day, a child home sick or something, I would still be able to buy groceries for the next day." And I thought, yeah, that's quite a hope.

Don't people call you a Marxist for writing as you do? The Wall Street Journal *says you're trying to stoke a class war.*

Yeah, well, look, I didn't start the class war that's going on here. The class war that's been coming from the side of the extremely wealthy, it's been happening for a while. But it's a class war that has been very one-sided. Unions are weak in our country. They should be leading the charge against this. But the squeezing of people on wages and then on benefits—that's a big thing in the middle class, you know, that your health insurance package, your pension is gone. College tuitions are rising. Despite that kind of squeeze there has not been enough fightback.

You gave the commencement address at Haverford College. And your last line in that speech was, "Go out there and raise some hell." What, practically, can people do about this issue?

The first thing to remember is that there are ways of making change by working together. We sort of lose that idea, that this American culture has been full of wonderful examples of people working together—*collectively* is the old word—to make change. The civil rights movement, it wasn't just a couple of, you know, superstars like Martin Luther King. It was thousands and thousands, millions I should say, of people taking risks, becoming leaders in their communities. The women's movement wasn't only Gloria Steinem and Betty Friedan. It was, again, millions of women coming together and saying, "We're going to make change here. We're going to march. We're going to demand different legislation."

You have been not only a journalist but an activist. I've seen you marching with poor people in Michigan, handing out leaflets on the living wage, demonstrating with immigrants. Why did you decide to cross the line between explaining the world and trying to change the world?

I can't really distinguish these things. If I get incensed about some injustice, I will not just sit at my desk. I might want to march. I learn a lot in those situations. A year ago I was at the picket line of janitors at the University of Miami. These were janitors earning $6 and change, and now they were on a hunger strike. I listened to them, I took notes, and that's part of me as a journalist.

A janitor, I understand, is the fastest-growing job in America, right?

Yeah, it is. And that's something to think about when we're told, "Oh, don't worry about the class polarization in America and the shrinking middle class and things like that. You just have to get an education to get ahead." Get an education to get ahead when the fastest-growing jobs have been in things like janitorial services and food services and home health.

It's been said the mark of a truly educated person is to be deeply moved by statistics. You are very educated. Let me read you a statistic and you tell me if this moves you and why. Since 1979, the share of pretax income going to the top 1 percent of American households has risen by seven percentage points, to 16 percent. At the same time the share of income going to the bottom 80 percent has fallen by seven percentage points.

The polarization is accelerating. The people at the top are getting an ever-greater share of the wealth.

They drive everybody's prices.

Yeah, they're also in a better position to control the electoral process, the political process.

Contributions to candidates, right?

You are talking about families who can buy a congressman or households that can buy a congressman compared to households that can barely put dinner on the table. We don't have democracy anymore. What some of us have been saying, at least to the Democratic candidates, is, "Cut that bond. Cut that bond to the wealthy. Try being a populist. We don't have the money on our side. We have the numbers—people. That top 1 percent may have a huge disproportionate share of wealth but their numbers are small. We still count." Well, I was going to say we still count votes. I hope we still count votes here.

You majored in science. You went to Rockefeller University and were doing graduate work with cell biology as your focus. How did you start getting involved with poor people?

It partly has to do with my own personal family background. I came from a blue-collar family that was quite poor when I was born and remained so even as my father became upwardly mobile and made it possible for me to go to college.

What did you bring from science to journalism?

To me it was sort of a natural. Because science is about asking questions, getting to the bottom of things, investigating. And so I immediately took to investigative journalism, which was the first kind of journalism I did.

And your last book, Dancing in the Streets: A History of Collective Joy, *is fascinating. You did amazing research into festivals, celebrations, carnivals— all the ways human beings collaborate to have fun. What did you learn about collective joy?*

I'm interested in what bonds people together, what brings us together in good ways. And there's not a lot known about that. We spend a lot of time, scholarly time, thinking about love and sex, but very little about the kind of joy that can take over a crowd of people or a group of people, in festivity, in ecstatic ritual of some kind, in celebration. So that drove me into this book. Because I think we have to recapture that joy if we are going to make positive change together. ∾

MARTÍN ESPADA

Martín Espada grew up in the tough, racially mixed neighborhood of East New York in Brooklyn, where, as he recalls in one of his poems, "There were roaches between the bristles of my toothbrush."

Roaches were a mere nuisance compared to the racists he encountered when the family moved to a suburb on Long Island. The teenage son of the only Puerto Rican family in the community, "I caught absolute hell. It was much more traumatic than anything that ever happened to me on the so-called mean streets of East New York."

He began writing poetry at an early age and kept at it as he studied history as an undergraduate at the University of Wisconsin and earned a law degree from Northeastern University. Discovering poetry and politics to be "all in the same spectrum," Espada vowed to use both to speak "on behalf of those who don't have an opportunity to be heard." He worked in bilingual education law and became a legal advocate for tenants in Boston, explaining to an interviewer, "While waiting for my cases to be called, I would sit on a staircase in the courthouse, scratching poems on a yellow legal pad."

In 1982, Espada published his first collection, The Immigrant Iceboy's Bolero. Sixteen books of poems, essays, and translations would follow— including Imagine the Angels of Bread, A Mayan Astronomer, and The

Republic of Poetry—*winning for him honors and acclaim as "the Latino poet of his generation." His latest collection is called* The Trouble Ball.

　　Espada now teaches poetry and English at the University of Massachusetts Amherst, but because he has never forgotten what it means to love a country that isn't sure what it thinks about you, he can often be found helping the children of new immigrants find the poetry in their own experience. When I heard that he was coaxing poems from ninth graders at DreamYard Prep, a small public school in the South Bronx, we sent a crew to film the experience, and I asked Martín to join me for this conversation.

—Bill Moyers

How do you explain all that energy that feeds you and those kids?

Behind it, I think, is all the hope that most young people have regardless of circumstance; that if they make themselves heard somehow things will change, somehow they will be empowered by this experience. It seems to be an extraordinary statement, given the way poetry in this culture is so often mocked and marginalized, and designated as trivial or meaningless. But the fact is, I meet people all the time who tell me, "Poetry saved my life. Were it not for poetry, were it not for this poem, were it not for this poet, I would be somewhere else. I would have made other choices. I was in prison when I read your work. I was a dropout when I read your work. And I decided to become a poet myself. I decided to go back to school. I decided to get a job." There are very tangible outcomes as a result of feeling inspired. And we have no way of knowing this, as poets, when we put our words into the air. Paradoxically, even the most political poem is an act of faith, because you have no way of quantifying its impact on the world. The fact is, we write these poems and put them into the environment, into the atmosphere, and we have no idea where they're going to land. We have no idea who's going to breathe them in, have no idea what effect it's going to have on an individual life unless that person materializes and says, "Poetry saved my life."

What do you mean when you say that "poetry humanizes"?

It makes the abstract concrete. It makes the general specific and particular.

We can never look at "the immigrant" the same way if we're reading or hearing the poetry that humanizes the immigrant.

What about these kids from the Dominican Republic, Guatemala, El Salvador, Puerto Rico? They've got a tough life ahead of them. They've got to get a job. They've got to make money. Shouldn't they be doing something more practical than writing poetry?

Well, for me, poetry is practical. Poetry will help them survive to the extent that poetry helps maintain their dignity, helps them maintain their sense of self-respect. They will be better suited to defend themselves in the world. They have to realize that their lives are the stuff of poetry. They have to be given license to write poetry about themselves and what they know before they'll do it. To that extent, poetry can be taught. Obviously there are certain things that can't be taught, one of which is that sense of urgency. You have to have something to say.

Your father, Frank Espada, came to this country from Puerto Rico. As a teenager, he joined the Air Force and was stationed in Texas. Then he became a political activist. What's the story there?

He was going to spend Christmas furlough with his parents in New York City. When he got on the bus, my father, who is a dark-skinned Puerto Rican, sat at the front. And by the time they got to Biloxi, Mississippi, on the coast, he was the only person on the bus. It was the middle of the night and they changed drivers. The new driver came on and saw my father sitting there in the front, and immediately instructed him to go to the back of the bus. My father, being nineteen years old, having grown up in East Harlem, wasn't about to take that from anybody, so he used a colorful expletive in response. The driver returned with two cops and my father was arrested. He appeared before the judge and the judge said, and I quote, "Boy, how many days you got on that furlough?" And my father said, "I have seven days." And the judge said, "I hereby sentence you to seven days in the county jail." My father says that that was the best thing that ever happened to him, because he decided then and there what to do with the rest of his life. At the age of nineteen, he figured out he wanted to fight this sort of thing. And so, when he got out of the military, that's exactly what he began to do. He got involved with the civil rights movement and later on became a political activist in many areas as a leader of the Puerto Rican community in New York.

Which brings us to the poem you wrote about your old apartment building....

This is called "Return."

RETURN

245 Wortman Avenue
East New York, Brooklyn

Forty years ago, I bled in this hallway.
Half-light dimmed the brick
like the angel of public housing.
That night I called and listened at every door:
In 1966, there was a war on television.

Blood leaked on the floor like oil from the engine of me.
Blood rushed through a crack in my scalp;
blood foamed in both hands; blood ruined my shoes.
The boy who fired the can off my head in the street
pumped what blood he could into his fleeing legs.
I banged on every door for help, spreading a plague
of bloody fingerprints all the way home to apartment 14F.

Forty years later, I stand in the hallway.
The dim angel of public housing is too exhausted
to welcome me. My hand presses
against the door at apartment 14F
like an octopus stuck to aquarium glass;
blood drums behind my ears.
Listen to every door: There is a war on television.

It wasn't enough to write poetry like that. You went on to law school.

When I graduated, I simply went to work in Boston's Latino community. I worked in the field of bilingual education law, which was very unusual, and, later on, housing law. I was a tenant lawyer.

Tenant lawyer. Law as a political tool.

Absolutely.

Poetry as a political tool?

Absolutely.

How so?

Both involve advocacy. Speaking on behalf of those without an opportunity
to be heard. Not that they couldn't speak for themselves given the chance.
They just don't get the chance. And to me, there's no contradiction between
being an advocate as a lawyer and being an advocate as a poet. I mean, to
me, it was all in the same spectrum.

What's that old term—poetic justice?

For me, all justice is poetic. First of all, because it is so beautiful. To see justice done: there's something about that I can't even put into words. Or for
that matter, when you see it happen in a courtroom, there's someone there,
again, ordinarily silenced and suppressed by that system, who has an opportunity to speak or to speak through you. When that person is vindicated
and justice is done, to me, there's no feeling like that.

Your latest book, The Republic of Poetry, *was short-listed for the 2007
Pulitzer Prize. Do you think that, politically, Americans have the imagination to see ourselves as a republic of poetry, where, as you say, we work these
distinctions out before they reach the level of bigotry, prejudice, and exclusion?
Or is that utopian?*

I would never want to underestimate the racism in this society. We talk
about borders all the time. In fact, for Latinos, the true borders of our experience have always been the borders of racism. Having said that, I also
believe that we don't necessarily see the situations in which solidarity happens. We don't see the situation where somebody reaches out to someone
else. Does that make the news? Do we hear about that? How would our
perspective on this crisis change if we saw and heard more of that kind of
news? I mean, we have to deal with this paradox that there are more than
forty million Latinos in this country and yet we're invisible. If you remember when legislation was introduced into Congress that essentially would
criminalize so-called "illegal immigrants," there were enormous demonstrations in the streets in New York, in L.A., in Washington, D.C. And the

common denominator of the response was shock, not just at the fact of the demonstrations, but at the dimensions of them. Where did they all come from? Now, the question is: why is it that these forty million people were invisible the day before those demonstrations? To me, all that shock that was registered—"Look at all the Latinos!"—sounded a little bit like Custer at Little Big Horn: "Look at all the Indians." You know? That sense of shock and surprise was a perfect expression of this invisibility that we endure.

You have in The Republic of Poetry *some very powerful poems about war, prompting me to bring some news clippings that I have kept on this subject. Death among Latino soldiers in Iraq ranked the highest compared to other minority groups. One of the first U.S. soldiers to die in Iraq was an orphaned Guatemalan who at the time of his death was not even an American citizen. And two out of every three Latinos now believe that U.S. troops should be brought home from Iraq as soon as possible. What do those stories say to you?*

What those stories say to me is that the war in Iraq is a Latino issue. In fact, that the war in Iraq is probably one of the most important issues facing Latinos, because of our position in society. Latinos are more likely to be exploited in a time of war, more likely to go to the front lines, more likely to become cannon fodder, more likely to be killed or wounded. Because of more limited economic alternatives, we're more likely to take that step and to join an army in a time of war, with the vague promise that somehow this will improve our conditions. We have to have a clearer sense of who the enemy really is, who's really causing the suffering. And those statistics demonstrate that process is, in fact, happening. Latinos understand that this war is doing damage to our community, and they're responding.

There's a poem in The Republic of Poetry, *"Between the Rockets and the Songs," about New Year's Eve 2003, which would have been almost nine months after the invasion of Iraq. Read this and tell me about it.*

BETWEEN THE ROCKETS AND THE SONGS

The fireworks began at midnight,
golden sparks and rockets hissing
through the confusion of trees above our house.
I would prove to my son, now twelve,
that there was no war in the sky, not here,

so we walked down the road
to find the place where the fireworks began.
We swatted branches from our eyes,
peering at a house where the golden blaze
dissolved in smoke. There was silence,
a world of ice, then voices rose up
with the last of the sparks, singing,
and when the song showered down on us
through the leaves we leaned closer, like trees.
Rockets and singing from the same house, said my son.
We turned back down the road,
at the end of the year, at the beginning of the year,
somewhere between the rockets and the songs.

Again, this was an actual incident. It was New Year's Eve. There was this great noise outside, this brilliant light. My son became very nervous.

At that time, he was twelve years old. I knew that he was making these connections. He expressed this to me. He believed that we were being bombed. He believed that the war was happening on our street, the war he had been seeing on television, the war we had been protesting, the war we had all been talking about. And so I decided to show him that on one level, anyway, there was nothing to be afraid of. We took a walk until we found the source of the light and the source of the noise. And remarkably, it stopped and then the singing began. To me, that moment felt like the choice that we're now all confronted with as a society. Are we going to choose rockets or are we going to choose songs? Are we going to choose war or are we going to choose peace? Are we going to choose violence or are we going to choose poetry?

We are at that crossroads, not only my generation, but my son's generation and the generation at that school in the Bronx, where those teachers are showing those kids, taking them by the hand and saying, "Here are the rockets and here are the songs. Choose the songs." ∽

JOHN GRISHAM

The novelist nailed it before many journalists did: if you don't think the courts are friendly enough, buy them off. You need money, of course, but the corporations in John Grisham's The Appeal *have greenbacks to spare, and soon have the state supreme court in their back pocket. As one of their law firm's operatives brags, "When our clients need help, we target a Supreme Court justice who is not particularly friendly, and we take him or her out of the picture."*

Grisham describes this judicial heist so graphically that Janet Maslin in The New York Times *called* The Appeal *"his savviest book in years." It couldn't have been more timely: practically every week brings word of fresh assaults on the independence of our judiciary. In thirty-nine states, judges have to run for office. That's more than 80 percent of the state judges in the country. Over the past thirty years judicial elections have morphed from low-key affairs to extravagantly financed crusades, as wealthy vested interests anonymously pour huge sums of money into the election of judges whose civil decisions directly affect corporate America.*

In the decade leading up to publication of The Appeal, *judicial campaigns raised $200.4 million, more than twice the amount collected in the previous ten years. Small wonder 97 percent of elected state justices in a recent survey to acknowledge being under pressure to raise money to win or stay on the bench.*

The 2010 decision by the right-wing majority of the United States Supreme Court, allowing corporations to flood campaigns with unlimited funds, further threatens judicial independence. "No state," says former justice Sandra Day O'Connor, "can possibly benefit from having that much money injected into a political campaign." Read The Appeal *and you will understand why.*

Now world famous, John Grisham was a small-town lawyer and state legislator who never wrote a book until he was thirty. Since then his books have sold nearly a quarter of a billion copies in twenty-nine languages. Among them are A Time to Kill, The Firm, The Pelican Brief, The Client, The Rainmaker, *and* The Testament. *With* The Appeal, *Grisham, a devout Baptist layman and veteran Sunday school teacher, reads like an Old Testament prophet sounding the trumpet for justice.*

For all his success, John Grisham is not a very public man. He keeps a low profile and makes few speeches. So I was surprised to read that he was going to make a keynote address in Atlanta, Georgia, before the first meeting of the New Baptist Covenant, a group formed by former President Jimmy Carter to unite Baptists "around an agenda of Christ-centered social ministry." We spoke around the time of that speech, just as The Appeal *was published.*

—Bill Moyers

—∽∾∽—

You so rarely give speeches that I'm curious as to why you chose this gathering in Atlanta for a forum.

I didn't have much of a choice. The phone rang, and it was Jimmy Carter. And I'd never talked to him before. He invited me to come down, and I told him I probably couldn't do it because my next book, *The Appeal*, comes out that week. He said, "Well, can I be pushy?" You know, I don't know how you tell a former president they can't be pushy. I said, "Sure," and he said, "I really want you to come." I said, "Okay, I'll be happy to do it."

Tell me about The Appeal.

It's got more politics than anything I've written, tons of politics, tons of legal intrigue. All my books are based, in some degree, on something that really happened. This is about the election of a supreme court justice in the state of Mississippi. Thirty-some-odd states elect their judges, which is a bad system, because they allow private money, and it's just like a campaign. You got corporate people throwing money in. You got big individuals. You got, you know, cash coming in to elect a judge who may hear your case. Think about that. You've got a case pending before the court and you want to reshape the structure of the court just to get your guy elected. And that's happened in several states. Big money comes in, takes out an unsympathetic judge, replaces him with someone who may be more friendly to you. And he gets to rule in your case.

This is the corporation that dumps the toxic poisons into the stream, ruins the community's drinking water?

Yes, Chapter One is a verdict where this big chemical company has polluted this small town to the point where you can't even drink the water. It's become a cancer cluster; a lot of people have died. And so there's a big lawsuit. And that's the opening of the book. Then it's all the intrigue about what that company does, because the guy who owns that company doesn't like the composition of the state supreme court. And he realizes he can change it.

By buying an election, buying the judge. Judges in Mississippi are often determined by the most money that goes into the campaign. What are the practical consequences for citizens?

In Mississippi, the court has now been realigned in such a way where you have a hard-right majority. Six or seven. Two or three dissents. When you've got a majority you only need five. Virtually every plaintiff's verdict is reversed. So if your neighbor's son gets killed in a car wreck and there's a big lawsuit and there's a big verdict against the negligent party, or if your friend is injured by a negligent doctor or a hospital, whatever, you're pretty much out of luck.

So the court is now decidedly biased, in your judgment, in favor of the powerful.

Oh, it's not in my judgment. It's a proven fact. You can read the state supreme court decisions in Mississippi and Alabama, and both states have a hard-right majority. And so people with legitimate claims are not always, but generally, out of luck.

Isn't there any outrage among all those good Christian folks, as my mother would say, who live there—those ordinary folks?

No. Because the Chamber of Commerce sells it, corporate America sells it, and the Republican Party sells it as a way to protect business, economic development, economic growth. "Look at our state. We frown on lawsuits. We frown on unions. This is a good place to do business." That's how you sell it. Sounds good. It's how every politician does it down there. And you end up with a court that's very unsympathetic to the rights of victims, to the rights of consumers, to the rights of criminal defendants. Yeah, that's what happens when those types of people are elected.

What's your sense of why these Christian folks, so many Baptists, vote for the party that is in fact the party of money?

They live poor and vote rich. The brilliant thing the Republicans did was get all these guys under one tent. From your traditional Republican base—wealthy Republicans, your country club Republicans, your corporate Republicans—and bring in the NASCAR bubbas and all those folks, and then get the religious right. All these good Christian folks. Get them all under one tent. All voting, really, for one purpose, and that's to protect, you know, the rich folks. That's worked beautifully for the Republican Party.

Predators show up in just about every one of your novels. The little guy does get screwed until one of your protagonists shows up to take on the case. I grew up in a small town, too. You're describing small-town justice.

Yes, sir. That's what I know. I was there, but I also study it. Watched it, you know, by reading about cases. *The Innocent Man*, you know, is the most recent example, and why I never wanted to write a nonfiction book. It's a whole lot more fun, a whole lot easier, to create stuff than to go research a bunch of facts and have to do the hard work. And I try to avoid hard work if at all possible.

The Innocent Man is your first foray into nonfiction—you did deep research into how Ron Williamson and another man were wrongly convicted of a 1982 murder. Eleven years later, DNA evidence proved their innocence, freeing Williamson from death row.

We've sent 130 men to death row to be executed in this country, at least 130 that we know of, who later have been exonerated because they were either innocent or they were not fairly tried. Including Ron Williamson, the guy I wrote about. Well, you know, if that doesn't bother you, go to death row. Go see a death row. Your first reaction is, how could someone survive here? How could you live? You're in a very small cell, just a few feet by few feet. How do you keep your sanity? They do, most of them. They function, they survive. There are very, very harsh conditions, and perhaps they should be. I'm not saying prison should be an easy place. But imagine, it's tough enough if you're guilty. If you're a serial murderer, it's tough enough. But think if you're an innocent man, if you know you didn't do the crime, and the guy who did do the murder is still out there. You're serving his time, and nobody's listening to you. Nobody's listening to you. Those are powerful stories.

The prosecutor was reelected unopposed, despite the fact that the town knew he had convicted the wrong man.

Wrongful convictions happen every week in every state in this country. And they happen for all the same reasons. Sloppy police work. Eyewitness identification is the worst type, almost. Because it's wrong about half the time. Think about that. Eyewitness identification has sent more men to prison than probably anything else. Sloppy prosecutions. Junk science. Snitch testimony. It happens all the time. You get some snitch in a jail who wants out, and he comes in and says, "Oh, I heard your defendant confess." And they'll say, "Well, okay, we'll reduce your time and we'll let you out if you'll testify at trial." There should be rules governing snitch testimony.

There are five or six primary reasons you have wrongful convictions. All could be addressed. All could be fixed with the right statutes. The human cost of wrongful convictions is enormous. But the economic cost is huge, too. Keeping a guy in prison costs $50,000 a year. Executing one costs a couple million. It varies from state to state.

Wow!

It's expensive to crank up the machinery of death.

What would you do with someone who's for sure guilty?

Oh, listen, I have no sympathy for violent criminals. And this country was so sick of violent crime—that's one reason we've reacted the way we do. And we still have the death penalty. And we still have two million people in prison in this country right now. Our prisons are choked, they're so full, and most of them are nonviolent. We're spending somewhere between $40,000 and $80,000 apiece to house them, every guy in prison. Now, somebody's not doing the math here. You know, we're spending all this money on these people. But for the violent people, the murderers, there are some criminals who do not belong outside prison. I'm not in favor of the death penalty, but I'm in favor of locking these people away in maximum-security units where they can never get out, they can never escape, they can never be paroled. Lock the bad ones away, but you've got to rethink everybody else. You've got to rethink the young kids who are in there because of, you know, crack cocaine. I mean, they need help. They serve five years, they get out, and do the same thing over and over again. The system's getting worse.

As the years have gone by, I've caught myself more and more taking on an issue, whether it's the death penalty, or homelessness, or big tobacco, or insurance abuse, or whatever. When I can take an issue and wrap a novel around it and make it compelling, make the pages turn and make it very suspenseful, and get the reader hooked on the book, and also get the reader, for the first time, maybe, to think about a problem from a different viewpoint, those are the best books. The more books I write, the more I seem to think about social injustice, and the stories I have for future books, there are a lot more ideas dealing with what's wrong with our systems. And maybe how to fix them. Not that I know how to fix them. But I can sure show you what's wrong with them.

You paint a pretty dark portrait of what it's like to be poor, to be marginalized, to be in the minority.

I didn't live it myself, but when you grow up in Mississippi and Arkansas, you see it. You can still see it now, in the Deep South and in other areas. For almost ten years I practiced law in a small town in Mississippi. And my clients were working people and poor people. Victims. People who lost their jobs, who lost their insurance. But, also, people accused of crimes. That's shaped my life. Because I was always fighting for these people against, you know, something bigger. The legal experience was formative. I would never have written a first book had I not been a lawyer. I didn't dream of writing.

When I was reading Steinbeck in high school I was going to be a professional athlete. I had no talent but a lot of big dreams. That didn't work out. I couldn't even play in college. I never thought I was going to be a writer. It came later in life, after I'd practiced law for a few years.

You seem to be talking more politics, writing more politics, which is something risky for a writer, because your readers may not agree with your politics.

Yes, I guess it's risky. I think we're all caught up in politics. With the war going how could you not be caught in politics? A bad war. A lot of the issues of the day are political issues. As a society, we just have this insatiable appetite now for more and more politics. We've got the twenty-four-hour cable shows. Everybody's an analyst. Everybody's an expert, you know. So we get caught up in it.

You once called the Iraq War "a moral abomination."

I did. Still do. We attacked a sovereign nation that was not threatening us. What was our justification? I don't know. We were lied to by our leaders. It wasn't what they said it was. Estimates are half a million Iraqis have died since the war started. They wouldn't be dead, I don't think, had we not gone there. How do you get out? We lost four thousand very brave soldiers who would love their country, and would go fighting where they were told because they're soldiers. Tens of thousands of shattered lives. We're not taking care of the veterans when they come home. The social cost of this is enormous.

The brutality of war, and the battles of politics, couldn't be further removed from A Painted House. *You tell the story of a little boy growing up on a cotton farm in rural Arkansas. Is it autobiographical?*

It's very autobiographical up to a point. The setting is very accurate. The first seven years of my life I was on a cotton farm. I remember the Mexican farmworkers living in the top of the barn. I remember playing baseball with Juan. We had the same name. I remember the floods, losing crops. The house in the book was my grandparents' house. We didn't live with them. We lived not too far away. And the church stuff, Black Oak Baptist Church, that's where we went. It was in town. My mother was a town girl. She grew up in Black Oak. My father was a country boy—they were five miles apart, but, you know, the social structure in these little towns is very important. And my mother said one time she got in a big fight with a kid who lived out in the country. And as the ultimate insult, this little girl said to my mother, "Yeah, but you live in a painted house." Meaning that you're kind of an uptown snooty girl because your house is painted. And it was very real, very true. Mother's told that story for years. And that was always the title from day one.

How is it so many southerners become good storytellers and good politicians?

I think anytime you have a geographical location, a region where you have had and still may have a lot of suffering, a lot of conflict, you're going to have good stories. You're going to have great writers. Because there's so much material. You look at the tortured history of the South, the cruelty, the war, the poverty—all the violence in the history of the South gives rise to great stories.

There's also the conversation. I remember my mother talking across the back fence to Miss Platt, who was our landlord. I remember the voices of the people coming home from the theater at nine o'clock, at ten o'clock at night, walking just five yards from my bed. I went down to the courthouse square and heard the white farmers on one side of town telling their stories and the black farmers on the other side of town telling their stories. It was hard to come out of there and not have stories ratcheting in your head. You remember that?

Well, I can remember my father telling stories his grandfather told him. And these were poor folks with no television, maybe radio, no telephones. They talked, they talked, they talked. They told stories.

What about the sermons? Did you hear a lot of sermons?

Well, good gosh, yeah. I heard them all, from the long sermon on Sunday morning when you're sitting there soaked with sweat, to the revivalists, the evangelists who'd come to town for the big crusades, the tent crusades where the whole town would show up. And it was kind of exciting at times and boring at times. But I've heard a lot of sermons.

Were you "born again"?

Sure. When I was eight years old—First Baptist Church in Parkin, Arkansas. I felt the call to become a Christian. I felt the need to. I talked to my parents. I talked to my pastor. And I accepted Christ when I was eight years old, just a little small boy. And like most of the kids, you know, in my church, and my brothers and sisters, that was very much a part of growing up.

And when you look back half a century later, how do you think that moment has played out in your life and in your work?

Well, you know, once you make that conversion, you are and always will be something different, a different person. I can't say it impacts what I choose to write. But it certainly impacts how I write. The great secret to *The Firm*, and this is what, you know, people don't realize—

Your second book—

The first printing was fifty thousand copies, which is nothing to sneeze at. People read that book, and when they finished it, they realized they could give it to their fifteen-year-old or their eighty-year-old mother and not be embarrassed. It sold a zillion copies because of that. My books are exceptionally clean by today's standards. There are things I don't want to write, can't write. I wrote a sex scene one time and showed it to my wife. And she burst out laughing. She said, "What do you know about sex?"

Spoken like a true Baptist.

The content of my books, the language, even the violence, is something that is easy to stomach. And I would not, because of my faith, write any other way. ✒

SUSAN JACOBY

In the spring of 2010, a Harris Poll reported some astonishing statistics on how Americans view President Obama. Sixty-seven percent of Republicans said he is a socialist. So did 12 percent of independents and 14 percent of Democrats. Fifty-seven percent of Republicans believed him to be a Muslim, as did 29 percent of independents and 15 percent of Democrats. Forty-five percent of Republicans, 24 percent of independents, and 8 percent of Democrats refused to believe he was born in the United States. And to 24 percent of Republicans, 13 percent of independents, and 6 percent of Democrats he "may be the Antichrist."

The right-wing propaganda offensive against the president—a relentless and ruthless barrage of toxic misinformation constantly pumped into the nation's bloodstream by Fox News, Rush Limbaugh and his imitators on talk radio, hypocritical partisan apparatchiks like Newt Gingrich, and ranting bloggers—was intended to smear Obama beyond recognition. His face—whitened like a clown, with lips painted bright red like the Joker in Batman— *showed up on protest signs at right-wing rallies, alongside others in which the president was depicted as Hitler, complete with mustache and swastika.*

These shock troops in the right's war on Obama, with their unscrupulous pursuit of the lowest common denominator of public discourse, are the latest vanguard in the headlong flight from reason that characterizes our time. The writer Susan Jacoby, a specialist in American intellectual history, believes that Thomas Jefferson got it right when he said, "Whenever the people are well informed, they can be trusted with their own government," and says this flight from reason affects far more than politics. She describes a calamitous dumbing down of American culture, "an overarching crisis of memory and knowledge," that affects everything from scientific research to decisions about war and peace. And she concludes that the verdict is out on whether Americans "are willing to consider what the flight from reason has cost us."

The program director of New York's Center for Inquiry, Jacoby makes the case in her book The Age of American Unreason. *Among her earlier work,* Wild Justice *was a Pulitzer Prize finalist, and* Freethinkers: A History of American Secularism *was chosen by* The Los Angeles Times *and* The Washington Post *as one of the notable books of the year.*

—Bill Moyers

—⁓—

How is this flight from reason, as you describe it, playing out?

In an age of unreason you tend to focus on very small personal facts as opposed to big issues. But even more than that, lack of knowledge and unreason affect the way candidates speak about everything. For example, obviously the health care situation in this country is very important. All of the candidates say it is. But people don't know how health care is handled in other countries. How many people, for instance, have the right to choose their own doctors in this country? In other words, without a base of knowledge of how things are, you can't really have a reasonable talk about how things ought to be. You can say, "Oh, we don't want a program that will prevent people from choosing their own doctors." Well, are we able to choose our own doctors? I'm not. I have to choose within a managed care network.

You describe what's happened to our political language. You shudder when politicians talk not about people but about the "folks." What's wrong with that?

What's wrong with it is that "folks" used to be a colloquialism. It was the kind of thing that you'd talk about mostly in rural areas, mostly in the South and the Midwest. People talked about "folks." It was not considered suitable for public speech. If you used it in the classroom, your teacher would get after you, because it wasn't considered appropriate language. But think about our political language in the past and today. Just think about the Gettysburg Address: "We highly resolve that these dead shall not have died in vain—that this government, of the folks, by the folks, and for the folks, shall not perish from the earth." This is patronizing. It's talking down to people. I read all of FDR's fireside chats; I could not find a single reference to "folks." You know why? Because addressing people as "folks" is talking down to them. It's not dignifying them. When you call people "citizens," you're calling on them to rise above the lowest common denominator. You really need to think about what's being said when people are called "folks." It's encouraging you not to do too much.

Not to expect anything special.

Politicians are terribly scared of saying, "We really need to expect more of people."

You mentioned Franklin Roosevelt.

I want him back.

You talk about how during World War II, when he would have a fireside chat, he would ask the people listening to get a map of the world and spread it out in front of them so that as he talked about the battles that were going on they would be with him in terms of the place, the geography, the strategy of what was going on. Can you imagine a president doing that today?

No, I can't. Doris Kearns Goodwin talks about this extensively in her book *No Ordinary Time*. Maps sold out. You couldn't buy a map before Roosevelt's fireside chat the February after Pearl Harbor because millions of Americans went out and bought maps. And they sat there by the radio and followed what he was talking about. But one of the big mistakes today is that we talk about our political culture as if it were something separate, something different from our general culture. What I say in *The Age of American Unreason* is, no, that's wrong. Our political culture is a reflection of our general culture. It is as much shaped by our general culture as it shapes our general culture.

Now to return to FDR, which I'm really glad you asked about—it's been forgotten now in the mythology of World War II that even when the

Nazis invaded Poland and attacked England, an overwhelming majority of Americans were opposed to American involvement in the war. The reason they came around is not just Pearl Harbor. Franklin D. Roosevelt spent several years trying to educate a resistant public about the stake that America had in the future of Europe. The draft extension six months before Pearl Harbor, in the summer of 1941, passed by one vote. Imagine what would have happened if the army had been disbanded, if FDR had not made all those educational efforts, where we would have been six months later when Pearl Harbor was attacked. May I say that everybody talks about who's equipped to be commander-in-chief, a word presidents didn't used to use. I hate the word.

And why do you hate it?

Because the president is only the commander in chief of the armed forces. He's not the commander in chief of us. It's a word that in the past presidents didn't use except in a strictly military sense. What's far more important than being commander in chief is being educator in chief. And Franklin Roosevelt and Abraham Lincoln would not have succeeded as commanders in chief if they hadn't first succeeded as teachers in chief. To be nonpartisan about it, Bill Clinton and George W. Bush are two of the biggest failures as teachers in chief of any presidents we've ever had. Bush at foreign policy, obviously. It's great to bring people along with you when everybody's in favor of the war, as they were in 2003 because there was this desire to strike back at somebody, anyone, for 9/11. So Bush just said, "Oh, yeah. Saddam Hussein had something to do with 9/11." And people believed it.

And Clinton? What about Clinton?

Everything in my view that's being written about the failure ten years ago of the Clinton health care program, in relation to Hillary Clinton, is wrong. Its failure is usually attributed to their failure to bring the insurance industry groups to the table, all of the interest groups in advance. No. The reason that health care reform was dead on arrival was that the American people hadn't been educated and prepared for any kind of change. Bill Clinton just announced his plan, which had been developed more or less secretly, without much public participation. The health insurance industry jumped in with its Harry and Louise commercials. I'll bet everybody remembers Harry and Louise, and nobody remembers a detail of the Clinton plan, the health care plan. It is the job of the president to get his message out before Harry and Louise. Bill Clinton didn't do that.

You also write about the difference it makes to talk about troop *and* troops *instead of* soldier *and* soldiers.

Very Orwellian. *Troops* used to be a word reserved only as a collective noun. We would say, "Allied troops have landed at Normandy." *Troops* meant a massive military operation. We never talked about a soldier who was killed in action as a *troop*. We don't lay a wreath at the Tomb of the Unknown Troop. We lay a wreath at the Tomb of the Unknown Soldier. That kind of euphemistic language—talking about *troops* takes individuality away from them.

They become an abstraction.

They become an abstraction, right. Not an individual soldier who is dying. And, by the way, I offer a theory about how this substitution happens. And it's not very Machiavellian at all. It's part of, again, how dumb our culture has become. I think some PR person somehow decided that *soldier* could mean only a man. And they were looking for a noun that sounded more neutral. It's utterly stupid, of course; a soldier can be a man or a woman. But my guess is that some dopey PR person suggested this. And somebody in the army said, "Great." And the newspapers just went along.

So what prompted this book?

In a way it was an outgrowth of *Freethinkers: A History of American Secularism*. After *Freethinkers* was published I welcomed the opportunity to go out and speak across the country, to educate people about a secular tradition that has been lost, downgraded, and denigrated. I soon found my audiences consisted almost entirely of people who already agreed with me. Conservatives report exactly the same experience. This was not always the case in our country. In the nineteenth century, Robert Ingersoll, who is known as "the Great Agnostic," had audiences full of people who didn't agree with him. But they wanted to hear what he had to say. They wanted to see whether the devil really has horns. Now what we have is a situation in which people go to hear people they already agree with. What's going on is not so much education as reinforcement of the opinions you already have.

Why is it we're so unwilling to give a hearing to contradictory viewpoints? Or to imagine that we might learn something from someone who disagrees with us?

I think it is part of a larger thing that is making our culture dumber. We have over the past forty years resorted to shorter and shorter and shorter attention spans. One of the most important studies I've seen was by the Kaiser Family Foundation. They found that, on average, children under six spend two hours a day watching television or video—it's called "infantainment"—but only thirty-nine minutes a day reading or being read to by their parents. I don't see how people can learn to concentrate and read if they watch television when they're very young as opposed to having their parents read to them. The fact is when you're watching television, whether it's an infant or adult, or staring glazedly at a video screen, you're not doing something else.

What does it say to you that half of American adults believe in ghosts? I take these numbers from your book. One-third believe in astrology. And four-fifths believe in miracles.

The flip side of this is that half of Americans don't believe in evolution. And these things go together. Because what they do is they place science on a par almost with folk beliefs. If I may inveigh against ourselves, I think the American media in particular has a lot to do with it. Because one of the things that really has gotten dumber about our culture is the way the media constantly talks about truth as if it were always equidistant from two points. Sometimes the truth is one-sided. After the 9/11 terrorist attacks there was a huge cover story in *Time* magazine in 2002 about the rapture and end-of-the-world scenarios. There wasn't a singular secular person quoted in it. They discussed the rapture scenario from the Book of Revelation as though it was a perfectly reasonable thing for people to believe. It's exactly like saying, "So-and-so says, 'Two plus two equals five.' But, of course, mathematicians say that it really equals four." The mathematicians are right. The people who say that two plus two equals five are wrong. The media blurs that constantly.

You call it a kind of dumb objectivity. What does it say to you that nearly two-thirds of Americans want creationism based on the Book of Genesis to be taught in our public schools along with evolution?

It's that evolution is just a theory, it's just another opinion. Just as some people believe that the account of the six days of creation in Genesis is literally true, some people believe we're descended from lower animals. In other words, it places belief on the same level as science, subject to proof. I should say, however, that it may also mean that a lot of Americans aren't exactly sure what creationism means. Because, in fact, the recent Gallup poll shows that only 30 percent of Americans believe that every word of the Bible is literally true. Many—most—Americans believe the Bible is divinely inspired. But you can believe the Bible is divinely inspired and still believe in evolution, but you can't believe that the Bible is literally true and still believe in evolution. There's a wonderful book, *Religious Literacy* by Stephen Prothero, which cites a poll that half of Americans can't name Genesis as the first book of the Bible. This is part of the dumbing down of our culture. One of those books that 50 percent of Americans apparently aren't reading is the Bible, or they would know that Genesis is the first book of the Bible. It's sort of like, "I don't know what Genesis is, but I believe it."

Doesn't this also say something about the level of science education in our public schools?

I think it says everything about the level of education in our schools. One out of every five Americans still believes that the sun revolves around the earth. But you shouldn't have to be an intellectual or a college graduate to know that the sun doesn't revolve around the earth. There's been a huge failure of education. I do agree with many cultural conservatives about the emphasis on African American history, women's history, and so on. These are all great additions, and necessary. But what they've done in addition to adding subjects is to place less emphasis on the overall culture that everybody should know. People getting out of high school should know how many Supreme Court justices there are. Most Americans don't. This feeds back into our current political process. You wonder why more of the American public doesn't understand it. Well, if you don't know that there are nine judges, then you don't know that George W. Bush's last two judicial appointments, Samuel Alito and John Roberts, put us one vote away from having a Supreme Court that's likely to overturn *Roe v. Wade*. But you have to know there are nine justices to know how really important the composition of the Supreme Court is in the next election. Our schools are doing a bad job of teaching history and science.

You claim that right-wing intellectuals are dangerous because they have com-
mand of a vocabulary that makes wishful thinking sound rational.

One of the great successes of the intellectual right is that they have succeeded brilliantly during the last twenty years at pinning the "intellectual"
label solely on liberals, so that a lot of people think that to be an intellectual
means that you are a liberal alone. And one of the reasons that I think that
right-wing intellectuals are so dangerous is they've been so clever at doing
this. They've been much more clever than liberal intellectuals have been.
They've made it look like liberals are the only "elites." But right-wing people
get huge salaries from business-financed right-wing foundations. They're
not the elites? Of course they're the elites. I object to their ideas; I don't
object to the people. But the liberal intellectual community is really caught
asleep at the switch by these people. One of the points I make in *The Age of
American Unreason*, which is why I think I'm going to get killed from both
the right and the left, is that antirationalism in America is not the province
of either the right or the left. It's the province of both. When you talk to
right-wing intellectuals about the Iraq War, it doesn't matter to them that
it hasn't worked out. They still think it was right. And the evidence of how
it got started, on false pretenses and so on, doesn't matter to them.

They make wishful thinking sound rational. It's the same thing when we
hear that the surge is working. Well, the surge is working as long as we have
those troops there. There are fewer people being killed in suicide bombings every day because we have a lot more young soldiers there in harm's
way. How many people were killed in suicide bombings in Baghdad before
America entered the war? I believe the answer is none. So what they're doing is comparing apples and oranges.

*You're pretty hard on some liberal intellectuals, too. You say they won't ac-
knowledge the political significance of public ignorance: "Liberal intellectuals . . . tended during the past eight years to define the Bush administration as
the root of all evil, and see an outraged citizenry ready to throw the bums out
as the solution." And you say that's the cheap and wrong way out. Right?*

It's the cheap way out and the wrong way out for this reason: Over and over
we have heard from candidates who supported the war and changed their
minds. "We were lied to," they said. "If we'd known then what we know
now we wouldn't have done it." They say to the public, "You were lied to."

But the deeper conversation we need to be having is why were Americans so willing to be lied to—not only average citizens, but politicians. There was a National Geographic–Roper poll of Americans between ages eighteen and twenty-four—only 23 percent of college-educated young people could find Saudi Arabia, Iraq, Iran, and Israel on the map, four countries of ultimate importance to American policy. This was a map, by the way, that wasn't blank; it had the names of the countries lettered on it. They didn't know where the Middle East is! Only 6 percent of high school graduates could name those countries. This is nothing to be bragging about. Surely this has something to do with why as a country we have such shallow discussions.

You say left-of-center intellectuals have focused on the right-wing deceptions employed to sell the war in Iraq rather than on the ignorance and erosion of historical memory that makes serious deceptions possible and plausible. Talk about the power and importance of memory.

Well, first of all, one of the things that we don't remember is what our Constitution actually says. If we don't know what our Constitution says about the separation of powers, then it really certainly affects the way we decide all kinds of public issues.

George Orwell talked about important knowledge like that being flushed down the memory hole. When that happens, the people in power can rule without any reference to the past.

For example, what the right wing says about judges is that our unelected judges are overstepping their powers. They talk as if judges have no right to interpret the Constitution. But that is exactly what the unelected federal judiciary was set up to do. It says so in the Constitution. People confuse the fact that they may not like certain judicial decisions with the right of judges to interpret the Constitution—indeed, the duty of judges under our Constitution to interpret the Constitution.

By ignorant, you mean "lack of knowledge," "unaware." You don't mean "stupid," which means "dimwitted."

No.

But I can't imagine a politician succeeding by saying, "We're an ignorant culture and an ignorant people."

No, but I can imagine a politician succeeding by saying, "We as a people have not lived up to our obligation to learn what we ought to learn to make informed decisions." I can imagine candidates saying, "And we in the Congress have been guilty of that, too." Because it's not just the public that's ignorant. We get the government we deserve. You wouldn't say to people, "You're a dope." You would say, "We have got to do better about learning the things we need to know to make sound public policy." We can't learn the things we need to know from five-second sound bite commercials. We can't learn the things that we need to know from a quick hit on the Internet to see the latest person making a fool of themselves on YouTube. We can only learn the things we need to know from talking to each other and from books. We've become satisfied with too little. We've become satisfied with the lowest common denominator. ∾

JIM YONG KIM

When the trustees of Dartmouth College chose Dr. Jim Yong Kim to be the school's seventeenth president—the first Asian American to head any Ivy League institution—they knew he would bring the woes of the world with him to the idyllic New Hampshire campus, and they were more than okay with it. They were, in fact, counting on him to challenge Dartmouth's students, as he had recently challenged a graduating class of young doctors, to act as if "the world's troubles are your troubles."

It's no pious sentiment on his part. Kim has seen the world's hurt up close and made an extraordinary life's work out of helping to heal it. As a founding trustee of the global organization Partners in Health, he has worked for twenty-three years with the legendary Paul Farmer on a crusade to transform health care for the poor worldwide. He once supervised all of the World Health Organization's work related to HIV/AIDS, co-founded the Global Health Delivery Project in collaboration with Harvard University's medical and business schools, and developed the Web-based "communities of practice" (GHDonline.org), which enable health practitioners from Haiti and Peru to Lesotho and Siberia to engage in real-time problem solving.

Born in Seoul, Korea, and raised in Muscatine, Iowa, where he was quarterback of the football team, point guard on the basketball team, and valedictorian, Jim Yong Kim graduated magna cum laude from Brown, where he had thought of becoming a philosopher. His father's imperative to "get a skill" instead spurred him on to Harvard, where he earned both a medical degree and a doctorate in anthropology. He became chairman of the school's Department of Global Health and Social Medicine, director of its François-Xavier Bagnoud Center for Health and Human Rights, and chief of the Division of Global Health Equity at Brigham and Women's Hospital in Boston. Oh, yes—in addition to his administrative duties, writing, and re-search, Dr. Kim taught overflowing classes of students. All of this accomplished by the time he was fifty!

So what do you do when you are already one of Time's *one hundred most influential people in the world, one of* U.S. News and World Report's *"best American leaders," and a MacArthur Foundation "genius"? Well, if you are Jim Yong Kim, you take on yet another challenge—decamping to the hills of western New Hampshire and the presidency of one of America's oldest colleges, founded in 1769 on the colonial frontier and poised now to take on "the world's troubles."*

—Bill Moyers

You have spent the last twenty-five years of your life working with the sickest and the poorest people in the world. And here you are, sitting in the corner office of a wealthy, elite school with fewer than six thousand undergraduate students. What in the world did you tell the search committee?

The call from the search committee was entirely unexpected. I was minding my own business, working with colleagues who were interested in global health, but also colleagues at the Harvard Business School and the systems engineering department at MIT, to try to figure out how to make health care programs in developing countries work more effectively. Dartmouth came out of the blue and said, "Would you look at this job?"

One of the reasons I took the job was my experience with Paul Farmer, who was chronicled in the book *Mountains Beyond Mountains*. He's one of my heroes and my closest friend in the world—a great public health advocate who has made a lot of personal sacrifices in his life. They call him the modern-day Albert Schweitzer. He is a person who works tirelessly for the health of poor people, and I have been very touched by the extent to which young people are motivated and moved by his life story.

There's always a sense in young people that they want to do something great, but a lot of them don't think they can make a difference. That's really why I am at Dartmouth, to tell young people, "A few committed souls can change the world." You know the famous Margaret Mead line that you should never doubt the capacity of a small group of committed souls to change the world; indeed, it is the only thing that ever has. I am at Dartmouth to give them that message.

But that's not the most popular message right now. When you told those young doctors graduating from medical school last May, "The world's troubles are your troubles," that's the last thing many people in America want to hear, because we have so many of our own troubles right here at home.

I don't think that I would exclude our troubles. One of the projects that I started just before leaving Harvard was an effort to improve the health care of Native Americans in New Mexico. The life expectancy of certain Native American groups in the United States is one of the great moral crises that we face, life expectancies that are at times even lower than life expectancy in some of the developing countries that I work in, in the forties and fifties in some communities. So the world's troubles are right here as well.

There's something else. I was tantalized by the notion of reaching back into the undergraduate curriculum and trying to think hard about what it would take to train a group of young people who would leave the college energized, inspired, and really thinking there's no problem that they couldn't tackle. This is a good time to get them thinking about climate change, the crisis in the health care system in the United States, as well as global health problems. What do you need to do to prepare yourself for a meaningful life, tackling those kinds of problems?

From your perspective, what's wrong with our health care system?

For many, many years, we've been working under the fantasy that if we come up with new drugs and new treatments, we're done. The rest of the system will take care of itself. In my view, the rocket science in health and health care is how we deliver it. Unfortunately, there's not a single medical school that I know of that actually teaches the delivery of health care as one of the essential sciences.

What we've learned about organizations is that it is very difficult to get a complex organization, a group of people, to work consistently toward a goal, especially a goal as complex as providing great health care. In the business world, if you don't do it well, the market gets rid of you. You go out of business. But many hospitals that are executing very poorly persist for a very, very long time. My own view is that we have to fundamentally rethink the kind of research we do and the kind of people we educate so that they'll think about the complexity of delivery as a topic that we need to tackle as a science.

Complexity of delivery?

Yes. Just think about a single patient. A patient comes into the hospital. There's a judgment made the minute that patient walks into the emergency room about how sick that person is. And then there are relays of information from the triage nurse to the physician, from the physician to the other physician who comes on the shift. From them to the ward team that takes over that patient—there are so many transfers of information. Yet we haven't looked at the transfer of information the way that, for example, Southwest Airlines has. Apparently they do it as well as any company in the world. It seems that Southwest Airlines has taken seriously the human science of how you transfer simple information from one person to the next. In medical school, and in the hospitals that I've worked in, we've mostly done it ad hoc. Sometimes we do it well, sometimes we don't do it well, but we haven't treated it as a science despite knowing that transfer of information is critical to good patient care.

What we need now is a whole new cadre of people who understand the science, who really are committed to patient care, but who then also think about how to make those human systems work effectively. We've been calling it, aspirationally, the science of health care delivery. And we do it at Dartmouth. Thirty years ago, one of our great faculty members, Jack Wennberg, started asking a pretty simple question: why is there variation in the number of children who get their tonsils taken out between one county in Vermont versus another? Because one of his children was in school at one place, another of his children was in the school in another place.

In one place, almost everyone had their tonsils out. And in another place, almost no one did. And of course, he found that there happened to be a doctor in one of the counties who liked to take tonsils out and benefited from it. So he kept asking this question about outcome variation. He called it the evaluative clinical sciences.

That's a fancy name. What does it mean to the layman?

It means, how do you evaluate clinical outcomes? How do you understand variation in doctors' practices, for example? And ultimately, how do you fix the problems? Why is the Medicare reimbursement rate almost a third in the Mayo Clinic area in Minnesota of what it is in Miami?

Why have we been so resistant to doing this? It sounds so sensible.

I've noticed over the years that when it comes to our most cherished social goals, not only do we tolerate poor execution, sometimes we celebrate poor execution. Sometimes it's part of the culture. You know: "These folks are trying to solve this terrible problem, they can't keep their books straight, they really don't know what they're getting, they don't measure anything, but they're on the right side, so that's okay." I think we're in a different time.

What can we learn from the health care partnerships you've spent the last twenty-five years creating around the world?

One is that community health workers—members of the community who help people go through very difficult treatment regimens—can work anywhere. We did it first in Haiti, then we did it in Peru, and then in Africa. But most remarkably, we've also implemented that program in Boston, and are now thinking of implementing it on the Navajo reservation in New Mexico.

And in essence, it means what?

It means that for people who are, say, taking HIV medications that are very difficult, that they have to take every day, that they have to really be careful about, with nutrition, et cetera, that having someone who just visits every day, just to make sure that you're taking your medicines and you're doing okay, has a huge payoff down the line in terms of overall health outcomes. Almost a decade ago, we found a group of patients living with HIV in Boston who were really falling through the cracks. We implemented almost an identical program to the one we developed in Haiti, and we've had really astounding results. The cost of their care has gone down, and they're back working, and they're productive members of society. They're not landing in the emergency room when their disease gets out of control.

We've got to bring the best and the brightest to work on health care delivery and the only way to do that is to get more people thinking about it every day. Right now, the physicians who are running these hospitals have never been trained in the skills they need to run such complex enterprises. Most of them have never been trained in systems thinking, in strategy, in management.

One of the big disappointments to a lot of people is that the White House seems to have made a deal with the drug industry not to use the power of the government to negotiate lower drug prices through Medicare and Medicaid. I know you learned something about negotiating for lower drug prices when you were at the World Health Organization, right?

It's a very complicated business. Of the three major killers—HIV, tuberculosis, and malaria—the only disease for which we have really good drugs is HIV. It's very simple why—there's a market in the United States and Europe. So we know that market incentives to drive drug delivery are critical. We have to maintain them somehow, because if you don't have market incentives, we have almost no new drugs. Now, having said that, I've worked a lot with the drug companies to say, "Okay, so make as much money as you can on the HIV drugs in the first world. We will work with you to protect those markets and protect your intellectual property. On the other hand, in those areas where you make no money anyway, work with us to make those drugs available." And they've done that for HIV drugs in a way that's really quite astounding.

We've got to make sure that the incentive for the drug companies to make new drugs is still there, but at the same time, be reasonable about making sure that people have access to them.

There was a strain of TB that could be cured by a drug, but the drug was so expensive that poor people couldn't afford it in the developing world. What did you do about that?

We looked at the cost of these drugs for a complete cure for a patient living in the developing world. When we started, it was about $25,000. But what we later learned was that the only reason they were so expensive is because they were only sold in first world countries. So we got everyone who was interested in purchasing these drugs. We went to Doctors Without Borders, we went to other health organizations and said, "Can you help us get the

Indian and Chinese drug industry to start making these drugs?" And they did it. Now, the real key was at Eli Lilly and Company, which was making two of the drugs. They came on board and said, "You know what? We're going to help you with this program. We don't make any money off these drugs, they were off patent a long time ago. We're going to actually help you find manufacturers in those countries that can make these drugs at a lower cost."

It's one of the greatest acts of corporate philanthropy I've ever seen, Eli Lilly and Company helping us craft the overall response to drug-resistant tuberculosis. We're not there yet. If there were a market for tuberculosis drugs, then I think we'd have lots of new drugs. But because there's not one in the developed world, we're still struggling.

So we've learned a couple of things. One, intellectual property is important—but the drug companies, if you keep working with them, they'll see that there are great philanthropic and humanitarian achievements that they can claim for themselves by helping to make them accessible. We're not there yet, but the Gates Foundation, for example, is working very hard to fill the holes that the market is not filling. We've all got our fingers crossed, hoping that Bill and Melinda Gates will be successful in getting us these new drugs and vaccines.

But when you see health fairs where people who are so poor in this country go because they can't afford to have a toxic tooth pulled, how do you justify spending that much effort and that much money in Africa and Haiti and South America when we have such desperate need in this country?

They're two very different problems. Both of them break my heart. In the developing countries what we're doing is taking annual expenditures on health care from $2 or $3 per person up to maybe $15, $20, or $30. In the United States, where we're spending, on average, $7,000 per person per year, we should be able to find a way to provide health care for everyone. And I think we can do that fairly quickly if we put our minds to it. An example of the problem with health in the developing world is drug-resistant tuberculosis. The majority of the cases of drug-resistant tuberculosis in the United States are among the foreign-born, but it is not a smart idea to think that those kind of diseases are over there, and we're immune from them. We're not. In terms of infectious diseases and other health problems, we are one planet.

Yes, but friends and viewers write or say to me, "Moyers, don't bring us any more bad news. We don't want to see any more starving children in Rwanda, sick children in the Congo, or dying children in Haiti. If Bill Gates can't save them, there's nothing we can do." What keeps you from getting depressed?

For twenty-five years, in working with Partners in Health, we've really seen some tremendous changes. Haiti suffers from so many problems, including deforestation, poor health care, poverty, all these different kinds of problems, but in our one little area, not only have we built a health care system that now sees almost two million patients a year, but the trees have come back.

We just sort of did this almost quixotic little project where we kept planting trees. And the area around our clinic looks almost like the rain forest that it once was. So in going to those really difficult situations, first of all, it brings out a kind of humility that I don't feel unless I go and see the most excruciating thing on the face of the earth, which to me is a mother who can't feed her child. Having the experience of seeing those things does something to me as a person, to my soul. But then in seeing the possibilities, the programs that can turn things around, that's the most inspiring thing that I've ever seen.

Where does this passion come from in you? If an anthropologist walked in here and said, "Who is that person, where is he from?" what's the answer?

I've been very fortunate. You know, my father came by himself, across the North Korean border, when he was seventeen and hadn't seen his brothers or sisters or parents since then. He died some time ago, but never saw any of his relatives that he left behind in North Korea. My mother was a refugee in war-torn Korea and was plucked, because she was a good student, to come to Scarritt College in Tennessee. So there have been so many accidents of luck that have gotten me to this position. We first came to Dallas, Texas. My father had been a well-established dentist in Korea, but then had to do dental school all over again, because they didn't recognize Korean degrees. So he got his dental degree from Baylor's dental school, and then we moved to a small town in Iowa where I grew up and graduated from high school. My mother, who lived through war, graduated from Scarritt College and was given the great opportunity of completing her master's degree in divinity with Reinhold Niebuhr and Paul Tillich at Union Theological Seminary.

Two great theologians of the twentieth century.

Absolutely. It was one of the most exciting intellectual environments in the country at that time, in the 1950s. So we always had the sense from my mother that we should do something great, that there are great things to be done in the world. She would read to us the speeches of Martin Luther King in 1968. She even gave me Booker T. Washington to read when I was in grade school. So I had exposure to a lot of great thinkers. She kept trying to convince us that we had a responsibility in the world.

Now, my father was a dentist, one of the most practical people on the face of the earth. When I came back from my first semester at Brown University, he picked me up at the airport and we were driving home and I said to him, "Dad, I think I'm going to study philosophy." So he slowly pulls his car over to the side of the road, looks back at me, and says, "Look, when you finish your residency, you can do anything you want." It was clear: if I was going to make it in this country as an Asian American, he said, "You're going to need a skill. You can do anything with that. Whatever you do after you have that skill is okay." But, he said, "I can't go to my grave without knowing that you have some way of supporting yourself if everything else falls through."

Were you the only Asian family in that little town?

We were.

What was that like?

Well, we were comfortable economically. But if you go to a mall, just up the road, where they don't know who you are, of course, back in those days *Kung Fu* was the big exposure to Asian culture. So you know, everyone would come up to us and either be fearful or mocking. So racism was there. But I've come to understand that the racism that we felt wasn't the kind of racism that impacted African Americans in the South in the '30s and '40s and even more recently. It was different. I think I developed a sensitivity for people who are marginalized and outcast, but I don't have any illusions about me being an oppressed person. My father was a dentist, my mother was a philosopher. We loved Iowa Hawkeye football, so we had a great time there.

And you went on to train as an anthropologist as well as in medicine. What do you think the eye of an anthropologist sees that a physician on his or her own might not see?

In medicine, what we're trained to do is to look for patterns, to build order out of great complexity, out of very subtle signs and symptoms, and then have a plan where you can act. Anthropologists are a little bit different; we don't often act on what we see. So I'm sort of in the middle now. I do the ethnography, to try to get a sense of what the culture is. If you want to know what anthropologists do, one of my great professors, Sally Falk Moore, once said that it's very simple. You walk into a room and you say, "Who are these people and what do they want?" So if you're constantly asking that question, over time, you build up a sense of how a particular social system works. That's always what we've done. What is it that we need to do to actually change policy around HIV treatment or drug resistant TB treatment? That anthropological piece of it, linked to a physician's approach to solving a problem and putting a solution on the table, taking people through difficult times—that's been a very good combination for me. ～

W.S. MERWIN

A poem by William S. Merwin is a finely crafted thing. So is Merwin's life. He began the crafting of it at the age of eighteen, when Ezra Pound told him, "If you want to be a poet you have to take it seriously . . . and you have to do it every day." And "the way to do it is to learn a language and translate. You can learn a foreign language, but the translation is your way of learning your own language." Merwin listened, and went off to Princeton to study Romance languages. He began his career as a translator in England, France, and in Majorca, Spain, where he tutored the son of poet Robert Graves. He and started to jot down ideas for poems on "useless paper, scrap paper," which he keeps until he "can find out where it goes from there."

His first book of verse, A Mask for Janus, *was chosen for the Yale Younger Poets Prize by none other than W.H. Auden, whom Merwin later angered when, in 1971, he won the Pulitzer Prize and donated the money to the antiwar movement. Over the past half century Merwin kept winning major awards as he produced more than twenty-five volumes of poetry, a score of translations, ten works of prose, several verse plays, and a memoir,* Summer Doorways. *In 1976, he moved to Hawaii to study Zen Buddhism. He later married Paula Schwartz, and the two of them built a solar-powered home on an abandoned pineapple farm. Together, inch by inch, they restored the surrounding tropical rain forest, proving that nature, too, like a poem, can be a finely crafted thing.*

In July 2010, W.S. Merwin was named the seventeenth poet laureate of the United States, officially known as the consultant in poetry to the Library of Congress. We talked when he came to New York to accept his second Pulitzer Prize for his latest collection, The Shadow of Sirius.

—Bill Moyers

—◦◦◦—

Sirius is the Dog Star, the most luminous star in the sky, twenty-five times more luminous than the sun. Yet you write about its shadow, something no one has never seen, something invisible to us.

That's the point. The shadow of Sirius is pure metaphor, pure imagination. As we talk to each other, we see the light, our faces. But we know there's the other side that we never see. It's the dark, the unknown side, that guides us and that is part of our lives all the time. It's the mystery, always with us. And it gives depth and dimension to everything else.

"The Nomad Flute" is the first poem in the book. Would you read it?

THE NOMAD FLUTE

You that sang to me once sing to me now
let me hear your long lifted note
survive with me
the star is fading
I can think farther than that but I forget
do you hear me
do you still hear me

does your air
remember you
o breath of morning
night song morning song
I have with me
all that I do not know
I have lost none of it

but I know better now
than to ask you
where you learned that music
where any of it came from
once there were lions in China

I will listen until the flute stops
and the light is old again

"I have with me all that I do not know. I have lost none of it." We carry with us what we do not know?

We always do that. The most valuable things in our lives come out of what we don't know, Bill. And that's a process that we never understand. I think poetry always comes out of what you don't know. Now, I tell students knowledge is very important. Learn languages. Read history. Read, listen—above all, listen to everybody. Listen to everything that you hear. Every sound in the street. Every bird and every dog and everything that you hear. But know that while all of your knowledge is important, there is something you will never know. It's who you are. Who are you, Bill?

I would have to write a poem to try to get at that. And it would not be a very good poem. This line, "The star is fading"—what am I to make of that?

Whatever you want to. I mean, whatever the star is. Your star or the star that has lighted your life. It's also the morning, you know? The star fades in the morning. And you watch the star fade, and finally you don't see it. But you can think farther than that—farther than the star. You can think farther. But finally your thought comes to an end—lost in the what, we don't know, in the vast emptiness and unknown of the universe.

What intrigues me about Sirius is that while it appears to be a single star, it is in fact a binary system.

Yes.

Far more complicated than a single star. So that old truism is indeed true— there's always more than meets the eye?

Yes. And that's why I say that poetry arises out of the shadow of Sirius, out of that unknown, and speaks to what we do know. Shakespeare does it all the time. The novelist Russell Banks had a wonderful device that he used in teaching. He told me that he will give people a text—Chekhov's short story, or Conrad—and then ask them, after they have read it, "Where does the language leave the surface?" Of course, you can't do that with Shakespeare. Shakespeare's never on the surface. Shakespeare's always below the surface and above the surface.

That's difficult for me to grasp.

Look at the beginning of *Hamlet*, the characters on this bitter cold night. There's a sound, and the person coming onstage challenges the other one, saying, "Who is there?" Now, in the normal scheme of things that's wrong— it's the sentry who is supposed to challenge the newcomer. So you think he gets it wrong. Now, the original *Hamlet* apparently lasted five hours. People stood all that time and listened. Many of them couldn't read and write. And they were just absolutely hypnotized by that language. With Shakespeare, there's something from below the surface that's happening all the time. And even if you don't get every word, if you don't rationally understand every word that's going on—and we don't—something gets through. The poetry gets through. The power of those long soliloquies in *Hamlet*, or of Lear on the heath, or Prospero's speech about "We are such stuff as dreams are made on"—I've seen practically illiterate high school children watching a film in which there are a few lines of Shakespeare, and they put down the popcorn and sit up. They've never heard anything like this. He's got it. He's got some magic that—

Well, I don't understand all of your poetry, but I "get" it.

That's the important thing.

So what makes a poem work?

I don't know. I'll never know what makes a poem work.

But you once said that if a poem works, it is its own form.

Well, one of the things about poetry—and this is different from prose— when a poem is really finished, you can't move words around. You can't say, "In other words, you mean . . ." No, that's not it. There are no other words in which you mean it. This is it. And if it doesn't work, it doesn't work. But if it does work, that's the way it is.

Poetry can be quite physical. More so, at times, than prose.

It is. Poetry begins with hearing. You don't have to hear prose. You can read it off the front page of *The Times* and not hear a thing. But you can't read a sonnet of Shakespeare without hearing it. You hear "Shall I compare thee to a summer's day?" And you get it.

Poetry's really about what can't be said. Nobody finds words for grief. Nobody finds words for love. Nobody finds words for lust, or for real anger. These are things that always escape words.

Long ago, I gave up asking poets, "What do you mean by that?" Because they often don't know. The meaning is my response to it, isn't it?

That's part of it. But there are many shades of that meaning. And you certainly must have your own meaning, your own response to it. If you don't, you're not getting anything, are you? Your take on the poem is essentially what it's for. I mean, it is your poem. When you really get a poem, don't you feel you're remembering it? That you've discovered it yourself? In fact, you might have written it yourself.

You're on to something important. There is a quality to your poems—they can make me feel very vulnerable. And at the same time they are profoundly exhilarating. As if, here at this very late age, I'm connecting to something primordial. Like the mist rising over an ancient lake I once slept beside in East Africa. I hadn't thought of that lake or those mists in a long time. But as I read poem after poem in your book, I was reconnected.

I'm so happy to hear that, Bill.

But how do you explain it?

Oh, I don't explain.

The poem unlocks some experience.

It does in me. And that's something that I've felt ever since I was a child. I was very lucky. It's very important for parents to read to children—not just prose but poetry. Because listening to poetry is not the same as listening to prose. And those children who've grown up hearing a parent reading poems to them are changed by that forever. They have that experience forever. They always have that voice. They always hear it. My father was a minister. And I didn't remain a Christian. But—

Why?

I found the Apostle's Creed wasn't for me. I didn't believe it. But as a child I had to go to church several times a week. I didn't listen to his sermon so much, but I listened to him reading the Psalms and reading the Bible from the pulpit. And I was fascinated by the language. I was fascinated by hearing the Psalms. I still know many of the Psalms by heart.

What's your favorite?

Oh, "Have mercy upon me, O God, according to thy loving kindness." That certainly would be one of them. And the Shepherd's Psalm. You know—

The Twenty-third Psalm—

"The Lord is my shepherd"—

"The Lord is my shepherd, I shall not want." Yes, one of the first I learned. Is it true you wrote hymns for your father? At age five?

As soon as I could write with a pencil, I was writing these little hymns and illustrating them, and I thought they should be sung in church. But they never were.

Is that when you first began to engage with language?

That was part of it. And my mother read to me children's poetry. She read Robert Louis Stevenson's *A Child's Garden of Verses*. There are poems of Stevenson's that I still remember.

A CHILD'S GARDEN OF VERSES

Dark brown is the river,
golden is the sand.
It flows along forever,
with trees on either hand.
Green leaves a-floating,
castles of the foam,

Boats of mine a-boating—
where will all come home?

It's a beautiful poem. I still love it. Stevenson was a wonderful poet. And his last poem that he wrote from Samoa—"Blows the wind today . . ."—that's a wonderful poem. Homesickness. A poem of great homesickness.

When we confirmed this meeting, you suggested I read a poem in here called "Rain Light."

That's a very close poem to me:

RAIN LIGHT

All day the stars watch from long ago
my mother said I am going now
when you are alone you will be all right
whether or not you know you will know
look at the old house in the dawn rain
all the flowers are forms of water
the sun reminds them through a white cloud
touches the patchwork spread on the hill
the washed colors of the afterlife
that lived there long before you were born
see how they wake without a question
even though the whole world is burning

"Even though the whole world is burning." As it is.

Yes. It is burning, and we're part of the burning. Part of the doing it. Part of the suffering it. Part of the watching of it, helplessly and ignorantly. We know it's happening. It is our lives that are burning. We're not the person we were yesterday. Or twenty years ago.

Or when we were young. You have a poem in here called "Youth" that drives this home.

Well, when I was young, I didn't recognize youth. I was too young. And I write that I was looking for "you" all the time. And, of course, I couldn't find you, because you were right there. And it was only when I began to lose you that I began to recognize you.

There's a line from another poem of yours—I'll paraphrase it—where you talk about, "We no more are aware of aging than a bird is aware of the air through which it flies."

Yes. Youth, too. Youth is something that we don't understand as long as we have it. It's only when it's gone. But there are many things in life that are like that. Only when we move away from it do we get some perspective. When we've moved beyond them we can't touch them anymore. They're out of reach. I'll read that one.

YOUTH

Through all of youth I was looking for you
without knowing what I was looking for

or what to call you I think I did not
even know I was looking how would I

have known you when I saw you as I did
time after time when you appeared to me

as you did naked offering yourself
entirely at that moment and you let

me breathe you touch you taste you knowing
no more than I did and only when I

began to think of losing you did I
recognize you when you were already

part memory part distance remaining
mine in the ways that I learn to miss you

from what we cannot hold the stars are made

"From what we cannot hold, the stars are made." What can you tell me about that line?

Stars are what we can't touch. They guide us. And in a sense they are part of us. But we can't hold them. We can't possess them.

I can hear in my head Robert Kennedy speaking about his brother at the 1964

Democratic Convention, a few months after John F. Kennedy had been assassinated. He quoted from Romeo and Juliet:

> . . . when he shall die,
> Take him up and cut him out in little stars,
> And he shall make the face of heaven so fine
> That all the world will be in love with night
> And pay no worship to the garish sun.

Isn't that wonderful?

The stars seem to provide us with a glance of immortality.

There are so many myths, Bill, where the hero or heroine or the god or goddess at the end is simply transformed to become a constellation, always to be there, guiding lights from there on, forever in the sky.

This goes back a long time. Sirius, the star for whom you named your book, was closely associated with the Egyptian goddess Isis.

Yes. One of the great themes that runs through poetry is the feeling of loss. Not being able to hold or keep things. I mean, grief is the feeling of having lost, of having something being out of reach. Gone. Inaccessible. As I said before, I think poetry's about what can't be said, and that language emerges out of what could not be said, out of this desperate desire to utter something, to express something inexpressible. You see a silent photograph of an Iraqi woman whose husband or son or brother has just been killed, and you know that if you could hear, you would be hearing one long vowel of grief. A senseless, meaningless vowel of grief. And that's the beginning of language right there. That inexpressible sound. It's utterly painful beyond expression. And the consonants are the attempts to break it, to control it, to do something with it. I think that's how language emerged.

From perhaps the first woman in a cave who wakes up in the morning and puts her hand on her mate's cold body and knows instantly something profound is gone.

Yes.

There arises this need, you say—

Yes, yes.

—to express it. In a wail and in a word. Well, that helps me to understand why a lament seems to run through so many of your poems. You're an affirming person, but there's grief in many of your poems. Years ago we filmed you reading at the Dodge Poetry Festival. The poem was called "Yesterday." After that broadcast aired, several young men told me they went home and called their fathers.

Yesterday

My friend says I was not a good son
you understand
I say yes I understand

he says I did not go
to see my parents very often you know
and I say yes I know

even when I was living in the same city he says

maybe I would go there once
a month or maybe even less
I say oh yes

he says the last time I went to see my father
I say the last time I saw my father

he says the last time I saw my father
he was asking me about my life
how I was making out and he
went into the next room
to get something to give me

oh I say
feeling again the cold
of my father's hand the last time

he says and my father turned
in the doorway and saw me
look at my wristwatch and he

said you know I would like you to stay
and talk with me

oh yes I say

but if you are busy he said
I don't want you to feel that you
have to
just because I'm here
I say nothing

he says my father
said maybe
you have important work you are doing
or maybe you should be seeing
somebody I don't want to keep you

I look out the window
my friend is older than I am
he says and I told my father it was so
and I got up and left him then
you know

though there was nowhere I had to go
and nothing I had to do

I have missed my father often since his death almost twenty years ago, but I never missed him more so than when I heard you read that poem.

It's wonderful to know that a poem I've written connects with somebody else's experience. And that it becomes their experience. That's the way it should be.

Your poetry has become more personal in these later years.

Oh, I think, just getting older. I wanted each book to be distinct from the others. I look back at earlier books and realize I couldn't write those poems now. Each book was necessary in order to write the next one.

I've always wanted, through all of them, to write more directly and more simply. At one time in the early '60s there were critics who said, "Oh, Merwin is so impossible to understand. And clearly he doesn't want to be understood." At the same time, though, schoolteachers would come up to me and say, "I've been giving your poems to the children." And I would ask them, "What do they make of them?" And they answered, "Oh, they get along fine with them." I thought, "Fine, if the children get them." And I asked one of them, "What year do you teach?" She said, "Second year." Well, I thought, "If the young children get them, that's all that matters." Then a friend of mine said to me, "Oh, Bill, in fifteen years people will think you're extremely simple to read." I hope that's what's happened.

To what extent has the very personal nature of so many of your later poems been influenced by your embrace of Buddhism?

I don't know the answer to that, Bill. I don't because I don't know the alternative. Did the aspirin cure your headache? Or would you have got over it anyway? I don't know.

You do manage to see light in the darkness.

If we don't, we're in ultimate despair, with nothing left to be said. All of these things have been true always. We humans have been cruel and dishonest. We have been hopelessly angry and greedy. All of our faults have always been there. All of our failings. We haven't worked our way out of them. It's one reason I am skeptical of saints—people who are said to be past all human failings. I don't think so. And that's all right. I think that we should forgive ourselves and forgive each other if we possibly can. It's very difficult sometimes.

What about this poem in your new book? "Still Morning." Read it for me, please.

STILL MORNING

It appears now that there is only one
age and it knows
nothing of age as the flying birds know
nothing of the air they are flying through
or of the day that bears them up
through themselves
and I am a child before there are words
arms are holding me up in a shadow

voices murmur in a shadow
as I watch one patch of sunlight moving
across the green carpet
in a building
gone long ago and all the voices
silent and each word they said in that time
silent now
while I go on seeing that patch of sunlight

"That patch of sunlight." Where did you first see it?

Union City, New Jersey, in a church that was torn down many, many years ago.

Your father's church?

Yes, and I was being lifted up. May even have been when I was baptized. Very, very early—but I still remember it. Still remember the man in a brown suit. I later asked my mother, "Who was the man in the brown suit who was holding me?" And she said, "Oh, yes. That was Reverend So-and-So. He had come for a visit. And he said he would lift you up and hold you for the ceremony." I never saw him again, but I remember being held up and watching the green carpet and that patch of sunlight.

That happened where you grew up in New Jersey, across the Hudson River from where we're sitting right now. Here's another poem in your book from those years. You call it "The Song of the Trolleys."

Oh yes, there was a trolley car that went right past our house in Union City.

You seem to have the world in your ear.

Well, as I said, I believe poems begin with hearing. One listens until one hears something. People will ask me, "What are you listening to? And what are you listening for?" And I say, "That's what you have to find out." First you have to learn how to listen.

I had a portent the other day of our meeting. We took our two small grandchildren to the Central Park Zoo. Entering the rain forest preserve, we looked up and there's a quote from W.S. Merwin. Did you know it's there?

No.

It says, "On the last day of the world, I would want to plant a tree." Why would you want to plant a tree?

I guess it's because I would like to be putting life back into the world, rather than taking life out of it all the time. We do a lot of that, you know? I've lived on Maui for thirty-five years. And I feel very, very lucky to be there. The remnants of an ancient culture fascinate me. But it's where I could garden. I could be surrounded by a garden all year round. See life growing all around me. We live in a small valley leading down to the sea, and I love to get up well before daybreak, before the birds are awake. It's so beautiful in the morning. There are these lovely sounds. Sometimes late at night, I just stop everything before I go to bed and listen to the valley. People say it's a silent valley; it's so quiet. But listen and you hear the sound of the valley.

Which brings me to one of my favorite poems in the book. Read "The Long and Short of It."

The Long and the Short of It

As long as we can believe anything
we believe in measure
we do it with the first breath we take
and the first sound we make
it is in each word we learn
and in each of them it means
what will come again and when
it is there in meal and in moon
and in meaning it is the meaning
it is the firmament and the furrow
turning at the end of the field
and the verse turning with its breath
it is in memory that keeps telling us
some of the old story about us

And the experience there?

I think we know the experience every time we draw a breath. It's there in the beat of our hearts and in our breathing. And in the rhythm of our days. It's the basis of our lives and goes on evolving. It's mysterious. And we think we can measure it, but we know perfectly well with the other side of our minds that we can't measure it at all.

Sometimes when I look at the moon I think about how it's the same moon seen by Hadrian and Ovid and—

Oh, yes.

—and Shelley and Keats and Byron and Neruda.

I often think that.

This constancy of our gaze through the centuries.

There's a great poem by a Chinese poet by the late Tang Dynasty who wrote about seeing that same moon during a rebellion when everyone was getting killed. And he said, "This is the moon that guided me through the streets as I escaped. That led me to find my way out into the mountains. And here it is." He said, "I ask myself what can I believe everywhere." He said, "I believe the moon everywhere."

That it's—the constancy.

The constancy. What makes a blade of grass come up between the stones of the sidewalk? I'll never forget the great assurance I felt when my mother explained that the earth was under the sidewalk.

Do you think often of death?

I think we all think about death. And there's a connection to this feeling about words. Words come not from the threatening dark but the nourishing dark. The nourishing darkness. The dark and the light are always with us.

Let's close with another favorite of mine, one you wrote for your wife, Paula. How long have you two been married?

Oh, twenty-seven years. I was never sure that monogamy would overtake me. But it did when I met Paula.

And you wrote this poem to her late in spring.

We were in the old farmhouse in France. I was sitting in the little garden house that I built there years ago, and Paula was working in the garden.

To Paula in Late Spring

Let me imagine that we will come again
when we want to and it will be spring
we will be no older than we ever were
the worn griefs will have eased like the early cloud
through which the morning slowly comes to itself
and the ancient defenses against the dead
will be done with and left to the dead at last
the light will be as it is now in the garden
that we have made here these years together
of our long evenings and astonishment

And I thought, "This is it. It never gets better than this, you know?" ⌇

MIKE DAVIS

There was pandemonium among conservative polemicists when President Obama proposed a spending stimulus in response to the economic crash that occurred on George W. Bush's watch. Never mind that the Bush administration had just bailed out Wall Street, expanded government health care for the elderly, and turned huge surpluses into vast deficits. Suddenly, with a Democrat in the White House, a cry of "The Socialists Are Coming! The Socialists Are Coming!" resonated from right-wing ramparts all across cable, radio, and the blogosphere.

CNBC's resident showboating screwball, Jim Cramer—who, as God is my witness, refers to his viewers as "Cramericans"—was practically foaming at the mouth: "Guess who he's [Obama] taking his cues from? No, not Mao! Not Pancho Villa! . . . No, he's taking cues from Lenin! And I don't mean the 'All We Need Is Love' Lennon. I'm talking about we'll-take-every-dime-Cramericans-have Lenin."

Easy there, Jim. Better stick to decaf.

Odds are none of the swashbuckling paranoiacs on the right even know a socialist. It just so happens I do, and while he is sometimes controversial, you can bet your bottom dollar—if Obama hasn't already confiscated it—he's not on any White House guest list. Mike Davis describes himself as an "international socialist," which means he's come a distance, metaphorically, from his days as *a meatcutter and long-haul truck driver, although he's never forgotten what it takes to earn a living bloodying your hands on gristle or steering an eighteen-wheeler overnight.*

Mike Davis currently teaches creative writing at the University of California, Riverside, and writes books, good ones. In Praise of Barbarians: Essays Against Empire *is his latest. Two earlier histories of Los Angeles and southern California—*City of Quartz *and* Ecology of Fear—*were bestsellers and must reading for anyone with an interest in the social and economic development of the now-tarnished Golden State. When we spoke, six months after the financial meltdown of September 2008, California's economy had tanked, with one of the country's highest number of foreclosures and unemployment above 10 percent and climbing. Worse than much of the country, California was a financial earthquake off the Richter scale.*

—Bill Moyers

Did you ever imagine our financial system would be in such a sudden free fall?

No. And I found myself in the position of, say, a Jehovah's Witness, who believes the end is nigh but then one morning wakes up, looks out the window, and the stars are indeed falling from heaven. It's actually happened: the end is nigh! So no, I never imagined such catastrophes.

You've described this as the mother of all fiscal crises. Are the people you know frightened right now?

Oh, people are terrified, particularly where I teach in Riverside County. People have no idea where to turn. Our campus—University of California, Riverside—has the largest percentage of working-class students in the U.C. system. Their families have scrimped and saved. They've worked hard to get into courses that pointed toward stable careers and jobs. And now those futures are apparently incinerated.

You wrote an essay on TomDispatch.com in which you asked, "Can Obama see the Grand Canyon?" What's with the metaphor?

Well, the first explorers to visit the Grand Canyon were overwhelmed. They couldn't visualize the Grand Canyon because they had no concept for it. That is, there was no analogue in their cultural experience, no comparable landscape that would allow them to make sense of what they were seeing. It actually took ten years of heroic scientific effort by John Wesley Powell and some great geologists like Clarence Dutton before the Grand Canyon was seen in the sense that we understand it now: as a deep slice in earth history. Before then you just had confused images and feelings of vertigo.

I raise this to ask: Do we really have an analogy for the current crisis? Do we have the concepts to understand its profundity? Here we are seemingly on the brink of a second Great Depression, which is occurring at a time of epochal climate change. It's occurring at a time when the two major benchmarks for global social progress—the United Nations millennial goals for relieving poverty and child mortality, on one hand, and the Kyoto goals for reducing greenhouse emissions, on the other—are clearly not going to be achieved. This would be a time of fierce urgency in any sense. And on top of that, we are facing a meltdown of the world economy in a way that no one anticipated. No one counted on a financial calamity of this order to happen in such a synchronized, almost simultaneous way across the world.

So you wrote: "Like the Grand Canyon's first explorers, we are looking into an unprecedented abyss of economic and social turmoil that confounds our previous perceptions of historical risk. Our vertigo is intensified by our ignorance of the depth of the crisis or any sense of how far we might ultimately fall." That was five or six months ago. Any sense of how far we might ultimately fall?

No. I don't think anyone does. Nobody's seen the bottom here. We're working largely on the basis of hope and faith and crossing our fingers. We've invested in one person—the president—an almost messianic responsibility.

What's Obama done right so far?

I think what he's done most right is to push through the stimulus package, which I argue is primarily a relief bill, because obviously you can't talk about stopping the decline if you're going to allow the public sector—the local public sector, schools and public services on a state and local level—to collapse, as they are. You have to shore that up. Not that the stimulus is sufficient to address the totality of the fiscal crisis across the span of local governments, but it puts a Band-Aid over it. It extends unemployment compensation—gives a little more money to people who are out of work. My father was on WPA in 1935 . . .

Works Progress Administration, one of Franklin Roosevelt's creations.

Right. Of course, there's a big difference today. Every dollar he was paid by the federal government—98, 99 cents of it—went for products that were made in the United States or grown in the United States. One of my nephews just lost his job in Seattle. He takes his unemployment money down to Walmart or Sam's Club and buys stuff from China. Probably 40, 45 cents of the stimulus goes to the Chinese or the Korean economies. So the stimulus in this country, Keynesian stimulus, doesn't necessarily have the multiplier effect—if it doesn't create as many jobs or raise demand to the extent that it did during the 1930s when the United States had the largest, most productive industrial machine in the world. It could make almost anything. The question then was solely how to put the workers and machines back at work.

Today, after dismantling so much of our manufacturing base, so much of our national wealth, so much of our employment, is dependent on services linked to the financial role of the United States. But unlike Roosevelt, who could undertake institutional reforms that would reduce the control of banks over industry, now we're part of an integrated, interlocked system where what we can do on a national scale is ultimately limited by our creditors and by the dollar. Every part internationally has become so interdependent that it's hard to think about a general recovery without some kind of simultaneous and coordinated effort. And that seems to be utterly utopian at this moment.

In that essay, you asked the question "Is Obama FDR?" Well?

I'm prepared to concede that in terms of his character, his moral beliefs, his empathy and compassion for Americans, but above all in his understanding of the urgency and the unparalleled nature of this situation, yes, I mean, he could be Roosevelt. He could be Lincoln. But Bill, the obvious real heroes of the New Deal were the millions of rank-and-file Americans who sat down in their auto plants or walked on freezing picket lines in front of their factories. They made the New Deal possible. They provided the impetus to turn Washington to the left. We would be talking very differently about the legacy of Franklin Delano Roosevelt if it hadn't been for the incredible insurgency of labor and other ordinary Americans in the 1930s.

The garment workers left the Socialist Party, for example, and moved into the Democratic Party, giving Roosevelt an infusion of fresh blood.

A lot of them joined the American Labor Party in New York because they could not, in good conscience, ever pull that lever for Tammany Hall Democrats. You see, they wanted to support Roosevelt without supporting the Democrats. In the 1930s, of course, you had vigorous third parties often in power on state levels—the Farmer-Labor Party, the Commonwealth Federation, the Non-Partisan League. And you had militantly progressive Republicans from the heartland like George Norris and Bob La Follette, who in the current Senate would sit to the left of Bernie Sanders. Far more than FDR or even John L. Lewis, they were heroic crusaders against corporate greed and concentrated economic power. They exposed illegal monopolies, war profiteering, and violence against labor. For the first and only time in modern American history, they shined a populist light on the inner sanctums of the banks, particularly the vast spiderweb of secret power over an industry spun by the House of Morgan.

And that hasn't happened to Wall Street in this current crisis. The most fundamental, straightforward questions are not yet being asked: Who are the counterparties who own the credit default swaps? Who are the main creditors of these banks? As we bail out these big institutions with tens of billons of dollars of tax money, the public doesn't have any idea who's actually benefiting. Who are the parties that stand to gain?

Why don't we have that pressing inquiry and demand for accountability that we had in the 1930s?

In the 1930s we had an interesting coalition between a progressive middle class including, at that point, a lot of farmers still and a dynamic labor movement, even though it was divided, and a journalistic and literary culture that was in constant debate with the left. The left was all-important in the '30s. And I'm talking about not just the Communist Party but social democrats of all kinds. They weren't that significant a force politically, but they were significant intellectually. They were asking deep and profound questions about the nature of economic power, economic institutions. And this was leading in turn, if not to sweeping reforms, at least to big questions about who holds power, and how does economic power influence political decisions in Washington—all the things that today most Democrats and most Republicans are afraid to explore.

Why are they so afraid?

Because they're the beneficiaries of the system. In some cases I think the president has come to accept that there's really only one way he can operate, and that's through accommodating himself to the forces that exist and cutting compromises he sees as inevitable. They may talk about bank nationalization, but it's nothing more than salvaging the banks for the private sector rather than talking about the possibility of public ownership. It's really that we've lost so much of the reform conscience in America—this sense of the possible. We treat political positions as if they're entirely relative. We let Rush Limbaugh define what a liberal or a socialist is. You see, I think New Deal liberalism has a relatively precise historical benchmark definition.

Which is?

FDR's fourth-term election, when he ran on the idea of an Economic Bill of Rights for Americans, something that Lyndon Johnson believed in and tried to renew. And if you were to advance any agenda right now for how to get us out of this crisis, it would be to resurrect this concept of the real social citizenship, an economic Bill of Rights, and the need to strengthen the power of labor in the economy. The postwar "golden age" of the '50s and '60s was a period when unions were powerful enough to be major institutions of the macro economy. Wages were tied to productivity. Unions played a dynamic and incredibly central role in the American economy, which, of course, they lost in the late '70s and under Reagan. It was the strengthening of labor, the power of ordinary people in the unions that made the accomplishments of the New Deal possible. Remember, these were people who almost doubled the size of the American economy during the Second World War.

*There's a chorus of voices—*The Wall Street Journal *editorial page, conservative talk radio, Fox News, Lou Dobbs, CNBC's Kudlow and Cramer—all blaming Obama for the bad economy. How can the right thrive on such amnesia?*

What could be more absurd than the people who brought this country to its knees now being the chorus of dissenters? The fact that they are the lightning rod for popular anger is worrisome, because if these bailouts and stimulus fail, if the country sinks deeper into what could be a very long period of stagnation, if popular anger is monopolized by the demagogues on the right, you could see a real resurgence of the more rabidly extremist wing of the Republican Party, especially the anti-immigrant economic nationalist wing.

When you live near the border of southern California, as I do—or in the southern cities and areas of the Midwest—you can see the John Birch Society and its ilk being invigorated into the Republican Party. The vacuum left by the fall of the Soviet Union has been filled by good old-fashioned nativism—immigrant-bashing. No group is so vulnerable right now as the immigrants whose labor has sustained the California economy for the last generation, legal or unlegal.

They have the fewest entitlements. They have the weakest safety net. And their jobs are the ones that are being impacted most directly because they work in construction services or industries that are highly sensitive to the business cycle. Some have gone back to Mexico. But it doesn't make sense for most people to go back. The border economy has really collapsed. The tourist economy along the border is dead. The *maquiladoras*, the border assembly plants, are laying off. These people took huge risks to get to the United States, and they're expected to go back to a country where there are even fewer jobs and fewer hopes?

How are people surviving? Well, in some cases, they cram five into a room. They're standing in front of Home Depots hoping for a job and hoping they won't get picked up by the police or the immigration service. But it's very likely our southern border and Mexico are going to become further destabilized than they already are. And this will provide more ammunition for the right-wing myth of the economic crisis as a stab in the back: blame immigrants, blame liberals, blame the imaginary "socialism" of bank rescue plans that are in fact fully endorsed by capitalist journals like *The Economist* or the *Financial Times*.

There's so much talk from the right raising the specter of socialism. I thought I might as well talk to a real socialist about what the term means. I cannot find anyone in this country advocating the abolition of private markets or nationalizing the major industries. Is anyone you know arguing for supplanting capitalism?

I am.

You are?

Look, I'm a kind of old-school socialist in the way that Billy Graham's an old-school Baptist. I do genuinely believe in the democratic social owner-ship of the means to production. But that's religion. That's the religious principle.

And in practice?

Well, the role of the left—or the left we need in this country—is not to come up with utopian blueprints of how we're going to run an entirely al-ternative society, much less to express nostalgia about authoritative bureau-cratic societies like the Soviet Union or China. I think the left's mission is really to try to articulate the common sense of the labor movement and social struggles on the ground. So, for instance, you know, where you have the complete collapse of the financial system, and where the remedies pro-posed are privileging the creditors and the very people responsible for that, it's a straightforward enough proposition to say, "Hey, if we're going to own the banking system, why not make the decisions and make them in alliance with social policy that ensures that housing's affordable, that school loans are affordable, that small business gets credit?" Why not turn the banking system into a public utility?

Now, this doesn't constitute an anticapitalist demand. But it's a radical demand that asks fundamental questions about our institutions, about who holds the economic power. During the savings and loan crisis in the 1980s there was a period when the Resolution Trust Corporation was organized to buy up the abandoned apartments and homes and then sell them at fire sale rates to private interests. For a year or two it had the means of resolving much of the housing crisis in the United States. Why shouldn't the federal government basically turn that housing stock into a solution for people's housing needs? Sell them directly to homeowners at discounts or rent them out? In other words, the role of the left is to ask the deeper questions about who has power, how institutions work, and propose alternatives that seem more commonsensical in terms of satisfying human needs and equality in this society.

Frankly, President Obama and the liberal Democrats that still exist should actually welcome a revival of the left. It only strengthens them in a way. It's like being Martin Luther King without having Malcolm X. The problem with the Democrats is they fold. They end up conceding power and a veto ability to the Republicans when they don't need to do so. I'd welcome something of the spirit of Roosevelt when he took on the right wing of his own party as well as the right wing of the Republican Party.

FDR was called a socialist. They said he was conducting a class war. Now Obama is being accused by conservatives of launching a class war because he wants to return the tax rate to 39.9 percent, where it stood in the Clinton era. How would you have him deal with this charge of class war?

You deal with it by saying, "Yeah, we want class war, too." And here's what class war means—the only possibility of getting this country out of the crisis, the only possibility that really deep-set reforms can occur, including the protection and renewal of the productive base of the economy, is for working people to become more powerful. We need more protests. More noise in the street. At the end of the day, political parties and political leaderships tend to legislate what social movements and social voices have already achieved in the factories or the streets—in the civil rights demonstrations, for example. The problem is that so many progressives, so many liberals, now treat the new president as if he were *El Commandante*. We line up and follow his leadership. He, meanwhile, is maneuvering in a relationship of forces where people on the left, progressives, even the Black Caucus don't account for that much. He's appeasing Blue Dogs. He's having to deal with Republicans, and to an absolutely unnecessary extent, he's following the template of the Clinton years. And of course the Clinton years were the years of the closest collaboration between the financial industry and the White House that produced financial deregulation.

The best thing the president has done is the stimulus. The worst thing has been to continue the bailout along the same lines that were initiated by Bush's treasury secretary, Paulson. The majority of the American people truly rejected that bailout. They see it as rewarding the very people who ignited the crisis in the first place.

So what would you have us do?

Deglobalization, as people call it.

Reversing history?

Well, history can be reversed. The saddest thing about my own dad, who was a meat-and-potatoes guy, 1930s straight unionist, loved Roosevelt, is that he grew up in the early twentieth century believing in American history. Every time the American people struggled and won a new right, okay, that became a foundation for another struggle. Then, in the Reagan years, he saw history going in reverse. His union pension fund went bankrupt. The particular industry he worked in basically became defunct. And it was harrowing to me to see my father, who was the most patriotic guy I ever knew, struck by the realization that we're always fighting for principles and rights and they can be taken away. History can go in reverse. But by the same token, where does it say in the Bible that we should live in a globalized economy where the world's run by Wall Street or the authoritarian leaders of China? I haven't seen that text, have you?

No, but people with ideas like yours have been marginalized. No coverage in the press. No participation in the public debates. I'm curious—what made you so radical?

Well, in my case, there really was a burning bush. And that was the civil rights movement in San Diego, where I grew up, in the '50s and '60s. And when I was sixteen my father had a heart attack. I had to leave school for a while to work. And the black side of my family by marriage, they got me to come to a demonstration of the Congress of Racial Equality—CORE—in front of the Bank of America in downtown San Diego. It literally transformed my life, just the sheer beauty of it and the sheer righteousness of it. Now, I won't claim that every decision or political stance or political group I joined as a result of the civil rights movement was the right one. But it permanently shaped my life. Another turning point in my evolution toward the left was a conversation with an old friend of yours, a great Texas populist newspaper editor, Archer Fullingim. I was in Austin for a spell in 1967 and listened in awe as Fullingim gave a great speech about corporate power and the media. Many of my friends were becoming Marxists of one exotic stripe or another, but I was more interested in the history of the Peoples Party of the 1890s. Fullingim's electrifying speech reinforced my romantic belief in a Populist revival, so I made a pilgrimage to see him in southeast Texas. He was sitting on his porch out in Kountze, capital of the Big Thicket country, carving a gourd. I said, "Archer, can we revive the Populist Party? Can you lead the Populist Party?" And he looked at me. And he said, "Son, you're one of the dumbest pissants I've ever met." He said, "The Populist Party is history. Corporations run this country. And they run the Democratic Party. And you better figure out this stuff for yourself." And it's what I've been trying to do since.

Listen, to be a socialist in the United States is not to be an orphan, okay? It's to stand in the shadow of an immense history of American radicalism and labor, but with the responsibility to ensure its regeneration. I actually think the American left is about to receive a huge blood transfusion in the next year or two. It has to, because the existence of the left, of radical social and economic critiques, with an imagination that goes beyond selfishness, is necessary to have any kind of serious debate in this country.

You wrote recently, "I believe great opportunities lie ahead for the rebels of the world to swell our ranks and take the fight forward. A new generation of young people is discovering that their political engagement counts." Where are you seeing that?

Well, I have no difficulty finding hope. Hope kind of seeks me out. I've seen things in my life that I couldn't really believed had happened: black working people in the South standing up for themselves, antiwar GIs opposing stupid wars. When you've see such things like these happen in your life, you can never be pessimistic. There's an enormous legacy of the American left and of American radicalism in general that has to be nurtured and continued and passed down for new generations to shape in new ways. ❧

REVEREND JEREMIAH WRIGHT

There was a Jeremiah Wright before there was a Barack Obama, and it turns out, as you will see, that we actually had encountered each other, briefly, in 1965. But I was first aware of him as a churchman more than twenty years later, when the PBS documentary series Frontline went to Chicago to profile the minister who had become pastor of Trinity United Church of Christ.

The young and well-educated Reverend Wright could have had his pick of large, prosperous congregations but instead chose one with eighty-seven members in a largely black neighborhood of working-class and poor people on the South Side of the city. By the time Frontline showed up, the congregation had grown by thousands. There were soup kitchens for the hungry, day care for children, drug and legal counseling for the afflicted, and mentoring for the young. Jeremiah Wright called on the faithful to remember "the lowest, the least, the left out," and they did.

Wright was a builder, but he was also a boat rocker: he preached against corrupt politics, gang violence, and white supremacy. And he worked to build his people's pride. He installed stained-glass windows depicting the biblical stories that took place in Africa. And he asked parishioners to rededicate themselves to God, the black family, and the black community, to live up to Trinity's motto: "Unashamedly Black and Unapologetically Christian."

A young Barack Obama came to Chicago in the mid-'80s and went to work *on the South Side as an organizer. He was a religious skeptic who sought out Jeremiah Wright for his knowledge of the neighborhood. Soon he was attending Sunday services. In his book* Dreams from My Father, *he described his first service at Trinity:*

> *People began to shout, to rise from their seats and clap and cry out, a forceful wind carrying the reverend's voice up into the rafters. . . . And in that single note—hope!—I heard something else; at the foot of that cross, inside the thousands of churches across the city, I imagined the stories of ordinary black people merging with the stories of David and Goliath, Moses and Pharoah, the Christians in the lion's den, Ezekiel's field of dry bones. Those stories—of survival, and freedom, and hope—became our story, my story; the blood that spilled was our blood, the tears our tears; until this black church, on this bright day, seemed once more a vessel carrying the story of a people into future generations and into a larger world.*

In 1988 Obama was baptized at Trinity as a Christian. Twenty years later, his membership would become a political liability, as incendiary sound bites lifted out of context from Wright's sermons became fodder for Obama's opponents and the media: Wright suggesting the terrorist attacks of 9/11 were payback for American policy, Wright repeating the canard heard often in black communities that the U.S. government had spread HIV among the residents, Wright seemingly calling on God to damn America.

"That's not the man I know," my friend James Forbes told me on the phone after a week in which those inflammatory excerpts—most of them a few seconds in length—dominated the news. Forbes, one of the country's most influential preachers and now senior minister emeritus of New York City's historic Riverside Church, befriended Wright years ago through the fellowship of their faith. "You should interview him," Jim said. "Arrange it," I answered. And he did.

Jeremiah Wright and I met in New York at the height of the controversy. It was his first television interview during this period. We agreed to talk at length, and to end up dealing specifically with the controversial views that were now dogging him—and Obama—in endlessly repeated sound bites. First, however, I wanted to know about the man, the ministry, and the church.

—Bill Moyers

Let's start with first things first and provide my viewers with some background about you. I'm sure they want to know more about you than we've seen in those fleeting video clips. When did you hear the call to ministry? How did it come?

I was a teenager when I heard the call to ministry. I grew up in a parsonage. I grew up a son of, and grandson of, a minister, which also gave me the advantage of knowing that there were more things to ministry than pastoring. I had no idea that I'd be preaching or pastoring a church at that teenage year. As a matter of fact, I left Philadelphia for Virginia Union University. It was during the civil rights movement, and that movement showed me a side of Christianity that I had not seen in Philadelphia. I had not seen Christians like those I saw in Richmond, Virginia, who loved the Lord, who professed faith in Jesus Christ, and who believed in segregation, saw nothing wrong with lynching, saw nothing wrong with forcing Negroes to stay in their place. I knew about hatred. I knew about prejudice. But I didn't personally know Christians who participated in that kind of thing.

And how did you react?

It made me question my call. It made me question whether or not I was doing the right thing. It made me pause in my educational pursuit. I stopped school in my senior year, and went into the service.

You served six years in the military—two as a marine, and four in the navy as a cardiopulmonary technician. That's where our paths crossed for the only time. I have a photograph of President Lyndon Johnson recovering from gallbladder surgery at Bethesda Naval Hospital. You're right there beside him, behind the IV pole, monitoring the president's heart. And right behind you is a very young me. I was the president's press secretary.

That's right. And you know the president had to be operated on early and be out of surgery before the stock market opened. He wanted the world to know he was wide awake and talking. So the rest of us had to show up to scrub in at three o'clock in the morning. When he awakened, we did not move him to recovery as we would other patients. We kept him right there for security reasons, Secret Service all around, all over the operating suite, and nobody else allowed in there.

After about an hour and a half, I went to get some coffee. And as I was coming back from the lounge, I saw guys talking into their wristwatches. I was nodding to them, speaking to them, and as I turned to go back into the operating room, they grabbed me, knocked the coffee out of my hand—it burned me—twisted my arm up behind my neck, and one of them starts screaming into his phone: "I got him. I got him." I thought: "Got him? Got him? Who's him?" And I'm screaming in pain. Right then my assistant comes running up. He sees me jacked up that way and he starts laughing. I said, "Joe, don't laugh. Tell them who I am." And Joe says to the agent, "He's part of the team. He's been here all morning."

Standing right there beside the president of the United States!

Guy looked at me, pulled my mask up over my face. "Oh, *yeah*."

Quite a story—and I never heard it. After the military you graduated from Howard University and went to the University of Chicago Divinity School for a master's in the History of Religions. Then came the invitation by that struggling little church on the South Side of Chicago to be its pastor. When you looked out on that handful of worshippers that first Sunday morning—eighty-seven members, I understand, although I'm sure all of them weren't there—

Oh, yes, they were. They all knew this new kid with the big natural hairdo was going to be there. They made sure to show up.

What did you see in that church and what did you think you had to do?

Well, actually, a good friend of yours, and one of my professors at the University of Chicago, Dr. Martin Marty—

Longtime friend, one of our distinguished historians of religion in America.

Marty put a challenge to us back then. This is the late '60s, early '70s. I'll never forget. He said, "You know, you come into the average church on a Sunday morning and you think you've stepped from the real world into a fantasy world. Pick up a church bulletin and you will see what I mean. You leave a world with Vietnam in it, with all that's going on." Today, he'd say, "You leave a world with Iraq in it, and four thousand American boys and girls dead, and one hundred to two hundred thousand Iraqi dead, you leave the world of the hungry, suffering, and life as it is in the Lower Ninth Ward in New Orleans, and you come in your church and pick up the bulletin and it says there is a ladies' tea on the second Sunday, the children's choir will be doing this and that, and so on, and you will wonder, how come the church bulletin doesn't relate to the world to which those very church members are going back after the benediction?" Well, it hit me. And it hit me several different ways.

Number one, what about the prophetic voice of the church that's not heard? What are we to do with the ministry? Take our church. We were started by a white denomination and we were meant to be an integrated church. Ten years later that hadn't happened. What do we do in ministry that speaks to the reality around us? Martin Marty made me think about such things. He put the challenge to me.

Marty told me you launched a strenuous effort to help the members of that church overcome the shame, and I'm quoting him, "they had so long been conditioned to experience." What was the source of that shame?

What Carter G. Woodson calls the "Mis-Education of the Negro." That whole idea that Africa was ignorant, Africans were ignorant; there was no African history, no African music, no African culture; anything related to Africa was negative. Therefore, you were ashamed to be African, even African American. Chinese come to the country, they're Chinese American. Koreans come, they're Korean American. With us, the shame of being a descendant of Africa was a shame that had been pumped into the minds and hearts of Africans from the 1600s on, even aided and abetted by the benefit of those schools started by the missionaries, who simply carried their culture with them into the South so that European culture and Christianity became synonymous. So that to become a Christian, you had to let go of all vestiges of Africa and become European, become New Englanders and worship like New Englanders. People were made to feel shame for being black.

My predecessor at the church, Dr. Reuben Sheares, started using the phrase "unashamedly black and unapologetically Christian," so coming out of the 1960s, we didn't have to apologize for being black or for being Christian. Remember, many persons in the African American community teased us black Christians for following a white man's religion. We learned in this church that no, we don't have to be ashamed of being African American, and we don't have to apologize for being Christians.

When Trinity Church says it is unashamedly black and unapologetically Christian, is it embracing a race-based theology?

No, it is not. It is embracing Christianity without giving up our African past. A lot of missionaries to other countries assumed their own culture was superior, that Africans had no culture of their own. And they said, "To be a Christian, you must be like us." Right now, you can go to Ghana, Nigeria, Senegal, and see Christians in 140-degree weather who have on a tie—because wearing a tie was what it meant to be a Christian, as on Sundays in New England. And the missionaries said, in effect, "We have the only sacred music. You must sing our music. You must use a pipe organ. You cannot use your instruments."

They were taught to sing the great Anglican hymns and sing them the way the English and Americans sang them, right?

Correct, correct. And make sure you use correct diction. Well, African Americans in the late '60s started saying, "No, no, no, no, no, no, no." I was a soloist in the concert choir at Virginia Union in the early '60s. We were not allowed to sing anything but anthems and spirituals. The same thing with the Howard University concert choir. The same thing with all the historically black choirs until '68. Can you believe that for a long time there was no gospel music at Howard University—an all-black school? There was no jazz major. The white universities were giving Count Basie and Duke Ellington degrees. We didn't even have a blues course. It goes back to when the missionaries had not allowed us to teach our own music. And in the '60s, as you'll remember, all across the country and all across denominational lines, college-age kids started saying: "No more. *No más. Nada más.* We're going to do our culture, our history. And we're not going to say one is superior to the other. We are different, but different does not mean deficient. We're different like snowflakes are different. We're proud of who we are"—that's the statement my congregation was making. It's not about a race-based theology.

So, contrary to some of the rumors that have been circulated about Trinity, God is not exclusively identified with only the black community?

Of course not. What we have in our church is what people call "multicultural" these days. We have Hispanic members, members from Cuba, from

Puerto Rico, from Belize—all of the Caribbean islands, in fact. We have members from South Africa, from West Africa, and we have some white members.

What does the Sunday morning worship service mean to them?

It means hope, for one thing. Like David says in the Book of Psalms, I would have fainted unless I lived to see the goodness of the right in this life. Don't tell me about heaven. Tell me there's a better way in this life. We're not about Edward Albee or Camus's theater of the absurd. We're not about Shakespeare—full of sound and fury, signifying nothing. We're about God and people of goodwill working hard together to do something about conditions in this life. We tell ourselves we can change, we can do better. We remind ourselves that before Martin Luther King and the civil rights movement, we did not have a Civil Rights Act. We did not have a Voting Rights Act. See? Change is possible. That's what our church says. So our people come looking for hope. They've been getting their heads whipped all week. And we try to move them from hurt to healing.

You're talking about members of Trinity who are experiencing unemployment, a daily struggle, discrimination. They come from the real world to worship.

They come for encouragement, to not just talk about heaven "by and by," but to learn that we are not alone in this struggle, and that the struggle can make a difference. Not to leave that world and come to church pretending that we are now in some sort of fantasy land, but that we serve a God who enters history on the side of the oppressed, that we serve a God who cares about the poor, that we serve a God who says "inasmuch as you've done unto the least of these, my little ones, you've done unto me." This God says, "I'm with you in the ongoing struggle."

As I understand it, black liberation theology reads the Bible through the long experience of people who have suffered, who then are able to say to themselves that we read the Bible differently because we have struggled. Is that a fair bumper sticker of liberation theology?

I think that's a fair bumper sticker. I think that the terms "liberation theology" and "black liberation theology" cause more problems and red flags for people who don't understand it.

When I hear about "black liberation theology" as the interpretation of scripture from the vantage point of the oppressed, well, that's the Jewish story.

Exactly, exactly. From Genesis forward. These are people who stayed on message through Egyptian oppression, Assyrian oppression, Babylonian oppression, Persian oppression, Greek oppression, Roman oppression. See, because of that, their understanding of what God is saying is very different from the Greeks, the Romans, the Egyptians. And that's why the prophetic theology of the African American church is different.

Here's where the trouble comes, though. The Hebrew prophets loved Israel. But they hated the waywardness of Israel. And they were calling Israel out of love back to justice, not damning—

Exactly.

Not damning Israel, right?

Right. In fact, if you look at the damning and the condemning—well, look at the book of Deuteronomy, it talks about blessings and curses, how God doesn't bless everything. God does not bless gangbangers. God does not bless dope dealers. God does not bless young thugs who hit old women upside the head and snatch their purse. God does not bless that. God does not bless the killing of babies. And when you look at blessings and curses out of that Hebrew tradition, that's what the prophets were saying, that God is not blessing this. God calls them through the prophets to repentance. "If my people, who are called by my name," God says to Solomon, "will humble themselves and pray, seek my faith and turn from their wicked ways, then will I hear from heaven." That's God talking, not Jeremiah Wright.

Well, you know that one of your most controversial sermons is the one that ended up with the sound bite "God damn America." Here's a portion:

> *REVEREND JEREMIAH WRIGHT, APRIL 13, 2003: Where governments lie, God does not lie. Where governments change, God does not change. And I'm through now. But let me leave you with one more thing. Governments fail. The government in this text comprised of Caesar, Cornelius, Pontius Pilate—the Roman government failed. The British government used to rule from East to West. The British government*

had a Union Jack. She colonized Kenya, Ghana, Nigeria, Jamaica, Barbados, Trinidad, and Hong Kong. Her navies ruled the seven seas all the way down to the tip of Argentina in the Falklands, but the British government failed. The Russian government failed. The Japanese government failed. The German government failed. And the United States of America government, when it came to treating her citizens of Indian descent fairly, she failed. She put them on reservations. When it came to treating her citizens of Japanese descent fairly, she failed. She put them in internment prison camps. When it came to treating citizens of African descent fairly, America failed. She put them in chains. The government put them in slave quarters, put them on auction blocks, put them in cotton fields, put them in inferior schools, put them in substandard housing, put them in scientific experiments, put them in the lowest paying jobs, put them outside the equal protection of the law, kept them out of their racist bastions of higher education, and locked them into positions of hopelessness and helplessness. The government gives them the drugs, builds bigger prisons, passes a three-strike law, and then wants us to sing "God Bless America?" No, no, no. Not God bless America; God damn America! That's in the Bible, for killing innocent people. God damn America for treating her citizens as less than human. God damn America as long as she keeps trying to act like she is God and she is supreme!

What did you mean?

When you start confusing God and government, your particular government with God, then you're in serious trouble, because governments fail people. And governments change. And governments lie. And that is the context in which I was illustrating how governments since biblical times, up to our time, how they failed and how they lie. And when we start talking about "my government right or wrong," I just don't think that goes. Governments that want to kill innocents are not consistent with the will of God. You are made in the image of God, not in the image of any particular government. We have the freedom in this country to talk about this publicly, whereas some other places, you're dead if you say the wrong thing about your government.

You can almost be crucified for saying certain things in this country.

That's true. That's true. You can be crucified by corporate-owned media. But as I just said, you can be killed in other countries by the government for saying that. Dr. King, of course, was vilified. And most of us forget that on April 4, 1967, a year before he was assassinated, he came here to New York City's Riverside Church and talked about racism, militarism, and capitalism. He became vilified. He was ostracized not only by the majority of Americans and by the press, he was vilified by his own community. They thought he had overstepped his bounds. He was no longer talking about civil rights, sitting down at lunch counters and all that—he was talking about the war in Vietnam.

President Johnson was furious at him for that. That's where they broke.

And that's where a lot of the African American community broke with him, too. He was vilified by Roy Wilkins and by Jackie Robinson. He was vilified by many of the Negro leaders who felt he had overstepped his bounds talking about an unjust war. And that part of King is not lifted up every year in all the memorial services. "I have a dream" is lifted up, and passages like that—sound bites, if you will—from that March on Washington speech. The King who preached, "I've been to the mountaintop, I've looked over. And I've seen the Promised Land. I might not get there with you," that part of the speech is talked about, but not the fact that he was in Memphis siding with garbage collectors who wanted a raise. Nothing about Resurrection City, nothing about the poor—

Resurrection City was the march in Washington for the poor.

For the poor. That part of King is not talked about. It's been off-limits for forty years now.

Why do you think so many Americans don't seem to want to acknowledge that a nation capable of greatness is also capable of cruelty?

I come at that as an historian of religion. We are miseducated as a people. And because we're miseducated, you end up with the majority of the people not wanting to hear the truth. They stick with what they were taught. James Washington, a church historian now deceased, says that after every revolution, the winners of that revolution write down what the revolution was about so that their children can learn it, whether it's true or not. They don't learn anything at all about the Arawak. They don't learn anything at all about the Seminole, or the Cherokee Trail of Tears. No, they don't learn that. What they learn is that in 1776 there was one black guy in the fight against the British. They weren't taught that the words "We hold these truths to be self-evident, that all men are created equal" were written by men holding slaves. No, keep that part out. Don't learn that. So people cling to what they were taught. And when you start trying to show them they have a piece of the story, here's the rest of the story, you run into vitriolic hatred because you're desecrating our myth, you're desecrating what we hold sacred. And when you're holding sacred a system of miseducation that has not taught you the truth, then you don't understand the meaning of *condemn*, d-e-m-n, d-a-m-n. They don't understand the root, the etymology of the word in terms of God condemning the practices that are against God's will and God's people. What is happening today is that I am talking about truth. Reading the scripture or the hermeneutics of a people.

Hermeneutics is an interpretation. It's the window through which you're looking. See, the story is framed through this window, and if you only see it through this window, you don't take into account the world seen through another window. Your story is informed by and limited by your hermeneutics. The theologian James Cone put it this way: the God of the people who are riding on the decks of the slave ship is not the God of the people who are riding underneath the decks as slaves in chains. If the God you're asking to bless slavery is not the God to whom other people are praying, "Get us out of slavery," it's not like Notre Dame playing Michigan. You're not flipping a coin and hoping God blesses the winning team, no. The God who is perceived as allowing slavery, allowing rape, allowing misogyny, allowing sodomy, allowing the murder, the lynching of people—that's not the God of the people being lynched and sodomized and raped and carried away into a foreign country. Same thing you find in the Hebrew Bible. Those people who are carried away into slavery have a very different concept of what it means to be the people of God than the ones who carried them away.

And they ask: "How can we sing the song of the Lord of a foreign land?" You used them in one of your sermons.

Yes, I did. I was trying to show how we felt anger. I felt anger. I felt hurt. I felt pain. In fact, September 11, I was in Newark, New Jersey, across the river from the World Trade Center. I was trapped in Newark because when they shut down the airlines, I couldn't get back to Chicago. I saw the second plane hit from my hotel window. And I had members who lost loved ones both at the Pentagon and at the World Trade Center.

So I know the pain. And I had to preach to my people that Sunday. I had to preach. They came to church wanting to know, where is God in this? Using Psalm 137, I tried to show them how the people who were carried away into slavery were very angry, very bitter, moved, and in their anger wanting revenge against the armies that had carried them away to slavery. That text ends up saying, "Let's kill, let's bash their babies' heads against the stones." So you move from revolt and revulsion to wanting revenge. You move from anger with the army against you to taking it out on the innocents. You even want to kill babies. That's what's going on in Psalm 137. The Hebrew people wanted revenge. And that's exactly where we are. We want revenge. But God doesn't want to leave you there. God wants redemption. God wants wholeness. And that's the context, the biblical context, that I used to try to get people sitting in that sanctuary on that Sunday after 9/11, who wanted to know, "Where is God in this? What is God saying? Because I want revenge."

Here is part of that sermon:

> REVEREND WRIGHT, SEPTEMBER 16, 2001: *The people of faith have moved from the hatred of armed enemies, these soldiers who captured the king, those soldiers who slaughtered his son and put his eyes out, the soldiers who sacked the city, burned the towns, burned the temples, burned the towers, and moved from the hatred for armed enemies to the hatred of unarmed innocents, the babies, the babies. "Blessed are they who dash your baby's brains against a rock." And that, my beloved, is a dangerous place to be. Yet that is where the people of faith are in 551 BC, and that is where far too many people of faith are in*

2001 AD. We have moved from the hatred of armed enemies to the hatred of unarmed innocents. We want revenge. We want paybacks, and we don't care who gets hurt in the process. I heard Ambassador Peck on an interview yesterday. Did anybody else see him or hear him? He was on Fox News. This is a white man, and he was upsetting the Fox News commentators to no end. He pointed out. Did you see him, John? A white man. He pointed out—an ambassador!—that what Malcolm X said when he got silenced by Elijah Muhammad was in fact true. America's chickens are coming home to roost! We took this country by terror away from the Sioux, the Apache, the Arawak, the Comanche, the Arapaho, the Navajo. Terrorism! We took Africans from their country to build our way of ease and kept them enslaved and living in fear. Terrorism! We bombed Grenada and killed innocent civilians, babies, non-military personnel. We bombed the black civilian community of Panama with stealth bombers and killed unarmed teenagers and toddlers, pregnant mothers and hardworking fathers. We bombed Gaddafi's home and killed his child. "Blessed are they who bash your children's head against a rock!" We bombed Iraq. We killed unarmed civilians trying to make a living. We bombed a plant in Sudan to pay back for the attack on our embassy. Killed hundreds of hardworking people, mothers and fathers who left home to go to work that day, not knowing that they would never get back home. We bombed Hiroshima! We bombed Nagasaki, and we nuked far more than the thousands in New York and the Pentagon, and we never batted an eye! Kids playing in the playground, mothers picking up children after school, civilians—not soldiers—people just trying to make it day by day. We have supported state terrorism against the Palestinians and black South Africans, and now we are indignant? Because the stuff we have done overseas is now being brought back into our own front yards! America's chickens are coming home to roost! Violence begets violence. Hatred begets hatred and terrorism begets terrorism. A white ambassador said that, y'all, not a black militant. Not a reverend who preaches about racism. An ambassador whose eyes

are wide open, and who's trying to get us to wake up and move
away from this dangerous precipice upon which we are now
poised.

You preached that sermon on the Sunday after 9/11. That was almost seven
years ago. This year, when people saw some sound bites from it, they were
upset because you seemed to be blaming America. Did you somehow fail to
communicate?

The persons who have heard the entire sermon understand the communication perfectly. The failure to communicate is when something is taken out of context like a sound bite for a political purpose and looped over and over again, looped in the face of the public. Those who are doing that are communicating exactly what they want to communicate—to paint me as some sort of fanatic or, as a learned journalist from *The New York Times* called me, a "wackadoodle." It's to paint me, to say something's wrong with me; there's nothing wrong with this country. We're perfect; we have no blood on our hands. I say it again, that's not a failure to communicate. The message that is being communicated by the sound bites is exactly what those pushing those sound bites want to communicate.

What do you think they wanted to communicate?

I think they wanted to communicate that I am unpatriotic, that I am un-American, that I am filled with hate speech, that I have a cult at Trinity United Church of Christ in Chicago. And—hint, hint, hint—guess who goes to his church? Hint. That's what they wanted to communicate. They know nothing about the church. They know nothing about our prison ministry. They know nothing about our food-sharing ministry. They know nothing about our senior citizens' homes. They know nothing about all we try to do as a church and have tried to do, and still continue to do as a church that believes what Martin Marty said, that the two worlds have to be together—the world before church and the world after the benediction. And that the gospel of Jesus Christ has to speak to both of those worlds, not only in terms of the message preached on a Sunday morning but in terms of the lived-out ministry throughout the week.

When you began to see those very brief sound bites circulating as they did,
what did you think?

I felt it was unfair. I felt it was unjust. I felt it was untrue. I felt those who were doing that were doing it for some very devious reasons, to put an element of fear and hatred into the "game" and to stir up the anxiety of Americans who still don't know the African American church, know nothing about the prophetic theology of the African American experience, who know nothing about the black church, who don't even know how we got a black church in this country in the first place.

What's happened at the church since this controversy flared?

Our members are very upset, because they know it's a lie, the things that are being broadcast. Church members have been very supportive. But they're upset by the behavior of some of the media—picking up church bulletins to get the names and addresses and phone numbers of the sick and shut-in, calling them to try to get stories. One lady they called was in hospice. Our members are very upset about that. Very upset. They know it's happening because of the political campaign. What have we gotten into here? Some people—Christians, some of them—threatening us, quoting scripture, telling us how they're going to wipe us off the face of the earth in the name of Jesus.

There have been death threats?

Yes, there have. Both on myself and on my successor, Pastor Moss, and bomb threats at the church.

Did you ever imagine that you would come to personify the black anger that so many whites fear?

No. I did not. I have been preaching since I was ordained forty-one years ago. I've been reminding people since all this happened of the stance I took in standing against apartheid along with our denomination back in the '70s and how putting a "Free South Africa" sign in front of the church put me at odds with the government. Our denomination's defense of the Wilmington Ten* put me at odds with the establishment. Being at odds with policies is

---

*The Wilmington Ten were a group of civil rights activists imprisoned on charges of arson and conspiracy arising from a firebombing and riot in Wilmington, North Carolina, in 1971. Their convictions were overturned in 1980.

nothing new to me. But taking bits and pieces of sermons I preached six, seven, ten, fifteen years ago and turning them into a media event—not the full sermons, but snippets and sound bites making me the target of hatred— that is something very new and something very, very unsettling.

I know how in times like this music is very important to you and your congregation.

It is. I told you earlier that I struggle with how to take a people who are hurting and bring them to healing. How do you take a people who are suffocating with hate and give them hope? Well, a part is through the musical tradition. The blues is key. We learned how to sing the blues. That's why our suicide rate wasn't much higher, because we started singing the blues. Well, people sitting there in the pews every Sunday, they know that tradition. That's a part of what helps us hold it together.

You said something about suicide?

Blacks learned how to sing the blues rather than just give up on life. A guy's wife walks out on him with his best friend and he's crushed. Instead of going out and taking a gun and killing, he sings a song. "I'm going down to the railroad to lay my poor head on the track. I'm going down to the railroad to lay my poor head on the track. And when the locomotive comes, I'm gonna pull my fool head back." He's not giving up life over this. Life goes on beyond this. Pain is just for a moment. This whole notion about what we're going through is only a season. "And this came to pass, didn't come to stay." That's what the blues do. And that's what the music tradition does. So, trying to keep that as an integral part of worship is crucial for us.

So what blues are you singing right now?

"Don't know why they treat me so bad." I'm singing the sacred blues, the songs of our gospel tradition. That I'm so glad trouble don't last always. That "what man meant for evil, God meant for good."

"What man meant for evil, God meant for good."

That's a quote from Joseph, in the Book of Genesis.

And what do you take it to mean?

That human beings many times do things for nefarious purposes. And God can take that and turn it—make something good out of it. For instance, using that Joseph passage, when his brothers sold him into slavery, they thought for sure that their daddy was going to get them. And Joseph reassured them by saying, "No, no, what you meant for evil, God has turned into something good. I'm not trying to do revenge or payback. God is about restoration. And I restore you. As brothers, we're all brothers."

Sure, those sound bites, those snippets were taken for nefarious purposes. But God can take that and do something very positive. In Philadelphia, as you know, Barack Obama made a very powerful speech about our need as a nation to address the whole issue of race. That's something good that's already starting because of those guys playing these sound bites; something very positive may come out of it. God can take what they meant to hurt somebody and help our nation come to grips with truth, to help a nation come to grips with miseducation, to help a nation come to grips with things we don't like to talk about.

In the twenty years that you've been Obama's pastor, have you ever heard him repeat any of your controversial statements as his opinion?

No. No. No. Absolutely not. I don't talk to him about politics. At a political event he goes out as a politician and says what he has to say as a politician. I continue to be a pastor who speaks to the people of God about the things of God.

Here's a man who came to see you twenty years ago wanting to know about the neighborhood. At the time Barack Obama was a skeptic about religion. He sought you out because he knew you knew the community. You led him to the faith. You performed his wedding ceremony. You baptized his two children. You were for twenty years his spiritual counselor. In that speech in Philadelphia the other day, he was obviously trying to have it both ways in responding to the controversy over you. He condemned statements by you that "have caused such controversy." He said they express "a profoundly distorted view" of America and are not only "wrong but divisive." But he also defended you. He said—and this is a direct quote—"Not once in my conversations with him have I heard him talk about any ethnic group in derogatory terms, or treat whites with whom he interacted with anything but courtesy and respect." He praised your learning, your patriotism, your faith and compassion. And he said that while "we can dismiss Reverend Wright as a crank or a demagogue," the whole controversy reflects the complexities of race that the country has yet to work through. How did it go down with you when you heard Barack Obama say those things?

It went down very simply. He's a politician, I'm a pastor. We speak to two different audiences. And he says what he has to say as a politician. I say what I have to say as a pastor. Those are two different worlds. I do what I do. He does what politicians do. What happened in Philadelphia, where he had to respond to the sound bites, he responded as a politician. But he did not disown me because I'm a pastor.

Even some of your admirers say it would be wrong to gloss over what Martin Marty himself—who loves you—called your "abrasive edges." For example, Louis Farrakhan lives in the south part of Chicago, doesn't he? You've had a long, complicated relationship with him, right?

Yes.

And he's expressed racist and anti-Semitic remarks. Some indefensible things—

Twenty years ago.

Twenty years ago, but indefensible, no?

The Nation of Islam and Mr Farrakhan have helped more African American men to get off drugs, more African American men to respect themselves, more African American men to work for a living instead of gangbanging. Turning people's lives around. Giving people hope. Now, he and I don't believe the same things in terms of our specific faiths. He's Muslim, I'm Christian. We don't believe the same things that he talked about all those years ago. But that has nothing to do with what he has done in terms of helping people change their lives for the better. When Louis Farrakhan speaks, black America listens. They may not agree with him, but they're listening.

What does it say to you that millions of Americans, according to polls, still think Barack Obama is a Muslim?

It says to me that the miseducation or misinformation or disinformation of the corporate media still reigns supreme. Thirty-some percent of Americans still think there are weapons of mass destruction in Iraq. You tell a lie long enough, people start believing it. What does the media do? "Barack *Hussein* Obama! Barack *Hussein* Obama! Barack *Hussein*." It sounds like Osama, Obama. That's why many people still think he's a Muslim.

The United Church of Christ—our denomination—has called for a "sacred conversation" on race in America. What are the steps that can be taken to move race relations forward?

There are many. Let's start with the paradigm about how one sees God. Your theology determines your anthropology. And your anthropology— how you see humans—determines your sociology. Let's look at how we've come to see race based on an understanding of God who is said to see others as less than important. You know, there are plenty of passages in our sacred scriptures that are racist. They're in the Vedas, the Babylonian Talmud, in the Koran, they're in the Bible. How do we grapple with these passages in our sacred texts? The same way you grapple with that passage in the book of Judges where it's all right for a preacher to have a concubine and cut her up into twelve pieces. We have to argue with our texts that are anti-Semitic. That old Christian notion, "the Jews killed Jesus." We have to come to grips with these texts that were written by certain people at certain times with certain racist understandings of others who were different. We have to understand that "different" doesn't mean deficient. Barack Obama talked about the need to start a new conversation. Let's have the conversation we need to have.

Note: There was more I wanted to hear about from Jeremiah Wright, including his relations with Jews and his views on Israel, but at this point our interview was interrupted by Wright's daughter, who was acting as his media advisor. She came into the studio and announced that he had to leave. The reverend didn't seem to be in any hurry to go—he seemed comfortable in the intimate space where we talked—but no sooner had we resumed the conversation than his daughter reappeared with his security detail (traveling with him because of earlier death threats) and insisted our time was up.

The following Monday, at the National Press Club in Washington, the reverend delivered a statement that he had carefully prepared for an audience who obviously had never attended a service like that one described by Obama, people Wright knew to be "completely outside the black religious experience."

He wanted them to understand the theme of transformation—"God's desire for changed minds, changed laws, changed social orders . . . a changed world." But during the question period that followed—no longer surrounded by an adoring congregation and unaccustomed to a throng of inquiring reporters—Wright was rattled. The quiet and composed man I had met on Friday grew querulous, aggrieved, and, at moments, incomprehensible. It was a disastrous performance. The next day Obama denounced Wright, and a month later, the candidate resigned his membership in Trinity Church. ~

BARRY LOPEZ

When Barry Lopez accepted the National Book Award for Arctic Dreams back in the mid-1980s, I clipped an article about the occasion from The New York Times and dropped it into a file labeled "Worth Pursuing," as was my habit then and now. More than a score of years later, heading for the final weeks of the Journal, while thumbing through the bulging folder, I came upon that now yellowed clipping. Our paths had not crossed in all these years—we seemed always to be traveling in different directions—but I realized the moment had come for a conversation.

Throughout that time, Barry Lopez had kept writing—nonfiction and novels, essays and short stories, volumes of prose about travel, photography and language—setting a gold standard for those of us journalists whose self-proclaimed mission is to explain things we don't understand. Barry did it the old-fashioned way: going out to see for himself. He became as familiar with the playas of Texas and the deserts and canyons of the American Southwest as he did with the frigid extremes at both poles. But always he returned home to western Oregon to write with what one reviewer called "the snap and hiss of a campfire." Natural landscapes have fascinated him since he was a boy, but he also explores the interior journeys that shape our own private worlds.

As another reviewer wrote, Barry Lopez "restores to us the name for what it is we want." He would be my final guest on the Journal, which meant

*a trip back to the asphalt and skyscrapers where he had spent part of his
childhood.*

—*Bill Moyers*

—∞∞—

*How is it to be back in the canyons of New York City after all the time you've
spent in the far places of the world?*

I like it here. There is a shade of blue in the sky here that I always associate with the city. Whenever I see it, driving in from the airport or on
a winter evening, just moonlight and the blue and the canyons below the
buildings—well, Bill, it intensifies my sense of hope to see a vibrant aggre-
gation of human imaginations underneath this mantle of a blue sky. I don't
have a sense, "Oh, my God, I'm coming into Sodom and Gomorrah," some
dead-end place for humanity. A city like this, it's the best we can do. It's
uplifting.

*Paradoxically, as you talk I'm thinking about the clear blue sky over New
York on the morning of September 11. One of the most beautiful mornings you
could hope for. My wife and I were looking out the window in awe of it when,
just a couple of miles away, terrorists were driving those two planes into the
World Trade Center. I will always associate the blue sky with that moment.
You've written about "courting the imagination." How does such a paradox—
the beauty and the terror—affect your imagination?*

You have to see the paradox as a large truth, and as a caution. We have a
way of talking about beauty as though beauty were only skin deep. But
real beauty is so deep you have to move into darkness in order to understand it. It's just what you said. You're talking to your wife and this blue
sky goes gray. Horror overtakes us. You can't separate those two things.
But we have to be as aware of the beauty as we are of the darkness. I visit
Auschwitz, or I go to Sumatra soon after the great tsunami, and I realize
there's no hope for anyone who remains traumatized by such horror for
the rest of their life.

   You know, people say you shouldn't talk about certain things, because
others get nervous when you do. Torture, for example. But a person who
speaks in public of what is beautiful—that also makes people nervous,

especially people who maintain, for whatever reason, a jaded, cynical separateness from the world.

It also makes some people anxious when you speak of faith, because immediately they think, "Christian faith? Or Islamic faith? What kind of faith are you talking about?" If it's me, I'm not talking about any of those. I am talking about a belief in the capability of other people. When I'm in a place of physical danger—in Antarctica, for example, diving underneath the sea ice there—my faith is in my colleagues. And when I meet other writers, journalists who've worked at understanding the human dilemma for a long time, I have faith in those people. I trust them.

We say in my business—television production—"Trust the process," which means count on the people who are responsible for different phases of the work to do what they have to do to make it all come out all right. You do your bit, they do their bit, and the production goes on. That's the way life goes, too.

It is. I have to think there have been times in your own life as a journalist when you've lost faith or looked into a situation that made you feel you were never going to recover from it, but you do. And you do because somebody reached out to you. A letter. A phone call. There's a circle of people who stay in loose touch who renew your sense of what we have to do, say, about addressing the fate of the earth. We all like to root for the home team. I like to root for humanity, and I want to believe that we can come to a state of grace. That we can do better than we're doing now. I believe fiercely in that. And I meet people in every corner of the world who affirm it.

You said once that for all of us living in North America, nature is the oldest metaphor in our story. Is that still true?

That's our ancestral stuff. When people experienced an emotion for which they had no language, they had to find a referent out there in the world for it. Our stories began where we used animals and wind and light as a context in which to develop ideas that were very complicated. That's how people began to communicate. When you're in wild or underdeveloped environments, with traditional people, their relationship to the wind—the wind is alive for them. It has a soul. And it's an I–Thou, not an I–it, relationship because the wind is part of their moral universe. Some of those people have a sense—well, of holiness, of the Great Mystery of which they believe they are a part. We've created instead a world in which we have excluded from our moral universe everything but ourselves. Nature has become our separated "other"—we've said, "If it doesn't serve us, kill it, move it, destroy it, crush it. Make it serve us. If it doesn't, it's no good."

What we're trying to do now is to wake up to what humanity has known for longer than 10,000 years, namely, that you can't direct the play. The play is not directable. You must participate in the play. You must get out of the director's role of telling everybody what to do and how to behave and who can be on stage. You must put all that aside and step onto the stage with other men and women. And say, "We're in this together." We need to discover an arrangement that allows us to care for each other. But we can't exclude—we can't make nature the banished relative, no part of the human family.

That's a classic metaphor: life's a play and we all are actors on its stage. All of us have walk-on parts in this unending drama.

And who is to say one person has a walk-on part and someone else is the star? What happens if a person speaks imperfect English in a culture like ours, is not articulate, but can dance in a way that makes you shiver? Why is that a walk-on part? Take television—God bless television, but you can turn on the television every day and see people who assume an expertise that they clearly don't have. The kind of expertise we need is not a more facile grasp of policy, but a more complex love of humanity.

But some people are hard to love, Barry.

I'm not talking about [the Liberian dictator] Charles Taylor, or Idi Amin, or Hitler, or Stalin, or any of these reprehensible human beings. What they did, we must condemn. But humanity is also Michelangelo, Darwin, Epictetus. I mean, if you have the Bach cello suites in your head at the same moment that you're looking at a gas chamber at Auschwitz, you somehow hold on to the possibility of understanding what we're actually enmeshed in.

Well, this of course is the puzzle, isn't it? In that "high civilization" of Germany, Hitler's generals strolled in their gardens, listening to Bach and Beethoven, while a mile away the gas chambers were working overtime.

They lacked the imagination to see that their own humanity was being destroyed there. What I am trying to say is those six cello suites that Bach wrote are an homage to the other side of humanity, where there's beautiful proportion and rhythm. Use that fuel to open yourself up, even when—especially when—other things have broken your heart.

We talk about wilderness. I spend a lot of time in "wilderness." We've lived forty years in rural Oregon. Have you ever seen a wilderness calendar with anything but lyrical images? Nature's not just a lyrical experience, a kind of Bierstadt painting. Nature is the full expression of life, and you have to be present to all of it, the flooding, the earthquake. And you have to ask yourself, why does the Dalai Lama still laugh? Why does Desmond Tutu, with whom I once worked, why is he capable of such laughter, given how he saw his own people treated during apartheid? I think part of the answer is that people like Desmond Tutu find a way between the darkness and the light to be fully alive.

I understand you are working on another book, one that takes you from the cradle of humanity in South Africa to Australia, from Antarctica to the Galapagos.

Yes, and let me tell you what has hit me about all that traveling. Somebody asked me once, "How can you talk so much about community when you're gone from your place in Oregon so often?" And I tried to think of what I'd learned living there, in my chosen place, that helps me answer that question without feeling guilty. The answer was right in front of me. For forty years, about two hundred yards from the front of the house where I look down on the river, Chinook salmon have spawned. Every year they come back. They have to run a gauntlet, but they're there every year. No one in their right mind would say that those salmon, who come and go, aren't members of the community. The community couldn't survive without them. And that was the moment I thought, "Well, I'm just like them. I'm rooted deeply here. This is my home. But I go like they do out into the ocean. And I try to bring back a story. They're fulfilled by their travels, and so am I. My work is to go out there and look and come back and say what it is that I saw."

It intrigues me that way out there, in the far corners of the world, you see humanity clearer than many of us who are right here.

Here's the deal. I had really good teachers. They awakened in me a capacity for metaphor. Science is a way of knowing, dance is a way of knowing, writing is a way of knowing—that's what they taught me. And when I am walking on the ground out there—my body is paying attention through its senses. That means the earth, too, is a teacher. The Inuit people, the Yup'ik and Inupiaq Eskimo or Pitjantjatjara people in Australia—all have different ways of trying to understand the Great Mystery. You don't talk when you're out there, they say, you listen. And the most important lesson you're taught is that you are not the center. This is what Copernicus was trying to introduce. Are you going to be able to manage this idea that the sun doesn't revolve around us, but we revolve around the sun? We're still feeling the reverberations of that. Darwin told us that all life is on the move, though in no particular direction. When you're walking the earth, it's talking to you about that. You listen.

In my files, Barry, I have kept an account of remarks you made some twenty-five years ago when you received the National Book Award for Arctic Dreams. *And you mentioned then a word you came upon when you were once visiting in Japan.*

I was with a novelist named Kazumasa Hirai, a wonderful storyteller. And I asked him, "What do you mean when you say you're a storyteller?" And Kazumasa-san told me the Japanese use the word *kotodama* to carry the sense of something ineffable. He said your job as a storyteller is to be the caretaker for that ineffable part of the world, the spiritual interior of the world. Storytelling is the best protection we have, I think, against forgetting the spiritual interior of our lives, of all lives.

I was talking to a mutual friend of ours one night, someone who's always been an affirmative and optimistic fellow, and he said, "Moyers, for the first time in my life"—and he's in his fifities—"I'm beginning to think this America I believed in won't work. That the forces arrayed against justice and fairness are so great that we're going to go down."

Later that very night, I came across something you wrote some time ago: "There are simply no answers to some of the great pressing questions. You continue to live them out, making your life a worthy expression of leaning into the light." What a good phrase: "leaning into the light." Where are you today on the path between confusion and conviction?

Bill, people think that if you've written a book and somebody's given you a pat on the back for it, you're all settled, you know—everything's fine. But the truth is, I am frightened all the time. An old question from my childhood comes back: "Who cares what you have to say?" So, my path is the same path it's always been. It's a path through confusion and a lack of self-confidence, through embarrassment with my imperfection. But at the same time, I know I have seen things that have dropped me to my knees in a state of awe. Knowing that those things are there, I do my best to be a witness to them, to write carefully about them, to break through.

In recent years I've come to a better understanding of the virtue of reverence than I have ever had before, and here I'm borrowing from an American philosopher named Paul Woodruff. I read his book *Reverence: Renewing a Forgotten Virtue*. He says that reverence is rooted in the understanding that there is a world beyond human control, human invention, and human understanding, and that no matter how sophisticated our technologies for probing reality become, the Great Mystery will be there forever. It's not ours to solve. When you come upon something incomprehensible, some dimension of this Great Mystery, reverence brings you to your knees. You can open up to it and come out of your own little small tiny place in the world and realize what it is to be fully alive, a part of all life evolving.

But I'll tell you something about Paul Woodruff. He was in Vietnam at its worst. And I wonder if he would ever have understood this sense of reverence if he hadn't seen the savagery.

Absolutely. Back to what we were saying earlier. How do you introduce yourself to the darkness in the world? And how do you walk away from it and have something to offer besides reasons for despair and grief? He did just that when he wrote that wonderful book.

You know, I have seen truly horrible things. Truly horrible things in the world. And in those moments I broke down and was given to despair. Despair is the great temptation, but I thought, "If I have any kind of self-respect, I cannot allow myself to fall apart. I must find a way to put myself back together. If I can discover a language that will help someone else who is broken in half, if I can tell them a story that sticks, that helps them heal, well, then I'm okay."

One of the characters in your book Resistance *is a woman dying of Parkinson's disease, who hands her daughter Viktor Frankl's book* Man's Search for Meaning *and says to her, "Now's the time for you to read this book."*

She thinks her daughter is grown-up enough to understand. It's the same thing that you just described with Paul Woodruff, don't you think? That the parent sees in the child the moment in which the child can appreciate that there is another response to the horror besides self-destruction and despair. That we can enter the bleakness that human beings are capable of, creating, and not allow it alone to define what it means to be human.

There's a story, Bill—I don't remember the philosopher, the Greek philosopher—about Zeus and Prometheus. In this account, Zeus says to Prometheus, "Okay, you stole fire. That's great for you. Now your people have technology. Wonderful. But two things are missing here, if you wish your people to thrive. I am offering you justice and reverence. If you don't take these two things to heart, your fire—your technology—will fail you. It will be your undoing."

So lean into the light.

Yes, lean into the light. ∾

SELECT BIBLIOGRAPHY
OF GUESTS INTERVIEWED

MICHELLE ALEXANDER
The New Jim Crow: Mass Incarceration in the Age of Colorblindness (The New Press, 2009)

KAREN ARMSTRONG
Twelve Steps to a Compassionate Life (Knopf, 2010)
The Case for God (Knopf, 2009)
Muhammad: A Prophet for Our Time (Atlas Books/HarperCollins, 2006)
The Great Transformation: The Beginning of Our Religious Traditions (Knopf, 2006)
Buddha (Viking, 2001)
The Battle for God (Knopf, 2000)
Islam: A Short History (Modern Library, 2000)

ANDREW BACEVICH
Washington Rules: America's Path to Permanent War (Metropolitan Books, 2010)
The Limits of Power: The End of American Exceptionalism (Metropolitan Books, 2008)
The New American Militarism: How Americans Are Seduced by War (Oxford University Press, 2005)
American Empire: The Realities and Consequences of U.S. Diplomacy (Harvard University Press, 2002)

BENJAMIN BARBER
Con$umed: How Markets Corrupt Children, Infantilize Adults, and Swallow Citizens Whole (W.W. Norton, 2007)
Fear's Empire: War, Terrorism, and Democracy (W.W. Norton, 2003)
Jihad vs. McWorld (Times Books, 1995)

DOUGLAS BLACKMON
Slavery by Another Name: The Re-enslavement of Black People in America from the Civil War to World War II (Doubleday, 2008)

ROBERT BLY

My Sentence Was a Thousand Years of Joy: Poems (HarperCollins, 2005)

The Maiden King: The Reunion of Masculine and Feminine (co-authored with Marion Woodman; Henry Holt, 1998)

Sibling Society (Addison-Wesley, 1996)

Iron John: A Book About Men (Addison-Wesley, 1990)

A Little Book on the Human Shadow (edited by William Booth; Raccoon Books, 1986)

Kabir, Try to See This! Versions (Ally Press, 1976)

GRACE LEE BOGGS

The Next American Revolution: Sustainable Activism for the Twenty-first Century (with Scott Kurashige; University of California Press, 2011)

Living for Change: An Autobiography (University of Minnesota Press, 1998)

Conversations in Maine: Exploring Our Nation's Future (co-authored with James Boggs and Freddy and Lyman Paine; South End Press, 1978)

DAVID BOIES

Courting Justice: From NY Yankees v. Major League Baseball *to* Bush v. Gore, *1997–2000* (Hyperion, 2004)

THOMAS CAHILL

A Saint on Death Row: The Story of Dominique Green (Nan A. Talese, 2009)

Mysteries of the Middle Ages: The Rise of Feminism, Science, and Art from the Cults of Catholic Europe (Nan A. Talese, 2006)

The Gifts of the Jews: How a Tribe of Desert Nomads Changed the Way Everyone Thinks and Feels (Nan A. Talese, 1999)

How the Irish Saved Civilization: The Untold Story of Ireland's Heroic Role from the Fall of Rome to the Rise of Medieval Europe (Nan A. Talese, 1995)

JAMES CONE

Strange Fruit: The Cross and the Lynching Tree (Orbis Books, 2011)

Risks of Faith: The Emergence of a Black Theology of Liberation, 1968–1998 (Beacon Press, 1999)

Martin & Malcolm & America: A Dream or a Nightmare (Orbis Books, 1991)

MIKE DAVIS

Evil Paradises: Dreamworlds of Neoliberalism (co-edited with Daniel Bertrand Monk; The New Press, 2007)

Planet of Slums (Verso, 2006)

Dead Cities: And Other Tales (The New Press, 2002)

Ecology of Fear: Los Angeles and the Imagination of Disaster (Metropolitan Books, 1998)

City of Quartz: Excavating the Future in Los Angeles (Verso, 1990)

Prisoners of the American Dream: Politics and Economy in the History of the US Working Class (Verso, 1986)

ROSS DOUTHAT

Grand New Party: How Republicans Can Win the Working Class and Save the American Dream (co-authored with Reihan Salam; Doubleday, 2008)

Privilege: Harvard and the Education of the Ruling Class (Hyperion, 2005)

MICKEY EDWARDS

Reclaiming Conservatism: How a Great American Political Movement Got Lost—and How It Can Find Its Way Back (Oxford University Press, 2008)

Behind Enemy Lines: A Rebel in Congress Proposes a Bold New Politics for the 1980s (Regnery, 1984)

BARBARA EHRENREICH

Bright-Sided: How the Relentless Promotion of Positive Thinking Has Undermined America (Metropolitan Books, 2009)

This Land Is Their Land: Reports from a Divided Nation (Metropolitan Books, 2008)

Bait and Switch: The (Futile) Pursuit of the American Dream (Metropolitan Books, 2005)

Nickel and Dimed: On (Not) Getting By in America (Metropolitan Books, 2001)

LOUISE ERDRICH

Shadow Tag (HarperCollins, 2010)

The Porcupine Year (HarperCollins, 2008)

The Plague of Doves (HarperCollins, 2008)

The Last Report on the Miracles at Little No Horse (HarperCollins, 2001)

The Blue Jay's Dance: A Birth Year (HarperPerennial, 1995)

Love Medicine: New and Expanded Version (New York: Henry Holt, 1993)

MARTÍN ESPADA

The Lover of a Subversive Is Also a Subversive: Essays and Commentaries (University of Michigan Press, 2010)

The Republic of Poetry (W.W. Norton, 2006)

Alabanza: New and Selected Poems, 1982–2002 (W.W. Norton, 2004)

Rebellion Is the Circle of a Lover's Hands (Curbstone Press, 1990)

JAMES K. GALBRAITH

The Predator State: How Conservatives Abandoned the Free Market and Why Liberals Should Too (Free Press, 2008)

Created Unequal: The Crisis in American Pay (Free Press, 1998)

NIKKI GIOVANNI

Bicycles: Love Poems (William Morrow, 2009)

Rosa (illustrated by Bryan Collier; Henry Holt, 2005)

The Collected Poetry of Nikki Giovanni: 1968–1998 (chronology and notes by Virginia C. Fowler; William Morrow, 2003)

Love Poems (William Morrow, 1997)

VICTOR GOLD

Invasion of the Party-Snatchers: How the Holy-Rollers and Neo-Cons Destroyed the GOP (Sourcebooks, 2007)

Looking Forward (by George Bush with Victor Gold; Doubleday, 1987)

The Body Politic (co-authored with Lynne Cheney; St. Martin's Press, 1980)

I Don't Need You When I'm Right: The Confessions of a Washington PR Man (William Morrow, 1975)

RICHARD GOLDSTONE

International Judicial Institutions: The Architecture of International Justice at Home and Abroad (co-authored with Adam M. Smith; Routledge, 2008)

For Humanity: Reflections of a War Crimes Investigator (Yale University Press, 2000)

JANE GOODALL

Hope for Animals and Their World: How Endangered Species Are Being Rescued from the Brink (with Gail Hudson and Thane Maynard; Grand Central, 2009)

The Ten Trusts: What We Must Do to Care for the Animals We Love (co-authored with Marc Bekoff; HarperSanFrancisco, 2002)

Beyond Innocence: An Autobiography in Letters: The Later Years (edited by Dale Peterson; Houghton Mifflin, 2001)

Reason for Hope: A Spiritual Journey (with Phillip Berman; Warner Books, 1999)

WILLIAM GREIDER

Come Home, America: The Rise and Fall (and Redeeming Promise) of Our Country (Rodale, 2010)

The Soul of Capitalism: Opening Paths to a Moral Economy (Simon & Schuster, 2003)

Secrets of the Temple: How the Federal Reserve Runs the Country (Simon & Schuster, 1987)

JOHN GRISHAM
The Confession (Doubleday, 2010)
Ford County: Stories (Doubleday, 2009)
The Associate (Doubleday, 2009)
The Innocent Man: Murder and Injustice in a Small Town (Doubleday, 2006)
The Last Juror (Doubleday, 2004)
The Brethren (Doubleday, 2000)
The Rainmaker (Doubleday, 1995)
The Client (Doubleday, 1993)
The Pelican Brief (Doubleday, 1992)
The Firm (Doubleday, 1991)

JIM HIGHTOWER
Swim Against the Current: Even a Dead Fish Can Go with the Flow (Wiley, 2008)
Thieves in High Places: They've Stolen Our Country—and It's Time to Take It Back (Viking, 2003)
If the Gods Had Meant Us to Vote They Would Have Given Us Candidates: More Political Subversion from Jim Hightower (HarperCollins, 2000)
There's Nothing in the Middle of the Road but Yellow Stripes and Dead Armadillos (HarperCollins, 1997)

SUSAN JACOBY
Never Say Die: The Myth and Marketing of the New Old Age (Pantheon, 2011)
Alger Hiss and the Battle for History (Yale University Press, 2009)
The Age of American Unreason (Pantheon, 2008)
Freethinkers: A History of American Secularism (Metropolitan Books, 2004)

SIMON JOHNSON
13 Bankers: The Wall Street Takeover and the Next Financial Meltdown (co-authored with James Kwak; Pantheon, 2010)

ROBERT KAISER
So Damn Much Money: The Triumph of Lobbying and the Corrosion of American Government (Knopf, 2009)
The News About the News: American Journalism in Peril (co-authored with Leonard Downie Jr.; Knopf, 2002)

JIM YONG KIM
Dying for Growth: Global Inequality and the Health of the Poor (co-edited with

Alex Irwin, John Gershman, and Joyce V. Millen; Common Courage Press, 2002)

MAXINE HONG KINGSTON
I Love a Broad Margin to My Life (Knopf, 2011)
Veterans of War, Veterans of Peace (editor; Koa Books, 2006)
The Fifth Book of Peace (Knopf, 2003)
China Men (Knopf, 1980)
The Woman Warrior: Memoirs of a Girlhood Among Ghosts (Knopf, 1976)

SARA LAWRENCE-LIGHTFOOT
The Third Chapter: Passion, Risk, and Adventure in the 25 Years After 50 (Farrar, Straus and Giroux, 2009)
The Essential Conversation: What Parents and Teachers Can Learn from Each Other (Random House, 2003)
Respect: An Exploration (Perseus Books, 1999)
The Art and Science of Portraiture (co-authored with Jessica Hoffmann Davis; Jossey-Bass, 1997)
Balm in Gilead: Journey of a Healer (Addison-Wesley, 1988)

JOHN LITHGOW
I Got Two Dogs (illustrated by Robert Neubacker; Simon & Schuster Books for Young Readers, 2008)
Marsupial Sue Presents the Runaway Pancake (illustrated by Jack E. Davis; Simon & Schuster Books for Young Readers, 2005)
I'm a Manatee (illustrated by Art Hoyt; Simon & Schuster Books for Young Readers, 2003)
The Remarkable Farkle McBride (illustrated by C.F. Payne; Simon & Schuster Books for Young Readers, 2000)

BARRY LOPEZ
Resistance (Knopf, 2004)
Field Notes: The Grace Note of the Canyon Wren (Knopf, 1994)
Crossing Open Ground (Scribner, 1988)
Arctic Dreams: Imagination and Desire in a Northern Landscape (Scribner, 1986)
Giving Birth to Thunder, Sleeping with His Daughter: Coyote Builds North America (Sheed Andrews and McMeel, 1977)

W.S. MERWIN
The Shadow of Sirius (Copper Canyon Press, 2009)
Migration: New & Selected Poems (Copper Canyon Press, 2005)

The First Four Books of Poems (Copper Canyon Press, 2000)
The River Sound: Poems (Knopf, 1999)
The Second Four Books of Poems (Copper Canyon Press, 1993)

NELL PAINTER
The History of White People (W.W. Norton, 2010)
Creating Black Americans: African-America History and Its Meaning, 1619 to the Present (Oxford University Press, 2006)
Sojourner Truth: A Life, a Symbol (W.W. Norton, 1996)
Exodusters: Black Migration to Kansas After Reconstruction (Knopf, 1977)

MICHAEL POLLAN
Food Rules: An Eater's Manual (Penguin, 2009)
In Defense of Food: An Eater's Manifesto (Penguin, 2008)
The Omnivore's Dilemma: A Natural History of Four Meals (Penguin, 2007)
The Botany of Desire: A Plant's Eye View of the World (Random House, 2001)
Second Nature: A Gardener's Education (Atlantic Monthly Press, 1991)

WENDELL POTTER
Deadly Spin: An Insurance Company Insider Speaks Out on How Corporate PR Is Killing Health Care and Deceiving Americans (Bloomsbury Press, 2010)

PHILIPPE SANDS
Torture Team: Rumsfeld's Memo and the Betrayal of American Values (Palgrave MacMillan, 2008)
Lawless World: America and the Making and Breaking of Global Rules from FDR's Atlantic Charter to George W. Bush's Illegal War (Viking, 2005)
From Nuremberg to the Hague: The Future of International Criminal Justice (editor; Cambridge University Press, 2003)

JEREMY SCAHILL
Blackwater: The Rise of the World's Most Powerful Mercenary Army (Nation Books, 2007)

DAVID SIMON
The Corner: A Year in the Life of an Inner-City Neighborhood (co-authored with Edward Burns; Broadway, 1997)
Homicide: A Year on the Killing Streets (Houghton Mifflin, 1991)

HOLLY SKLAR
Raise the Floor: Wages and Policies that Work for All of Us (co-authored with Laryssa Mykyta and Susan Wefald; (Ms. Foundation for Women, 2001)
Washington's War on Nicaragua (South End Press, 1988)

554   SELECT BIBLIOGRAPHY

A Bound Man: Why We Are Excited About Obama and Why He Can't Win
(Free Press, 2007)

*White Guilt: How Blacks and Whites Together Destroyed the Promise of the
Civil Rights Era* (HarperCollins, 2006)

A Dream Deferred: The Second Betrayal of Black Freedom in America
(HarperCollins, 1998)

The Content of Our Character: A New Vision of Race in America (St. Martin's
Press, 1990)

JON STEWART

The Daily Show with Jon Stewart *Presents Earth (The Book): A Visitor's Guide
to the Human Race* (co-authored and co-edited with David Javerbaum, Rory
Albanese, Steve Bodow, and Josh Lieb; Grand Central, 2010)

The Daily Show with Jon Stewart *Presents America (The Book): A Citizen's
Guide to Democracy Inaction* (co-authored and co-edited with Ben Karlin
and David Javerbaum; Warner Books, 2004)

Naked Pictures of Famous People (Rob Weisbach Books, 1998)

SAM TANENHAUS

The Death of Conservatism (Random House, 2009)

Whittaker Chambers: A Biography (Random House, 1997)

E.O. WILSON

The Leafcutter Ants: Civilization by Instinct (co-authored with Bert Hölldobler;
(W.W. Norton, 2011)

Anthill: A Novel (W.W. Norton, 2010)

The Superorganism: The Beauty, Elegance, and Strangeness of Insect Societies (co-
authored with Bert Hölldobler and illustrated by Margaret C. Nelson; W.W.
Norton, 2008)

The Creation: An Appeal to Save Life on Earth (W.W. Norton, 2006)

On Human Nature: With a New Preface (Harvard University Press, 2004)

The Future of Life (Knopf, 2002)

REVEREND JEREMIAH WRIGHT

A Sankofa Moment: The History of Trinity United Church of Christ (Saint Paul
Press, 2010)

*Blow the Trumpet in Zion!: Global Vision and Action for the 21st-Century Black
Church* (co-edited with Iva E. Carruthers and Frederick D. Haynes III;
Fortress Press, 2005)

When Black Men Stand Up for God: Reflections on the Million Man March

(co-authored with Frank Madison Reid III and Colleen Birchett; African American Images, 1996)

ROBERT WRIGHT
The Evolution of God (Little, Brown, 2009)
Nonzero: The Logic of Human Destiny (Pantheon, 2000)
The Moral Animal: The New Science of Evolutionary Psychology (Pantheon, 1994)

HOWARD ZINN
The Bomb (City Lights Books, 2010)
Voices of A People's History of the United States, 2nd ed (co-authored with Anthony Arnove; Seven Stories Press, 2009)
A People's History of American Empire: A Graphic Adaptation (co-authored with Mike Konopacki and Paul Buhle; Metropolitan Books, 2008)
A People's History of the United States: 1492–Present (HarperCollins, 2003)
Marx in Soho: A Play on History (South End Press, 1999)

PERMISSIONS

INDEX